THE QUALIFYING ASSOCIATIONS

INTERNATIONAL LIBRARY OF SOCIOLOGY
AND SOCIAL RECONSTRUCTION

Founded by Karl Mannheim
Editor: W. J. H. Sprott

A catalogue of the books available in the INTERNATIONAL LIBRARY OF SOCIOLOGY AND SOCIAL RECONSTRUCTION, and new books in preparation for the Library will be found at the end of this volume.

THE QUALIFYING ASSOCIATIONS

A Study in
Professionalization

by

GEOFFREY MILLERSON

LONDON
ROUTLEDGE & KEGAN PAUL
NEW YORK: THE HUMANITIES PRESS

First published 1964
by Routledge & Kegan Paul Ltd
Broadway House, 68–74 Carter Lane
London, E.C.4

Printed in Great Britain
by Staples Printers Ltd, Rochester, Kent

CONTENTS

Preface   *page* ix

Acknowledgements   xi

1. PROFESSIONS, PROFESSIONALIZATION AND
   PROFESSIONAL ORGANIZATION
   The Problem of Defining a Profession   1
   Toward a Definition   9
   Professionalization   10
   Professional Organization   13
   The Development of Professional Organization   16

2. TYPES OF PROFESSIONAL ORGANIZATION
   Introduction   26
   The Functions of Professional Organization   28
   Types of Professional Organization   32
   Trade Associations   41
   Ambiguities and Variations in Professional
     Organization   42
   Some Factors Determining Distribution and Numbers
     of Associations   43

3. WHY ARE QUALIFYING ASSOCIATIONS FORMED?
   Obstacles to the Formation of Professional Organization   47
   Why Are Associations Formed?   50
   Conclusion   85

4. STRUCTURE OF QUALIFYING ASSOCIATIONS
   Legal Status   88
   Government of the Association   94
   Membership Structure   109
   Local Organization   115
   Conclusion   116

5. QUALIFYING ASSOCIATIONS AND EDUCATION
   Education, the Professions and the New Qualifying
     Associations, 1800 to 1850   120
   Education and the Qualifying Associations,
     1850 to 1900   124
   Training and Education—the Position Today   130
   Examinations   135
   Qualifying Associations and Education   139

Contents

6. QUALIFYING ASSOCIATIONS AND
PROFESSIONAL CONDUCT
Introduction   *page* 148
What is Professional Conduct?   148
The Sociological Determinants of an Ethical Code   150
Qualifying Associations' Concern with Professional
   Conduct   159
The Nature of the Code   164
The Problem of Implementing a Code   170
Investigation of Unprofessional Conduct   171
The Role of Professional Ethics   175

7. THE QUALIFYING ASSOCIATION IN SOCIETY
The Development of Associations   181
The Nature of Qualifying Associations   188
Dilemmas of Qualifying Associations   194
The Role of Qualifying Associations   204
The Wider Contributions of Associations in Society   211

8. CONCLUSION

APPENDICES

A List of Qualifying Associations in England and
   Wales   221

Chronological List of Existing Qualifying and Non-
   Qualifying Associations in England and Wales   246

Notes   259
Index   297

TABLES

1.1. Analysis of Elements included in Various Definitions
of Profession   *page* 5
4.1. Qualifying Associations which possess Royal Charters   92
4.2. Relationship between Size of Council and Number
of Committees   103
4.3. Number and Percentage of Councils possessing
Different Types of Committees   104
4.4. Changing Requirements for Different Membership Grades 111
4.5. Membership Growth in Certain Qualifying Associations
1900 to 1960   117
5.1. Qualifying Associations established in England and Wales
between 1800 and 1850, with Year of First
Examination   121
5.2. Qualifying Associations established in England and Wales
between 1850 and 1900, with Year of First
Examination   126
5.3. Years in which National Certificates and Diplomas
were introduced   143
5.4. Number of External Education Committees on which
Certain Qualifying Associations were represented
in 1961–62   145
6.1. Analysis of Statements abstracted from Ethical Codes   166
6.2. Analysis based on Table 6.1 of Elements found in Ethical
Codes of Various Qualifying Associations   167
6.3. Professions Registered by Statute arranged in
Chronological Order of Registration   172
6.4. Number of Cases dealt with by the Disciplinary
Committee of the Institute of Chartered Accountants
in England and Wales, indicating Action taken, for
the Years 1949–62   176
6.5. Analysis of Offences committed by Members of the
Institute of Chartered Accountants in England and
Wales and Disciplinary Action taken by Council
during the Years 1949–62   178
7.1. Main Examples of Consolidation among Qualifying
Associations in the Twentieth Century   203

vii

CHARTS

6.1. Structural Elements determining Need for introducing
    an Ethical Code within an Occupation   *page* 152
6.2. Structural Elements determining Possibility of introducing
    an Ethical Code within an Occupation   155
6.3. General Procedure for Investigating Unprofessional
    Conduct   174

PREFACE

IN Britain, comparatively little has been written about professions. Apart from the classic studies of Carr-Saunders and Wilson, and the Webbs, plus passing comments from various authors, the field does not appear to have attracted much attention. There are historical accounts of a few professions (such as teachers, architects and nurses) and numerous histories of organizations, but not a great deal more.

This book looks at one important aspect of professionalism, the way to professional status through organization. It describes the Qualifying Association, a type of organization which attempts to qualify individuals for practice in a particular occupation. By setting more or less rigid entrance requirements, in terms of age, education and training, examination success and experience, these associations aim to provide a qualification.

The modern Qualifying Associations first appeared during the nineteenth century. Early organizations demonstrated their ability to transform an occupation slowly, raising standards, improving training and education, and even more important— building the occupation's status. Undoubtedly, notable achievements encouraged other occupations to exploit the same means. As a result, this type of association became the apparent symbol of professional status. Consequently for the last hundred years, groups of individuals have formed Qualifying Associations, thus laying claim to the designation 'profession'. Because approximately one hundred and sixty such associations now exist in England and Wales alone, their whole nature grows increasingly confused and suspect, their value seems distorted. A closer inspection of structure and work reveals extensive variations in standards. Quite clearly, they are not all of equal merit. Some associations deserve the designation 'professional', others do not. But what is the significance of the elusive terms 'profession' and 'professional'? These concepts are not easily defined.

Preface

In order to gain a better understanding of the 'Qualifying Associations', it is necessary to start with some examination of the idea of professionalism. Chapter One considers the problems of presenting a definition of 'profession', the basis of the process involved in professionalization, and the general development of professional organization. In fact, the system of professional organization contains several types of association. The various forms are outlined in Chapter Two. The rest of the book concentrates on an analysis of the Qualifying Association: the background of development; structure; educational functions; control over membership, and so on.

While many aspects of structure and work separate the 'best' associations from the mediocre or indifferent, there are numerous organizations in the middle range, which make a useful contribution to their particular occupations. Really, the complete set of Qualifying Associations forms a hierarchy, split up into several strata. All kinds of real and unreal distinctions lead to the divisions. Yet it would be a misguided exercise to try indicating the position of each association.

Much abuse of the system has produced a battery of useless, unnecessary, badly managed associations. Nevertheless the total effect has been beneficial. The range and depth of improvement throughout society is beyond dispute. The object of this book is to offer an account of these bodies, in the hope that such a study will help to further comprehension of the complex process of professionalization.

GEOFFREY MILLERSON

ACKNOWLEDGEMENTS

MANY people have contributed directly or indirectly to this book. In particular, I would like to thank Professor D. V. Glass, Dr Asher Tropp and Dr Stephen Cotgrove, who helped at various stages with their comments and criticisms.

My greatest debt is to the associations themselves, who proved continuously willing to supply information, discuss problems and offer every possible aid. I acknowledge with special thanks the permission given by associations listed in Appendix I, to publish certain facts about their structure. These associations are indicated thus(*), among the following organizations which supplied information: *Advertising Association*, Architectural Association, Association of Average Adjusters, Association of Certified and Corporate Accountants*, Association of Consulting Engineers, Association of International Accountants*, Association of Occupational Therapists*, Association of Psychiatric Social Workers, British Association of Accountants and Auditors*, British Boot and Shoe Institution*, British Dietetic Association*, British Institute of Management*, British Institution of Radio Engineers*, British Optical Association*, Building Societies Institute*, Chartered Auctioneers' and Estate Agents' Institute*, Chartered Institute of Loss Adjusters*, Chartered Institute of Patent Agents*, Chartered Institute of Secretaries*, Chartered Insurance Institute*, Chartered Land Agents Society*, Chartered Society of Physiotherapy*, Chemical Society, College of General Practitioners, Corporation of Insurance Brokers*, Corporation of Secretaries*, Faculty of Architects and Surveyors*, Faculty of Auditors, Geological Society of London, Hotel and Catering Institute*, Illuminating Engineering Society, Incorporated Advertising Managers' Association, Incorporated Association of Architects and Surveyors*, Incorporated Association of Cost and Industrial Accountants*, Incorporated Institute of British Decorators and Interior Designers*, Incorporated Society of Auctioneers and Landed Property Agents*, Institute of Actuaries*, Institute of Almoners*, Institute of Arbitrators, Institute of Bankers*, Institute of Biology*, Institute of Book-keepers*, Institute of Brewing*, Institute*

Acknowledgements

of British Foundrymen*, Institute of British Photographers*, Institute of British Surgical Technicians*, Institute of Builders*, Institute of Ceramics*, Institute of Certificated Grocers, Institute of Chartered Accountants in England and Wales*, Institute of Chartered Shipbrokers*, Institute of Company Accountants*, Institute of Cost and Works Accountants*, Institute of Credit Management, Institute of Directors, Institute of Fuel*, Institute of Hospital Administrators*, Institute of Housing*, Institute of Landscape Architects*, Institute of Legal Executives*, Institute of Linguists*, Institute of Marine Engineers, Institute of Marketing and Sales Management*, Institute of Meat, Institute of Medical Laboratory Technology*, Institute of Metals, Institute of the Motor Industry*, Institute of Municipal Treasurers and Accountants*, Institute of Office Management*, Institute of Packaging*, Institute of Personnel Management*, Institute of Petroleum*, Institute of Physics and the Physical Society*, Institute of Practitioners in Advertising*, Institute of Printing*, Institute of Printing Management*, Institute of Public Cleansing*, Institute of Public Relations*, Institute of Public Supplies*, Institute of Quarrying*, Institute of Quantity Surveyors*, Institute of Refrigeration*, Institute of Registered Architects, Institute of Road Transport Engineers, Institute of Sewage Purification*, Institute of Shipping and Forwarding Agents*, Institute of Statisticians*, Institute of Taxation*, Institute of Traffic Administration, Institute of Transport*, Institute of Travel Agents*, Institute of Weights and Measures Administration*, Institute of Welding*, Institute of Welfare Officers*, Institute of Works Study*, Institution of Agricultural Engineers*, Institution of Chemical Engineers*, Institution of Civil Engineers*, Institution of Electrical Engineers*, Institution of Engineers-in-Charge, Institution of Engineering Designers*, Institution of Gas Engineers*, Institution of Heating and Ventilating Engineers*, Institution of Locomotive Engineers*, Institution of Mechanical Engineers*, Institution of Metallurgists*, Institution of Mining and Metallurgy*, Institution of Municipal Engineers*, Institution of Plant Engineers*, Institution of Production Engineers*, Institution of Public Health Engineers*, Institution of Railway Signal Engineers*, Institution of the Rubber Industry*, Institution of Structural Engineers*, Institution of Water Engineers*, Institution of Works Managers*, Institutional Management Association*, Iron and Steel Institute, Law Society*, Library Association*, Market Research Society*, Museums Association*, National Association of Estate Agents, Pharmaceutical Society of Great Britain*, Plastics Institute*,

Acknowledgements

Purchasing Officers Association*, Rating and Valuation Association*, Royal Aeronautical Society*, Royal Astronomical Society, Royal College of Obstetricians and Gynaecologists*, Royal College of Physicians of London*, Royal College of Surgeons of England*, Royal College of Veterinary Surgeons*, Royal Geographical Society, Royal Horticultural Society, Royal Institute of British Architects*, Royal Institution of Chartered Surveyors*, Royal Institute of Chemistry*, Royal Institution of Naval Architects*, Royal Photographic Society, Royal Society of Arts, Royal Statistical Society, Society of Chiropodists*, Society of Commercial Accountants*, Society of Dairy Technology*, Society of Engineers*, Society of Glass Technology*, Society of Radiographers*, Society of Remedial Gymnasts*, Textile Institute*, Town Planning Institute*, Valuers Institution*, Worshipful Society of Apothecaries of London, Zoological Society of London.

All material collected from the above organizations, during the research, has been deposited in the British Library of Political and Economic Science.

Chapter One

PROFESSIONS, PROFESSIONALIZATION AND PROFESSIONAL ORGANIZATION

THE PROBLEMS OF DEFINING A PROFESSION

OF all sociological ideas, one of the most difficult to analyse satisfactorily is the concept of a profession. Perhaps three basic problems account for the confusion and uncertainty. Firstly, there is the semantic confusion, resulting from wide and excessive use of the word. Secondly, there are the structural limitations enforced by attempts to devise fundamental characteristics of a profession. Thirdly, there is the adherence to a static model, rather than an appreciation of the dynamic process involved in professionalism.

Semantic Confusion

Concepts such as family, status, class, and morals have also become confused through popular and often misguided use, but at least these have attained some sociological stability. 'Profession', 'professionalism' and 'professionalization' have been less fortunate.

In popular usage, 'profession' and 'professional' appear to have a variety of meanings. Thus, the word 'profession' may be used as a polite synonym for 'job', 'work', 'occupation'. The question 'What is your profession?' may really be considered, by the inquirer, as a genteel form of 'What's your job?'. Alternatively, the description is applied to anyone neatly dressed, who does not apparently wear special clothing for work, and who is concerned with clerical operations. So the term becomes attached indiscriminately to any, and every, type of 'black-coated' and 'white-collar' occupation. A further source of trouble arises from the difference between 'professional' and 'amateur', used in sport and leisure time activities. Here, the amateur is one who performs certain tasks, on a part-time basis, for the intrinsic pleasure obtained from them, and not for any financial reward or profit. The professional regards the same process as a full-time occupation, providing the main income. Another connotation of 'professional' implies the successful completion of a task with great skill. The results are indistinguishable from those obtained by using skilled personnel, who consider that type of work as their major occupational activity.

A second form of semantic confusion comes from the addition of prefixes and qualifying words. Numerous versions have been developed—for example, pseudo-, semi-, quasi-, sub-, auxiliary, marginal, liberal, learned. Only some expressions have assumed any extensive use. Often, the origins are impossible to trace, because the term is employed without definition, suggesting that the reader already knows the true meaning and value. Many times, the intention is to derogate attempts, by members of an occupation, to establish professional status for themselves. Those struggling are judged to be unworthy of the classification. Sometimes the addition is helpful. Sometimes the description is official. But on most occasions, the real aim is to escape the thought that all professions are equal. Differences, it is felt, must separate professions from non-professions, new from old, acceptable from unacceptable. If anything, these represent strivings toward *a* definition, and *the* characteristics distinguishing a profession from other occupations, without resorting to an actual definition.

Thirdly, confusion arises from the indiscriminate use of the term 'profession' to describe dissimilar concepts. As M. L. Cogan[1] points out, 'profession' is employed (*a*) to differentiate one occupation from another, (*b*) to designate a formal vocational association, (*c*) to describe a licensed vocation. In a later paper,[2] Cogan suggests that confusion arises from three levels of definition: (*a*) a historical and lexicological definition, (*b*) a persuasive definition, attempting to redirect attitudes, (*c*) an operational definition, offering a basis of guidance for the professional. This analysis is less helpful. Few definitions fit easily into one of these three classifications; sometimes the best category cannot be determined. In fact, most definitions contain up to three parts: (*a*) a historical element based on the traditional professions, (*b*) an idealistic element to act as an incentive, (*c*) a realistic element relating ideal and tradition to current form and practice.

Finally, confusion arises from an incomplete, or a mistaken, image of an occupation. For example, the description 'engineer' is applied to anyone from a lathe-setter, to a trained and qualified technical expert. A librarian is a person who issues tickets and stamps books, in a public lending library. Little difference would be seen between an insurance underwriter and an insurance agent, who collects small premiums from door to door. A pharmacist is described as a 'chemist', although a chemist really performs a different function.

Structural Limitations

In order to define and delimit occupations to be considered as professions, various writers have offered the characteristics of a profession. Such aids suffer from disabilities.

Firstly, the authors begin as historians, accountants, lawyers, economists, engineers, philosophers, sociologists, etc. As a result, group affiliations and roles determine the choice of items, and bias. Usually, the measures are presented with their own occupations in mind. The lawyer emphasizes the fiduciary nature of the professional-client relationship, the depth of learning, the cordial colleague relationships and sense of public service.[3] The accountant may stress the organized control over competence and integrity, the value of practical experience and so on.[4]

Secondly, the influences of one author upon another can be traced. In the end, too few would seem to have actually considered the problem afresh. Many rely upon the same formulae, containing slight additions. Carr-Saunders and Wilson is the classic study, from which most authors have taken their postulates.[5] The Webb's survey[6] and the passionate aside of R. H. Tawney[7] also provide starting points.

Thirdly, characteristics and definitions have been moulded to fit arguments. More accurately, special characteristics have

3

emerged from special considerations. For example, Tawney attacks the functionless property derived from the capitalist system of industry, and suggests the subordination of industry to the community's needs. To reform industry, he proposes changes, which rest on a comparison of industry and the professions. Professions are organized for the performance of duties. Similarly, industry must aim to serve. Herbert Spencer's idea of a profession is strikingly unusual, yet this view flows from an organic theory of society.[8] Considering society as an organism, its members are subservient to the necessary functions to be performed. Groups within society are responsible for various functions—defence, the regulation and sustenance of life. Professions carry out a further general function: the augmentation of life. By curing disease, removing pain, etc., medical men increase life. Musicians and dancers 'exalt the emotions' and increase life . . . and so on, through poets, dramatists, authors, scientists and philosophers. Emile Durkheim's viewpoint develops from his belief in the trend toward, and growth of, group solidarity within society.[9]

Consequently, a mass of confusion stems from all analyses, which attempt to determine the occupational characteristics of a profession. Individual bias results from a strong occupational, or theoretical, outlook. Ready adoption of a few premises, from other people, has led to sterility. A further complication appears when authors speak in terms of ideals, either to spur on fellow practitioners, or to re-inforce their feeling of achievement.

Table 1.1 presents an analysis of characteristics put forward by a number of different commentators. Prevalence of particular aspects perhaps implies agreement, as well as blind acceptance from others. Interesting ornamentations occur outside the central theme.

Essential features expressed here are:
- (a) A profession involves a skill based on theoretical knowledge.
- (b) The skill requires training and education.
- (c) The professional must demonstrate competence by passing a test.
- (d) Integrity is maintained by adherence to a code of conduct.
- (e) The service is for the public good.
- (f) The profession is organized.

TABLE I.I. SHOWING AN ANALYSIS OF ELEMENTS INCLUDED IN VARIOUS DEFINITIONS OF PROFESSION

For references to sources see (10) in "Notes to Chapter One" at end

	1 Skill based on theoretical knowledge	2 Requires training and education	3 Competence tested	4 Organized	5 Adheres to a professional code of conduct	6 Altruistic service	7 Applied to affairs of others	8 Indispensable public service	9 Licensed (registered) community sanction	10 Definite professional client relationship	11 Fiduciary client relationship	12 Best impartial service given	13 Loyalty to colleagues	14 Definite compensation (i.e. fee, or fixed charge)	Other elements
Bowen	+				+										
Carr-Saunders & Wilson	+	+		+	+									+	
Christie		+			+										Practice modified by generalized knowledge
Cogan			+	+	+	+	+								
Crew						+	+	+							
Drinker	+	+			+	+					+		+		
Flexner	+	+		+	+	+	+								
Greenwood				+	+				+						
Howitt	+	+	+	+	+	+				+					Members prepared to contribute to professional development
Kaye	+		+		+										Guaranteed service raises association's prestige thus securing employment and improving income
Leigh	+	+			+										Application of principles to concrete professional practice: a complex process requiring exercise of disciplined individual judgement
Lewis & Maude	+			+	+						+				Independence
Marshall	+			+	+	+									Non-manual
Milne				+	+	+		+	+						
Parsons				+	+	+			+	+					
Ross	+			+	+							+			Profits not dependent on capital
Simon		+	+	+	+										
Tawney		+	+	+											
Webbs					+		+					+		+	
Whitehead	+			+			+								Foresight based on theory, theory based on understanding
Wickenden	+	+	+	+	+										Recognized status

Constantly underlying definitions, there are various senti-ments. For example, the professional is a noble, independent individual who places public duty and honour before all else. But neither the characteristics presented, nor the sentiments commonly supporting them, allow a realistic assessment of the professional situation. While some characteristics seem reason-able and realistic, others appear restrictive. Must a profession be organized? Must a professional pass an examination to show competence? Is a code of professional conduct always necessary to enforce integrity? Do professionals always operate a valuable public service? How many professionals are actually inde-pendent practitioners? These questions expose the third fundamental problem in defining a profession.

Dynamic Realism

Based on the first professions of the church, law and medicine, a traditional image of the professional evolved. He was a 'gentle-man', an independent practitioner dispensing a necessary pub-lic service of a fiduciary nature. His competence was determined by examination and licence. His integrity was ensured by observance of a strict ethical code. Unprofessional conduct could lead to complete deprivation from further practice. His training and education were institutionalized. Here was the model for all professions. Several criticisms might be made of this 'image'.

Firstly, the respectability of these professions, as a whole, only emerged in the eighteenth century, to be consolidated in Vic-torian England. Secondly, compulsory tests of competence were applied to these professions at a comparatively late date. Barris-ters were not subjected to a compulsory examination until 1872. Solicitors were examined from 1836. Medical practice was with-out regulation until 1858. Qualifications were not required for practice; and existing degrees and diplomas varied considerably in standard. Before the 1850s, no serious test was generally im-posed prior to ordination. Thirdly, high prestige of these profes-sions resulted from other elements besides control over the profession, and the vital nature of the service. (*a*) Practitioners became heavily involved in local affairs—government, justice, education, local banks, etc. (*b*) The legal and medical professions furnished valuable means of social mobility. Those from humble origins tended to stress their respectability.

As founded upon the traditional structure and work of law, medicine and the church, the professional ideal remains unsound. First, the majority of professionals are no longer independent practitioners, working by themselves. Over the last hundred years, the tendency has been for independent professionals to decline in number and proportion, even in the older professions.[11] Of course, some professions seem likely to contain a higher proportion of independent practitioners, either due to the nature of the work, or through special restrictions preventing partnerships and group practice. Second, not all professionals are involved in a direct, personal, fiduciary client-professional relationship. The close, confidential, single-client relationship found in legal, medical and spiritual matters, has a particular quality peculiar to those professions. Though confidential matters, concerning person and property, arise in many occupations, these are not quite the same. A strict, ethical code is not automatically required to protect public and professionals, in every type of professional service. Third, the mere formation of an organization, to certificate members and control professional conduct, does not immediately entitle the occupation to be designated as a profession. Fourth, a false impression is given of professional remuneration. While lawyers, doctors and surgeons have traditionally accepted fees, these charges have never been uniform. Practitioner's status mainly determined the size of fee. Even today, barristers' fees continue unregulated, beyond specification of a minimum retainer.[12] Fifth, training and education need not be institutionalized.

False assumptions about the nature of professionalism generate dilemmas. Firstly, by establishing a pattern of professionalization, many occupations organized themselves to achieve professional status. Qualifying Associations have been formed to professionalize particular types of work. As part of the process, examinations enable separation of competent and incompetent. Thus, organization and certification determine the essential qualities, which make a profession. Consequently, any occupation without these qualities is, theoretically, difficult to justify as a profession. Therefore an author, poet, painter, actor, musician, civil servant, Member of Parliament is not a professional. On the other hand, any collection of people forming a Qualifying Association acquires 'professional status'. To overcome this dilemma, prefixes and additional words are superimposed, to dilute aspired professionalism. Classifications of professions appear.[13] Another form of combat develops from inter-association competition. Association status symbols divide the 'professionals' from the rest. A Royal Charter, a Grant of Arms, a special licence to avoid the word 'Limited', members' services, an exclusive address—all efforts to elevate the association in a search for prestige.

Secondly, an apparent conflict of interest exists between 'business' and professional practice. This needs resolution.[14] Two assumptions are made in the argument. For the professions, the ethical problem entails matching the ideal of service and lack of interest in profit, with the question of payment for services. Competition means regulation, for professionals owe a duty to their clients, and to the community. For business, competition destroys any sense of unity or responsibility. Experience supplies training, not education in a theoretically based skill. Success measures competence, not an examination certificate. This may be a false antithesis based on incorrect assumptions. Even so, reconciliation has occurred through a mixture of the two. Professions have necessarily adopted business methods. Business has absorbed professionals, and adopted a more deliberate sense of responsibility.

Thirdly, the predominence of professionals as employees, especially in bureaucratic structures, creates a situation leading to possible alienation. Loyalty to strictly professional values may be replaced by observance of those emanating from the organization. The individual's role, in a bureaucratic organization, may conflict with a role determined by purely professional relationships. Any code of professional conduct, imposed by an external organization, may not coincide with the aims and methods of bureaucracy. Instead of being an independent, fee-paid principal, the professional is a salaried employee, who has to superimpose a duty to his association, upon any obligation to his employer. Also bureaucratization produces new specialists, and experts within specialist fields, which may have no equivalent outside the organization. As a result, they may fail to attain wide recognition as professionals, unless they already happen to be accountants, engineers, scientists or some generally known type of professional. Status ambiguity can follow.

To understand the concept 'profession', certain principles must be accepted:

(*a*) A profession is a higher-grade, non-manual occupation. Non-manual, in this context, implies that the intellectual, or practical, technique involved depends on a substantial theoretical foundation.

(*b*) The designation 'profession' is not a permanent monopoly of a few occupations. The term refers to a comparative status level attained after deliberate action by an occupation.

(*c*) Professional status is probably a dynamic quality. Elements composing status may change, owing to social and economic changes.

(*d*) An occupation does not have to be organized to become a profession. An organized occupation is not necessarily a profession. A well-defined area of study, or concern, must exist and be applied to give a definite service. To provide competent service, knowledge and experience must be obtained. Competence may be demonstrated by actual performance, or more conveniently for most occupations, by some standardized examination.

(*e*) Presence, or absence, of a code of professional conduct does not signify professional, or non-professional status. Some occupations require greater control than others, due to the nature of work involved. Some need a severe, comprehensive code, others do not. Need for a code depends on the professional situation.

(*f*) To achieve professional status, the occupation must be subjectively and objectively recognized as a profession. Subjectively, members of the occupation must be conscious of themselves as professionals. Objectively, those using the services, and the general public, must be willing to recognize and accept the occupation as a profession. Recognition can take the form of high remuneration, delegation of responsibility or authority, etc.

Professions, Professionalization

Definition of a Profession

It is a type of higher-grade, non-manual occupation, with both subjectively and objectively recognized occupational status, possessing a well-defined area of study or concern and providing a definite service, after advanced training and education.

PROFESSIONALIZATION

Professionalization is the process by which an occupation undergoes transformation to become a profession. As with other forms of institutionalization, professionalization entails conformity, internalization and sanction of specific norms, in this case, by members of a particular occupation. Forming an association is the easiest method of inducing a normative pattern. By assuming the structural features of established and acknowledged professional associations, the new organization hopes to enforce standards of competence and integrity.

Initially, the organization attempts to build solidarity, to construct a 'community' pattern differentiating the occupation from others. Ultimately, the aim is to create exclusiveness. Then potential members must proceed through stages of training, education and experience, before becoming eligible to be examined for membership. Existing members must also guarantee the acceptibility of the candidate. Once chosen as a member of the group, the individual must conform to the group norms and accept special obligations toward colleagues, clients and public. In return, group membership may be displayed by means of designatory letters, and protected descriptions, so conferring status upon the individual.

Within the process of professionalization, certain factors contribute to success.

(1) *Ability to achieve a definable basis of background knowledge and practice, plus a crystallization of the activities composing the occupational task*

An essential part of professionalization is the separation of the occupation from its milieu, enabling practitioners to profess a distinct speciality. Separation may be difficult, owing to the long-standing, permanent nature of the general occupational area. Alternatively, separation can be relatively easy, where there is an expanding field in a comparatively new occupational area. Law and engineering illustrate these two extremes.

The essence of separation is the capacity to present new forms of knowledge, or practice. These must be definable in theoretical terms. For example, there ought to be background knowledge, which differentiates the plant engineer from the production engineer, and the production engineer from the mechanical engineer. Besides conveying exclusiveness, a substantial quantity of minimum background knowledge restricts encroachment by any neighbouring specialists, and deters untrained and unqualified practitioners.

Translation of knowledge and practice into theoretical terms is valuable and very important. Special 'theory' impresses, thereby creating prestige for the occupation. Also theoretical concepts permit better standardization of work, preparation of textbooks and instructional matter, and easier teaching.

(2) *Opportunity to acquire knowledge and practice*

Special theory may be valuable, but it is purposeless, without some opportunity for acquiring the essentials. Means must be available to train personnel in the 'new' techniques. If training is institutionalized, then several subsidiary benefits may be derived. It develops into a method of raising standards of practice, of inducing uniform practice, of determining entrance of personnel into the occupation, of introducing certification. Institutionalized training allows greater control over status development of the occupation.

'New' subjects, devised by new professional or aspiring professional groups, suffer serious handicaps if they are not related to standard curricula in universities and colleges. Such a situation places a heavy burden upon Qualifying Associations to supply courses, teaching staff, even tuition material and textbooks. Inability to offer training facilities may discourage entrants to the occupation. On the other hand, if a new Qualifying Association simply demands and reshuffles a combination of 'old' subjects, then existing qualifications may be regarded as perfectly satisfactory by occupational entrants and potential employers.

(3) *Development of self-consciousness by emerging professionals*

Growth of self-awareness, probably constitutes the most important element contributing to professionalization. This display of self-consciousness is demonstrated in various ways, for example:

- (*a*) by dissatisfaction with available training and education for the occupation,
- (*b*) by attempts to standardize practice and to introduce theoretical analysis of work,
- (*c*) by concern with low standards, bad workmanship, indifferent handling of clients,
- (*d*) by attempts to establish co-ordination and co-operation between practitioners,
- (*e*) by protests about lack of recognition for the occupation,
- (*f*) by belief in the emergence of a new and different discipline with wide applications.

Such uneasiness and concern may appear in articles and correspondence to the Press, but it is more sharply expressed by formation of organizations. Different types of association can result from different types of situation and need. For example, the *British Medical Association* (as the *Provincial Medical and Surgical Association*) was established in 1834, as an association of qualified practitioners. The main purpose was to consolidate professional status, through determined effort. Formed in 1841, the *Pharmaceutical Society* aimed to counteract low standards and shortage of qualified personnel, by immediately organizing teaching and setting examinations.

Until members of an occupation realize their collective existence as a group, then movement toward professionalization cannot really begin. Yet, a plea for professional status remains insufficient. The 'cause' must be realized and recognized by society, in part or whole.[15]

(4) *Realization and recognition of the occupation as a profession, by those outside the occupation*

To achieve professional status, the occupation must be accepted as a profession by the whole, or part, of society. Appreciation of 'professional services' might be confined to a narrow section of society. For example, the general public does not normally encounter an actuary, a statistician, a radiographer, or a land agent. Therefore, it may be difficult to understand, and assess, their functions and claims to professional status. Alternatively, some new occupations obtain help from preconceived images. For example, a management accountant would be aided by the high status of accountancy, largely built up through the actions of the *Institute of Chartered Accountants* and similar bodies. A new type of engineer would start with an immediate advantage outside the engineering profession, due to the prestige established by leading engineering Institutions.

Recognition by society may take many forms: high remuneration; delegation of power and authority; use of services in preference to others; official acknowledgment of a separate existence; requests for advice; presentation of special status symbols and honours. Whereas in some occupations, individuals mainly accomplish recognition independently (actors, writers, musicians, etc.) and so contribute to a favourable public image of the whole, most occupations have to gain public estimation by means of an organized group. In the former case, acceptance of the individual depends on creativity and interpretation based on personality characteristics, and much less on special training and education. In the latter case, success of the individual is related to competence, or ability to ensure a standard, specific service. This depends on an understanding of, and conformity to, established theory and practice, founded upon special training and education.

Professional associations strive to acquire status for members on a collective group basis. Status of the individual is a function of group membership. Initial acceptance of the individual, in the economic situation, rests on an ability to exhibit affiliation to the group, and a willingness to offer associated guarantees. Success then depends on the individual's competence, personality characteristics, etc.

PROFESSIONAL ORGANIZATION

So far, it has been suggested that a profession is an occupation, which has achieved a special level of prestige in society. Professionalization is the process by which high status is attained. This process can be brought about by individuals acting independently of each other, or by individuals acting together as a group. Individuals, who obtain great personal prestige, may project that status on to their occupation. If individuals act together, improved status is easier to accomplish.

As professional associations concentrate on elevating their members' status, are these organizations a form of trade union and nothing more? A trade union is usually a registered, though unincorporated organization, representing members within a particular occupation, or close series of occupations, for the purpose of negotiating remuneration and working conditions. Thus a trade union is concerned with an aspect of economic status. These organizations are mostly affiliated to the Trades Union Congress. Their main object remains entirely protective, although some restricted educational programme may be available. No educational qualification is required for membership, demonstrating successful completion of specialized training, except that some unions demand evidence of completed apprenticeship. Employment in a particular occupation constitutes the only membership requirement. To gain benefits for members, trade unions are prepared to call strikes, to enforce membership, to conduct demarcation disputes, to advise members to work to rule.

In many respects, professional associations differ from trade unions.

(a) More than one type of professional association exists, each type determined by special functions.

(b) Professional associations tend to be multi-functional and concerned with social and economic status, as opposed to the single function of trade unions.

(c) They are usually incorporated under the Companies Acts, or by Royal Charter.

(d) Only a certain type of professional organization directly concerns itself with negotiations over remuneration and working conditions. Even then, there are few of these associations, and they tend to be much smaller than trade unions generally. They keep to one narrow occupation, and never force membership upon workers. Traditionally, they dislike resorting to the drastic action methods of trade unions, because of possible damage to the professional image. Associations, which qualify by examination,

14

do not attempt any direct intervention in questions of remuneration or working conditions, either the action is considered 'unethical', or conditions of incorporation apply restraints. There are one or two exceptions to this rule. Also, some associations devise scales of charges for members.

(*e*) In one type of professional organization, the Qualifying Association, there is more than one membership grade. Corporate membership indicates an examined level of competence.

(*f*) Professional associations may contain employers, employees and self-employed practitioners, all as members of one organization.

(*g*) Apart from special cases, compulsory membership is not a condition of employment, although employers may prefer membership of certain associations, as a sign of suitable qualification. An exception is found in law. A barrister must be a member of an Inn of Court, in order to practise. On the other hand, a solicitor must take the *Law Society's* examination to be admitted, but he does not have to join the *Law Society* to practise. A Registered Medical Practitioner does not have to belong to the *British Medical Association*. A teacher need not join the *National Union of Teachers*. Any business concerned with the dispensing and retail sale of drugs and poisons must be under the personal control of a registered pharmacist. This means qualifying as a Member of the *Pharmaceutical Society*. Generally speaking, there are no professions completely controlled by particular associations.

While qualifying professional associations have comparatively little in common with trade unions, in some ways, they resemble the medieval craft guilds. For example, structure of guild membership corresponds quite closely to that found in the Qualifying Association, viz. apprentice-journeyman-master in the guild, student-professional-senior professional in the modern association. Government in the medieval guild was less democratic, as Wardens were elected by, and from, the Masters. But in the craft guild, training was controlled and apprentices tested before admission as journeymen. And guilds regulated standards of service and competence.

Despite similarities to medieval craft guilds, only two modern professions can be traced back to guild origins: the pharmacists via the apothecaries and grocers; the surgeons back to their connection with the barbers.[16] The traditional reluctance of professionals to be considered tradesmen, may have prevented wider organization as guilds.

THE DEVELOPMENT OF PROFESSIONAL ORGANIZATION

Before the Nineteenth Century

Following the Norman Conquest, certainly by the end of the twelfth century, the Church had gained a considerable hold over the country's wealth and property, and all forms of intellectual activity.[17] This monopoly faded as the Friars began teaching in towns, and opportunities for literate men increased outside monasteries. Also a contempt for the clergy was generated in the late Middle Ages, as monastic discipline declined, and an obvious gulf grew between rich and poor ecclesiastics. Finally, Henry VIII dissolved the monasteries from 1536 to 1539.[18] But a strong link already joined the Church and the work of physicians, lawyers, secretaries, surveyors, architects, teachers and diplomats. Anyone seeking entrance to, or promotion in these occupations, automatically took holy orders, or minor orders. Nevertheless, during the twelfth and thirteenth centuries, the clergy were prohibited from practising medicine and law.[19] As medicine became more secular, this led to a division into physicians, surgeons and apothecaries, then toward organization. Teachers, and to some extent physicians, continued to be connected to the Church through universities still dominated by ecclesiastics.

Law was the first secular profession to be organized. During the second half of the twelfth century, establishment of a permanent court at Westminster encouraged full-time, 'professional' pleaders or *narratores* to appear. These men undertook to conduct a case before the Court of Common Pleas. Pleading became increasingly technical and intricate, especially after the introduction of juries at the beginning of the thirteenth century. Accordingly, laymen tended to rely on the specialists. From the narratores came the *serjeant counters*, later called *serjeants-at-law*.

The serjeants quickly monopolized all pleading in higher courts. Early in the fourteenth century, the Crown began appointing judges from the outstanding serjeants. And by the fourteenth century, anyone wanting to practise common law became either an apprentice to a serjeant, or a pupil of a senior clerk of Chancery.[20]

For their own convenience, the serjeants' apprentices, the Chancery clerks and the serjeants all formed societies. They rented certain Inns to be used first as hostels, then later to house collegiate societies. Each Inn was governed by Benchers, consisting of Judges and senior serjeants. Serjeants were elected from Readers, who conducted the education of apprentices. Below the Readers were the utter-, or outer-barristers, consisting of the better apprentices, or students, especially chosen to argue in moots, or mock trials. Judges, assisted by Benchers, gradually restricted the right to plead before a higher court, to those who had already proved themselves by arguing in moots.[21] These *Inns of Court* represent the first real professional organization, being established by 1400.

The medical profession continued practically unorganized until the sixteenth century, when the *Company of Barber-Surgeons* and the *Royal College of Physicians of London* were both formed. Except in the larger towns, apothecaries and surgeons were too few to organize independent guilds, so they tended to associate with other types of workers.[22] The London surgeons formed an unincorporated guild in 1435, then in 1495, the barbers surrendered their powers over surgeons. In 1530, the *Barbers' Company* was reorganized, and a Statute of 1540 united the barbers and surgeons into the *Company of Barber-Surgeons*.[23] For a brief period in 1421, London physicians and surgeons formed a conjoint College, or Faculty. This broke up owing to strong disagreement between the physicians and surgeons.[24] By the end of the fifteenth century, the medical profession was in a deplorable state, due to the large number of untrained, unskilled practitioners and quacks. An Act of 1511 failed to induce regulation. The first substantial organization of physicians was the *Royal College of Physicians of London*. On 23 September 1518, Henry VIII founded the College on the advice of Cardinal Wolsey, and resulting from a petition by Henry Linacre at his own expense. The Bishop of London's power to examine physicians was trans-

17

ferred to the College by Royal Charter. Statutes confirmed the Charter.[25]

The eighteenth century produced several new societies, some later developing into professional organizations. After foundation of the *Royal Society* in 1660,[26] no other permanent, influential society appeared until the *Society of Antiquaries* in 1717.[27] Unfortunately, during the eighteenth century, both societies lost their early enthusiasm and declined into uninspiring gentlemen's clubs. Then in 1754, came the *Society of Arts*, founded to finance competitions in order to encourage new inventions, art, technical and scientific improvements. Membership became very fashionable.[28]

Almost for the first time, a school of English painting began to emerge in the early eighteenth century. This led to organization. Several teaching academies appeared, and a successful exhibition in 1746, caused a number of artists to hold further exhibitions at the *Society of Arts*. Disagreements with the Society created a split. Some artists continued to exhibit there, the more eminent ones left to form the *Society of Artists of Great Britain*, incorporated by Royal Charter in 1765. As a result of further quarrels, a scandal and a struggle for control of the Society, Sir William Chambers left. Chambers drew up plans for a new society, and in 1768, he obtained George III's approval for foundation of the *Royal Academy*.[29]

Another society of consequence, and a prelude to the future, was the *Society of Gentlemen Practisers in the Courts of Law and Equity*. Over the centuries, attorneys steadily developed away from serjeants and barristers. Originally, the attorney's function was to be present in court, either to plea for his client, or to acknowledge pleas put forward by the narratore, on behalf of his client. From the thirteenth century, his functions slowly expanded, at the same time he was excluded from pleading before any principal court. By the seventeenth century, attorneys were superior legal clerks, responsible for receiving clients' instructions, conveyancing, drafting pleadings. Barristers concentrated on pleading cases before courts and acting as consultants. Solicitors emerged in the fifteenth century, as a form of land agent. Their work demanded a good knowledge of law, so by the seventeenth century they had risen to a place beside the attorneys.

At first, attorneys possessed their own Inns, the *Inns of Chancery*, but in the fifteenth century these came under the control of the *Inns of Court* and were allowed to decay. Attorneys multiplied, so leading to attempts at restricting their numbers. A Statute of 1729 proved the most successful regulating Act, for then all attorneys had to be examined by judges and entered on Court Rolls. Yet the measure was only partially useful, because judges were unpaid for their services, therefore examinations tended to be perfunctory. The *Society of Gentlemen Practisers* was founded by London attorneys, as a voluntary, independent society in 1739. It tried to improve practice by exposing untrained attorneys and any guilty of illegal practice, also to resist encroachment by other groups.[30]

Toward the end of the eighteenth century, many different societies appeared: medical societies associated with physicians, surgeons and apothecaries; societies of medical students in London hospitals;[31] the *Linnean Society*, founded in 1788, for the study of botany and zoology.[32] Most important of all were the dining clubs of the last two decades.[33] Though most of these clubs eventually failed, they represented the early signs of expanding professionalism in the nineteenth century. In London, these small societies began as a means of discussing business and maintaining contact.

By the end of the eighteenth century, professional organization was not strongly developed. To become a barrister, one needed to enter an *Inn of Court* as a student. No provision was made for education. No test was administered before call. The *Inns of Court* functioned merely as exclusive clubs. Besides the *Society of Gentlemen Practisers* in London, solicitors had formed provincial societies, as a convenient method of maintaining some social and business contact.

The medical profession continued only superficially organized. In London, the *Royal College of Physicians* retained complete control over non-surgical practice. Fellowship being confined to Oxford and Cambridge graduates in medicine, or holders of foreign medical degrees. Surgeons belonged to the *Company of Surgeons*, which had broken away from the *Company of Barber-Surgeons* in 1745. Throughout the eighteenth century, apothecaries steadily took more interest in the general practice of medicine. As a result, the *Society of Apothecaries* in London began orientating examinations and teaching toward the study of medicine.[34]

Why was professional organization so undeveloped? This is not an easy question to answer. The population of England and Wales grew very slowly until about mid-eighteenth century. It stayed small and widely distributed in self-contained, rural communities, with few sizable towns. Industry developed on a craft basis. Small-scale trade did not demand complex systems of accounting, insurance, shipping and finance. Any specialists, such as doctors, surgeons, apothecaries, attorneys, engineers, surveyors, accountants, architects, etc., were either geographically isolated from each other, or too few in number to require, or enable, regulation of competition and service. Further, except in the case of law, nothing actually prevented unqualified and untrained practitioners from offering service. Often, specialist occupations did not enjoy the benefits of common techniques, founded on a firm theoretical base. No regular training existed, apart from experience obtained by working with an established practitioner. No measures of competence existed, apart from individual conscience, the satisfaction of clients and a constant demand for services. If anything, experience engrained by apprenticeship was widely regarded as the best method of training. It applied to medicine, law, architecture, engineering and so on. Possibly the system of pupilage instilled them with a feeling for individual practice, instead of need for belonging to an organized group. Strong social class divisions may have cut across occupations, preventing unity of the profession as a first step to organization. Members of professions were certainly divided by social origins, and by social class position of clientele.

Very likely, the eighteenth century marks the true beginning of the professions. During the first half of the century, both doctors and lawyers suffered heavy lampooning in plays, pamphlets and novels. They were quacks and pettifoggers, exploiting other people's misfortunes for their own betterment. They were conniving untrustworthy rascals. The English clergy, beset by patronage, non-residency, pluralism and poor livings, was treated without much respect. Incumbents were either well-meaning, dedicated, starving wretches, or rich, pleasure-seeking, avaricious men who did not seem to take their vocation very seriously. The Church, law, the army, the navy, and the civil service functioned in an infested state of patronage and complex sinecures. Over the century, respectability and public estimation developed for the professions, probably owing to increasing involvement of practitioners in local affairs.[35]

The Nineteenth Century and After

Several changes took place in the nineteenth century. Old organizations were reformed and new associations came on to the scene.

Firstly, older organizations found themselves driven to reform, chiefly from within. After 1860, the *Royal Society* was transformed from a 'club' dominated by amateurs and non-scientists, into an exclusive society for eminent professional scientists, with membership signifying a level of distinction in science.[36] The *Royal College of Physicians* revised its constitution. Voting rights were extended, transfer from Licentiate to Fellow became possible, complete revision of examinations took place and a new Member grade was introduced.[37] In 1800, the *Company of Surgeons* obtained a Royal Charter to secure reincorporation as the *Royal College of Surgeons of London*, but Council remained self-electing until 1843. Another Royal Charter in 1843 extended franchise, created a new Fellowship grade and renamed it the *Royal College of Surgeons of England*.[38] By the Apothecaries Act 1815, the *Society of Apothecaries* gained jurisdiction over the whole of England and Wales. Now the Society's examinations were almost entirely concerned with medical subjects.[39] For nearly the rest of the century, the double qualification (L.S.A., M.R.C.S. and later the L.M.S.S.A.) was sought by aspiring general practitioners—a new type of comprehensive medical man.

The *Inns of Court* remained structurally unchanged, though education and preparation of Bar students gradually received more attention. Following a brief experiment in 1833, lectures were introduced in the 1840s, only to lapse again in a short time. The Solicitor-General convened a meeting of Benchers in 1851, and as a result, the Inns set up the joint *Council of Legal Education*. The Council established a permanent lecture system and a voluntary examination. The examination became compulsory in 1872. A general meeting of the Bar in December 1883, led to formation of the *Bar Committee*, replaced in 1894 by the *General Council of the Bar*. This was a consultative, representative body with limited powers and no authority over individual Inns.[40]

Secondly, many more study societies appeared in the nineteenth century, all based on the same pattern as the eighteenth century *Society of Antiquaries* and *Linnean Society*, viz. the *Geological Society* (1807), the *Royal Astronomical Society* (1820), the *Zoological Society* (1824), the *Royal Geographical Society* (1830), the *Royal Entomological Society of London* (1833), the *Chemical Society* (1841) and so on.[41]

Initially in most organizations, membership contained a heavy concentration of peers, 'gentlemen', parsons and doctors, undoubtedly due to the fact that they constituted the leisured, educated section of society.[42] A great many doctors and clergymen were amateur botanists, zoologists, astronomers and geologists. These associations represented a need for the means to study and discuss subjects on a serious level, in the absence of cheap authoritative books, informed magazines and accessible libraries. For practically the whole century, science and many specialized subjects could still serve as hobbies, which did not entail very deep, intricate pre-instruction. In several associations, the same people seem to have been involved in the foundation.[43] Perhaps the middle classes joined these organizations, as an expression of their keen search for self-improvement, also because membership began to convey some social status. Smaller, local societies sprang up throughout the country.[44]

However, many of the London societies changed in structure and function. From small metropolitan associations, they expanded into national organizations. Membership became increasingly 'professional'. Treatment of subjects grew more technical. Plurality, membership of more than one society, was less evident toward the end of the century.[45] These organizations were no longer low-level discussion groups for middle-class amateurs, and an educationally favoured, leisured élite. Instead, they had become steadily more important as meeting places for trained specialists, who relied on the facilities for communicating new information.

Thirdly, a new type of professional organization evolved. This was an association devised to improve professional status, working conditions and the nature of the profession, by gathering together established professionals, without providing for student-professionals. No unqualified or non-practitioners were admitted. No attempt was made to qualify anyone to practise. Study functions seemed incidental to the main purpose of driving the occupation to higher status. The first important organization appeared in 1832. This was the *Provincial Medical and Surgical Association*, to maintain 'the Honour and Respectability of the Profession generally in the Provinces'.[46] Besides collecting statistics and publishing technical information, the Association worked diligently toward securing registration for the profession, achieved in the Medical Act, 1858. The P.M.S.A. became the *British Medical Association* in 1856.

Many smaller, less effective bodies have been created since the P.M.S.A. Yet none has been quite as successful as the B.M.A., or the *National Union of Teachers* (founded in 1870 as the *National Union of Elementary Teachers*).[47]

Fourthly, the most notable and spectacular development in the nineteenth century, proved to be the rise of the qualifying professional associations. The first of these was the *Institution of Civil Engineers* in January 1818. Although the Institution neither examined entrants, nor regularly published any technical journal until 1836, it cannot be regarded as a 'Study Association'. It started with three grades: Members, Honorary Members and Associates—a fourth (Corresponding Members) being added in November 1819. Members were practising Civil Engineers, Associates were training to be Civil Engineers and Honorary Members were those interested in Civil Engineering. Late introduction of examinations (in 1897) does not indicate an absence of the qualifying function. Rather it reflects a reliance upon pupilage. To qualify as a civil engineer, training usually meant taking up an apprenticeship with a practising member, who later vouched for the pupil after a suitable period.

In 1834, there came the *(Royal) Institute of British Architects*. This followed a progressive movement to organization, spread over some fifty years. Once again, pupilage became the accepted form of training; voluntary examinations eventually began in 1862. The *Pharmaceutical Society* appeared in 1841, composed of chemists and druggists, who had taken over the original work of the apothecaries. Unlike the civil engineers and architects, the pharmacists did not rely completely on pupilage, they quickly started examinations.

Three other Qualifying Associations were founded before 1850: the *Royal College of Veterinary Surgeons* in 1844, the *Institution of Mechanical Engineers* in 1847 and the *Institute of Actuaries* in 1848. The Mechanical Engineers did not set examinations, for they continued the Civil Engineers' example. On the other hand, the Actuaries rapidly prepared examinations, while the *Royal College of Veterinary Surgeons* was already connected with the veterinary colleges of London and Edinburgh.

All these associations will be examined in greater detail in later chapters.

One important organization not mentioned so far is the *Law Society*, founded in 1825 as '*The Society of Attorneys, Solicitors, Proctors and others not being Barristers practising in the Courts of Law and Equity of the United Kingdom*'. By this time, the eighteenth-century *Society of Gentlemen Practisers* had almost faded away, its effective days long since passed. The *Law Society* was also a voluntary organization, aiming to improve the state of the profession. Many felt a need for organized training and examination of solicitors, and a few years after formation, the Society was proposed as an examining body. It declined to act, suggesting the Bench ought to be responsible for examination. However, on the introduction of examinations in 1836–7, the Society supplied representatives first to one examining board (the Common Law Courts Examining Board), then later to the other (the Chancery examining authority in 1846). Finally, in 1877, the *Law Society* became fully responsible for all solicitors' examinations.[48]

From mid-century, the number of Qualifying Associations multiplied, especially from the 1880s. The movement spread to other types of engineers, surveyors, chemists, librarians, accountants, auctioneers, company secretaries, and on into the twentieth century. No simple explanation accounts for this phenomenon. Expansion was not a response to improved educational facilities. On the contrary, associations found themselves faced by inadequate methods of preparing their students for examinations. Similarly, associations did not appear just as a direct result of the progress of industrialization.

Professionalization, as a process, diffused through many

occupations by means of the Qualifying Association. This type of association demonstrated an ability to convert occupations into professions. But the formation of an association *per se* has never immediately, or sometimes even ultimately, brought professional status to an occupation. Professionalism has continued to grow in the Study Associations, owing to an expansion of trained and qualified specialists in pure and applied science, astronomy, archaeology, etc. Study Associations have turned into centres for communication and discussion of research. Increasing complexity of technical detail eliminates any amateurs not well-grounded in the subject. Yet some societies remain part professional and part amateur, because the subject-matter serves as an interesting leisure-time activity. Geography, astronomy and certain biological subjects are examples. Developing professionalism also shows itself in the expanding number of protective associations, though such organization can only consolidate status.

Of all forms of professional organization, the Qualifying Association seems the most significant and the most interesting. But why is it significant? Where does it fit into a general pattern of professional organization? Why are Qualifying Associations formed in the first place? How does the association work? Has it affected the educational structure? Having determined members' competence, how far do associations proceed to ensure integrity? These are some of the questions to be considered in the following chapters.

Chapter Two

TYPES OF PROFESSIONAL
ORGANIZATION

INTRODUCTION

CHAPTER ONE outlined the beginning of a number of different organizations. Obviously they were not all formed for the same purpose. A variety of objects can be found, perhaps undergoing change and emphasis over time. Some began as associations to protect occupational standards and status. In other organizations, 'professionalism' evolved as membership consisted more of full-time practitioners, less of interested amateurs.

In medicine, both the *Royal College of Physicians* and *Royal College of Surgeons* were designed to serve one purpose—to provide a qualification. Alternatively, the *British Medical Association* was conceived to organize qualified practitioners, in order to protect the medical profession.[1] Chemistry offers another example. The *Chemical Society* does not qualify anyone to style himself as a 'chemist', purely on the basis of being a Fellow. The Society aims at 'the general advancement of Chemical Science by the discussion and publication of new discoveries and the encouragement of chemical research'. On the other hand, the qualifying body for chemists is the *Royal Institute of Chemistry*.[2]

Yet another kind of organization is the *Royal Society*. Founded for the promotion of science, membership until mid-nineteenth century contained anyone interested and willing to support the objects, scientist or non-scientist. Then membership was slowly restricted to distinguished scientists. Today, election to the Society has become an honour in the scientific world, awarded in recognition of contributions to science. As in the case of the *Royal Academy*, and the *British Academy*, Fellowship is bestowed from inside. Aspiring members do not apply directly for Fellowship. Election is by no means certain.

Another society mentioned in Chapter One was the *Royal Society of Arts*. Here, the main object is 'the encouragement of Arts, Manufactures and Commerce'. Candidates for election to Fellowship must be proposed by three Fellows, at least one of whom knows the candidate personally. In special cases, the Council can nominate Fellows. Regardless of the Society's past achievements, present valuable services, or distinguished membership, entrance is relatively easy providing the application is properly supported. There are no qualification restrictions. The same can be said of several study societies: the *Royal Geographical Society*, the *Royal Astronomical Society*, the *Zoological Society*.

Taking all these associations and societies, they constitute a pattern of services for professionals. Some supply the means of qualifying as a particular sort of worker. Some give an opportunity to keep up to date with a subject, or study the subject further. Some seek to protect the professional, by acting as an organized voice of the profession against other forces. Some are able to recognize professional achievement, by carefully selecting candidates to join a distinguished membership. But these purposes are not insular, selfish aims devised to arm the professional against the public interest. Those using professional services benefit through higher standards of qualification, the stricter control of professional conduct, the organized supply of information to the professional.

In order to understand the vast system of professional organization, it is worthwhile separating the different types of association. Types of association can be based on an analysis of the predominating objects of the organizations, backed by an estimate of structure and work.[3] So, looking at all associations, some objects will be present in one type of association yet absent in another, and the objects will define the work and structure of the organization. Going further, some objects form the definite aims of the association, then these aims result in the fulfilment of other objects. For example, one main aim may be examination of entrants, thereby qualifying them to be recognized as mechanical engineers, chemists, accountants and so on. This central object can lead to the elevation of professional status, as the qualification becomes acceptable as a reliable standard. Similarly, a body of qualified professionals can draw upon expert opinion generated by members, thus forming a source of advice to the public, inquiry committees and various organizations. All the aims of associations can be divided into primary and secondary functions: primary functions being the direct aims; secondary functions being indirect aims following on from primary functions.

Primary Functions

(1) *To organize*

Clearly, this is the most fundamental aim of an association. Discounting any selfish desire for self-advertisement or power, on the part of the founders, their immediate aim is to gather together all those within a particular occupation, or all persons with a particular interest. Histories of many organizations show initial formation to be a selfless task, performed by dedicated men (and women), who hope to build an improved foundation for study, for protection, for raising standards.[4] Few associations have been created, or maintained, without the active determination of founders, Council and Executive Officers.

Yet a majority of members of any association seem notoriously ungrateful and apathetic, once they have joined. They acquire membership and this first stage of 'belonging' becomes an end in itself, rather than a means to a further end. Therefore, the organizing function extends beyond the period of foundation. It is a continuous process, making members conscious of being organized and receiving benefits. Without a two-way exchange between organizers and membership, the association hardly performs its organizing function properly. Also, the association organizes to carry out other aims: to qualify, to study, to protect. Any failure to promote such objects, internally or externally, means a partial failure of the organizing function.

(2) *To qualify*

Not all associations aim at qualifying their members to act in a certain capacity. Those associations intending to furnish a qualification may have difficulty introducing examinations. But tests of competence are necessary to build professional status, as well as professional standards. Even then, examinations are not enough; the qualification must be accepted inside the occupation, as good evidence of knowledge and experience.

(3) *To further study of a subject and communicate information obtained*

Extent of this function varies tremendously from one occupation to another, from one subject area to another. For example, in science, output of new knowledge steadily expands, constantly forcing the pace for rapid and accurate communication. Good co-ordination is a necessity. Since 1941, a joint subscription policy has operated for members of the *Royal Institute of Chemistry*, the *Chemical Society* and the *Society of Chemical Industry*. In 1960, the amalgamation of the *Physical Society* and *Institute of Physics* seemed partly aimed at greater co-ordination. Another agreement was reached in 1961, between the *Institute of Metals, Iron and Steel Institute* and *Institution of Metallurgists*. The *Institution of Mining and Metallurgy* joined the group subscription scheme in 1963.

Nothing like this has happened outside the fields of science and technology. Biology, as a general field, has more associations concerned primarily with study than any other subject, possibly except for medicine. On the other hand, in accountancy, many aspects of social work, insurance, commerce, the flow of new knowledge is much slower, information being largely confined to an application of a few techniques, or reassessment of old methods.

In any organization, study facilities depend on many factors; available finance, subject-matter, members' needs, alternative sources of information. Facilities can involve: lectures and discussion meetings, study groups, conferences, conventions, visits, library, museum, publication of a journal, books, pamphlets, etc.

(4) *To register competent professionals*

Associations, which qualify members, often maintain a register or publish a membership list, serving as a register of those considered competent. Occasionally, a Registrar will be found in an association, although the occupation is not registered by Statute. This indicates the serious aim to distinguish qualified from unqualified. The list of corporate members provides a useful guide, for anyone wishing to employ specific professional services.

(5) *To promote and preserve a high standard of professional conduct*

A real need for a code of ethics depends on the nature of the professional task. A formal code is useful, perhaps essential: where the professional works as an individual, rather than in a mass organization; where he is concerned directly with the life and property of others. In fact, few professional organizations possess formal codes. Most associations tend to use a general proviso in the Bye-laws or Articles of Association enabling appropriate action by Council, if a case of unprofessional conduct arises. An elaborate code may be missing, but an association can still be conscious of the need to preserve a uniform system of conduct and practice.

Secondary Functions

(1) *To raise professional status*

Elevation of professional status might be mistaken for the central object of many professional organizations. However, improvement in status can only result from primary aims, viz. promotion of examinations, enforcement of an ethical code. Standing of a professional group must depend ultimately on the quality of service offered by the individual; to some extent, this will depend on the association's standards. If an organization intends to gain advantages for members, success can only follow demonstrated public benefit. Ability to secure wide publicity and make a resounding impact can bring a professional group to public notice, so creating a general awareness of the group's existence. But public awareness must not be confused with public estimation. The whole problem of professional status becomes complicated by the constant tendency of associations to measure themselves against each other. Considerable effort seems to be spent on raising the association's standing in the eyes of other associations; consequently devices and procedures have developed, probably with little meaning or value beyond the world of professional organization.

(2) *To control entry to the profession*

Unless there are legal restrictions on practice, a professional association can seldom completely control entrance to the profession. An association can be said to control entrance to a profession; in a registered occupation, with the association as the central registration authority; or if the association awards the essential qualification. For example, Pharmacists and the *Pharmaceutical Society*, Patent Agents and the *Chartered Institute of Patent Agents*, certain associations of Medical Auxiliaries. Even then, they cannot prevent the qualification, admission and registration of any individual, if all the basic requirements have been satisfied. Outside the regulation possible in a registered profession, associations can hardly control entrance to the occupation. To become an accountant, it is worth taking the examinations of the *Institute of Chartered Accountants*, or *Association of Certified and Corporate Accountants*. Indeed, to act as an auditor to public companies, one must be a member of the Institute or Association. But only a small proportion of accountants are in 'public' practice. Many people practise as 'accountants' in commerce and institutions, without attempting to join either body, though some are members of lesser accountancy organizations. One does not have to join the *Royal Institute of Chemistry* to be a chemist, or the *Institution of Mechanical Engineers* to be a mechanical engineer. Nevertheless, if an association's qualification has attained sufficient recognition, employers may insist upon employees being members, or taking the examinations, in order to hold a particular post. They may prefer membership of one association to that of another, or prefer a member of a professional association to a university graduate. This attitude tends to be reinforced, where employers and administrators are themselves members of specific associations.

(3) *To protect the profession and the public*

Through insisting upon a qualified membership, adhering to a common practice, controlled by an elected body drawn from members, an association can present some guarantee to both professionals and those they serve. This may be a guarantee of fair competition and maintained concern over professional matters for the professional, and a possible source of redress against unreasonable charges, or abuse of trust, for the lay-public. Limitations occur if the association is not connected with a closed profession, or if disqualification from membership does not prevent further practice.

(4) *To act as an interest, or pressure group, on behalf of members*

All professional organizations can be assumed to act as the concerted voice of a professional group, but not all associations can directly pursue the betterment of remuneration and working conditions. They may be prevented: legally, by Articles or Byelaws involved under incorporation; temperamentally, by a reluctance to interfere in such matters. Accordingly, associations principally devised to qualify, or to study, usually act as interest groups—not pressure groups. Associations aimed to protect remuneration and working conditions of the professional are normally pressure groups.

(5) *To encourage social activity and co-operation between professionals*

Most organizations relax occasionally from their more serious endeavours. Formal and informal social contacts are important, if just to remind individual members, without seeming to indoctrinate, that they belong to a corporate body which exists for their benefit and well-being. The Annual Dinner serves as a fillip to the feeling of corporate pride, allowing distinguished members and non-members to sing the praises of the association. On a smaller scale, lesser meetings create and sustain formal and informal relationships between officials and members, between professionals themselves, aiding communication of advice, information and even polite admonishments.

(6) *To provide welfare benefits*

Some associations, especially those which qualify, manage a benevolent fund, established by donations, to help necessitous members or dependants of deceased members.

TYPES OF PROFESSIONAL ORGANIZATION

Using differences in function as a starting point for analysis, types of professional association can be determined. Essentially, the term professional organization refers to any association, which directly aims at the improvement of any aspect of professional practice: for example, by providing a qualification, by controlling conduct, by co-ordinating technical information, by pressing for better conditions of employment.

In the following analysis, four basic types of organization are proposed, with two types further subdivided. The types are:

(1) The Prestige Association:
    (*a*) The Exclusive Prestige Association,
    (*b*) The Non-Selective Prestige Association.
(2) The Study Association.
(3) The Qualifying Association.
(4) The Occupational Association:
    (*a*) The Co-ordinating Association,
    (*b*) The Protective Association.

Each type of organization will be described with respect to: aims; membership structure and requirements; government and committee structure; work; effect. Examples will be given of each kind of association.

(1) *The Prestige Association*

This description implies the sense of honour and distinction bestowed on an individual, through election to a closed group, membership of which is generally regarded as conferring special prestige. More accurately, the type ought to be subdivided into two: the *Exclusive Prestige Association* and the *Non-Selective Prestige Association*. The former is exclusive because of careful, rigorous selection of special candidates. The latter is non-selective because election does not rest on demonstrated skill, ability or achievement in a specialized branch of knowledge, or activity. The second classification will be considered in another section.

Aims

Usually, aims are wide. The *Royal Society*, in the first Charter (1662), is stated to be formed 'for further promoting by authority of experiments the science of natural things and of useful arts'; the second Charter (1663), abbreviates the aim even more, viz. 'for Improving Natural knowledge'. The *Royal Academy*'s 'Instrument of Foundation' in 1768, described it as the 'Royal Academy of Arts in London for the purpose of Cultivating and Improving the Arts of Painting, Sculpture and Architecture'. In a third example, the *British Academy*, it is 'for the promotion of Historical, Philosophical and Philological Studies'.

Membership Structure and Requirements

Membership structure is quite simple. The *Royal Society* has two main classes: Fellows and Foreign Members (there are also three Royal Fellows). The *British Academy* consists of Fellows, Corresponding Fellows, plus a small special class of Honorary Fellows. In the *Royal Academy*, two main classes exist: Academicians (including Senior Academicians) and Associates, with a small class of Honorary Academicians and one Honorary Academician Extraordinary.

Requirements are difficult to specify. Neither interest in the association's work, nor great achievement within the field necessarily determines election to membership. One does not apply to become a member, rather one is informed of having been elected to membership. In pure and applied science, election to Fellowship of the *Royal Society* would be considered high recognition of service to science. Artists, perhaps those progressing through middle age, would regard election to the *Royal Academy* as a mark of honour.[5]

Two important elements preserve exclusiveness: firstly, the size of membership is restricted, usually by Royal Charter; secondly, election is sought after by those outside, and carefully controlled inside.[6]

Government and Committee Structure

Government is uncomplicated: a Central Council elected by members and from members; possibly some standing committees to manage certain activities (Finance, Library, Publications). The *Royal Society* has an exceptional committee structure. Apart from the Council and Council Standing Committee, there are about a hundred sub-committees dealing with allocation of money for research, expeditions, exchange visits, preparation of publications, collation of scientific information. These committees involve a large proportion of the Fellows.

Work

If the aims seem wide, so too is the range of work. The *Royal Academy*'s function divides into two main areas, the teaching of art and staging of art exhibitions.[7] The scope of the *British Academy* spreads even wider: support for publications and research outside the Academy; administration of grants for archaeological research; extensive meetings.[8] The *Royal Society*'s work spans almost the whole of science, through publications (chiefly the 'Philosophical Transactions' and 'Proceedings'), administration of grants for research, co-ordination of research, and shared responsibility for the government of various institutions.[9]

Effect

Distinguished public service, a carefully fostered tradition, very deliberate selection of candidates—these factors put the *Prestige Association* on a special level of professional organization. If an association's status is recognized and accepted by society, as well as by the professional world, then membership confers status upon the individual. If it recruits from a professional élite, awarding a mark of merit, then even higher status may result.

(2) *The Study Association*

These societies consist of individuals willing to further knowledge of a subject in a narrow field of inquiry. They may be highly specialized groups dealing with complicated technical details, requiring an initial depth of knowledge and training, in order to appreciate the study. They may be societies connected with subjects demanding far less technical knowledge and training, therefore open to both general and expert discussion. Thus at one extreme will be found the *Chemical Society*, the *Royal Statistical Society*, the *Palaeontographical Society*—at the other, the *Zoological Society*, the *Royal Geographical Society*.

Aims

The whole aim is to study and promote a specific subject by holding regular meetings, producing publications, providing a library and sometimes by other means. The *Royal Meteorological Society* 'for promotion of the science of meteorology in every aspect'; the *Royal Astronomical Society* for 'the encouragement and promotion of Astronomy'; the *Zoological Society* for 'advancement of Zoology and Animal Physiology and for the introduction of new and curious subjects of the Animal Kingdom'; the *Chemical Society* for the 'general advancement of Chemical Science by the discussion and publication of new discoveries and the encouragement of chemical research'.

Membership Structure and Requirements

In most cases, they have only a single class of members (Fellows). Some add a special class of Honorary Fellows for distinguished members, perhaps an Associate of Junior Membership grade based on age, lower subscription, fewer privileges. Requirements for membership constitute a bare minimum: interest in the subject; recommendation by one to three existing members, known to the candidate personally.

Government and Committee Structure

Committee structure depends on size and work of the society. It may consist of a Council only, or there can be a Council plus Standing Committees to manage Finance, Library, Publications, possibly committees for special projects as well. Councils tend to be much smaller (twenty to thirty people) than in *Qualifying Associations*.

Some societies have a more complex committee structure. In 1959, the *Zoological Society* had seven committees on which non-Council members also served (Animal Welfare and Husbandry, Collections Policy, Education, Gardens and Parks, Prosectorial, Scientific, Zoological Record). The *Royal Geographical Society* has six committees: Finance, Library and Maps, Education, Research and Expeditions, Survey. Both the *Zoological Society* and *Royal Geographical Society* have heavy outside educational programmes, an uncommon feature among *Study Associations*.

Work

A society's work depends greatly on size of membership, geographical distribution of membership and subject. Many
societies are limited to a series of lecture-meetings held during
certain months of the year, and a regular publication ('Journal'
or 'Transactions'). Most of them consist of 2,000 members or
less, though some are very big (*Royal Horticultural Society, Royal
Geographical Society, Chemical Society, Zoological Society, Geological
Society, Royal Meteorological Society*).

Effect

As already suggested, subject-areas vary in complexity. A more
complicated and technical subject is likely to attract professionals
only, or those sufficiently trained to understand lectures and
publications. *Study Associations* covering a more general field, or
a technical subject more accessible to amateurs, attract non-
professionals as well as professionals. Now, a danger arises
because some members may use the designatory letters as a
'qualification', or an uninformed, unsuspecting public might
regard the abbreviation as an indication of 'qualification'. The
Study Association then becomes a *Non-Selective Prestige Association.*
'Non-Selective' as election is fairly certain, providing the candidate follows the correct procedure. A 'Prestige Association', in
that members may try using the designatory letters to create
prestige, or an air of intellectual status. These remarks do not
imply the degradation of a society's objects, or any other internal
failure. Trouble arises from possible abuse by some members,
intentional or otherwise.[10]

Examples

Practically all the *Study Associations* of National importance are
listed in Appendix IIb.

(3) *The Qualifying Association*

While the first two types were designed to improve knowledge of
a subject, the *Qualifying Association* aims to examine and qualify
individuals, wishing to practise in the subject. This additional

object vastly expands the role of an association, giving it a key position in the system of professional organization.

Aims

Many *Qualifying Associations* act in a dual capacity, behaving as an association to qualify and study. A central aim is the advancement of a subject-area and/or the technique involved in its practice. New aims spring up by the side of any qualifying function, extending toward the control of professional conduct and the elevation of professional status.

Membership Structure and Requirements

Other types of associations are basically uni-grade, the *Qualifying Association* is multi-grade. Grades of membership separate the senior professional, professional and aspirant professional. Divisions rest on examination levels, age, position of occupational responsibility, experience. Requirements for membership become more complex: interest is not enough, pre-eminence is not a necessary pre-requisite. The main requirement consists of an ability to pass the association's examination(s), or obtain suitable exemption—backed by age, experience and responsibility.

Government and Committee Structure

Multiple functions and increased membership size demand a more elaborate governmental structure. Central government is on a much larger scale, including many standing committees to manage admissions, education, examinations, publications and so on. Additionally, local organizations (branches, local societies) and specialized sections within the association make the internal pattern of government even more complicated.

Work

Associations contribute to training and education of professionals; to the organization of research; to the publication of research and aids to practice; to providing expert advice.

Effect

Success of earlier *Qualifying Associations* encouraged those in other occupations to seek professional status, by adopting similar methods. Proliferation has developed overlapping, confusion for the public, feeble imitation and some consolidation.

Examples

Almost all the associations in England and Wales are shown in Appendix IIa.

(4) *The Occupational Association*

In a sense, all associations connected with a distinct occupation are 'occupational' associations. However, the true *Occupational Association* organizes professionals, without attempting to qualify them. There are two sub-types.

The *Co-ordinating Association*: an association of qualified professionals working in a narrow professional field, which co-ordinates the professional activities of members, without extensive negotiations or the application of pressure techniques to improve working conditions or remuneration of members.

The *Protective Association*: an association of qualified professionals working in a comparatively wide professional area, which provides an organized means of exercising pressure to protect and improve the working conditions and remuneration of the individual professional.

Aims

Primarily, the aim is to organize qualified professionals. *Co-ordinating Associations* enable specialists to discuss occupational problems, which are too parochial to be satisfactorily treated in more general associations. Are *Protective Associations* entirely narrow-minded professional trade unions? As explained in Chapter One, there are many differences distinguishing professional associations from ordinary trade unions. Some *Protective Associations* appear to behave solely as trade unions, pressing for higher incomes and benefits. Others perform valuable public services, which must help to discount any unpleasant impression that they are purely self-centred. Of course, such actions may be deliberately planned to gain extra support. But perhaps this is an ungenerous attitude. Certainly the *British Medical Association* undertakes a great deal of work for the public good. It has campaigned strongly against quacks and patent medicines; introduced codes of ethics to guide practitioners; organized and published expert advice for the general public; fought for improved public and industrial health services.[11]

Membership Structure and Requirements

The majority have only one class of members. Qualified professionals, or those working in that narrow area, are eligible for membership.

Government and Committee Structure

Enormous variation occurs in government, anything from a simple organizing committee, to an elaborate system of committees.

Work

The work of *Occupational Associations* is hard to assess. Many are small, much of the work does not attract public attention, or receive wide publicity. Two of the largest and most powerful organizations dominate the scene (the *British Medical Association*, and the *National Union of Teachers*). Distribution of this type of organization is uneven throughout the professional world. Some fields do not appear to have them (accountancy, surveying, management), although there may be more specialized associations. Some areas have associations, but professionals do not seem to use them (chemistry, engineering). Some fields are swamped by organization (teaching, medicine).

Effect

Professionals have always regarded trade unionism as dangerous and unnecessary. By tradition, the professional does not bargain or discuss fees. To descend to the market place might disturb the delicately balanced superiority of his position. To quarrel over payment may destroy the ideal of public service. Bureaucratization and mass employment have removed many qualms; in medicine and teaching, 'union' consciousness grows. Chemists, physicists and engineers, although subject to bureaucratization, have operated in a 'sellers' market' during recent years, which may help to account for their lack of interest in unionism. How far will professionals go, before they adopt true trade union tactics? Strikes, working to rule, compulsory membership, demarcation disputes—all have been used, or threatened, but such action can harm the reputation of any professional group.[12]

Examples

CO-ORDINATING ASSOCIATIONS: *Society of Medical Officers of Health, County Surveyors' Society, Society of County Treasurers.* (Central and Local Government Officers are very prone to organization.) PROTECTIVE ASSOCIATION: *British Medical Association, National Union of Teachers, Engineers Guild, British Association of Chemists, Association of Official Architects, National Pharmaceutical Union.*

TRADE ASSOCIATIONS

A Trade Association is not a professional association.[13] However, trade associations' activities involve professionals. In England and Wales, there are over 1,300 of them, surmounted by the two giants—the *Federation of British Industries* and the *National Union of Manufacturers*.[14] Services range through exhibitions, advertising on behalf of the industry, journals, abstracts, films, market information and statistics, research, and on to education.[15] Depending on the nature of the association and the industry concerned, professionals will be found as representatives on committees. As representatives of trade associations, they gain special access to government departments, advisory committees and comparable high levels of administration and advice. Trade associations connected with highly technical industries, offer a great deal of useful information and advice.[16]

Types of Professional Organization

Patterns of professional organization are intricate. A typology can only allow a partial, approximate analysis, as 'pure' types will not always be clearly identifiable in each occupation. Associations seldom perform just one function. The most complicated type of organization, the *Qualifying Association*, attempts to qualify, to advance the subject, to control professional conduct and so on.

Some organizations remain difficult to analyse, owing to the traditional structure and role built up over time. The *Inns of Court*, the *Royal College of Physicians of London*, the *Royal College of Surgeons of England* and the *Law Society* are all special problems.

The *Inns of Court* continue as voluntary, unincorporated, independent societies, outside the control of any external authority. Each Inn consists of Bar Students, Barristers and Benchers. Each Inn supports the *General Council of the Bar* and the *Council of Legal Education*. Each Inn is governed by self-electing Benchers. Only the Inns have the power to qualify a barrister, by admitting him to the Bar. Only the Inns can disbar a barrister, though the Bar Council investigates and gives advice in cases of unprofessional conduct. The Bar Council also issues general directives about unethical conduct. In May 1962, the *Inns of Court Executive Council* was established, to consider matters referred to it and with powers to make decisions binding on the Inns. Also, the *Council of Legal Education* now has full authority to decide on all matters connected with legal education, without reference to the Inns. Once called to the Bar, a barrister remains a member of his Inn for life; he can only resign by petitioning for voluntary disbarment.

The *Law Society* began as a voluntary society. Under the Solicitors Act, 1843, the Society was made responsible for maintaining a Register of Solicitors. Responsibility for all solicitors' examinations came in the Solicitors' Act of 1877. Under the Act of 1933, powers were given to make rules of professional conduct. The Disciplinary Committee consists of past and present Council members, appointed by the Master of the Rolls. The Society instituted lectures in 1833. By 1854, lectures on Common Law, Equity and Conveyancing were being delivered twice weekly, and from these courses, the Law School developed. To become a solicitor, one has to enrol as a student with the *Law Society*, serve articles which are registered with the Society, and take the Society's examinations.[17] Having been admitted as a solicitor, it is not necessary to become a member of the Society.

The old medical corporations retain several vestiges of their ancient origins, while the *Royal College of Obstetricians and Gynaecologists* assumed much the same structure on foundation in 1924. Neither the *Royal College of Physicians*, nor the *Royal College of Surgeons* established a regular journal, although both founded excellent libraries.[18] After the Medical Act 1886, the two Royal Colleges introduced a conjoint examination (the L.R.C.P., M.R.C.S.). Post-graduate examinations are held independently for Membership of the *Royal College of Physicians* (M.R.C.P.) and Fellowship of the *Royal College of Surgeons* (F.R.C.S.). Fellowship of the *Royal College of Physicians* is obtained through election by existing Fellows. Except for distinguished persons, admission to the Royal Colleges is solely by examination. Thus they provide either an additional qualification, or an alternative to a university degree. Post-graduate qualifications are even more important. All three Colleges maintain a multitude of research and investigation committees, to co-ordinate and encourage medical research. Sections of the *Royal College of Surgeons* also examine dentists (for the L.D.S. R.C.S.) and anaesthetists (F.F.A. R.C.S.). In the case of all the Royal Colleges, members are merely diploma-holders, without access to the kind of facilities normally found in qualifying bodies.

SOME FACTORS DETERMINING DISTRIBUTION AND NUMBERS OF ASSOCIATIONS

Distribution of different types is not even throughout every professional field. Some areas do not have distinct *Study Associations*, for example, accountancy, insurance, management, banking. Pure and applied science, particularly biology, abound with *Study Associations*, yet there are only two *Qualifying Associations*—one for chemists, the other for physicists. For the artist, painter and sculptor, there appear to be numerous *Exclusive Prestige Associations*, but no other type. Teaching has a large number of *Pro-*

tective Occupational Associations and very little else. Medicine has every type of association, except the *Exclusive Prestige Association*. In Engineering, the emphasis is on the *Qualifying Association*, at the same time, this area shows the highest differentiation (about two dozen specialist associations).

What kind of factors help to determine the uneven spread and number of different types?

(1) *Emphasis on Theoretical, or Advanced Practical Elements*

Where a strong, expanding, theoretical base exists, more *Study Associations* are likely to be found. Both science and medicine possess considerable numbers of *Study Associations*, contrasting with every other professional field. Where emphasis stresses qualification alone, and individuals simply require a means of demonstrating a specific level of acquired knowledge and practice, then study aspects play a minor role, especially if the theoretical foundation does not expand much. This situation applies in the non-technological sides of commerce and industry.

(2) *Possibility of Subject being treated on Amateur and Full-time Employment Level*

Some subjects can be approached on two levels: by individuals regarding the subject as a source of interest, a part-time study or hobby; by others, who consider the subject as a basis of full-time, paid employment. Co-existence of two-level treatment fosters the growth of *Study Associations*, for example, in a wide range of biological subjects, geography, geology, astronomy, archaeology.

(3) *Clarity of Separation within the Study Area or Occupation*

Where internal divisions are practical, obvious or necessary, then there will be a greater tendency to form additional organizations in the same area. Fragmentation represents a dangerous threat to any type of association, as dispersion may affect potential size of membership, finance and services, or influence.

Separation does not necessarily follow increasing specialization. In science and medicine, specialization has caused an expansion of *Study Associations*, yet existing *Qualifying Associations* remain unchallenged. Partly this must be due to academic teaching of these subjects. Variations, introduced by different levels of teaching and types of institutions, have extended the number of *Protective Occupational Associations* in teaching.

(4) *Nature of Professional Service*

Where a direct professional-client service is provided, and/or life and property are directly concerned in the service, then standards must be maintained and competition controlled, to protect both professional and client. This requires a particular type of association: the *Qualifying Association*.

(5) *Existence of Reliable Qualifications and Educational Facilities*

Adequate provision of qualifications and educational facilities reduces the likelihood of *Qualifying Associations* forming. Lack of facilities and absence of suitable qualifications have contributed to the establishment, and development of associations in commerce and engineering. Absence of higher educational facilities in the nineteenth century, encouraged expansion of national and local *Study Associations*.

(6) *Size of Potential Membership*

Size of potential membership constitutes the greatest limitation on the number and distribution of associations. As subject-matter becomes more specialized, so the potential number of members is reduced. Some occupational areas possess wider occupational scope than others, for example, accountancy, chemistry, mechanical engineering, management. Larger occupations allow better opportunities for organization, for example, teaching, engineering, science, medicine. At the same time, the nature of the main employer may encourage or discourage growth of associations. Central and local government employees readily form organizations.

(7) Degree of Monopoly and Exclusiveness of Existing Associations

Monopoly of an organization can be strengthened externally: by registration of the profession and recognition by employers; by maintaining a high standard of meetings and publications; by successful negotiation with various bodies. Ultimately, status and monopoly of associations must depend on membership, members being attracted by the qualification's value, useful publications and meetings. Prestige of an association arises from good service to the professional and public, consequently, achieved status can grow immense, solid—and difficult for a new association to rival. Any new association faces the competition of older, well-established organizations.

Chapter Three

WHY ARE QUALIFYING
ASSOCIATIONS FORMED?

AT first sight, one might automatically assume that all Qualifying Associations were formed to acquire professional status for a particular occupation. Naturally, the long-term objective of all Qualifying Associations is to enhance occupational prestige, but this requires time, money and considerable effort. So, in many cases, status-seeking was not the immediate cause of formation. Much less sophisticated reasons are often found.

OBSTACLES TO THE FORMATION OF PROFESSIONAL
ORGANIZATION

As suggested in Chapter One, there are certain elements which contribute to the professionalization of an occupation. Briefly, these are:
  (1) a definable basis of background knowledge and practice, plus a crystallization of activities,
  (2) opportunity to acquire such knowledge and practice,
  (3) self-consciousness on the part of the emerging professionals,
  (4) realization and recognition of these professional services outside the occupation.

Apart from the absence of such essentials, other difficulties can prevent or obstruct formation of professional organization, consequently delaying professionalization. Establishment of a Qualifying Association has proved the surest path toward achieving professional status, because it enables differentiation of qualified from unqualified, promotion of institutionalized training, emphasis on speciality, development of uniform standards of practice and so on. Alternatively, the Protective Occupational Association, if powerful enough, has shown itself more capable of making a direct attack on two important determinants of professional status, viz. remuneration and conditions of employment. Normally, Qualifying Associations consider these areas closed to them.

If organization is the best method of transmuting an occupation into a profession, what can prevent organization? In fact, there are numerous obstacles.

(1) *Small numbers of practitioners*

Insufficient numbers may not necessarily prevent organization, although development can be hampered. Optimum sizes cannot be calculated, but a small number of practitioners, or interested people, may restrict the potential size and scope of organization. Some occupations and subjects offer a far greater possible membership than others. Small membership can mean inadequate finance and limited facilities. Also, there is the danger of widening the association's appeal, to attract those from bordering specialities. This can dilute the association's effort, even mislead it. Yet, small associations possess advantages: there is a greater chance of members knowing each other; the association is more likely to reflect total membership opinion; activities may be better adjusted to members' needs; government is less likely to be dominated by an oligarchy.

(2) *Geographical isolation*

Especially in the late eighteenth and early nineteenth centuries, geographical isolation was a serious handicap to organization. Imperfect and expensive transport affected attendance at meetings, both in terms of audience size and the area from which members could be attracted. Slow and expensive postal services, coupled with the lack of cheap copying and printing facilities reduced opportunities to establish and maintain wide contact. Few associations could be considered 'national', the majority were metropolitan or local. During the nineteenth century, isolation continued, but the gradual accumulation of practitioners in certain areas led to the formation of local organizations for engineers, accountants and architects. However, most associations began in London, remaining predominantly metropolitan for many years. Today, wide and scattered distribution of membership may still render association activities ineffective.

(3) *Underdevelopment of subject-matter and/or practical technique*

Where occupational practice is based on undeveloped, or shallow, theory and technique, then this can be a serious handicap. Firstly, it encourages untrained and unqualified practitioners, and tempts other specialists to encroach. Secondly, training is a problem. Unless actual practice can be translated into regular theoretical terms, textbooks may not be written and teaching can be handicapped. Thirdly, there may be a loss of prestige.

(4) *Rivalry between occupations and organizations*

Where a specialism overlaps existing professional areas, then it may be hard to form, or justify the formation of, a new organization. In the case of Qualifying Associations, this has happened in accountancy, various aspects of engineering and technology, commerce and surveying. The problem is that new associations will have to compete with established organizations. Older associations may already possess considerable status, and in the face of advancing knowledge, they may be quite capable of extending their activities.

(5) *Insufficient internal, or external, pressure to form an organization*

If individuals are satisfied with unorganized, unregulated practice and training, then they may be unwilling to belong to any association. This situation occurred for insurance brokers, managers, estate and land agents, and advertising agents. On the other hand, pressure from the outside can encourage formation of organization, through official criticism, press comments, etc. If pressure, or encouragement is absent, and if the specialism is not acknowledged or used, then organization may not follow.

(6) *Great variations in: quality of service provided; training received by practitioners; level of study; type of employment; social origins*

Such differences can create barriers and prevent comprehensive organization: 'respectable' practitioners may decline to join those felt to be less respectable; better trained and/or qualified personnel may resent joining with those less fortunate; senior members in an occupation may prefer to form their own association. These, and similar conflicts, lead to rival organization, splinter-groups and delayed organization.

(7) *Undeveloped governmental, industrial or commercial structure*

More complex employment structure stimulates the growth of organization; medical services and teaching provide two important examples. Bureaucratization precipitates specialisms, enabling specialist groups to be formed. Linked with this factor is the nature of the employer. A high-level, depersonalized, public or local authority may create unity amongst part, or whole, of the employees.

(8) *Absence of enterprising individuals*

Perhaps the most important element in the birth and growth of any association is the presence, or absence, of suitable enthusiastic organizers. The history of every association is the record of one or more devoted individuals, whose spark ignited a movement, or revived a decaying structure. Without these individuals, there could be no organization.

WHY ARE ASSOCIATIONS FORMED?

Non-Qualifying Associations

For non-qualifying associations, the reason is relatively uncomplicated: interest or protection; furtherance of the subject or of professional standing. Appeal is comparatively narrow, limited by the association's main function: to study, to co-ordinate, to protect.

Prof. John Cohen and co-workers analysed the 'mode of generation' of 220 national learned and scientific societies.[1] They found that nearly half the societies resulted from the efforts of a single individual, or a handful of people. About one-sixth appeared as a break-away from an existing organization. The rest were founded: to launch or support a journal; to preserve a library, private laboratory, collection of specimens, or to dispose of some fund; to regenerate a dying organization; to bring together a group of workers previously in contact informally; to raise professional defence against hostile interests.

Formation of other types of non-qualifying associations has never been analysed on a general level. Yet, once again the importance of an individual or small group of individuals is apparent, this time motivated by the need to co-ordinate or protect.

Qualifying Associations

No simple, direct relationship connects the evolution of industrialism, the development of national education, and the changing social structure with the foundation and development of Qualifying Associations. To expound reasons for formation in terms of broad general factors is too approximate. It is as unrealistic as any attempt to suggest that the discovery of the wheel 'caused' the invention of the steam locomotive.

True, the industrial revolution produced engineers, who made machines, which enabled large-scale production to expand. In turn, large-scale production demanded company formation, which created a need for the accountant and company secretary. This long, logical string of speculation and assumption could be stretched to cover most occupations. Further distortion would be introduced, by assuming that foundation dates of associations can be easily linked to occupational development and professionalization. To expose the problem, three examples will be given.

Why was the *Institute of Chartered Accountants in England and Wales* formed in 1880? It resulted from the joint action of five existing accountancy bodies. Why were these associations formed? Following the example of Scottish accountants in the 1850s, respectable accountants in Manchester, Sheffield, Liverpool and London decided separately to organize themselves. The aim was to combat public indignation and horror at the large number of incompetent, unscrupulous, untrained moneygrubbers, who openly practised as accountants. Why were there so many bad, dishonest accountants? The Companies Act 1862 made company formation much easier. Though many sound companies were started, numerous bad companies were formed by inexperienced promoters and shareholders. Expansion of company formation and liquidation encouraged anyone with a slight knowledge of book-keeping, to set up as an accountant, to prey on developing and dying companies.

A second case is the *Institution of Surveyors*, founded in 1868. Why was it formed—rather, why was it not formed earlier? Surveying is an old craft. Whenever man has built on a large scale, some kind of surveying was required. Canal construction in eighteenth-century England, plus the rapid development of railways and estates in the nineteenth century must have employed many surveyors. Why did they not become organized? Probably there were two main contributory factors. Firstly, the isolation and movement of personnel due to the type of work. Secondly, the limited demarcation of surveying from other occupations—for architects acted as surveyors, so did builders and civil engineers.

Finally, to take pharmacists. Eighteenth-century apothecaries became more and more interested in the general practice of medicine. The *Society of Apothecaries* steadily changed the whole character of training and their examinations. By the 1820s, emphasis was quite heavily concentrated on medicine. As a result, chemists and druggists evolved to take over the sale and dispensing of drugs. Between 1790 and 1820, chemists and druggists plus non-medical apothecaries organized themselves four times. Each occasion was a protest against intended legislation. Each time, the organization was disbanded once satisfaction had been obtained. Why? Why was the *Pharmaceutical Society* successfully established in 1841? These men were retail or wholesale sellers and dispensers scattered throughout the country. Foundation of the Society resulted from strong feelings generated by a complex situation. On one side was the threatened control of the occupation by non-pharmacists, proposed in the Hawes, Ewart and Hutton Medical Bill of February 1841. Also important was the determination of Jacob Bell and his fellow enthusiasts.

These three illustrations display the limitations and inadequacy of general explanations. Seeking to understand 'why' Qualifying Associations were formed, two features stand out. Firstly, forces within the confines of the occupational area are more crucial, than those operating in society as a whole.

Secondly, not every association adopted the standard formula for developing professional status, although the methods were probably understood. Jacob Bell, writing in 1842, clearly showed his grasp of the principles:

> . . . the most effectual method which any class of men can adopt for securing their political rights, and advancing their professional standing, consists not in disputation and warm argument, but in a steady and persevering attention to intellectual improvement, and the establishment of such regulations as are calculated to ensure collective privileges by increasing the amount of individual merit.[2]

Eventually, it must be accepted that there is no simple clear-cut answer to the question 'Why are Qualifying Associations formed?' Each association has its individual, immediate causes founded upon its own past. Occasionally, these elements resemble a set of circumstances unearthed in the case of another association. Some associations were formed because the members wanted to consolidate, or to build-up their occupational status. Some were founded merely to provide a means of maintaining contact with fellow-workers. Some were driven into existence by new and promising developments, or by the actions of other organizations.

Reasons for foundation are not readily classified, owing to mixed aims at formation and the inevitable changes occurring during development. Additionally, the complete truth may not be revealed. Sometimes the story of creation is lost, disguised, rationalized—even, at times, too commonplace to record or elaborate. Unless it has the approval, co-operation and uncritical comment of more senior, long-established bodies, no association will normally expose its weaknesses, its humble origins, its fight to achieve recognition. Even if generally approved, every association has to realize that co-operation and assistance offered by a similar association will only be carried to certain lengths. Inter-associational struggles for status are seldom so intense among non-qualifying associations. Finally, detaching the story from an historical context presents a further problem, owing to the multitude of factors which have to be discarded.

Why are Qualifying Associations formed then—to improve status, to qualify in order to raise status . . . ? In fact, these are partial answers emerging over time. Immediate causes can be various.

(1) *A Search for Status*

Some associations were conceived in an all-out attempt to achieve status for an occupation. Some associations were formed in order to consolidate status for an occupation. Here, the difference lies in the stage of status-development existing at the time. Where numerous respectable, trained practitioners are already present, they will probably try to consolidate their position, by keeping out and restraining untrained, less respectable personnel.

(a) *Founded to Achieve Status*

The Chartered Society of Physiotherapy (1894)

The use of massage became increasingly popular from the 1880s. Some trained Swedish masseurs and remedial gymnasts came to this country. But expanding demand encouraged many unsuitable, badly trained people to practise as masseurs. A scandal developed: 'houses of ill-fame' advertised themselves as 'massage establishments'; medical men grew worried; questions were asked in the House of Commons and protective legislation was suggested.

In 1892, the first training school began advertising in *Nursing Notes*. The *British Medical Journal* of 14 July 1894 warned its readers against the use of massage, because of the large number of unscrupulous practitioners. In the summer of 1894, four women met to discuss the problem. They decided to form a society, in order to restore the good name of massage. A self-elected Council of nine began preparations for a society and arranged for articles on massage to be published in *Nursing Notes*. By February 1895, the '*Society of Trained Masseuses*' was established. On 23 February the Society held an examination and the seven successful candidates raised total membership to seventeen. With co-operation from the medical profession, the Society gradually accomplished their task of making the profession respectable.[3]

Why Are Qualifying Associations Formed?

The Chartered Land Agents' Society (1902)

The *Land Agents' Society* was established in 1902 to give land agency the status of a profession.

> In 1902 when the Society was formally founded, land agents were living down the idea that failures in other walks of life made good land agents; also that the main qualifications of a land agent were the possession of a genial manner and the ability to wear riding breeches at any hour of the day with distinction![4]

There was also a real need to provide an opportunity for land agents to meet and discuss mutual problems, as most of them were isolated from, and unknown to each other. Col. Halifax Wyatt, agent for the Earl of Sefton, called a meeting in London on 9 October 1901, after consulting E. G. Wheler (Commissioner for the Duke of Northumberland), and four other agents. (Some years earlier, Wheler had tried to start an Association of North Country Land Agents.) Once properly founded, membership grew rapidly to nearly 900 in four years. Local branches quickly formed. Examinations were introduced in 1921, following a demand by members.

The Institute of Municipal Treasurers and Accountants (1885)

During the nineteenth century, local government became steadily more complex, as *ad hoc* committees were created locally to meet new contingencies. By 1883, there were 27,069 taxing authorities and eighteen different kinds of rates. A town dweller could live in four different local government areas, governed by six different authorities, subject to four different rating systems. Rural areas could be worse. Local government legislation, promised in 1882, did not materialize until 1888, but the Municipal Corporations Act, 1882, gave greater freedom to provide municipal services. Local government accounting expanded.

Early in 1885, John Elliott (Borough Accountant of Rochdale) discussed with the Borough Accountant of Rotherham, the desirability of forming an association for municipal treasurers and accountants, to confer on common problems. A preliminary meeting with other borough and city accountants led

55

Elliott to contact every treasurer or accountant of every city or borough with over 20,000 people throughout England and Wales. Sixty favourable replies, or three-quarters of those contacted, encouraged the promoters to meet and found the *'Corporate Treasurers' and Accountants' Institute'*, adopting a draft constitution.

Ben Jones, the first elected Chairman, pointed out the necessity of such an association to protect and improve the status of local government treasurers and accountants, who suffered the indignity of having their returns certified by Town Clerks, and who were ineligible to become Chartered Accountants, unless in private practice.[5]

(b) *Founded to Consolidate Status*

Contrasting with the movement to achieve status, when little or no status was present initially, some associations were formed to consolidate and increase status for a growing body of 'respectable' practitioners. Essentially, organization aimed at eliminating unqualified, disreputable elements, by establishing a contrast between them and the better type of professional.

Associations formed during the first half of the nineteenth century fit into this category, viz. the *Institution of Civil Engineers* (1818), the *Royal Institute of British Architects* (1834), the *Pharmaceutical Society of Great Britain* (1841), the *Royal College of Veterinary Surgeons* (1844), the *Institute of Actuaries* (1848). Quite possibly, the *Royal College of Physicians* and the *Royal College of Surgeons* might be earlier examples. Was the *Institution of Mechanical Engineers* (1847) another case? This will be considered later. Anyway, the associations for architects, civil and mechanical engineers were obviously founded for something more than affording an opportunity to meet regularly. The fact that they delayed introducing examinations does not demonstrate a pure study function later transformed into a qualifying function. Rather they relied on pupilage as the method of training, assuming it was sufficient if the principal vouched for his pupil's competence, at the end of training. Also, provision of more than one grade of membership separated various levels of attainment: the distinguished untrained; the aspiring pupil; the trained, working professional.

Why Are Qualifying Associations Formed?

The Institution of Civil Engineers (1818)

The Institution was the first modern Qualifying Association, though a long time elapsed before it could be fairly described as exclusively professional, or even qualifying. Over forty years before, a *Society of (Civil) Engineers* had met regularly in London to discuss engineering. However, this Society was really an informal dining club, playing no part in the Institution's formation.

On 2 January 1818, eight men assembled at the Kendal Coffee House, Fleet Street. H. R. Palmer addressed them, stressing the need for a source of information, or instruction, for Civil Engineers; he emphasized the value of discussing practical problems and recording the results of experience. They resolved to form the '*Institution of Civil Engineers*' for 'facilitating the acquirement of knowledge necessary in the civil engineering profession and for promoting mechanical philosophy'.

Subsequent development of the Institution is interesting, because it helped to establish a general pattern, which was to be adopted by other associations. Having founded the Institution, the members continued to meet weekly from November to March, initially in coffee houses until February 1820, then in hired rooms. The first technical paper was read in April 1819. Abstracts of papers appeared in *The Atheneum*, until selections were published in *Transactions* (1836, 1838, 1842 then more regularly). Records of discussions at meetings were issued from 1837 in *Proceedings*.

Multi-grade membership was introduced at the beginning: Honorary Members; Members and Associate Members. Corresponding Members were added in November 1819. A grade of Graduate Members was created in 1837, mainly for 'apprentice' civil engineers; at the same time the class of Corresponding Members was dissolved.

Though examinations were established comparatively late, the Institution certainly acted as a qualifying body. A Student grade replaced the class of Graduate Members in 1867. Associates were divided in 1878, professional civil engineers became Associate Members, non-professionals remained Associates. Associate Membership examinations started in 1897, following a general movement toward more systematic investigation of

57

candidates, which began in the late 1880s. Before this examination, acceptance of candidates for membership was based entirely on recommendations by corporate members. A certificate was required indicating that the Student had undergone suitable training as a Civil Engineer. The Institution might also request essays and drawings.[6]

The Royal Institute of British Architects (1834)

Before the Institute was founded in 1834, several previous attempts had been made to form an organization for architects. The *Architects Club* was a select body of nineteen architects, founded in 1791 to discuss professional matters. It did consider some aspects of professional conduct and charges. It tested some fire-resistant materials. But serious discussion disappeared after a few years, and it became a Dining Club. The *London Architectural Society* of 1806 was less exclusive and more disciplined. Members had to submit annually an original architectural design and an essay, or pay fines. Meetings were held fortnightly and two volumes of essays appeared (1808, 1810). In the 1810s, architects' discontent with training facilities precipitated various unsuccessful schemes for establishing a school of architecture. Some years later in 1831, another *Architectural Society* was founded with ambitious plans for a British School of Architecture, containing a library, museum and periodic exhibitions. Ordinary members must have been trained for five years in an architect's office; articled pupils under 21 could join and use facilities.[7]

All these societies either failed, or dwindled away to nothing. The *Institute of British Architects* was to prove itself more permanent. Foundation of the Institute dates from a meeting of architects and surveyors in January 1834, to form a '*Society for the Promotion of Architecture and Architectural Topography*'. No agreement could be reached on the Society's objects and conditions of membership. A number of architects, dissatisfied with the meeting, felt the need to introduce a standard of professional conduct. They decided to form a separate society, eventually called the '*Society of British Architects*'. The prospectus outlined a code of conduct, and provided for Fellows (architects of five years standing) and Associates (required to take an examination). The remaining architects, mostly architect-surveyors, disliked the clause in the prospectus which prohibited members acting as surveyors except on their own work. They formed the *'Society of Architects and Surveyors'*. Members of the *'Society of British Architects'* refused to drop the clause, and finally a meeting between the two societies backed the decision. Thus defeated, the *'Society of Architects and Surveyors'* faded into obscurity.

Now the stage was set for foundation of the *'Institute of British Architects'*. On 4 June 1834, eight men met to form the new Institute, nominating and inviting five others as members. Next day, all architects who had attended meetings earlier in the year were told that the Institute had been founded and the *'Society of British Architects'* disbanded.[8]

Membership consisted of three grades: Fellows, men over 30, principals practising Civil Architecture for over seven consecutive years; Associates, over 21, persons who had studied or practised for less than seven years; Honorary Members, eminent (and benevolent) men. Technical papers were given throughout the session. Publications began with the 'Transactions' in 1836, 'Proceedings' appeared later, then the 'Journal' from 1883. A register of assistants seeking employment was started in summer 1837. The first professional practice committee was set up in 1845, to enquire into professional charges and aspects of professional practice.

In May 1862, regulations were published for a voluntary architectural examination. The voluntary system was unsuccessful, as comparatively few took the examination (only forty-three candidates 1863–81). Since 1882, there has been a compulsory examination for all Associates. The Supplemental Charter of 1909 introduced a new non-corporate Licentiate grade, enabling older, experienced architects to be admitted without examination. By Council resolution of 7 December 1954, no more Licentiates have been admitted from 31 December 1955.[9]

The Pharmaceutical Society of Great Britain (1841)

As the apothecaries transferred more attention to medical practice, so a new kind of chemist and druggist began to appear in the eighteenth century. The *'General Pharmaceutical Association of*

Great Britain', formed by apothecaries in 1794, failed to induce regulation of druggists and eventually faded away, leaving affairs in the same state.[10] The Medical Stamp Acts of 1802 and 1812, which imposed duties on common medicines, ointments and glass, caused another temporary association to form. During progress of the Apothecaries Act, 1815, chemists and druggists appointed a committee to watch over their interests. They again paid attention to a Bill for controlling the sale of poisonous drugs in 1819. Through mis-application of the Medicine Stamp Acts, the *'General Association of Chemists and Druggists of Great Britain'* was formed in 1829, to assist anyone improperly prosecuted as a result of a legal anomaly. The Association was disbanded a few months later, when the law was rectified.[11]

Ultimately, chemists and druggists were firmly organized through opposition to a Bill for reforming the medical profession. Agitation for medical reform and registration of the profession began early in the century, accelerated by formation of the *'Provincial Medical and Surgical Association'*. Following a Select Committee of the House of Commons set up in 1834, to consider medical education and laws relating to the medical profession, much of the information was lost in the House of Commons fire. Enough material was collected to enable preparation and introduction of a Bill by Henry Warburton, Thomas Wakley and Benjamin Hawes. The Bill was withdrawn, the promoters separating to prepare further Bills. In February 1841, Hawes, Ewart and Hutton published a Bill to reform the medical profession. As no change affected pharmacy, the chemists took little notice. Then the Bill was modified, and a new clause prevented anyone acting as a chemist or druggist, unless licensed. Heavy penalties threatened the unlicensed. Chemists were to be controlled by a body on which they would not be represented.[12]

In London, leading chemists and druggists immediately formed a committee to watch the Bill's progress. But the committee could not decide on the future relationship of pharmacists to the medical profession. Finally, they agreed in April 1841 to establish a *'Pharmaceutical Society of Great Britain'*—'to benefit the public, and elevate the profession of Pharmacy, by furnishing the means of proper instruction; to protect the collective and individual interests and privileges of all its members in the event of any hostile attack in Parliament or otherwise; to establish a club for the relief of decayed or distressed members'. While the committee deliberated these matters over the weeks, Jacob Bell organized 'tea parties' at his house for pharmacists and medical men, to discuss the new Society. A general meeting of pharmacists on 15 April heard and approved the scheme for a *'Pharmaceutical Society'*. On 1 June, the constitution was adopted. On 17 June, Jacob Bell published a pamphlet 'Observations addressed to the Chemists and Druggists of Great Britain on the Pharmaceutical Society', about 2,000 copies were distributed all over the country. After the Council's first address in July, 5,000 copies were circulated.[13]

In December 1841, Council was informed of possible legislation to reform the medical profession; the Home Secretary said the Society would be told of any changes affecting pharmacists. No Bill was published, and the medical profession had to wait another seventeen years for reform.

On 12 January 1842, the President announced the foundation of lectures, also regulations for examinations and the appointment of examiners. These lectures were to develop into a School of Pharmacy. Membership expanded rapidly: 450 in September 1841, 800 in December, 1,958 in May 1842, by 1846 there were nearly 3,000. The Society successfully petitioned for a Royal Charter in November 1842. *The Pharmaceutical Journal* appeared in 1841 as a private venture of Jacob Bell, but he gave the rights to the Society. Legislation, beginning with the two Pharmacy Acts (1852, 1868) gradually strengthened the position of the Society.[14]

The Royal College of Veterinary Surgeons (1844)

In Feudal times, when household or Court duties were allotted to designated officials, the 'Marshal' superintended the maintenance of horses. The Marshal either treated sick horses, or directed treatment; veterinary practice was known therefore as 'Marshalcy'. A *'Guild of Marshals'* existed in fourteenth-century London, and in 1356 the Mayor and Aldermen granted them an ordinance to govern the craft. As marshalcy developed, so there was the rise of the 'Farrier'. Towards the end of the eleventh century, the general adoption of iron shoes for horses soon made horse-shoeing a necessary and highly esteemed craft.

Those practising the craft were called 'Farriers'. At first, Farriers only helped in marshalcy, but slowly they displaced the Marshals. By the end of the eighteenth century, veterinary surgery (a termed coined in the 1790s) was in the hands of farriers and cow-leeches (both generally described as 'ignorant' and 'brutal') and surgeons. A succession of disastrous animal plagues (1714, 1745, 1769, 1774) underlined the need for a trained class of veterinary surgeons.[15]

The *Oldham Agricultural Society* in 1785 began discussing methods of encouraging scientific farriery, and in 1788, they published an appeal for some establishment to provide teaching. On the Continent, veterinary colleges already existed, the first being set up by Louis XV in 1764 at Lyons. About 1788, George Vial St Bel (Sainbel), Professor of Veterinary Medicine at Lyons, visited England and outlined a plan for an institution to teach veterinary medicine. The next year, under the chairmanship of the Duke of Northumberland, a meeting of 'noblemen, gentlemen and scholars' resolved to erect a Veterinary College in London at their own expense, appointing Sainbel as Principal. In 1791, the college was built, but the death of Sainbel two years later, caused a great setback. Edward Coleman (1765–1839) became Principal. He was an energetic, charming, able man without much veterinary training, whose forceful, tyrannical ways not only helped to improve the status and training of veterinary surgeons, but produced a wide breach of opinion inside the profession. In 1823, William Dick, a past pupil of Coleman, opened the first veterinary college in Scotland.[16]

Reform of the profession began as a criticism of the Royal Veterinary College's administration under Coleman and the surgeon Sir Astley Cooper. Two veterinary surgeons, Joseph Goodwin and F. C. Cherry, had several meetings with Coleman early in 1827. Their suggested reforms, mainly concerning composition of the examining committee, were surprisingly accepted by Coleman and Cooper. Further meetings of the profession in April, led to a Memorial demanding veterinary surgeons as examiners instead of ordinary physicians and surgeons. This was rejected. Two veterinary periodicals begun in 1828, attacked the arbitary authority over veterinary surgeons. One publication soon ceased, while the other decided to withdraw from opposition. Teaching at the College remained inadequate. Changes were only possible after Coleman's death in 1839. Immediately, proposals were made for restaffing the College, and these were accepted.[17]

Organization of the profession started in 1840, when T. W. Mayer and his father, Thomas Mayer, drafted a Memorial to the London College, supported by many veterinary surgeons. One proposal recommended that the College obtain a Royal Charter 'to protect the qualified members from service in certain parochial offices, and to enable them to check the pretensions of incompetent and uneducated men'. The College Governors dismissed the idea of a Royal Charter, but agreed to help promote an Act of Parliament. This proved unsatisfactory, so in November 1840, the signatories of the original Memorial resolved to set up a Standing Committee to watch over professional interests, also to consider petitioning for a Royal Charter constituting a '*Royal College of Veterinary Surgeons*', composed of London and Edinburgh College graduates. The Edinburgh College approved the plan in 1841. A favourable view was received from the Home Secretary in 1842. But the London College refused to co-operate until 1843. The petition was modified, successfully presented, and the '*Royal College of Veterinary Surgeons*' was incorporated on 8 March 1844.

The Charter formed approximately a thousand certificated members of the Royal Veterinary College, London, and the Veterinary College, Edinburgh, into a corporate body. A Supplemental Charter in 1874 established the Fellowship (F.R.C.V.S.), an addition to the original class of Members (M.R.C.V.S.), also provision was made for the removal of members. In 1855, the Royal College tried unsuccessfully to confirm its powers by Act of Parliament. Another Bill in 1881 was passed and required the College to supervise education, to examine and to maintain a Register of Veterinary Surgeons.[18]

The Institute of Actuaries (1848)

Many life assurance organizations existed during the first half of the nineteenth century. Always there was a shortage of trained men. Occasionally, people from various offices did join together temporarily to carry out some common action. From the 1820s, an informal association gradually built up among more influential actuaries. About 1834, an '*Association of Managers of Scottish Offices*' was formed. In 1844, 1845 and 1846, Scottish members discussed formation of London organization, and offered help in establishing an English society.

General consideration of an English society first took place in London, in 1848. Opinion was divided. One small, compact, powerful section wanted only an association of managers in life assurance offices. The remainder, a larger, looser, less powerful group wanted a professional body for actuaries. Those belonging to the intensely respectable offices were unwilling to associate with just anybody. They preferred to shelve the whole idea. Instead of abandoning the scheme, a meeting of 10 June resolved 'to establish a scientific and practical Association amongst Actuaries, Secretaries and Managers of the Life Assurance Offices of Great Britain'. A draft plan outlining rules was circulated to every actuary and secretary whose name appeared in the *Post Magazine* Almanack for 1848. The scheme was slightly modified at a meeting in July.

An enrolment committee met initially on 13 July. In six weeks they scrutinized and enrolled 94 Fellows, 37 Associates. The Institute quickly became active: regular meetings were held; a library was started in 1850; the *Assurance Magazine*, later to be the Institute's official journal, began publishing the Institute's transactions. In April 1849, four examiners were appointed to prepare a syllabus for examinations. Council approved the draft in July and the first examination was held on 10 and 11 June 1850. New examinations were devised in 1851.[19]

The Royal Institute of Chemistry (1877)

In 1867, Fellows of the *Chemical Society* discussed conditions for admission: some considered Fellowship ought to confer distinction and demonstrate competency; others said the Royal Charter opened membership to anyone interested in chemistry. Council set up an inquiry committee. The committee recommended all applications to be signed by five, instead of three Fellows; candidates should declare 'qualification or occupation'; election by a majority of Fellows.[20] These changes did not appeal to practising chemists.

Why Are Qualifying Associations Formed?

During 1872, movement began for separating professional chemists from those merely interested in chemistry. Letters appeared in the *Chemical News*. The President of the *Chemical Society*, Prof. E. Frankland, called for an organization of chemists similar to the Royal Colleges in medicine, the *Institution of Civil Engineers* and *Inns of Court*. In 1875, a meeting was held 'to discuss the advisability of founding an institution to promote the education and protect the interests of professional chemists'. An organizing committee was set up.

Articles, editorials and letters continued to appear in *Chemical News* and *Nature* pressing for, and commenting on, a suitable organization for 'professional' chemists. Prof. Frankland suggested a special class of Fellows within the *Chemical Society*, consisting only of competent, practising chemists. The proposal was not widely supported. Finally, a circular was sent by an organizing committee to 124 well-known chemists, calling a meeting for 27 April 1876. The meeting appointed a committee to determine a scheme. In May, the committee decided on a provisional title '*Institute of Professional Chemists of Great Britain and Ireland*'. There would be one class of members, admitted by a Board of Examiners. Then, the committee consulted the *Chemical Society*'s Council, to see if an organization for professional chemists could be built into the Society. This was considered legally impossible under the Royal Charter.

In November, the organizing committee reported the *Chemical Society*'s decision to a general meeting. This committee was dissolved, and a third committee appointed to prepare for an independent association. Memorandum and Articles of Association were drawn up and submitted to the Board of Trade. When the *Pharmaceutical Society* was consulted, the Council objected to the proposed title ('*Institute of Professional Chemists*') and said the Society's examinations afforded sufficient guarantee of a chemist's competence. Accordingly, the title was changed to '*Institute of Chemistry*', and a proviso was added preventing any issue of membership certificates. Within months of incorporation, examinations were introduced. Censors were appointed to investigate unprofessional conduct.[21]

(2) Generation from Existing Associations

Surprisingly few Qualifying Associations have been established as a direct break-away from existing organizations. If a more general case is taken, viz. associations generated as a result of existing organization, then four different situations are found: a break-away from an existing association; a reaction to an existing association; existing associations helping to form a new association; existing associations joining together as a federation.

(a) *Break-away Associations*

Two early examples of break-away associations were the *Company of Surgeons* (later the *Royal College of Surgeons*) from the *Company of Barber-Surgeons* in 1745, the *Society of Apothecaries* from the *Grocers' Company* in 1617. In modern times, it has been a rare occurrence.

The Society of Architects (1884) (Amalgamated with the **R.I.B.A.** in 1925)

The Society offers the best example of a break-away group, although no longer surviving.

Under the Royal Charter of 1837, Associates of the *Royal Institute of British Architects* were not allowed to vote at meetings. Discontent grew increasingly as Associates composed the larger corporate grade. One Associate wrote to the *Building News* on 8 February 1884, proposing a Supplemental Charter to rectify the matter. Other letters suggested that this move was unlikely. Then a correspondent put forward the idea of a new '*Society of Architects*'. On 8 May, a preliminary meeting agreed to form a new society. On 23 June the '*Society of Architects*' came into being.

Apart from the internal conflict, which produced the Society, there was a movement toward Statutory Registration, organized by an 'Architects', Engineers' and Surveyors' Registration Committee'. Once formed, the '*Society of Architects*' took up the cause, soon absorbing the Committee. Several Parliamentary Bills were presented: for Registration of Architects, Engineers and Surveyors in 1886 and 1888; for Registration of Architects alone, six or seven Bills appeared during the 1890s. The R.I.B.A. remained aloof, completely dissociating itself from the movement. Council felt the Bills were too ambitious, and would extend full recognition to those not suitably trained.[22]

The Society continued independently, examinations were introduced and incorporation obtained in 1893. 'Registration of Architects' kept the Society and Institute apart, until the turn of the century, when R.I.B.A. members began to show interest in registration. Pressure from provincial societies started in 1904. A committee was set up to consider the whole problem, and in 1906 the R.I.B.A. Council resolved to work toward registration. Possible absorption of the Society was mooted, but past animosity prevented any action till after the 1914–18 war. In the early 1920s, three R.I.B.A. Council elections were fought on the issue of amalgamation with the Society. Eventually a decision was reached and in March 1925, the Institute and Society agreed that the Society's members should become R.I.B.A. members.[23]

But this was not the end of the struggle. Still many architects acted as surveyors, and amalgamation signalled the intended closure of the architectural profession, rejecting the architect-surveyor. Reacting against any severance of the two functions and amalgamation of the Society and Institute, two new organizations appeared: the *Incorporated Association of Architects and Surveyors* in 1925, and the *Faculty of Architects and Surveyors* in 1926. Today, both Association and Faculty consist mainly of surveyors. When the Architects (Registration) Act was passed in 1931, membership of neither association was recognized as a registrable qualification for architects.

(b) *A reaction to an existing association*

The best examples are to be found in accountancy. But traditionally, the *Institution of Mechanical Engineers* was supposed to have been formed as a reaction against the *Institution of Civil Engineers*. Probably this was not the complete truth.

The Institution of Mechanical Engineers (1847)

The event supposed to have triggered off the Institution's formation was the apparent humiliation of George Stephenson, by the *Institution of Civil Engineers*. Stephenson applied for membership and the Institution requested 'a probationary essay as a proof of his capacity as an engineer'. He declined to provide it.

Then on a wet afternoon in 1846, several railway engineers were driven to shelter in a plate-layers' hut at Blackwell, on the Bristol and Birmingham line. They discussed the effrontery of the Civil Engineers, which was an insult to Stephenson's work, and a slight on mechanical engineers in general. They decided that the time had come for mechanical engineers to establish their own Institution. J. E. McConnell, locomotive engineer of the Bristol and Birmingham Railway, arranged a meeting at his house. A circular was sent out suggesting the formation of an *Institution of Mechanical Engineers*. Response was satisfactory. A meeting on 7 October 1846 nominated a committee to draw up rules. On 27 January 1847, a general meeting was held in Birmingham to establish the Institution. There were seventy founder members, all prominent engineers, factory owners, managers, railway superintendents or chief engineers.[24]

Two grades of membership were given: Members, over 21, 'Managing Heads of Establishments where engines or machinery were made or employed'; Honorary Members, men whose scientific achievement or social position made them worthy candidates for membership. Every member was supposed to provide at least one technical paper every year, or pay £1 into the library fund. This rule was never enforced; it was removed in 1855. Meetings were held only four times a year. Membership grew slowly—201 members in 1847, 218 in 1855. A Graduate class was introduced in 1850, for engineers who had not yet reached a position fitting them for full membership. In fact, very few ever filled the requirements for this grade. A change in 1866 raised the minimum age of Members to 24, reduced the minimum age for Graduates to 18, introduced the Associate class. In 1876, a proposal was approved to move the Institution to London. Membership had now reached over 1,000. Regulations for membership were modified in 1907 and the Associate Membership grade introduced. Examinations were first held in 1913.[25]

The Society of Incorporated Accountants and Auditors (1885)
(Integrated with the Institute of Chartered Accountants in 1957)

Accountancy has a long history. During the fifteenth century, the Italians invented double-entry book-keeping. From the sixteenth century, many books on accounting were published in England. One of the earliest records of an English accountant at work dates back to the South Sea Bubble swindle around 1720-21. By the end of the eighteenth century, many accountants were listed in trade directories.[26]

From the middle of the nineteenth century, the number of public companies expanded rapidly, particularly after the Companies Act 1862. Between 1862 and 1893, 44,435 companies were registered, 20,074 died a natural death, amalgamated or became absorbed. In the 1862 Act, Section 92 said that an official liquidator, a disinterested person, had to be appointed on liquidation of the company. Section 93 stated that the official liquidator should be paid on a percentage basis, or as the Court directed. Much abuse followed and many unscrupulous people became 'accountants'. The Bankruptcy Act, 1869, abolished Official Assignees and appointed Trustees to distribute the debtor's estate. Creditors could appoint a committee to watch over the trustee; a Comptroller in Bankruptcy received the audited accounts. Even more abuse followed, as 'accountants' sought to snatch as much as they could from the remains of companies.[27] Finally, in the 1870s, respectable accountants in various English towns formed their own societies. In 1880, five associations obtained a Royal Charter to found the *Institute of Chartered Accountants in England and Wales.*

The Institute immediately introduced rigid standards. Except for founder members and practising public accountants with ten years' experience, entrance was by examination only. After a few years, every candidate for membership had to take the examinations. Four fundamental rules in the Charter provided a standard of professional conduct. More important, all students had to be articled to a member for five years, and members could not have more than two articled pupils.

Though these measures were admirable and necessary, many practising accountants found they could not join, without first taking the examinations. Also, the expense of becoming an articled pupil was restrictive. Inevitably, another association was formed—the *'Society of Accountants and Auditors'* in 1885. Quickly, the Institute attacked the Society, ridiculing its membership and intentions. But in time, the Society became as respectable as the Institute.[28]

Formation of the Society was only the beginning of expansion. In turn, the Society gradually prevented many capable accountants from joining, because entrance standards were raised. Once again, new accountancy organizations began to appear: the *'Institution of Certified Public Accountants'* 1903, the *'London Association of Accountants'* 1904, the *'Central Association of Accountants'* 1905. Now, both the Society and the Institute attacked the new associations.[29] Up to the outbreak of the war in 1939, eight other accountancy bodies were formed, apart from two associations for cost and works accountants. The major change was the amalgamation of the *'London Association of Accountants'* and the *'Corporation of Accountants'* (1891), to form the *'Association of Certified and Corporate Accountants'* in 1939. In 1941, the *'Institution of Certified Public Accountants'* was absorbed by the A.C.C.A.

(c) *Existing organizations helping to form an association*

Very occasionally, organizations in the same field will help to form a new association. Of course, apart from direct help with formation, many associations have assisted new associations by providing accommodation for meetings, etc.

The Institute of Physics (1918)

(Renamed the *'Institute of Physics and the Physical Society'* in 1960) In 1874, the *'Physical Society'* was formed by university scientists, as a means of discussing research in physics. By the beginning of the twentieth century, and as a result of the First World War, the physicist emerged as a distinct professional scientist. At the end of the war, the *'Institute of Physics'* was planned as part of a federation of societies connected with physics. Foundation took place on the initiative of the *Physical Society*'s Council, in collaboration with the *'Royal Meteorological Society'*, the *'Faraday Society'* and the *'British Institute of Radiology'*. Incorporated in 1920, the Institute served a distinct purpose. The Institute's meetings and publications were concerned mainly with applied physics, as opposed to the Society's interest in pure physics. The Institute became a qualifying body, while the Society remained a Study Association. After the 1939–45 war, membership and work of the two organizations increasingly overlapped, so discussion began about a possible merger. A scheme for integration was circulated in 1959, and the two bodies were amalgamated and reincorporated in 1960.[30]

The Institution of Metallurgists (1945)

Between the wars, there was only one appropriate qualifying body for metallurgists: the (*Royal*) *Institute of Chemistry*. The '*Iron and Steel Institute*' (1869), '*Institute of Metals*' (1908) and '*Institution of Mining and Metallurgy*' (1892) were important Study Associations, but not qualifying bodies. Many discussions had taken place in metallurgical societies, about the need for a Qualifying Association, without any result. Then in 1943, the Department of Scientific and Industrial Research (D.S.I.R.) set up a committee 'to consider and report on the steps that can be taken to secure and increase an adequate supply of metallurgists with special reference to post-war conditions'. At the same time, the *Iron and Steel Institute* and *Institute of Metals* had established similar committees.

In a letter to the Journal of the *Institute of Metals* for February 1943, Dr Marie Gayler suggested the formation of a professional body for metallurgists. Interest was aroused, and as a result of several meetings held in the Midlands, a draft constitution was forwarded to the *Institute of Metals* in December 1943. A deputation was invited to meet the Institute's Council in January, when it was stated that a committee had been appointed to consider the 'Supply, Training and Status of Metallurgists'. At the Annual Meeting of the *Iron and Steel Institute* in May 1944, the President announced that the two Institutes were jointly studying the possibility of assisting metallurgists to attain professional status. The *Institution of Mining and Metallurgy* declined to join in the discussion, because they felt their interests and activities were not closely involved. (In 1950, the Institution introduced its own examinations.) Councils of the two Institutes adopted a joint committee's report in July 1944. A joint meeting in December decided on the new organization's structure and work. On 28 November 1945, the inaugural meeting was held of the independent '*Institution of Metallurgists*'.[31]

A further development took place in 1959. At an Extraordinary General Meeting of the *Institution of Metallurgists*, amalgamation was proposed between the Institution, *Institute of Metals* and *Iron and Steel Institute*. After discussions in 1960, the three organizations shelved the idea of amalgamation, but agreed to establish a permanent Joint Consultative Committee, and a joint subscription scheme for all publications, as from 1962. In March 1963, the *Institution of Mining and Metallurgy* joined the consultative committee and subscription scheme.[32]

British Institute of Management (1947)

During the 1914–18 war, high-pressure production and the importance of checking costs resulted in extension of mass production techniques and cost accounting. Expansion in the numbers of cost accountants and production engineers, led to the postwar formation of the '*Institute of Cost and Works Accountants*' (1919) and the '*Institution of Production Engineers*' (1921). But the study of management had only continued slowly, since the work of Slater Lewis and Henri Fayol in the 1890s and 1900s. Yet in May 1911, the '*Sales Managers' Association*' was formed. This had been the idea of E. S. Daniells, an American who came to Britain in 1905, to sell Ingersoll watches. He wanted to draw sales managers together, to exchange thoughts on the problems of selling and raising the occupation's status.[33]

Early in 1914, E. T. Elbourne's book, *Factory Administration and Accounts*, was published. This was a detailed study of works management, organization and methods, and administration of accounts. After the war, interest in industrial administration began to stir—courses were started, conferences arranged. Probably, Elbourne was the first to suggest an organized body for those interested in industrial administration. A provisional committee of nine prepared for foundation of the '*Institute of Industrial Administration*' in 1920. From the start, activity was severely limited by lack of membership and finance. Slowly, in the 1930s, the Institute recovered.[34]

In September 1943, the Board of Trade wrote to the Institute, asking for ideas to assist the efficient development of post-war British industry. Primarily, the Institute indicated the need for a strong management association, and a research organization for the fundamental investigation of management problems.

The next year, in January, a document was circulated to the I.I.A. Council entitled 'Proposed British Institute of Management'. Representatives from thirty-seven organizations plus nine individuals attended a meeting in February, to discuss a new central association for management. They resolved to welcome 'a central organization initiated and supported by the Government, to stimulate the development and adoption of good management practice in association with industry and with existing organizations interested in management questions'.

In November 1945, the President of the Board of Trade appointed a committee under Sir Clive Baillieu ' . . . to formulate detailed proposals for setting up a central Institute for all questions connected with management'. The Committee recommended a central organization to be called the *'British Institute of Management'*, partly financed by the Exchequer for the first five years, established as a professional body. The I.I.A. supported the plan, though with some regret that a completely new association was to be created.

So the *'British Institute of Management'* was founded in 1947. Although an Education Committee was established, the B.I.M. felt unable to conduct all examinations, accordingly the I.I.A. was requested to act as the National examining authority for certain examinations. Then in 1948, discussions began about a merger of the B.I.M. and I.I.A., as their work clashed and the I.I.A. still suffered from financial troubles. By the end of 1948, negotiations were practically complete. Merger took place in two stages, spread over the period 1 January 1949 to 31 December 1951, allowing the I.I.A. to retain its legal entity until the B.I.M. established professional grades of membership. In 1950, some difficulties arose over the second stage, finally agreement was reached and integration achieved.[35]

(d) *Federation of existing Associations*

Always in the growth of organization, two long-term effects are noticeable: one is centrifugal, the other is centripetal. Some occupational areas contain an organizational system which remains fairly static over time, in others, the centrifugal effect dominates (as in engineering), or the two effects appear to alternate (as in accountancy and surveying). Federation demonstrates the centripetal force at work. Apart from the three examples considered here, there are also: the '*Institute of Brewing*' (1886); the '*Institution of Mining Engineers*' (1889); the '*Institute of Shipping and Forwarding Agents*' (1944).

Institute of Chartered Accountants in England and Wales (1880)

Accountancy expanded rapidly in the second half of the nineteenth century, attracting many untrained, disreputable characters eager to take advantage of the 'pickings'. Organization of accountants first took place in Scotland, where the different structure of law and Courts of Justice gave greater opportunity for accountants. Increasing numbers soon convinced them that organization was necessary. The '*Society of Accountants, Edinburgh*' was formed in 1853, followed by the '*Institute of Accountants and Actuaries, Glasgow*' in 1853 and the '*Society of Accountants, Aberdeen*' in 1867.[36]

In England, accountancy probably developed later than in Scotland, owing to the immature nature of company law. The first English association, the '*Society of Accountants*', was founded in 1870 by Liverpool accountants; then came the '*Institute of Accountants, London*' in 1870 (which founded the first accountancy journal in 1874—*The Accountant*), the '*Society of Accountants, Manchester*' in 1871, the '*Society of Accountants in England*', London, 1872, and the '*Society of Accountants, Sheffield*' in 1872.

In 1878, two associations introduced compulsory examinations, and the *Institute of Accountants (London)* promoted a Bill to incorporate an Institute for all practitioners in England and Wales. Later in 1878, the five English associations met and agreed to present a Bill registering all accountants in England and Wales. Opposition developed, all five societies then decided to petition together for a Royal Charter. On 11 May 1880, a Charter was granted incorporating the '*Institute of Chartered Accountants in England and Wales*'.[37]

The Chartered Insurance Institute (1897)

Early insurance organizations were formed entirely for commercial purposes. Marine insurers congregated at Lloyd's

Coffee House, London, in the eighteenth century. 'Lloyd's' was incorporated in 1771, as a society of marine underwriters, moving in 1774 to the Royal Exchange. Liverpool underwriters formed the '*Liverpool Underwriters' Association*' in 1802; managers of Edinburgh fire insurance companies formed an association in 1829; life assurance managers in Scotland founded the 'Associated Life Offices' in 1841. All these organizations were designed to improve and speed-up business, rather than to make individuals more efficient and better trained.

The first English non-commercial insurance Institute was founded in Manchester on 14 March 1877, at a meeting of District Managers of insurance companies. As a member wrote in 1879, it was 'an association, not representative but personal, designed to promote friendship and harmony, mutual information and guidance, and uniformity of action in individual cases'. Membership was restricted; employees of non-tariff companies were excluded, acceptance depended on seniority of position in one's office. To provide for junior members, another association was formed in 1883, the '*Junior Insurance Institute*' or '*Insurance Association of Manchester*'.

Other Insurance Institutes appeared in provincial towns and cities: Norwich 1886, Birmingham 1887, Leeds 1888, Bristol 1891, Newcastle upon Tyne 1896, Nottingham 1896 (also Glasgow 1881, Dublin 1885). By 1897, there were ten insurance Institutes. Even so, attempts to found a London Institute had failed in 1886, owing to the lack of interest shown by senior insurance officials. Provincial Institutes almost despaired of absent initiative in London. In 1895, the President of the Yorkshire Institute (Leeds) suggested possible action by provincial Institutes. Meanwhile the existing Institutes progressed, and James Ostler, President of the Manchester Institute, proposed amalgamation. Delegates from all Institutes attended a special conference in March 1897, and agreed on two proposals: to form a Federation of Insurance Institutes of Great Britain; to establish a common certificate of efficiency.

In August 1897, the Federation was declared in operation. Examination syllabuses were submitted and approved; local Institutes were urged to start classes in preparation for the first examination in May 1899. By 1907, additional Institutes had been formed in London, Liverpool, Belfast and Cardiff. These were duly admitted to the Federation, which became the '*Insurance Institute of Great Britain and Ireland*' in 1908.[38]

Institute of Personnel Management (1913)

The first women factory inspectors were appointed in 1893. Three years later, Miss E. M. Wood was employed at Rowntrees to look after the welfare of women and children. In 1909, Edward Cadbury arranged a three-day conference, for employers and managers interested in industrial welfare work. From the representatives of twenty-five firms, a small association was formed with Miss Wood as Secretary. The Trade Exhibition held at Olympia in 1912, gave welfare workers the chance to attract public attention, leading to another conference at York in June 1913. About fifty attended the conference and founded the '*Welfare Workers' Association*', as ' . . . an association of employers interested in industrial betterment and of welfare workers engaged by them'.

Outbreak of war in 1914 caused a set-back to the Association, three years passed before reorganization was complete. The 'Health of Munition Workers Committee', appointed by the Government in 1915, recommended women welfare workers for the many factories employing women and children on war-work. Demand for welfare workers led to rapid, inadequate training. By 1917, seven new, independent associations for welfare workers had emerged. Delegates from all associations were invited to a conference at Leeds in August 1917, when it was agreed to unite under the title the '*Central Association of Welfare Workers*'. The constitution was confirmed by 1918. Before the war had ended, the name was changed to '*Central Association of Welfare Workers (Industrial)*', to avoid misunderstandings about the Association's purpose.

Once again, in November 1919, the name was altered (to the '*Welfare Workers Institute*') owing to amalgamation with associations for men. Membership rapidly declined after the war (1919—700, 1921—250) probably through contracting demand for industrial welfare workers, and the large number who left the work. On incorporation in 1924, it was renamed the '*Institute of Welfare Workers*'. In 1931, the name became the '*Institute of Labour Management*'. The last revision came in 1946, when the present title was adopted.[39]

(3) *To co-ordinate the activities of existing practitioners*

Many associations were created just to co-ordinate, bringing together members in an occupation, without any greater pretentions. As they developed, aims were modified; associations extended their work to include education, publication and status building. Several examples can be given of the more senior members, in an occupation, joining together in order to discuss common technical problems, as well as to afford opportunities for maintaining social contacts.

The '*Quarry Managers' Association*' (now the '*Institute of Quarrying*') began in 1917 as a society for North Wales quarry managers. The '*Association of Managers of Sewage Disposal Works*' (now the '*Institute of Sewage Purification*') was formed in 1901. Although they both remain small, their attention has turned toward qualifying people, in their own fields. Similarly, the '*Institution of Gas Engineers*', now the major qualifying body in the gas industry, can be traced back to the '*British Association of Gas Managers*' established in 1863.[40] The '*Institute of Housing*' was founded in 1931 by a small group of Midlands Housing Managers, who had been meeting occasionally to discuss problems connected with their work. Because of the wide diversity of practice, and the lack of fundamental principles in local authority housing estate management, it was decided to form a national organization providing a guide to training and standards of efficiency, for entrants to housing management.[41] Both the '*Society of Remedial Gymnasts*' and the '*Association of Occupational Therapists*' appear to have started as co-ordinating organizations.

The '*Royal Institution of Naval Architects*' began in 1859, as a means of co-ordinating experience, carrying out experiments on a collective basis and examining work problems. Around 1860, naval architects were little more than superior shipwrights, and opportunities for technical training were almost non-existent. One serious mistake was made, the Institution introduced a 'non-professional' class of Associates. Within ten years, this class exceeded the number of actual naval architects.[42]

Closely allied with naval architects were the marine engineers. From 1869, marine engineers were admitted to the (*Royal*) *Institution of Naval Architects*. In 1870, C. E. Henwood unsuccessfully proposed changing the title to the 'Institution of Naval Architects and Marine Engineers', containing one section for marine engineers, another for naval architects. Finally, in 1889, the *'Institute of Marine Engineers'* was founded by several superintendent and sea-going marine engineers, to co-ordinate their work by holding meetings and publishing technical papers.[43]

To illustrate the process a little more, two associations will be considered in greater detail.

The Institute of Hospital Administrators (1902)

At the turn of the century, internal organization in hospitals was undergoing transformation, due to improved medical and surgical techniques, better standards of nursing and expanding demand for hospital services. But hospitals had grown up independently, in a spirit of isolation and rivalry, without any real exchange of problems, knowledge or experience of administration. Establishment of 'Hospital Funds' in the late 1890s had required improved efficiency and co-operation in administration as a pre-requisite of assistance, yet hospital administration standards continued to vary enormously from one institution to another. No special experience, or qualification, was demanded for hospital administrators.

In 1901, J. S. Neil, Assistant Secretary of the Great Northern Central Hospital, London (now the Royal Northern) suggested the possibility of an association of hospital officers. Following discussion with other Assistant Secretaries, a decision was made to establish the *'Hospital Officers' Association'*. Rules and a programme of meetings was drawn up by a Council. Membership was open to all types of hospital officers, and steadily the Institute grew (1903—95, 1904—141, 1907—206).

The Association's initial primary interest in co-ordination is illustrated by a statement of aims issued in 1905: 'First, to unite in a common bond all lay officers of hospitals without restriction on age, position or sex. Secondly, to promote good fellowship amongst them, and further in every possible way their mutual interests.'[44]

The Institute of Almoners (1903)

After discussions with the *Charity Organization Society*, a Miss

Why Are Qualifying Associations Formed?

Stewart was appointed the first Almoner in 1895, at the Royal Free Hospital, London. This was an experiment and she was paid by the C.O.S. The appointment had followed the report of a Select Committee of the House of Lords, set up in 1891 to investigate overcrowding in hospital out-patients' departments. It had also resulted from the continuous pressure of Sir Charles Loch, Secretary of the C.O.S. Between 1900 and 1910, fourteen additional appointments were made, mostly in London.

Almoners first organized themselves in 1903, as the *'Hospital Almoners' Association'* consisting of thirteen members. Training of almoners was arranged by the C.O.S.: six months with the C.O.S. and six months in a hospital almoner's office. To select candidates, the *'Hospital Almoners' Council'* was formed in 1907, composed mostly of C.O.S. members, one or two doctors and three almoners. By 1912, two certificates were awarded, one for 'Full' Almoners, the other for 'Assistant' Almoners. During the 1914–18 war, demand for almoners increased.

Subsequent to the war, trained almoners became more conscious of their organization. In 1920, a constitution was prepared for two organizations: the *'Hospital Almoners' Association'* to organize almoners, the *'Institute of Hospital Almoners'* to set examinations. Still, there were only fifty-one members. Eventually in May 1941, a Joint Committee was appointed to consider fusion of the two organizations. Following the report, the *'Institute of Almoners'* was constituted in summer 1945, to take over the work of both bodies.[45]

(4) *As a response to entirely new developments*

This is also an example of co-ordination, in a way, but resulting from entirely new and expanding fields, rather than from an attempt to co-ordinate specialists within a reasonably established, slow-moving occupation. Here is something more than a desire to meet occasionally, just to talk 'shop'. A whole new world of possibilities seems to have opened up; a real need is generated for information, technical discussion and training. A sign of the 'thirst' is shown in the enthusiastic and continuous response, often accompanying an association's foundation. Sometimes organization develops naturally, through wider application of new techniques, or the comparatively sudden exposure of a promising new field of activity. Sometimes organization is precipitated by circumstances.

(a) *Response to wider application of new techniques, etc.*

The best instances can be found among the engineering Institutions: the Electrical Engineers in 1871, the Structural Engineers 1908, the Production Engineers 1920, the Chemical Engineers 1922, the Radio Engineers 1925, the Agricultural Engineers 1938, and possibly the Plant Engineers in 1946. Before considering two examples in some detail, three cases might be taken briefly.

During the 1914–18 war, accelerated expansion of production methods caused a new branch of engineering to emerge—production engineering. This was based on the theory and techniques contributed by the work of F. B. Gilbreth and F. W. Taylor in the U.S.A., J. Slater Lewis and A. J. Liversedge in England, and Henri Fayol in France. At the end of 1920, H. E. Horner wrote to 'Engineering Production' proposing an organization for engineers specializing in manufacturing processes. Correspondence developed, interest led to a plan, and the '*Institution of Production Engineers*' was inaugurated in February 1921.[46]

Looking at another aspect of engineering, the First World War exposed the under-developed state of the British heavy chemical industry. No attention had been paid to the study of chemical engineering, in contrast to Germany and the United States. No British university taught chemical engineering. A serious shortage of explosives revealed the need for specialists concerned with the design, construction and efficiency of chemical plant. After the war, in 1922, industrialists, chemists and engineers joined together to form the '*Institution of Chemical Engineers*', assisted by various professional bodies. Once founded, the Institution placed full emphasis on a suitable qualification for chemical engineers. The first examination was held in 1925.[47]

Radio engineering provides a third example. Wireless communication had been demonstrated as a feasible proposition in the early years of the twentieth century, following the late nineteenth-century discoveries of Clerk Maxwell, Hertz and others, and the experiments of Marconi. In 1913, the '*Institute of Radio*

Engineers' was founded in New York. But no similar organization appeared in England, although the *Institution of Electrical Engineers* created a 'Wireless Section' in 1919, as its first specialized section. Attempts to found a separate *'British Radio Institution'* failed, as did the *'Radio Association'* of 1922. Transmission by the British Broadcasting Company began in 1922. Five years later, the Company became a public corporation. Regular broadcasting gave a new impetus to radio engineering, enabling a group of wireless engineers to form the *'Institute of Wireless Technology'* in October 1925. The Institute was renamed the *'British Institution of Radio Engineers'* in 1941. Progress was slow until the War, then steady expansion began, due to rapid advances in radio, radar, telecommunications and post-war developments in television and electronics, which quickly increased the number of trained engineers.[48]

Institution of Electrical Engineers (1871)

On 17 May 1871, a meeting was held in London 'to consider the expediency of forming a Society of Telegraph Engineers, having for its object the general advancement of Electrical and Telegraphic Science, and more particularly for facilitating the exchange of information and ideas among its members'. This was neither a surprising, nor an unnecessary development.

The electrical wire-telegraph had been successfully demonstrated in 1816 by Francis Ronalds. But even in 1837, when W. C. Cooke offered his telegraph, no one was interested. Improvements had to be made by Prof. C. Wheatstone and an experimental line laid, before the idea was accepted. Great publicity came in 1843, when a murderer was arrested, through use of a railway telegraph. From the mid-1840s, telegraph companies were formed. A submarine cable joined England and France in 1851, while many long-distance cables were laid in the 1860s, linking Europe and America, India, China and Japan. In Britain, the Telegraph Act, 1869, conferred a complete monopoly of all telegraphs on the Postmaster-General.

By 1871, the need was apparent for a society connected with the study of electricity and its uses. Cromwell and Alfred Varley had often discussed a possible plan, thus providing the impetus. Although only eight were present at the initial meeting in May, seventy-three applications for membership had already been received. Membership grew rapidly: February 1872—110, November 1872—260, January 1873—352. An unsuccessful petition for a Royal Charter in 1881, led to incorporation under the Companies Act in 1882, as the '*Society of Telegraph Engineers and Electricians*'. The name was changed to the '*Institution of Electrical Engineers*' in 1888.[49]

Institution of Structural Engineers (1908)

From the 1850s, and especially in the 1880s, reinforced concrete became an important structural material in France, Germany and the United States. In Britain, little interest was shown until 1897, when L. G. Mouchel opened an office and designed buildings using reinforced concrete. A flood of patents left builders and architects unable to decide between design merits of construction systems, and various types of deformed bars. In 1906, the 'British Fire Prevention Committee' appointed a special committee to investigate the use of reinforced concrete. Also in 1906, the R.I.B.A. with other organizations, set up a 'Reinforced Concrete Committee' to consider the proper conditions for using reinforced concrete in structures. These two events brought together men interested in this structural material.

A firm making reinforced concrete structures circularized similar firms, suggesting formation of a trade association, but some felt such an organization was an unsuitable solution. E. A. Sachs, Chairman of the British Fire Prevention Committee was invited to convene the nucleus of a widely based organization. Thus, on 21 July 1908, the first meeting was held of '*The Concrete Institute*' Council. In February 1909, the Institute was incorporated 'to advance the knowledge of concrete and reinforced concrete and direct attention to the uses to which these materials can be best applied', also to hold meetings and publish information.

In October 1912, a proposal was made to widen the Institute's scope, and an investigating committee recommended extension to cover all branches of structural engineering. Examinations were postponed until 1920. The name was changed to the '*Institution of Structural Engineers*' in 1922.[50]

Why Are Qualifying Associations Formed?

(b) Precipitated by circumstances

Perhaps many associations were precipitated by events, including some mentioned under previous headings—the *Pharmaceutical Society, Institution of Mechanical Engineers, Institute of Chemistry* and so on. Here, however, examples are considered of associations, which would probably not have appeared otherwise.

Royal Institution of Chartered Surveyors (1868)

No doubt, surveyors were bound to become organized, for surveying has been a specialist function for a considerable time. Yet, despite expanding activity in the late eighteenth century and nineteenth century, no permanent, successful organization appeared until the *'Institution of Surveyors'* in June 1868. A small *'Surveyors' Club'* was formed as a dining club in 1794. It still flourishes. A *'Land Surveyors' Club'* was founded in 1834, composed of surveyors and land agents to agricultural estates. In 1864, there emerged a *'Surveyors' Association'* consisting of general surveyors. Neither society managed to establish itself.

The precipitating factor was the great mid-Victorian surge in land development, estate management and valuation. A mass of Private Bills flowed through Parliament to sanction town improvements and extensions, and permit public works. Introduction of compulsory purchase of land, for provision of essential public services and improvements, created a need for skilled men to survey and value property. Land and quantity surveying were firmly established.

When founded in 1868, the *'Institution of Surveyors'* consisted of about 200 members. Membership grew slowly. There were only 500 members when a Charter was obtained in 1881.[51]

The Town Planning Institute (1913)

While the first Town Planning Bill (Housing, Town Planning, etc. Act, 1909) was being debated, Thomas Adams suggested formation of a professional body representing architects, surveyors, engineers and lawyers—the main professions concerned with town planning. After the Bill had been passed, Adams was appointed the first Inspector of Town Planning under the Act.

83

He approached Prof. Adshead, J. S. Birkett, H. V. Lanchester, G. L. Pepler, Raymond Unwin and others. Several discussions were held between 1910 and 1912. Eventually in July 1913, a provisional committee circulated a letter proposing a foundation meeting on 21 November. At that meeting, sixty-four members were nominated for election to various grades.[52]

(5) *To offer facilities beyond normal provision for meetings, etc.*

This is not a residual category. Sometimes the original aims of the association are unusual, going beyond the need to hold meetings, publish information and so on. Two examples can be given.

The Textile Institute (1909)

In 1907, two men working in the textile industry, George Moores and J. H. Lester, attended the Brussels Convention of the 'International Association for Testing Materials'. Impressed by the technical achievements displayed there, they decided to promote an association devoted to the application of science and scientific methods to the textile industry.

After two years' preparation, a formal meeting was held in July 1909, attended by sixteen men, who decided to found the '*Textile Institute*'. Besides 150 members, the Institute had the support of several distinguished people, including the President of the Board of Trade.

Two aims made the Institute different from other associations. It was intended to act as 'an authority for the determination and recognition of trade standards, usages, terms, definitions and the like' and 'to encourage original work and research dealing with natural and artificial fibrous material'. Since then, the Institute has prepared definitions and standard tests, produced text-books, and organized research groups in connection with all kinds of textile operations.[53]

The Royal Aeronautical Society (1866)

The Society is the only true example of a Study Association, which transformed into a Qualifying Association. When the

'*Aeronautical Society*' was formed in January 1866, the aim was far ahead of existing knowledge. On 12 January, six men met at the *Society of Arts* and resolved 'that it was desirable to form a Society for the purpose of increasing by experiments our knowledge of aeronautics . . .' Of these men, the Duke of Argyll (first President) was absolutely antagonistic toward the use of balloons; F. W. Brearey (first Honorary Secretary) had been inspired by Sir George Cayley's papers in *The Mechanics Magazine*, and his father had been a friend of Cayley.[54] At the first public meeting, on 6 June, F. H. Wenham read a paper on 'Aerial Locomotion and the Law by which Heavy Bodies impelled through the Air are sustained'—now considered a 'classic' in aeronautics. This remarkable Society was therefore concerned with heavier-than-air flight, rather than balloon flight, an outstanding position to hold in the mid-1860s.

Although kept alive for many years by a handful of enthusiasts, the Society continued to organize aeronautical exhibitions and present technical papers. Revival occurred in the early 1900s, when powered flight became a reality. Technical grades of Fellow, Associate Fellow and Student membership were introduced in 1911. Examinations began in 1922.[55]

CONCLUSION

The preceding classification does not attempt to construct a rigid framework, analysing complex reasons for foundation in over-simplified terms. Many examples overlap two, perhaps even more of the categories. Instead, the theme displays the flexibility and development common to most Qualifying Associations.

Today, an association can be easily formed; examinations may be introduced immediately as a membership requirement. Speed of development is faster, because many associations have trodden the same path in search of professional status, and the process of professionalization seems clear. Many occupations have become keyed to qualifications, as wider educational provision makes examination demands possible. Fifty or a hundred years ago, the situation was very different. Primary education was available, in some form; secondary education was limited; further and higher education were outside the reach of most people. Under such an educational handicap, the nineteenth-century associations tended to be formed with more modest objects.

Search for status does not seem so strong in every association. If certain questions are asked, then evidence accumulates to support such a belief. For example, how quickly and seriously did the association consider any educational function? How rapidly were attempts made to acquire recognized status-symbols of professional associations? How extensive were the efforts to gain recognition for the membership qualification? Did the association try to create a reputation for sound, expert advice by submitting memoranda to Government committees and departments, and other organizations? What efforts were made to gain public recognition? Answers to these kind of questions offer a test of status seeking.

Of the associations described, many began in a small way, merely drawing together individuals in the same basic type of work, affording an opportunity to meet. Probably no extreme and external social, or economic force determined the foundation. It would be misleading to forge a long chain of circumstances to demonstrate 'why' a particular association was formed. A glance at the chronological list in Appendix II does not suggest a simple link between associations and industrial development, or educational provision, or even size of occupation. Within a general pattern of structure and activity, considerable variations can be found in 'causes'. The resounding impression is of individual uniqueness, tempered by an adjustment to the social and educational climate of the time.

What can be said of these founders and early members? Some seemed conscious of inadequate training and education, therefore they sought to compensate for a badly constructed state system of education. Some seemed conscious of their position in society, as managers, or supervisory technicians, so banded together to convince themselves of their own importance. (This may be a harsh comment, yet in some cases, little evidence exists of outside activity to influence or serve others.) Some occupations had slowly developed into highly skilled work, consequently they contained trained men with achieved individual status, but unorganized and without a solid widely accepted professional status. Pharmacists, engineers, architects and actuaries are typical examples. Some occupations were comparatively new, but nevertheless they started at a high level of responsibility. Organization was used to achieve status appropriate to the dignity of the work. Perhaps the company secretary and insurance broker are two examples. Sometimes associations were produced by adjustments within an existing organizational framework. Members had become dissatisfied with an established association, through a failure of structure or work.

Analysis of the background to formation demands a distinction between factors internal to the occupational situation, and factors external, within the main social system. No doubt, internal factors are usually paramount. For example, those in the occupational area find a need for organized discussion of work, for the publication of reliable technical information, for a standardized measure of achieved training and education, for a means of establishing wider contacts, for reinforcing specialist demarcations. If the social system outside the occupation does not provide any means of satisfying such needs, then an association is very likely to appear.

Chapter Four

STRUCTURE OF QUALIFYING ASSOCIATIONS

LEGAL STATUS

ANY group of people may combine together to form a society, without undertaking incorporation. Remaining an unincorporated body brings disadvantages. Firstly, the society cannot sue, or be sued, in its own name. Secondly, property can only be held by means of a 'Deed of Trust', entailing election of trustees. Thirdly, officers of the society are not legally protected, so they may be individually liable. Fourthly, changes in the society's rules require unanimous agreement, unless there was a suitable proviso for amendments originally.

Methods of Incorporation

If an organization wishes to act as a trade union, then registration under the Trade Union Acts provides some protection and privileges. Alternatively, registration under the Friendly Societies Act gives a modicum of protection.[1] Otherwise incorporation is a necessary requirement. Besides the legal advantages gained, incorporation constitutes a prime adjunct in the search for professional status.

Three methods are available for incorporation: Act of Parliament; a Royal Charter; registration under the Companies Act. Before the Companies Act, 1862, incorporation could only be achieved via Statute or Royal Charter.

(1) Act of Parliament

To introduce a Private Bill, a petition is deposited at the Private Bill Office of the House of Commons prior to 27 November in each session. Agents for the Bill appear before the Examiners

88

of Petitions for Private Bills, to show that Standing Orders have been complied with, and that notice of petition has been given to the general public and interested parties. If the Examiners' report proves satisfactory, the Bill can be presented in either House. Presentation and First Reading being mere formalities; entrance to the House takes place on Second Reading. After the Second Reading, the Bill is referred to a Private Bill Committee, which amends the Bill as necessary, and reports back to the House. Then follows discussion and Third Reading. If successful, the Bill passes to the other House, where the same procedure occurs. Amendments, made in the second House, must be agreed to by the first House, or some compromise arranged. Having survived all these stages, the Bill receives Royal Assent.

Such a brief résumé cannot indicate fully the time, trouble and expense involved in presenting a Private Bill. The procedure is complex and uncertain, much depends on the existence and development of opposition, for the Bill can be blocked at any of several stages. In modern times, few professional associations have attempted to become incorporated by Statute.

The *Royal College of Physician's* powers were ratified by Act of Parliament in the sixteenth century.[2] The *Company of Surgeons* tried to obtain reincorporation in 1797. A Bill introduced into the Commons on 6 April, passed through all three stages within five days. Sent to the Lords, it moved rapidly to a Third Reading on 19 May, only to be blocked and virtually destroyed by one man (Lord Thurlow). Third Reading was postponed. Eventually, the Company dropped the Bill, achieving reincorporation by Royal Charter.[3] In 1878, the *Institute of Accountants, London* introduced a Bill to incorporate an association for accountants throughout England and Wales. This Bill was also withdrawn. The *(Royal) Institute of Chemistry* tried to dissolve and reincorporate the Institute by Statute in 1883, to overcome restrictions imposed through previous incorporation. The Bill was read for a first time in the Lords, then the Examiners said the objects sought were not satisfactory objects for a Private Bill. Once again, the Institute adopted the alternative of a Royal Charter.[4]

(2) *Royal Charter*

The grant of a Royal Charter remains one of the few personal rights of the Sovereign, it is also one of the oldest. The Privy Council can be traced back to the fourteenth century, with origins in Norman times. One of the most ancient functions of the Privy Council has been investigation of petitions, and preparation of Charters, either on petition to the Queen in Council, or upon direction of the Sovereign.

To obtain a Royal Charter, the Queen in Council is petitioned through the Privy Council. By an 'Order-in-Council', the Queen appoints an *ad hoc* committee to investigate the desirability of granting the petition. The 'Order in Council' is published in the *London Gazette*, enabling a notice of counter- or cross-petition to be presented by opposing bodies. Notice must be given within thirty days, accompanied by a fee. But the caveat can be lodged at any time within a year of the notice. All such objections are then forwarded to the petitioning body and must be answered. The *ad hoc* committee may also consult other Government Departments, especially the Board of Trade.

Once counter-petitions have been answered, a 'Decision-in-Principle' is given, which either rejects the petition, or begins negotiations for a draft Charter. Consultations continue until the *ad hoc* committee and petitioners reach agreement about the draft. If the draft Charter is accepted, another 'Order-in-Council' officially approves the committee's report and draft Charter. At the same time, the Home Secretary is instructed to prepare a Royal Charter for the Great Seal. After grant of the Charter, Bye-laws must be drawn up and approved by the institution's corporate members, and by the Privy Council. Usually, Bye-laws have to be submitted to the Privy Council within six months to a year. From first petitioning to the 'Decision-in-Principle' generally takes about nine or ten months. No reason is given for rejecting a petition. Nothing prevents a further petition at a later date.

Over the centuries, the function of a Royal Charter has steadily changed. In medieval England, a Charter signified Royal approval by awarding some monopoly power; then it became a more accessible form of incorporation, granting a legal monopoly for business or control; finally in modern times, the Charter has assumed new dignity, by affording a different level of incorporation. For the last hundred years, incorporation has been readily available through Companies Acts. Consequently, a Charter has developed into an inter-association status symbol, a distinguishing mark, acknowledging supremacy in a particular field and the ability to provide a sound public service. Table 4.1 lists the Chartered *Qualifying Associations*.

A Charter has always been an expensive undertaking.[5] It is never certain.[6] Success does not apparently depend directly on size of membership, subject, or length of establishment. More likely factors are:

(*a*) quality and extent of support, or opposition, for the petition,

(*b*) record of public service,

(*c*) respectability (control of entrance standards, professional conduct, etc.),

(*d*) existence of another association in the same field, already possessing a Royal Charter.

The ability to answer satisfactorily the arguments of the cross-petition is very important.

Incorporation by Royal Charter brings disadvantages, as well as advantages of increased status. The Privy Council must approve the Bye-laws and any changes in Bye-laws; a major change demands the extra expense of petitioning for a Supplemental Charter. Great care must be taken to avoid any purely selfish objects, for example, directly negotiating over members' remuneration, or working conditions. A Royal Charter binds the association more strongly to serve the public good. Restrictions may be imposed on the value of property held by the association, or on some other aspect of structure.

(3) *Incorporation by Companies Act*

The Companies Act, 1862, was the first such Act allowing any seven or more individuals, to form an incorporated company for any lawful purpose, providing they complied with the Act.

To obtain incorporation, the organization applies to the Board of Trade. Application cannot be refused, if all legal requirements have been met, but certain changes may be requested.[7] The association then becomes registered as a company, limited by guarantee and not having a share capital.[8] A 'Memorandum of Association', giving the institution's objects in detail, must be deposited with the Registrar of Companies, plus the

TABLE 4.1. SHOWING THE QUALIFYING ASSOCIATIONS WHICH
POSSESS ROYAL CHARTERS (ENGLAND AND WALES ONLY)

Year of foundation shown in parentheses. Present titles given.

Note: In addition the following have been granted Royal Charters:

1890	Institute of Journalists (1883)
1899	Iron and Steel Institute (1869)
1906	Institute of Directors (1903)
1910	Royal Institution of Naval Architects (1860)
1921	Institute of British Foundrymen (1904)
1946	Institute of Fuel (1927)

Many of the more important Study Associations ('learned societies')
obtained Royal Charters during the nineteenth century (about twenty-four).

Before 1880

1518	Royal College of Physicians of London
1800	Royal College of Surgeons of England (as Company of Surgeons 1745)
1828	Institution of Civil Engineers (1818)
1831	Law Society (1825)
1837	Royal Institute of British Architects (1834)
1843	Pharmaceutical Society of Great Britain (1841)
1844	Royal College of Veterinary Surgeons (1844)

1880 to 1890

1880	Institute of Chartered Accountants of England & Wales (1880)
1881	Royal Institution of Chartered Surveyors (1868)
1884	Institute of Actuaries (1848)
1885	Royal Institute of Chemistry (1877)

1890 to 1900

1891	Chartered Institute of Patent Agents (1882)
1898	Library Association (1877)

1900 to 1910

 1902 Chartered Institute of Secretaries (1891)

1910 to 1920

 1912 Chartered Insurance Institute (1897)
 1915 Institution of Mining Engineers (1889)
 1915 Institution of Mining and Metallurgy (1892)

1920 to 1930

 1920 Chartered Society of Physiotherapy (1894)
 1920 Institute of Chartered Shipbrokers (1911)
 1921 Institution of Electrical Engineers (1871)
 1925 Textile Institute (1910)
 1926 Institute of Transport (1919)
 1929 Chartered Land Agents Society (1902)
 1929 Institution of Gas Engineers (1863)

1930 to 1940

 1930 Institution of Mechanical Engineers (1847)
 1933 Institute of Marine Engineers (1889)
 1934 Institution of Structural Engineers (1908)

1940 to 1950

 1946 Royal College of Obstetricians and Gynaecologists (1929)
 1947 Chartered Auctioneers and Estate Agents Institute (1886)
 1948 Institution of Municipal Engineers (1873)
 1949 Royal Aeronautical Society (1866)

1950 to 1960

 1957 Institution of Chemical Engineers (1922)
 1959 Institute of Municipal Treasurers and Accountants (1885)
 1959 Town Planning Institute (1914)

After 1960

 1961 British Institution of Radio Engineers (1925)
 1961 Chartered Institute of Loss Adjusters (1941)

'Articles of Association' outlining the structure of the organization and means of implementing the aims. Under the Companies Act, if any company uses its income and property solely to promote its objects and not for profit, application can be made to the Board of Trade for a licence to omit the word 'Limited' from the title.[9] Most professional associations apply for exemption, regarding the step as a necessity on the road to professional respectability. Presumably, the word 'Limited' casts an unpleasant tone. Some associations take the licence as a form of recognition, exhibiting possession with pride.

Incorporation by the Companies Act offers the cheapest, easiest, most convenient method. It ensures a minimum of interference from the outside, plus a maximum level of legal protection.

GOVERNMENT OF THE ASSOCIATION

Government is in the hands of an elected Council, with a large part of the administration delegated to paid officials superintended and instructed by, and responsible to, the Council.

Constitution of the Council

Council is a representative, voluntary, elected committee of the association, consisting of honorary officers, who may be *ex officio* members, plus elected and/or representative members. In every case, composition, election or disqualification of members, proceedings, powers and duties of Council will be designated in Articles of Association, or Royal Charter Bye-laws. Standing Orders provide more detailed statements about procedure.

Considerable variations occur in the size, composition and election of Councils. Problems arise in connection with Council, some of these will be discussed later.

The Council's Powers and Duties

For a majority of associations, powers and duties are chiefly defined in the following way:

First, Council is elected to control, manage and advance the business and affairs of the association. Objects, exemplified in the Memorandum of Association or Royal Charter, outline the scope of action, viz. to establish examinations, library, to invest income, etc.

Second, within the provisions of the Articles, or Bye-laws, Council may regulate its own procedure for conducting business, delegating powers to Standing or other committees, and to any duly appointed officers. Often the number of regular meetings per year, and the necessary quorum validating meetings, is specified. Articles or Bye-laws may outline the method of calling Council meetings, the need to take minutes and compile an Annual Report for members. Outside these limits, Council decides on its own Standing Orders, and appoints its own committees.

Third, usually any *bona fide* act of Council, any Council Committee, or any Council member is valid, even if subsequently some defect is found in the appointment or continuance, of the committee or person, which serves as a disqualification.

Fourth, any act of Council approved by a General Meeting of members cannot be questioned, once approved. It must be considered as an act of the association.

Fifth, Council may vary any regulation, or Bye-law, providing there is no addition, or alteration, of any existing Bye-law.

Sixth, only Council can form, and provide regulation for, a local branch or section.

Seventh, Council can usually co-opt members, especially when a casual vacancy occurs. It can also appoint, remove and determine the remuneration and duties of paid officers of the association.

This summary of typical powers and duties of Council suggests extensive power, responsibility and 'untouchability'. But members of an association must delegate government to some kind of committee, for once the body expands beyond a few hundreds, government by general meeting or referendum becomes too slow and cumbersome. Council members remain unpaid volunteers elected directly or indirectly, by all corporate members. They are not usurpers. Every corporate member possesses the right to nominate candidates for election to Council, or to indicate matters demanding Council's attention. Whether or not members exercise these rights, forms another problem. If Council, officers and committees are to govern the association, elasticity must exist in the permitted types of action, and in the methods used to achieve specified objects.

Always, there are checks and safeguards: annual elections and annual general meetings; the paid secretariat; branch officers and committees; minutes and written records, open to inspection by members; the general vigilance of members. Almost without exception, Council takes great care to keep members informed through notices and summaries of minutes in the journal. Nevertheless, despite the many formal and informal balances, there are inherent problems in the structure and work of Council.

Some Problems connected with the Structure and Work of Council

(1) *Size*

Considering the structure of fifty-six associations,[10] nearly half of the Councils have fifty or more members, about three-quarters contain thirty or more members. A Council's size does not seem to depend directly on area of concern or size of organization, although the largest associations normally have the largest Councils. More likely, size relates to efforts toward: increased representativeness; retention of experienced senior personnel; securing distinguished people as Honorary Officers. Taking into account the power and responsibility of Council, large size appears to negate, or cast doubt on, the administrative ability of such a group. Frequency of regular meetings suggests further incapacity: of fifty-six Councils[10] (no information available in four cases), twenty-five meet six times or less a year (eighteen quarterly); only eight meet monthly, seven meet ten or eleven times each year. These facts might imply that Council serves as a 'rubber-stamping' committee, leaving real power in the hands of Honorary Officers (President, Vice-Presidents) and paid executive officers (Secretary, Assistant Secretaries, etc.).

But this conclusion ignores the real system of government. No entire Council could satisfactorily manage finance, admissions, examinations, branch liaison, publications and so on. Instead, responsibility must be spread over several committees, augmented (for day-to-day business) by the paid Executive Officers, with Council maintaining absolute control. Government by committee requires a reasonably sized Council, to prevent an excessive burden on individual members. After all, an association is a voluntary organization composed of men with full-time occupations, and usually the senior, busier men get on to the Council. Inevitably, a large Council tends to reconsider matters already thoroughly investigated by the Secretariat, or by another committee. Delegation means an obvious use of facilities, rather than a sign of ineffectiveness and irresponsibility. Finally, the problem of size is countered by the task of obtaining a full attendance at Council. To overcome absenteeism, most associations will not allow renomination of any members who attended occasionally during the previous year.

(2) *Democracy*

How democratic is the system of government? Here lies a complex problem, which subsumes many questions. Who has the right to vote? Who is eligible to stand for election? How representative is the Council? What are the in-built restrictions on democracy?

All fully paid-up corporate members enjoy voting rights. Election procedure is universal. Each year, Council nominates candidates to fill vacancies arising from retirement of elected Council members, usually one-third of the total. Corporate members may nominate candidates, usually within a specified time (normally three weeks). In fact, individual members might be deterred from nominating their own candidates. Looking at the fifty-six associations: twenty associations require one or two members to nominate a candidate, twelve specify three to five corporate members, but eleven require ten members for each candidate.

In a contested election, i.e. when nominated candidates exceed vacancies, a postal vote will normally be conducted of all corporate members. If the number of nominations equals the number of vacancies, then a formal election takes place at the Annual General Meeting, without a vote of all corporate members. (Some associations hold a postal ballot whether or not the election is contested.) Newer, smaller associations tend to rely completely on the Annual General Meeting, so that only members attending the A.G.M. vote for candidates. Of course, restriction of voting to the A.G.M. automatically disfranchises a large section of the membership. Yet disfranchisement also occurs in larger associations. In the same way, number of nominations equals number of vacancies and election takes place at the A.G.M.—not everyone attends, so a large proportion of corporate members is virtually vote-less. On the other hand, if an association despatches 10,000 voting papers and only one-third of members decide to reply, the undertaking is very expensive and disappointing, but quite democratic.

Election figures are seldom made public. Associations merely indicate successful candidates, sometimes unsuccessful ones as well. In many cases, Council elections would seem to be uncontested, routine events forming part of the A.G.M. agenda, possibly because of a complex nomination system, more probably due to general apathy. The standard practice of obtaining candidates furnishes one sign of apathy. Council members, Branch committee officers and association Executive Officers constantly look out for active, interested, voluble members and put their names forward. If suitable, these members will be invited to stand as candidates. Coupled with the problem of finding candidates, is the difficulty of making them known to the electorate. Doubtless it is hard to acquaint a widely scattered membership with the relative merits of candidates, when little or no description may be offered, or if a brief recital of qualifications, age and experience suggests hardly any difference between candidate and voter.

Many Councils elect Honorary Officers (President, Vice-President(s), Honorary Secretary, Honorary Treasurer) without any real reference to the corporate membership (twenty-eight out of fifty-six associations). A few (thirteen in fifty-six) resort to a postal vote, the other associations rely on the Annual General Meeting, when the meeting takes a formal vote on Council-nominated candidates. Thus, about four-fifths of associations leave election of Honorary Officers to Council. Again, this does not represent an unreasonable practice. It is a carefully controlled process by which Council members gain experience and succeed to office, after a period of ordinary Council service, after Council members have been able to demonstrate their value. Honorary Officers will be considered later.

Two other restrictions may add to, or detract from, the democratic nature of associations' government. Some associations (about a quarter of the fifty-six) impose a time-lapse on retiring Council members, so they must wait for a certain period (usually a year), before becoming re-eligible for election. Some associations prevent Council members from serving beyond a certain number of consecutive years (about a quarter of the fifty-six). Sometimes, Council members are drawn exclusively from the senior corporate grade (about a quarter of the associations). Therefore, many associations permit Council members to serve almost indefinitely, and some restrict Council membership to senior members in the association. Though undemocratic, in a way, it helps to attract and retain the most experienced members.

Membership inactivity may be due to apathy, or ignorance, alternatively it can signify confidence, satisfaction and trust. Invariably, mechanism exists to enforce democratic procedure and democratic representation.

(3) *Representativeness*

An association can be thought of as a three-dimensional structure, composed of different membership grades, in different areas of the country, in different types of work.

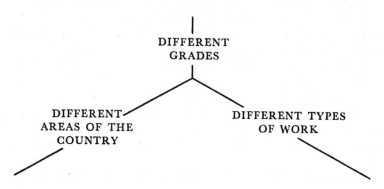

Ideally, any association ought to represent all aspects of the structure when determining the composition of the Council. However, careful attention to every structural element could produce insurmountable complications. Assuming the whole picture remains static, which it does not, then the various combinations could be immense. Take, for example, the *Royal Institution of Chartered Surveyors*. Examinations fall under five different

99

sections, representing the main types of work. There are about thirty Branches and Sub-branches. The Institution has two grades of professional members, plus three others. Difficulties arise even in simple cases. The *Institute of Chartered Accountants* has only two corporate grades (plus students) and two basic types of accountant (practising and non-practising), but a large number of local sections. Some compromise must be reached.

Most associations either discard complications resulting from different kinds of work, or seem less troubled by them. Three rare examples of associations making adjustments, are the *Institution of Municipal Engineers*, the *Chartered Society of Physiotherapy* and the *Library Association*. The Institution ensures that at least two Council members are Chief Engineers or Surveyors to County Councils, and at least two Chief Engineers or Surveyors to Rural District Councils.[11] The Society provides for teachers, private practitioners and National Health Service practitioners.[12] The *Library Association* ensures representation of university and special libraries.[13] Some associations endeavour to arrange a fair representation of different types of work, though the constitution does not stipulate any distribution.[14]

Similarly, the majority of associations do not make provision for separate representation of different corporate grades. About a quarter (of the fifty-six Council cited) specify a minimum number of a particular corporate grade to be on Council.[15] The *Town Planning Institute*, for example, does indicate the distribution: 15 Members, 5 Associate Members, 3 Legal Members, 1 Legal Associate Member, 1 Honorary Member, 1 Honorary Associate.[16] Chiefly, representatives of grades are found in the engineering Institutions. The *Institution of Metallurgists* is unusual, as certain Council members are elected by specific grades.[17]

Representatives from local sections or branches are commonly found on Councils (three-quarters of the fifty-six associations). These may be the local Branch Chairmen, or Secretaries, alternatively specially elected branch representatives. At least ten associations regulate branch representation on a proportional basis, thus larger branches send more representatives. In five cases, branch representatives constitute the whole Council, apart from the Honorary Officers. Branch representation obviously brings advantages and disadvantages. It forges a closer link between a scattered membership and Headquarters, allowing a better balance of opinion and preventing dominance by the Metropolitan area. On the other hand, local members may only indirectly elect representatives. For example, if elections take place at Branch meetings, electors must attend in order to vote. Also, many associations do not automatically assign a member to a local branch, which could mean disfranchisement. Such a situation puts the election into the hands of local active members, who may not represent local opinion.

Generally speaking, the sole membership variable adequately managed, is determined by geographical distribution. This means that some care must be taken to arrange proportional representation. Without deliberate allowance being made for different corporate grades, Council membership tends to consist predominantly of the senior grade. Again, real divisions may exist inside the association: between practising and non-practising, teaching and non-teaching; between very different types of work, or levels of responsibility; between people directly involved in the subject, and those working in another field entirely. Over- or under-representation of these elements may distort the policy and discussion of Council.

(4) *Continuity of Experience*

To function properly, a Council needs to draw upon past experience. Three sources are available: written records, the Secretariat, and past members of the Council. Of these, an efficient Secretariat offers possibly the best guide, although external to Council. Continuity of experience is preserved internally, by arranging for only a part of Council to retire each year, and by retaining Presidents as Vice- or Past-Presidents. In the fifty-six Councils analysed, three-quarters contained one or more Past-Presidents: in twenty cases, they continued to serve for limited periods (usually one to three years); eight associations keep all Past-Presidents as *ex officio* members for life. Retention of Presidents seems a valuable idea, except that ranged by the side of existing officers, they could represent a very solid, immovable body of opinion. Alternatives are the election of people outside the association to long-term Vice-Presidencies; election of Council members to the honorary offices of Honorary Secretary, or Honorary Treasurer, to serve a further period as *ex officio* members.

Experience is important, because of the nature of decisions required to be taken. But a Council consisting largely of long-service members possesses disadvantages. An entrenched Council may develop a low and blocked renewal rate; develop conservative tendencies; obstruct a progressive Secretariat, or interfere too much in the Secretariat's work; resist emergence of younger officers; forget the real views of ordinary members. Some balance has to be achieved, between the desire to make use of past valuable service, and the need to resist the prolonged, unchallenged employment of resolute officers and members.

(5) *Co-ordination of Work*

As a Council uses a system of inter-dependent committees, co-ordination becomes a problem. Several methods are adopted to overcome any difficulty. A small Council may function in slightly modified forms, to tackle various tasks. Commonly, members are allocated to, or agree to serve on, a limited number of committees—choice being based on interests and range of experience. Sometimes a limit restricts the number of committees on which the member may sit. Service of Council members on several committees creates an overlap, enabling views to be shared.

Dangers arise from delegation. Unless care is taken, certain people may find themselves diverted from more important committees. Any individuals, in contact with all committees, may be placed in an advantageous position. Separate committees can lose sight of the association's wider aims, through concentration upon a single objective.

Committees of the Council

Without any exception, Councils manage their affairs by means of a system of Standing and Non-Standing Committees. Standing Committees are the permanent committees, forming part of the continuous structure of administration.

Some relationship exists between size of Council and number of committees. Understandably, the larger the Council—the greater the number of Standing Committees, but if all committees are taken together, then small Councils can have many committees. In Table 4.2 below, eight Councils (containing twenty to thirty-four members) have seven or more committees. This is only made possible through co-option of non-Council members.

TABLE 4.2. SHOWING RELATIONSHIP BETWEEN SIZE OF COUNCIL AND NUMBER OF COMMITTEES

Size of Council	*Number of Committees*								
	3	4	5	6	7	8	9	10 *or more*	*Total*
19 *or less*			1		1				2
20 *to* 34	1	2	4	1	1	2	1	4	16
35 *to* 49	2		1	1		1		5	10
50 *to* 64		2		3	2		4	4	15
65 *to* 79			1	1	3		1	1	7
80 *to* 94	1					1	1	1	4
95 *& over*						1	1		2
Total	4	4	7	6	7	5	8	15	56

An association's area of concern does not seem to affect the number of committees. The number is mainly determined by the fundamental requirements of Council to control finance, education and examinations, admissions, publications, library, and discipline. Activity and responsibilities also account for the numbers of committees. For example, the *Pharmaceutical Society* has a small Council of twenty-four members, with a basic structure of four committees (Establishment and Organization, Education, Finance, Publications), plus four others. Outside these Standing Committees, there are eleven other special Council committees, reflecting the Society's responsibilities, viz. the British Pharmaceutical Codex Revision Committee, the British Veterinary Codex Committee, Committee to Nominate Boards of Examiners, etc. The *Textile Institute* has the most elaborate committee structure of any association. Multiplication arises from an extensive range of technical and research committees. Besides eleven organizing committees, the Institute has: eleven technical committees; a Textile Terms and Definitions Committee; a Unification of Testing Methods Committee; a Designs Competition Committee; a Textbook Committee; a Review of Textile Progress Committee; two joint committees with other organizations. In addition, numerous committees have sub-committees and panels. Elaboration of committee structure inside an association, sometimes results from efforts to study or improve facilities.

Great variations can be found in the committee arrangements of each association. Nevertheless, Table 4.3 shows specific kinds of committee recurring.

TABLE 4.3. SHOWING THE NUMBER AND PERCENTAGE OF COUNCILS POSSESSING DIFFERENT TYPES OF COMMITTEES

Title of Committee	*Number of Councils with Type*	*As percentage of all* ($N=56$)
Executive or General Purposes	33	60
General Purposes and Finance/Finance and House	18	37
Finance Committee (Separate)	29	52
Education and Examinations (together)	6	11
Education (Separate)	24	43
Examinations (Separate)	23	41
Membership and Examinations (together)	7	13
Membership or Admissions	27	48
Publications	30	54
Library and Publications (together)	7	13
Library	12	21
Disciplinary and/or Investigations	14	25

Two types of committee are continuously found: the General Purposes/Executive/General Purposes and Finance Committee (almost all the associations); Education/Examinations/Education and Examinations Committee (nine-tenths of associations). Functions, powers and duties are largely self-explanatory: the Admissions Committee deals with admissions of students and candidates for corporate membership, checking applications, qualifications, references, etc.; the Library Committee supervises the library and so on. Only the General Purposes/Executive Committee will be considered in any detail.

The General Purposes/Executive Committee forms the central committee of Council. Usually it consists of less than twenty senior members, representing about one-third to one-half (some-times less) of the Council. Terms of reference range widely, for the committee determines policy, deals with matters outside other committees' functions, acts for Council between meetings and may control finance. Though actual responsibility differs slightly from Council to Council, this committee might be con-sidered as a kind of inner cabinet, as many General Purposes Committees contain just the Honorary Officers and Chairmen of Standing Committees.

Committees vary in composition, though four regular patterns can be distinguished. They may consist of:

(*a*) all the members, or part of the Council acting *en masse*,

(*b*) only members of Council, but each individual serving on specific committees, sometimes the number for each member is restricted—e.g. not more than four,

(*c*) members of Council serving on committees, together with co-opted non-Council members from inside or out-side the association,

(*d*) co-opted non-Council members entirely, probably with Council members as Chairmen.

Types (*a*) and (*b*) are mainly confined to smaller, younger asso-ciations. Types (*c*) and (*d*) represent the normal procedure.

Members for different committees may volunteer, or be in-vited to serve. Selection can be in the hands of Honorary Officers, or more often, choice depends on committee chairmen. Some Councils leave members to nominate each other, then ballot for the names. In most cases, the President and often Vice-Presidents are *ex officio* members of all Standing Committees.

No clear, straightforward pattern of meetings is noticeable for Standing Committees. They may meet monthly, alternate months, on the day before Council meetings, or as necessary.

Unusual arrangements occur in some associations. For example, the *Institute of Municipal Treasurers and Accountants* maintains a nucleus of five to nine members for each of six Standing Committees, these members give their particular com-mittee preference. Two committees generally meet concurrently in different rooms. Council members, not in the nucleus of either sitting committee, may choose which committee meeting they want to attend. Thus, when an item of special importance is discussed, practically the whole Council may be present.

A recent trend has been the distribution of work into divisions, or distinct departments. In 1959–60, the *Royal Institute of British Architects* undertook a complete reorganization of administration along these lines.[18] The *British Institute of Management* also reformed its administrative system.[19] On amalgamation with the *Physical Society* in 1960, the *Institute of Physics* abandoned the old standing committee structure, separating the Institute's affairs into four sections, with a Vice-President responsible for each.[20] In 1961, the *Advertising Association* began reorganizing the committee structure. Besides the Executive Committee, there are three Divisions: the Administrative Division; the Advertising Investigation Division; the Services Division. The movement toward reorganization shows elsewhere, perhaps due to increasing size and sophistication. Break-down into divisions would seem a rational solution to the problem of expanding facilities, if coupled with an increase in the number of full-time paid officers, responsible for different aspects of work.

Honorary Officers

While every association has Honorary Officers, there is very little common practice. Over half (of the fifty-six associations) allow Council to elect Honorary Officers, over a quarter elect Honorary Officers at the Annual General Meeting, on Council's recommendation. Honorary Officers may consist of a President, Past-President(s), Vice-President(s), Honorary Secretary, Honorary Treasurer. Not all associations possess all these officers. Practically every association has at least one Vice-President (thirty-two out of fifty-two had four or more). Just over two-thirds have one or more Past-Presidents. About a quarter have an Honorary Treasurer. About two-thirds have an Honorary Secretary.

The President is a figurehead, ambassador, supreme director. His, or her, duties are seldom clearly designated, except for the function as Chairman of Council, even then, over a quarter of Councils have a separate Chairman. Appointment as President constitutes a two-way honour: an honour bestowed by the association; honour or prestige given by the individual to the association. For example, smaller, younger bodies may invite distinguished people from outside the association, to become

President. The aim is to enhance the association. Almost without exception, larger and older associations elect a distinguished past-member of Council. Several Councils elect the President from the Vice-Presidents, in strict rotation. Some associations appear to elect distinguished non-professionals to an honorary membership grade, and then invite them to serve as President.[21] Tenure of office rarely extends beyond a year, though some associations permit re-election. About a quarter of associations retain Past-Presidents indefinitely as *ex officio* Council members, providing they remain members of the association. More frequently, ex-Presidents continue for one to three years as Past-Presidents, then leave office.

A Vice-President is both deputy and assistant to the President. Again, a Vice-Presidency can be a reward for service on Council, or a means of enhancing the association, by the introduction of distinguished people from outside.

Two other offices give opportunities to reward Council members for good and loyal services, the posts of Honorary Secretary and Honorary Treasurer. While the Honorary Treasurer may have some importance as the formal controller and guardian of finances, the Honorary Secretary often seems anomalous, owing to the presence of a full-time paid Secretary.

Full-time Paid Executive Officers

No association can possibly function efficiently by complete reliance on casual, part-time help, furnished through Council and committees. The larger the association, the more it must employ full-time paid officers: to deal with day-to-day business; to filter-out applications for membership and inquiries; to prepare information; to maintain members' facilities. Obviously, extent of full-time executive staff depends greatly on the size, finance, activity, interests and facilities offered by an association. No accurate generalizations can be made about the numbers and types of officers, because requirements, and sometimes whims, are a personal reflection of individual associations. Each organization has a Secretary, perhaps one or more Deputy, or Under, Secretaries and usually one or more Assistant Secretaries. Then there can be an Education Officer, a Technical Officer, a Press/Public Relations/Publicity Officer, Librarian and so on. But the Secretary remains the most important officer.

It would be neither unfair to many associations, nor over-generous to many Secretaries, to suggest that he, or she, is often the keystone in the whole organization. Much of an association's long-term success and achievement ultimately depends on the vigour, enterprise, ability, resourcefulness and personality of the Secretary, especially in the early years or the developing periods of the association's life.

Formally, the Secretary's duties may be briefly outlined in the Royal Charter, or Articles of Association—responsibility for: taking minutes at Council and committee meetings; conducting correspondence of the association; superintending publications; collecting subscriptions and preparing accounts; supervision of the ordinary business of the association. Such a catalogue presents a pale understatement of his, or her, real duties and influence.

A thorough, detailed and intimate knowledge of the association's affairs, accumulated over a considerable period of time, makes the Secretary a valuable guide and mentor, watchdog and diplomatist. He, or she, may be expected to carry responsibility for making: decisions on routine applications for membership; preparation of material for Council and committees; preliminary considerations on problems of professional conduct; attention to a multitude of outside inquiries for the association's advice; implementation of the Council's policy. Like the President, the Secretary makes formal and informal visits to Branches, represents the association at outside functions (dinners, celebrations, conferences, etc.), serves on outside committees as the association's representative.

No real estimate can be given of the Secretary's relationship to Council, owing to variations from one association to another. Opportunities arise to lead and drive Council toward policy and decisions, yet this is not necessarily Machiavellian. Normally Council respects the Secretary's sound grasp of the association's affairs. Also, it must be remembered that paid staff and Executive Officers work directly under the authority and surveillance of the Secretary. While close contact must exist between certain officers and particular committees, the Secretary continues as the most important connection.

MEMBERSHIP STRUCTURE

Firstly, membership can be divided into corporate and non-corporate members. Corporate members are the qualified, constituent members of the legally incorporated association, possessing full rights and privileges, including the power to vote at meetings. Non-corporate members are the unqualified, or partially qualified members with limited rights and privileges, remaining outside the corporate body and unable to vote at meetings. Secondly, membership can be separated into three broad sections: senior professionals, professionals, aspirant professionals. The first two constitute the corporate members, the third non-corporate.

Roughly, two different membership patterns become discernable: the Fellow-Associate-Student type; the Member-Associate Member-Student type. No simple explanation can be given for the preference of one pattern, rather than the other, except for adherence to tradition. Engineering institutions traditionally follow the Member-Associate Member-Student type, while associations connected with 'business and commerce' retain the Fellow-Associate-Student base.

Outside these fundamental elements, two additional provisions are common. Firstly, just over half the associations have special grades of Honorary Membership for distinguished, long-standing members within the association and/or distinguished individuals outside. There may be one grade for both, or two separate classes. Secondly, about half the associations insert a Graduate, or Licentiate, non-corporate grade between corporate members and Students. This mainly applies to associations connected with science, engineering and technology. The extra non-corporate grade furnishes a special class for students, and others, who have met the qualifying examination requirements, but lack experience and/or age necessary for corporate membership.

Membership Requirements

Generalizations about membership requirements are bound to be approximate, owing to the variations found from one association to another. An analysis was made of requirements for the first corporate grade (i.e. Associate Member or Associate) in seventy associations.[22] This revealed certain characteristics. In nearly half the associations, the candidate must be at least 21, and 25 or over in about half. Practically all associations specify approved training of two to five years. About three-fifths stipulate definite employment in the occupation, often in a position of responsibility. In one-third of the cases, it would be necessary to register as a student, in order to take the examinations. But only nine do not grant partial or complete exemption from their examinations. The rest permit various exemptions via degrees and diplomas. Nearly half the associations provide modified late entry requirements, usually for those over 35. Modifications consist of reductions in the number of papers to be taken in the examination, a special examination, submission of a 'thesis' in place of the examination, a complete waiver of examinations. Finally, the application will have to be sponsored, generally by two members.

Taking the three divisions (Aspirant Professional—Professional —Senior Professional), each is separated from the others by four distinct requirements: age; examinations; professional training and/or experience; level of responsibility reached. Additional elements complicate the picture: examination exemptions at various levels; modified late entrance for those with experience and limited examination attainment; need to be proposed and supported by existing members. Table 4.4 indicates roughly the typical changing requirements, moving through the three stages.

The change from non-corporate to corporate membership marks the most important transition. Movement from the lower to the higher corporate grade may add little to achieved status. Unless the higher grade signifies a real advance in the eyes of members, they seem reluctant to transfer, paying a larger subscription for the same privileges. Some associations overcome hesitation by making the transfer automatic, once the member reaches the required age and possesses the appropriate experience in terms of years. Some associations make polite suggestions to eligible members. Significance of the transfer depends on the association. In associations connected with science, engineering and technology, eligible members (especially university and technical college teachers) appear to seek the higher grade. A

TABLE 4.4. SHOWING CHANGING REQUIREMENTS FOR DIFFERENT MEMBERSHIP GRADES

Requirements	Aspirant Professional		Professional	Senior Professional
	Student	*Graduate*		
Minimum Age	16–18	21	21–28	30–35 (Sometimes 23+)
Examinations	Preliminary Examination or equivalent—G.C.E. 'O' Level	Association's Final or equivalent. Occasionally this grade is used for students who have passed the Intermediate	Association's Final or equivalent	Association's Final or equivalent. Some Associations demand a further examination
Training and/or Experience	None Some Associations demand registration as student before candidates are eligible for examination	Usually 2–3 years' training	3–5 years' experience. Sometimes including the period of training (often in addition)	5–10 years' experience in a responsible position
Responsibility	None	None	Usually limited responsibility. For example: Engineer Surveyor or Assistant Manager, Accountant	In senior executive position—as Principal, Senior Engineer, Head of Department, etc., specified period

111

few associations regard the senior corporate grade as a 'post-graduate' level. They demand either evidence of substantial achievement in the profession, or that members must take a further examination. For example, in the following associations, members must take a Fellowship examination in order to transfer: *Institute of Actuaries, Chartered Insurance Institute, Institution of Metallurgists* (unless exempt), *Institute of Chartered Shipbrokers, Library Association* (until 1964, then by thesis).

Ideally, these various membership grades ought to represent different levels of achieved qualification (examinations), experience and attained responsibility. Indeed, they ought to be a safer indication of ability than a once-and-for-all examination, such as a university degree. Unfortunately this is not always true. On formation, a new association frequently cannot afford to demand that all new members pass the qualifying examination. For a period of years, experienced individuals enter without qualifying by examination, while younger candidates for membership must take prescribed examinations. Gradually, standards improve as the age limit for exemption from examinations is raised, as non-examination entrants are filtered more carefully. Eventually candidates enter by examination alone; transfer within depending on experience and responsibility. Retention of modified entrance for older, experienced, senior personnel can distort the value of membership, even establish resentment inside the association. There have been exceptions to this general pattern. For example, the *(Royal) Institute of Chemistry*, the *Pharmaceutical Society* and the *Institute of Actuaries* established examinations almost immediately on foundation, very carefully controlling non-examination entrants. Appendix I, Column 3, shows the year of first examination for many associations. Most associations ensure strict regulation of the lower corporate grade, at the same time, allowing individuals to enter the senior grade under special conditions.

Advantages obtained from Membership

What does the individual gain from membership of a Qualifying Association? Possible advantages can be classified under two broad headings. Firstly, membership demonstrates a definite achievement level in a specific occupational area. Secondly, membership offers access to a series of services, not otherwise widely available.

The first advantage needs further consideration. Probably, associations, as qualifying bodies, can be divided into four basic types. Membership provides:

    (*a*) the essential qualification for the occupation, it must be obtained in order to practise—this only happens in registered professions or where particular work is governed by Statute,

    (*b*) the best generally accepted qualification, preferable to others,

    (*c*) a satisfactory qualification, one of several available—opinion is divided about value,

    (*d*) a doubtful qualification, not widely accepted.

'Acceptance' and 'value' are not easy to define objectively, as they can relate to acceptance inside the profession, in surrounding professions, or in everyone's estimation. For the individual, one qualification may be sought rather than another, because examinations and entrance requirements seem less difficult, or for some inexplicable reason based on personal taste. Other factors complicate the issue. Many prospective members can gain exemption from examination requirements by means of a degree or diploma. Plural membership is also very common. Examination exemption and plural membership occur more and more frequently in associations connected with science, engineering and technology. But it would be wrong to conclude, that such action reflects the intrinsic qualifying value of the association. More likely, membership-seeking demonstrates a desire to amass a glowing façade of qualifications, or a recognition of valuable services offered by the association.

Membership certainly gives access to a variety of services, but the range and importance of facilities can be deceptive. No safe generalizations emerge. For example, Appendix I, Column 6, lists publication of a regular journal in practically every case. In fact, quality of these publications varies tremendously. A 'journal' can mean anything from a comprehensive, up-to-date, bulky, highly informative periodical, to a thin, chatty commentary spread between poorly written articles. Whether the 'journal' gives a useful service depends on so many factors: available funds; a continuous supply of good material; competition in the same field from similar publications; determination of the association. Fortunately, one enterprising publisher has realized the potential market, and undertakes to provide layout design, advertisements and help with general preparation. The result is an attractive, high quality journal. At least four associations sensibly use this commercial aid.

Other facilities exhibit an equally superficial impressiveness. A 'library' might consist of six to eight shelves of aged, unrepresentative books. At the opposite extreme, the libraries of the *Royal Institute of British Architects, Institute of Chartered Accountants, Chartered Insurance Institute* and *Pharmaceutical Society* offer extensive, comprehensive collections of wide reputation. A 'Yearbook' or 'Handbook' can be a list of members, or a membership list plus a valuable digest of essential information assisting in the member's everyday work.

All associations arrange meetings for their members. These meetings range through technical lectures and discussion groups, conventions, national and international conferences, joint meetings with other associations, visits, annual dinners, informal social functions. Again, huge differences are apparent. Some associations obtain national and international experts to speak, others circulate a rather sad collection of enthusiastic members, who try hard to give sound talks on 'technical' subjects.

Whatever the objective standard of publications, meetings and services as a whole, one ought not to decry or underestimate the sincere enthusiasm pervading all associations, large and small. If facilities are judged meagre and of poor quality, then it must be remembered that limitations are imposed by financial resources, by the type of membership, by support from members. Many associations could be improved, if ordinary members made more effort to participate in activities and to use facilities. Members often become passive receptors, paying an annual subscription, stacking unread journals in a corner and unopened notices in a waste-paper basket. Why is this? Perhaps one answer lies in the emphasis placed on examinations and the power of an association to qualify. Inevitably, members tend to look upon the association solely as a means of qualification.

Are there any other advantages for the individual? For example, controlled competition, uniform practice, reflected status. Some of these possibilities will be discussed later.

LOCAL ORGANIZATION

Almost all Qualifying Associations are national bodies, based on London, with a membership spread throughout the country, sometimes throughout the world. A widely distributed membership needs local organization. Thus every well-established, reasonably sized association has local branches, sections or societies.

A few associations contained local organization already in-built, owing to development as federations of existing local institutes or societies. Examples are the *Chartered Insurance Institute, Institution of Mining Engineers* and *Institute of Brewing*. In the case of mining engineers, they must be members of a Federated Institute, before being eligible for membership of the Institution. Most associations develop local branches on the initiative of Council, or through members feeling cut off from activities centred on Headquarters. Between the federated type of local organization and the branch superimposed by Council, there are occasional variations. For example, the *Royal Institute of British Architects* has 'Allied Societies' affiliated to it. These are local organizations of architects, with completely independent constitutions and administration. Each behaves as the accredited centre of R.I.B.A. activities for the district. Members of the R.I.B.A. are neither automatically members of an Allied Society, nor do they have to join.

Generally speaking, associations do not always regard branch membership as automatic. Some associations consider that members belong to a local branch, whether or not they actually attend any meetings. Some associations only recognize a member, as a branch member, if he takes the trouble to join a particular branch.

A Branch or District Society exists as an organized centre of local activities, providing facilities for members isolated from the main activities organized at Headquarters, adapting them to meet local needs. A Branch supplies a useful means for transmitting central Council recommendations and decisions, on domestic and technical matters. It also enables discussion and organization of opinion. Government of local organization by committees, with various officers, ensures a good training ground for future Council and central committee members.

Representation of local committees on the central Council provides a sound formal, and informal, link between headquarters and ordinary members.

Unfortunately, disadvantages sometimes result from local organization. Extent of autonomy presents problems. A correct balance must be fixed, determining those affairs which are the prerogative of central Council, and those which can be left in the hands of a local committee. Most associations allow local committees to carry out any action, except for admission and expulsion of members. Obviously any large, or serious, undertaking requires consultation with Headquarters.

Secretaries of some associations hold a special annual meeting for local secretaries, to discuss any ideas or problems. Representation of local organization on the central Council generates another source of possible discontent. Who is the best representative—the Chairman, the Secretary, or a specially elected representative? Should all branches have equal representation, or ought the number to depend on the size of the local organisation? Does the local representative truly represent local opinion, or merely reflect active Branch members interests? Answers to such questions must be determined with reference to individual associations.

CONCLUSION

To understand the structure of Qualifying Associations, it is necessary: firstly, to appreciate their competitive nature; secondly, to realize their voluntary basis.

Competition helped to create a traditional structure and a common aim to furnish similar facilities for members. The competitive struggle is for status, conducted on two planes: for the members and the occupation; for the association. While the two causes are linked, and an improvement in one area must influence the other, considerable effort seems to be diverted to inter-association prestige gathering and window-dressing.

The voluntary nature of associations is sometimes forgotten. Government remains in the hands of voluntary, part-time officers and committees, although full-time, paid officials execute general administration and day-to-day business. Yet the sheer volume and type of work involved in everyday administration transposes considerable power to full-time officers, establishing a measure of indispensability.

In reality, associations perform a series of tasks simultaneously. Firstly, they act as examining and qualifying bodies. This entails more than testing. It can mean supervision of training and education facilities, organization of classes and special information, even preparation of textbooks. Secondly, they furnish a continuous supply of technical information, in different ways, to many people, committees and organizations both inside and outside the occupation. Thirdly, they provide a way of keeping members in step with advancing knowledge.

Essentially, organizational structure has continued unchanged for the last fifty or a hundred years: government by committees of voluntary members; multi-grade membership; election of Council by corporate members; local needs supplied by branch organization. However, the majority of large associations have doubled in size, over the last twenty years. Now several organizations contain over 40,000 members and students. Table 4.5 indicates total expansion in a few associations.

TABLE 4.5. SHOWING MEMBERSHIP GROWTH IN CERTAIN QUALIFYING ASSOCIATIONS 1900 TO 1960

Title of Association	Approximate size of Total Membership in		
	1900	*1940*	*1960*
Institution of Mechanical Engineers	4,000	14,000	52,000
Institute of Bankers	9,000	37,750	48,600
Chartered Institute of Secretaries	1,300	25,000	47,000
Institution of Electrical Engineers	3,600	20,000	46,000
Chartered Insurance Institute	1,600	25,000	40,000
Institute of Chartered Accountants	3,000	14,300	38,300
Royal Institute of British Architects	2,000	11,000	26,000
Royal Institution of Chartered Surveyors	3,000	9,300	22,390
Institute of Municipal Treasurers & Accountants	213	2,100	9,000

More and more examination candidates appear each year. Today, the *Royal Institute of British Architects* examines about 1,900, the *Association of Certified and Corporate Accountants* nearly

4,000, the *Law Society* about 4,000, the *Royal Institution of Chartered Surveyors* over 5,000, the *Chartered Institute of Secretaries* and *Institute of Chartered Accountants* over 8,000, the *Institute of Bankers* about 30,000. In addition, associations must arrange for regular meetings, conferences, summer-schools, publications, etc.

Can the present structure of internal organization meet these large and expanding demands? The ready answer of many associations has been the appointment of more full-time officers, delegating more responsibility to them, then to break up administrations into divisions. More recently, some associations have created the special post of Director; a general chief administrator in addition to the Secretary. Delegation would seem to increase the authority and influence of the chief executive. Associations grow steadily away from the original idea of a voluntary organization, run by a band of part-time enthusiastic amateurs. But an association's income ultimately limits the size of full-time paid staff. Where associations cannot afford an adequate paid staff, increasing strain falls on existing personnel, or there must be an extension of the voluntary committee system, with more frequent meetings and longer sittings. Any expansion of committee work discourages busy, influential and capable people from taking part in government.

Is multi-grade membership a valuable, or a necessary element in the structure? No general answer can be given, as requirements differ from one type of occupation to another. Some indicator of technical experience and responsibility seems useful, and possible, in engineering and science, but limited in commerce. Students ought to be separated from qualified members. Perhaps special honorary and retired membership grades serve useful functions. But is it worthwhile having an extra noncorporate grade (Graduate or Licentiate), or more than one corporate grade? On the surface, the rationale appears founded on a combination of tradition and the maintained example of similar associations. As far as members are concerned, they pay a higher subscription for the same privileges, probably subsidizing facilities for the benefit of others. Foundation of an intermediate grade, between Student and the first corporate grade, rests on the grounds that the Graduate (or Licentiate) satisfies examination requirements, but lacks experience. Looking at the corporate grades, how many outside the association, or the occupation served, really appreciate the significant difference between a 'Fellow' and an 'Associate', or a 'Member' and an 'Associate Member'? Where a realistic adjustment of requirements and status separate corporate grades, then members may be prepared to take a further examination and apply for upgrading. Some associations seem to be drifting toward a merger of corporate grades, as differentials between senior Associates and Fellows fade, and transfer becomes practically automatic. In other associations (science, engineering, technology), junior and senior grades grow more sharply defined.

Chapter Five

QUALIFYING ASSOCIATIONS
AND EDUCATION

TRADITIONALLY, only very tenuous links connected the professions with universities, for the universities gradually lost any vocational aims after the Middle Ages. Teachers and ecclesiastics alone were in any sense university trained. However, before the nineteenth century, the clergy seldom faced examination before ordination. At Oxford and Cambridge, they took mathematics or classics and might attend lectures in theology. Oxford students could attend lectures of five theology professors, take an examination and receive a testamur. But no Bishop required such evidence for ordination. At Cambridge, no divinity professor gave lectures. From the 1840s, requirements slowly changed. Cambridge introduced a voluntary theological examination in 1843. Soon most Bishops expected Cambridge candidates to have passed the examination. From the 1850s, new theological colleges started to appear, setting a fresh standard for training.[1]

In law and medicine, training was not institutionalized. Pupilage gave the essential grounding. Teaching began in the late eighteenth-century hospitals. But these were nothing like the modern teaching institutions, instead, physicians and surgeons took paying pupils. At the beginning of the nineteenth century, the only hospital medical schools could be found at St Bartholomew's, St Thomas', Guy's and London Hospital, with some teaching at Middlesex, Westminster and St George's. Students tended to move round from hospital to hospital for clinical teaching and lectures. Also, several small private medical schools and schools of anatomy flourished.[2] Later, hospital medical schools in London became associated with the University of London, which began awarding medical degrees from about 1840.

Bar students had to belong to one of the *Inns of Court*, although the Inns failed to impose any strict training or examinations. Lectures were offered from the 1840s, and a voluntary examination introduced in 1853, becoming compulsory in 1872.[3] On the other hand, after 1836, solicitors had to take an examination before being admitted to the Court Rolls. The *Law Society* established regular lectures.[4]

Seven new associations appeared between 1800 and 1850.[5] What kind of attitude did they adopt toward education and certification? The associations may be divided roughly into two groups: those apparently not interested in formal education and examinations; those which quickly organized training and examinations.

TABLE 5.1. SHOWING QUALIFYING ASSOCIATIONS ESTABLISHED
IN ENGLAND AND WALES BETWEEN 1800 AND 1850, WITH YEAR
OF FIRST EXAMINATION

Founded in	*Association*
1800	Royal College of Surgeons of London (now 'of England') (Examinations already established by the College in its previous form—Company of Surgeons)
1818	Institution of Civil Engineers (Examinations: 1897)
1825	The Society of Attorneys, Solicitors, Proctors and others not being Barristers practising in the Courts of Law and Equity of the United Kingdom (Law Society) (Examinations established by the Courts of Common Law and Chancery 1836–7, taken over by the Society in 1877)
1834	(Royal) Institute of British Architects (Voluntary examination in 1863, compulsory in 1882)
1841	Pharmaceutical Society of Great Britain (Examinations: 1842)
1844	Royal College of Veterinary Surgeons (Examinations already held at the London and Edinburgh Veterinary Colleges. The Act of 1881 gave powers to examine)
1847	Institution of Mechanical Engineers (Examinations: 1913)
1848	Institute of Actuaries (Examinations: 1850)

Of the associations in Table 5.1, only two immediately planned and set examinations: the *Pharmaceutical Society* and the *Institute of Actuaries*. Probably many factors help explain the failure to set examinations. Firstly, architects and engineers regarded pupilage as the most suitable training. Secondly, examinations were not accepted in society as a necessary test of ability. Only the medical profession made use of examinations, and solicitors from the mid-1830s. Thirdly, no regular system of primary, secondary and higher education was generally available throughout the country, providing a sound educational background for potential examinees. Fourthly, membership of the associations was not considered necessary within particular occupations. Men could practise without demonstrating examined competence. Fifthly, though conscious of the lack of institutional training facilities, associations were not prepared to undertake teaching themselves.

For the *Royal College of Surgeons* and the *Royal College of Veterinary Surgeons*, the position was quite different. Many veterinary surgeons trained either at the London, or the Edinburgh Veterinary College, where examinations were established. The *Royal College of Surgeons* was a recast form of the *Company of Surgeons*, which already conducted examinations.

Introduction of examinations by the *Pharmaceutical Society* and *Institute of Actuaries* created problems. On foundation, the *Pharmaceutical Society* realised the value of examinations and the necessity to supply a means of adequate preparation. Measured ability was required to overcome a bad reputation fostered by a mass of untrained, ignorant, incompetent chemists and druggists. In the first Presidential Address of 12 January 1842, William Allen announced the establishment of lectures, appointment of examiners and regulations for examinations. To some extent, the Society probably felt impelled by the *Society of Apothecaries*, which already held lectures and examinations.[6] giving courses in materia medica, chemistry, pharmacy and botany. In July, regulations were published for two examinations: a minor examination for admission to the Associateship; a major examination for Membership. Before the end of 1842, The *Pharmaceutical Society* commenced lectures in February 1842, two candidates presented themselves for the minor examination.

The first successful candidate for the major examination appeared in February 1844.[7]

The story for the *Institute of Actuaries* proved entirely different. After foundation in October 1848, Council appointed four examiners in April 1849 to prepare a syllabus. By July, the plan was ready. In June 1850, the Institute held the first examination, consisting of two papers with thirty-five written questions. Six candidates passed the test. Next year, the Institute split the examination into two parts, each part being separated by at least a year, no candidate being eligible for the final unless over 21, with five years' experience in a life assurance company. And so examinations continued, usually with nine to twelve candidates. Unfortunately, the Institute's concept of education remained purely in terms of examinations. Only one hundred and thirty-three candidates appeared in ten years. Obviously examinees needed help to prepare, and in January 1857, T. B. Sprague proposed holding special classes. On acceptance of the scheme, Sprague was appointed tutor. A ten-week course was advertised and two students came forward. From this time on, the Institution faced the problem of preparing students for examinations, even by commissioning and publishing its own textbooks.[8]

Thus in both the *Pharmaceutical Society* and the *Institute of Actuaries*, tuition had to be organized in order to set examinations. Examination candidates could not be left to forage for themselves, as external facilities were almost non-existent. The *Law Society* also showed interest in examinations, despite an unwillingness to set them, suggesting instead that responsibility rested with the Courts of Common Law and Chancery. But in 1833, the Society began lectures. By 1854, lectures were delivered twice weekly in Common Law, Equity and Conveyancing, attended by an average of two hundred students.[9] From these beginnings, the Society's Law School developed, combining with a correspondence college in 1962, to form the 'College of Law'. In the same way, the *Pharmaceutical Society*'s 'School of Pharmacy' evolved from the first lectures, finally becoming part of London University in 1948.

EDUCATION AND THE QUALIFYING ASSOCIATIONS
1850 TO 1900

From the 1850s, the idea of examinations seemed to become more acceptable in society. Despite their antiquated administration and casual concern with education, both Oxford and Cambridge had helped to pioneer examinations. Cambridge instituted a written tripos, mainly mathematics, in 1780. A second tripos in classics was offered in 1824 for those successful in the mathematical tripos. In 1848, Cambridge introduced the moral and natural science triposes as post-graduate degrees.[10] Oxford began with written examinations, again mainly classics, in 1800 and an honours school in 1807. In 1852, honours schools were introduced in natural science, plus law and history together. When incorporated in 1838, the University of London received powers to award degrees in arts, law and medicine to students of constituent colleges.[11]

During the second half of the nineteenth century, many different organizations started examinations. The Union of Lancashire and Cheshire Institutes began in 1847, leading the (*Royal*) *Society of Arts* to consider examinations for the working classes. Following a favourable report from an investigating committee in 1853, the Society published a scheme. Only one candidate attended the first examination in March 1855, the next year showed a real improvement with fifty-two candidates. Subjects ranged through English Language and Literature, various sciences, History, Geography, foreign languages. By 1858, 1,100 were taking examinations at local centres. The Society introduced technological subjects in 1873, transferring them to the City and Guilds Institute in 1879.[12]

A new Royal Charter in 1858 enabled London University to award External Degrees, and in 1860, the University introduced two science degrees (B.Sc., D.Sc.). London Matriculation steadily became a popular and coveted certificate. Only sixty-nine passed 'Matric.' in 1840, in the 1890s the average was 2,000 a year. Examinations multiplied at the secondary school level. Founded in 1846, the College of Preceptors commenced examinations in three grades, in 1853. Oxford University introduced 'Local' examinations in 1857, for the benefit of public schools, followed by Cambridge in 1858. Foundation of the

Headmasters Conference of 'public' schools in 1870, led to the Oxford and Cambridge Joint School Examinations Board in 1873. The Science and Art Department began examinations in 1861. In 1870, the London Chamber of Commerce introduced courses in commercial education, and examinations in 1890.[13]

In summary, the situation showed a stronger emphasis on examinations within privileged educational institutions (public schools and universities), while more and more examinations became established outside, although unaccompanied by sufficient facilities for preparation.

By the 1880s, examinations had to be passed in order to become a barrister, solicitor, doctor, surgeon, clergyman, pharmacist, a merchant navy officer on a foreign-going ship, or a mine manager. Examinations barred entrance to the *Royal College of Veterinary Surgeons*, the *Royal Institute of British Architects* or the *Institute of Actuaries*. Competitive examinations were conducted by a Central Board, for admission to the Home or Indian Civil Service. A competitive examination governed entry to the Royal Military Academy at Woolwich, and a commission into the Army.

Bearing in mind this trend toward testing suitability, it was not surprising that associations formed after 1850, concerned themselves with examinations, especially in the 1880s and 1890s. Table 5.2 illustrates the pattern.

Of course, subsequent to the establishment of examinations, most associations admitted experienced men to their membership, without written examinations. In view of the undeveloped nature of national education, growing insistence upon examinations was an astonishing and bold step forward. Engineering institutions seemed less interested, perhaps owing to their reliance on the traditional method of selection based on pupilage and experience. Examinations had become accepted as an essential basis of professionalism. On the other hand, associations appeared much less concerned with instilling a sense of professional ethics. Only the *Institute of Chartered Accountants* and the *(Royal) Institute of Chemistry* made provisions immediately to regulate professional conduct.

Introduction of examinations had several effects. Firstly, compulsory examinations, or rigid entrance requirements, increased the reluctance of experienced professionals to join. Much

TABLE 5.2. QUALIFYING ASSOCIATIONS ESTABLISHED IN ENGLAND
AND WALES 1850 TO 1900, WITH YEAR OF FIRST EXAMINATION

(*Note:* These are all existing associations, listed under present titles. Defunct
associations are not included. Year of first examination given in parentheses)

Founded in	*Association*
1868	Royal Institution of Chartered Surveyors (1881)
1871	Institution of Electrical Engineers (1913)
1873	Institution of Municipal Engineers (1886)
1877	Royal Institute of Chemistry (1879)
1877	Library Association (1896)
1879	Institute of Bankers (1880)
1880	Institute of Chartered Accountants in England & Wales (1880)
1882	Chartered Institute of Patent Agents (1889)
1885	Institute of Municipal Treasurers & Accountants (1903)
1886	Chartered Auctioneers & Estate Agents Institute (1892)
1886	Institute of Brewing (1916, postponed until 1920)
1889	Institute of Marine Engineers (1935)
1889	Institution of Mining Engineers (1947)
1891	Chartered Institute of Secretaries (1897)
1894	Chartered Society of Physiotherapy (1895)
1897	Chartered Insurance Institute (1899)

	Other Associations
1860	Royal Institution of Naval Architects (Still relies on evidence of external qualifications)
1866	Institution of Gas Engineers (Formed as 'The British Association of Gas Managers', examinations only introduced in 1926, after the present Institution emerged in 1902)
1866	Royal Aeronautical Society (Formed as a 'Study Association', first set examinations in 1922)

depended on the necessity for the qualification in the occupation, plus recognition of the association awarding the diploma.
As a result, those in the occupation often did not bother to join,
or they sought alternative ways of joining, or they formed rival
associations. For example, membership of the (*Royal*) *Institute
of Chemistry* climbed slowly, in part due to the rigid entrance requirements, for even university graduates were not given com-

plete examination exemption until 1918. Rival associations became prevalent in accountancy and surveying. In accountancy, the *Society of Accountants and Auditors* was founded in 1885, because the *Institute of Chartered Accountants* demanded service under articles before candidates could take examinations. Possibly the examinations were too difficult and established accountants, lacking ten years' experience, were unwilling to sit for them. Rival associations appeared in at least two other fields, probably because of examinations and general requirements. The *Chartered Institute of Secretaries'* examinations started in 1897. In 1907, the *Incorporated Secretaries' Association* was formed, to be absorbed by the Institute in 1937. Insurance provides another example of rival organization. The *Faculty of Insurance* appeared in 1912, as an alternative to the *Chartered Insurance Institute*, to be amalgamated with the Institute in 1934.

Secondly, optional or voluntary examinations encouraged people to seek entrance by the easiest route. For example, the *Royal Institute of British Architects* instituted a voluntary examination in 1862. Before being made compulsory in 1882, only twelve examinations were held, only forty-three candidates passed with proficiency, yet total membership almost doubled to over 750.[14] Voluntary examinations, or examinations for one set of entrants alone, always present an awkward problem. A 'back-door' left open for entrance without examination may very well bring discontent. Members, who have submitted to the examination, resent the influx of non-examination candidates. A partly examined, partly unexamined membership casts doubt on the qualification's value and prevents consolidation of status. However, many associations have been forced to retain flexible entrance requirements, for a short or long period, in order to build up size.

Thirdly, perhaps most important of all, lack of adequate outside educational facilities forced associations to use their own resources, so helping in the preparation of examinees. Over the years, provision for study has caused associations to prepare textbooks, to found university lectureships and scholarships, to conduct elaborate tuition schemes, to establish teaching institutions. Some of these achievements will be considered later.

Possibly the *Institute of Chemistry* alone was able to introduce rigid examination standards with some confidence. The founders, at least half of whom were teachers of chemistry, showed their determination to organize examinations at once.[15] Expectations were based on the reasonably wide and expanding teaching of chemistry, coupled with the existence of substantial texts. Incorporated on 2 October 1877, the Institute's Council adopted an examination scheme in April 1878, and the first examinations were held in February 1879. In 1882, Council decided that all candidates for the Associateship, must show evidence of three years attendance at an institution approved by the Institute.[16]

The majority of associations were not so fortunate. Often they suffered from an absence or lack of teachers, teaching institutions and textbooks. In several cases, they had no firm theoretical background knowledge, no completely universal practice, which could be translated into theoretically structured concepts and methods. These factors handicapped teaching and resulted in syllabuses determined by 'accessible' subjects, rather than by subjects directed at actual practice. In addition, associations had to ensure a satisfactory level of general education by setting a preliminary examination in English, Elementary Mathematics, History, Geography, etc. A few examples illustrate what happened.

The *Chartered Insurance Institute* resulted from the federation of Insurance Institutes in 1897. An examination syllabus appeared in June 1898, and the first examination was held in 1899. Local Institutes were given responsibility for preparing students. In fact, insurance had become so heterogeneous that lectures and classes could not be provided in every subject. Lack of tutors and facilities largely left students to their own devices.[17] The *Chartered Institute of Secretaries* published a syllabus in February 1893. Preliminary and Intermediate examinations were first held in 1897, the first Final in 1900. For preparation, the Institute resorted to courses of lectures on company and mercantile law, book-keeping, political economy and preparation of accounts.[18] The *Institute of Municipal Treasurers and Accountants* set up a committee in April 1899, to consider methods of strengthening the Institute. The committee's report recommended examinations, but Council felt unable to deal with the problem, owing to their concern over incorporation. In August 1902, *The Financial Circular* published syllabuses. In October, the Editor passed on a request for tuition from 'several clerks desirous of sitting at the first examination'. For many years, the only oral tuition was provided through lectures arranged by Students' Societies. The London Students' Society began in 1903, their lectures being published in *The Financial Circular*.[19]

The situation gradually improved for associations connected with 'commerce', for some common subjects began to emerge— book-keeping, accountancy, aspects of law and commercial practice and so on. Very specialized associations still suffered. The *Library Association* is a good example. At the Annual Meeting in 1880, a resolution was passed asking Council to consider the best method of helping to train library assistants. Council appointed two committees, one after the other, and in 1882 their report was adopted. An examination scheme proposed a preliminary in general subjects, plus examinations in five subjects taken separately. The first examinations were held in July 1885, then irregularly until 1891. No instruction was offered, so although the idea of examinations was good, they caused a growing feeling of uncertainty about the syllabus. Four times, the Association revised the syllabus in the next fifteen years. Help was obviously needed by candidates. In 1895, J. J. Ogle started a 'Library Assistants' Corner' in *The Library*, dealing with notes and queries on practical librarianship.[20] Strong pleas were made for the regular instruction of library assistants.[21] Finally, in 1897, Council referred the matter to the Summer School Committee. The committee suggested classes in Cataloguing, Elementary Bibliography, Historical Printing. Council adopted the report. The Association provided a small grant, putting administration into the hands of a new Education Committee.[22]

Most of the associations formed in the 1900s and 1910s delayed examinations until after the First World War. By the mid-1920s and 1930s, they nearly all possessed examinations. Now imposition of a written test was less a heroic venture and more a fashionable necessity. Examinations, rather than experience alone, had become a requisite part of professionalism. More accessible secondary education, a firmer base of primary education, expansion of commercial and technical colleges, cheap printing and increasing production of textbooks—such factors enabled associations to hold examinations and stress the need for a theoretical background.

To set examinations and wait for candidates is hardly enough. Any association hoping to maintain and improve standards of entrance, must undertake supervision of candidates' training and education. Besides the need for a continuous watch on outside facilities, associations must often arrange aids for students. Supervision and provision vary considerably from one organization to another.

Supervision of Students

All associations have a student grade. About a third of Qualifying Associations require candidates to register as Students before taking the examinations. In the remainder, student membership is optional. Three possibilities are found, the aspirant professional (*a*) must be a student member and articled to an approved principal, or (*b*) must be a registered student, though not articled, or (*c*) can be a student member, choice being optional. Articled service, registered by the association, represents the extreme control.

Until the late nineteenth century, students of law or medicine often became the pupil of an established practitioner. Frequently a formal contract would be drawn up, binding the pupil to service and the principal to certain obligations. In fact, apprenticeship or pupilage supplied the basic training in most skilled occupations. Pupilage virtually disappeared with the institutionalization of training. Today, compulsory pupilage only remains for solicitors, patent agents and chartered accountants. Over the last fifty years, the Bar Council has advocated an obligatory period of service with an established barrister, for all those just called to the Bar. This is gradually coming into force. Additionally, all Bar Students must join an *Inn of Court* and keep twelve dining terms, dining at least six times each term.[23] A number of associations allow voluntary pupilage.[24] In the *Town Planning Institute*, a student must be articled before entering the examinations, unless exempt from the Intermediate examination.

Is pupilage the best form of professional training today? Many arguments exist for and against the system. For example, pupilage encourages a sense of responsibility in the articled clerk, or pupil, and ensures a supervised practical training. However, it can develop into a source of cheap, skilled labour. It can act as a means of controlling entrance to the profession. It can be a burdensome combination of full-time work and part-time study. Although premiums may not be paid, the years of articled service entail a reduced income for the pupil. To be effective, pupilage requires rigid supervision, otherwise little real training may take place.

Since the last war, the *Institute of Chartered Accountants* has tightened control over articled clerkship. Under the 1948 Supplemental Charter, Council obtained powers to include obligatory clauses in articles.[25] Now, Students must belong to a Students' Society, principals must give time to attend meetings, etc., and grant one month for full-time study before examinations. Still, students incur a serious strain. Just over half the candidates fail either the Institute's Intermediate or Final examinations. It has been calculated that an articled clerk of normal ability, hoping to pass the Institute's examination in five years, must undertake 3,000 hours homework, excluding the time for revision. Assuming six months' special leave (about 750 hours effective study), this leaves 2,250 hours spread over four and a half years, or 500 hours a year, excluding holidays, sick leave, etc. It means eleven hours a week study, plus full-time work. A consistent demand on will power and determination.[26]

Even if associations do not insist on articled service or compulsory registration, most of them require evidence of approved training and/or experience, before electing a successful examination candidate to corporate membership. As another supervisory safeguard, some associations inspect teaching institutions and approve specific teachers within them.[27] Some associations accept courses and local examinations as suitable exemption from their own examinations.[28] More often than not, associations require students to be employed in the particular occupation while studying, or to be taking an approved full-time course.

Practical training is essential and ought to be well-planned. Whether an association can demand certain patterns of training, or minimum periods of experience, depends on many factors: the various available forms of institutionalized and non-institutionalized training; the attitudes of employers; the attractions of bordering occupations; whether key members on the employer/administrative side are members of the association; how far association membership is necessary in the occupation, and so on. For example, the municipal engineer is employed solely by local authorities, and municipal engineers belong to the *Institution of Municipal Engineers*. As a result, the Institution has developed a scheme of practical training, which outlines a plan for the circulation of graduate-trainees and learners through departments. The Institution and *Institution of Civil Engineers* manage the scheme jointly. All intending municipal engineers must be accepted under the scheme.[29] Similarly, the *Institute of Housing* introduced a 'Model Training Scheme' for housing managers. It prescribes the various aspects of housing management, which ought to be covered during a period of approximately forty-four months, fitting into the Institute's examinations.[30]

Provision for Students

On the surface, it is difficult to appreciate the advantages of student membership. But one must remember that often for a nominal subscription, students receive the association's journal, they can use the library, attend lectures and conferences, obtain advice. These constitute the advantages of full membership without voting rights, or designatory letters, for a token payment.

While all associations have a student grade, not all of them contain special student societies inside the main organization. The *Institute of Chartered Accountants*, *Institute of Actuaries*, *Chartered Institute of Secretaries*, *Chartered Auctioneers and Estate Agents Institute* and several engineering institutions, all possess internal student organizations. They hold their own lectures, meetings and social functions, some prepare their own publications and arrange tuition for students.

Associations place few restrictions on students. Generally, no check is maintained on individual progress and diligence, except that a report may be required before entry to the examinations. It is rare for an association to insist on attendance at meetings. Some associations stipulate a maximum age for students, for example, they must not be over 25 or 28. Some require students to take the examinations within a specified time.

To be fair to students, the majority of associations give very little extra special service to them. They will receive the journal, notices of meetings . . . and there provision ends. And to be fair to associations, students regard their membership with a sense of minimum obligation.

Provision of Teaching Institutions

Associations have restricted financial resources. Income may be derived from subscriptions, sale of publications, social functions, conferences and legacies. Even bounded by limitations, some have gone far to establish teaching institutions. Often subsequent development proved slow and money had to be raised outside the association, all the same, these were notable achievements. Already, two examples have been mentioned: the *Law Society*'s School of Law, and the *Pharmaceutical Society*'s School of Pharmacy. A third nineteenth-century example was the *Architectural Association*'s School of Architecture, set up to compensate for the lack of training facilities in architecture.[31]

The 'College of Estate Management' at Kensington is another example of special provision. The idea originally came from Sir William Wells, President of the *Chartered Auctioneers and Estate Agents Institute*. He felt an institution was needed to train people for the various professions connected with the land—surveying, land agency, auctioneering, valuation, etc. Wells, with the Institute's help, persuaded London University to introduce an External Bachelor of Science Degree in Estate Management in 1918. Also the Institute supported Wells's suggestion for a college. Altogether over £56,000 was raised and the college was incorporated in 1919. Two years later, the *Surveyors' Institution* (now the *Royal Institution of Chartered Surveyors*) joined in the government of the college, followed by the *Land Agents' Society* in 1929.[32]

The *Library Association* was mainly responsible for initiating foundation of the School of Librarianship, at University College London. Classes previously arranged at the London School of Economics and Political Science, terminated in 1917 and created problems for the Association. Meanwhile the Education

Committee had been preparing a report on the training of librarians, which was later adopted by Council in March 1919. A sub-committee discussed a scheme with the University College authorities, to form a 'School of Librarianship'. On acceptance of the scheme, the Carnegie Trust gave an endowment. In October 1919, the School was established under a joint committee, providing a comprehensive series of day and evening classes.[33]

Shortage of suitable facilities has driven other associations to set up, or help sponsor special teaching. The *Chartered Insurance Institute* established a 'College of Insurance' in September 1957. This offers full-time courses lasting four weeks, for school-leavers, older entrants to insurance, insurance inspectors and various personnel working in insurance.[34] The *Institute of Welding* started a 'School of Welding Technology' in October 1957. The *Institution of Heating and Ventilating Engineers* took an active part in formation of the National College of Heating, Ventilating, Refrigeration and Fan Engineering, at the Borough Polytechnic, London.

Provision of Correspondence Tuition

Like the establishment of teaching institutions, correspondence tuition can be expensive. Also, if associations give courses, they are committed to continuous revision and to provision at reasonable cost, in contrast to correspondence schools organized as profit-making concerns. Correspondence tuition becomes very valuable, when theory and practice are too specialized to fit into other courses, or students are too widely dispersed and too few to form regular classes. It enables associations to maintain a uniform standard of teaching, and a greater link between actual examination requirements and teaching. Correspondence tuition has assumed considerable proportions during the last fifty years, especially in the field of commercial education. Some implications of the trend will be considered later. Here the provisions of three associations will be outlined.

The *Library Association* was the first to organize correspondence tuition for its own examinations. Between 1904 and 1908, courses were inaugurated in Library History and Organization, Practical Library Administration and Cataloguing. The scheme was enlarged to cover additional subjects in 1908. In 1930, administration of courses was taken over by the Association of Assistant Librarians' Section.[35]

Having organized oral classes for many years, the *Institute of Actuaries*, by 1925, was able to give courses for all parts of the examination except the preliminary. In 1925, after a further revision of the syllabus, the Examination Committee was asked to consider correspondence tuition. Finally, in 1937, the Actuarial Tuition Service was introduced, organized and administered jointly by the Institute and *Faculty of Actuaries* in Scotland. Today, the Service gives complete tuition, either by correspondence and weekly classes in London, or just by correspondence.[36]

Related to the same field, the *Chartered Insurance Institute* showed reluctance to start correspondence courses. Twice (1927, 1934) Council decided against providing correspondence courses, despite the fact that some 90 per cent of candidates prepared for the Institute's examinations by this method. Independently, a Federated Institute (London) set up a Tuition Committee, which early in 1941, prepared courses covering the basic principles of various branches of insurance. Later these facilities were extended to all Federated Institutes. Eventually the C.I.I. Council agreed to form the Institute Tuition Service. Since 1945 the Service has offered comprehensive postal tuition and oral classes.[37]

The London Students' Society of the *Chartered Institute of Secretaries* began postal courses in the mid-1920s. From 1928 to 1932, tuition was arranged in conjunction with a private correspondence school. Then the whole scheme was dropped and never revived, although the majority of examination candidates still use correspondence courses for preparation.[38]

EXAMINATIONS

The Nature of Examinations

Variations in syllabuses are too great to allow any detailed analysis, but some generalizations can be made. First, all associations demand evidence of an attained level of general education. Either students take the association's Preliminary examination, or they obtain exemption through the General Certificate of Education, Ordinary and Advanced Levels, or an equivalent. There seems little uniformity in these exemptions.[39] Second, examination for the first corporate grade may be divided into (*a*) an Intermediate and a Final examination, or (*b*) one whole Final examination, divided into parts. The Intermediate/Final pattern is found in commerce and the land profession; the multi-part final in engineering, science and technology. Third, though all associations expect evidence of practical training and experience, few of them actually set any practical test or examination. Naturally the need for a practical examination depends on the subject-matter.[40] Fourth, comparatively few associations (about a tenth) demand a further examination, before election to the higher corporate grade. Fifth, nearly half the associations modify examination requirements for mature, experienced candidates. Modifications range from special examinations, submission of a thesis, an oral examination, down to a complete waiver. Sixth, all associations permit partial, or complete, exemption from some, or all, the examinations. Exempting qualifications depend on the association and examination, usually they include university degrees and diplomas, a Diploma in Technology, Higher National Certificate or Diploma, or the Final examinations of similar associations. Some associations do not allow any exemption from the Final, while others just grant exemption for parts of the Final.

Preparation, supervision and assessment of examinations are normally the responsibility of the Examinations, or Examinations and Education Committee. Part of the work may be delegated to a full-time Education Officer, and external examiners may set and mark papers. Council must approve any change in the syllabus. If the change is drastic, then association members are often given opportunity to discuss and vote on the proposal.

Trends in Examinations During the Twentieth Century

(1) *Elimination of the Preliminary Examination*

Many years ago, all associations set their own preliminary examinations as a test of general education. Some Preliminaries were easier than others, despite the claimed equivalence to 'Matriculation' or the General School Certificate. Even at the beginning of the century (1911), the Board of Education expressed alarm at the vast number of examinations on the secondary school level. Quite unsuccessfully, the Board tried to induce uniformity. While many associations reached the point of accepting the Preliminary examinations of certain associations, little joint action followed. One exception was the Engineering Joint Examining Board established in 1938, eventually acting for the Institutions of Civil, Electrical, Marine, Mechanical, Municipal, and Structural Engineers and the Royal Aeronautical Society. The first common Preliminary examination was held in April 1942, the scheme continuing until Autumn 1960, when the last examination took place.

As a result of expanding secondary education, particularly since the 1939–45 war, associations have tended to abandon their own Preliminary examinations, asking instead for external evidence of general education (General Certificate of Education 'O' and 'A' Level, School Leaving Certificate, etc.). While the movement is an economy, as far as the associations are concerned, it does imply recruitment from those able to take the General Certificate of Education, or an equivalent. The step could be retrogressive. Also the possibility of taking separate subjects, plus numerous combinations of subjects, in the G.C.E. examinations has not helped to standardize the basic demands of associations. At least before the General School Certificate and Matriculation existed as 'package' certificates of special combinations of subjects. In addition, student entrance requirements appear to be rising, as the demand grows for Advanced Level passes plus Ordinary Level passes, rather than Ordinary Level alone.[41]

(2) *Increasing Exemption from the Final Examination*

Over the last fifty years, steadily increasing numbers have been admitted to associations with exemption from all examinations, via university degrees, Higher National Certificates and Diplomas, etc. The trend is mainly confined to associations connected with science, engineering and technology. Associations welcome and encourage the movement, especially the influx of university graduates. Outside these fields, few alternative qualifications exist to give partial or complete exemption (for example, in accountancy, banking, insurance).

The *Institution of Civil Engineers* illustrates the tendency. In the Institution before 1939, about half of those admitted to corporate membership were exempt from the examinations by a degree or equivalent, today the proportion is about three-quarters.[42] Probably the same figures apply to all the senior engineering institutions, and the two associations connected with pure science. Nearly 6 per cent of those seeking admission to corporate grades through exemption, are already corporate members of another institution.[43]

However, holders of Higher National Certificates and Diplomas, and the Final City and Guilds Certificate, appear to find it more and more difficult to obtain complete exemption from Final examinations. The implications of this trend will be considered later.

(3) *Greater Co-operation between Associations*

Inter-association co-operation is very uneven throughout different areas. Engineering Institutions have always shown a readiness to form joint committees. In 1901, the Institutions of Civil, Mechanical and Electrical Engineers, the *Iron and Steel Institute* and *Institution of Naval Architects* constituted a Joint Engineering Standards Committee, which became the British Engineering Standards Association, then the British Standards Institution incorporated by Royal Charter in 1929. Another indication of joint action is the National Certificate scheme. Also the Engineering Institutions' Part I Committee conducts a joint Part I examination, accepted by the Institutions for their three or four part graduate examinations.[44]

Outside engineering, extensive co-operation seems much less common, possibly for many reasons. Firstly, in some cases, rivalry prevents action, for example, the two main accountancy bodies, the two associations of secretaries. Secondly, subject-matter or treatment of subjects does not always overlap different associations. Thirdly, in the past, standards of different associations have not been similar. Fourthly, there is the desire to retain autonomy.

Generally, co-operation in examination policy only extends to recognition of each other's examinations, as a means of limited exemption. For example, in the case of the three major associations connected with the land profession, each recognizes the other two bodies' Finals as exemptions from the Intermediate.

Isolated examples of closer agreement can be found. The *Corporation of Insurance Brokers* inaugurated examinations in 1919, suspending them in 1939. During the war, Council negotiated with the *Chartered Insurance Institute* about the possibility of using the Institute's examinations. Since 1946, the Corporation has relied on the C.I.I. examinations, modified to include a General Branch suitable for insurance brokers.[45] A Town Planning Joint Examination Board was set up in 1930, to conduct the town planning examinations of five associations.[46] Another instance is the Advertising Joint Intermediate Examination of the *Advertising Association* and the *Institute of Practitioners in Advertising*. And in 1961, the *Plastics Institute* and the *Institution of the Rubber Industry* agreed to a Joint Examination Scheme to cover certain papers. The first examination was held in 1963.

QUALIFYING ASSOCIATIONS AND EDUCATION

Today, not counting multiple membership, there are approximately 625,000 corporate members and about 130,000 student members of the Qualifying Associations. These estimates demonstrate the importance of associations as a whole. Accordingly, the creation of a large number of independent qualifying organizations must have brought about changes in the social, educational and industrial structure of modern society. What are the changes? How effective have they proved to be? Effects can be considered under two main headings: the improvement of facilities for education; the benefit to the individual.

Improvement of Facilities for Training and Education

Qualifying Associations nearly always face a dearth of educational facilities. As previously indicated, in the nineteenth century some associations established their own specialized training institutions. In the twentieth century, few associations have tried to emulate these achievements, instead, more attention has focused on correspondence tuition and preparation of textbooks. Then there are the regular provisions: libraries, lectures, exhibitions, conferences, week-end courses, journals, special publications, joint meetings, research groups, visits, international conferences, refresher courses, local sections, special student societies. Every association provides one or more of these features, depending on need and available finance. They serve as a means of extending knowledge, circulating information, maintaining technical standards, quite apart from any role in the education of students and trained professionals. And sometimes the main objective of provisions seems to be the acquisition of inter-association prestige.

Demand for tuition in different geographical areas produced two effects. Firstly, an expansion of technical and commercial college courses to cover associations' syllabuses, consequently an increase in evening classes, in turn reinforcing the part-time principle in higher education.[47] Often members of the associations carry out the institutional teaching. Secondly, a growth of postal tuition, particularly for commercial subjects.

Correspondence courses appeared as a response to the new associations' examinations of the 1880s and 1890s, and as a means of preparation for the External Degrees of London University. Really postal tuition commenced in January 1840, when Isaac Pitman used the new 'Penny Post' to conduct shorthand courses by postcard. In 1880, a Scottish civil servant, C. E. Skerry, offered postal teaching for civil service examinations. Seven years later, Clough's College started a correspondence course for teachers. Introduction of compulsory examinations by the *Institute of Chartered Accountants* in 1880, caused a demand for tuition. Many advertisements appeared in *The Accountant* requesting help. Soon at least three regular announcements by lawyers offered personal and postal tuition. Other correspondence schools came into existence: the University Correspondence College in 1887, Chambers in 1885, Wolsey Hall, Oxford in 1894.[48] From that time, correspondence 'colleges' multiplied, although roughly nine major organizations dominate the scene today. They cover three main areas: most are concerned chiefly with commercial subjects; two specialize in tuition for university degrees; two concentrate on technical subjects.[49]

Most significant is the dependence of students on postal courses as a means of preparing for certain associations' examinations. From 50–90 per cent of candidates use postal tuition, to study for the examinations of associations connected with commercial and business subjects. Taking only six associations, they have together about 60,000 candidates a year for their examinations.[50]

Advocates of correspondence courses claim many advantages for the method: independent tuition at the student's own pace; no regular attendance times or unpleasant journeys to classes; development of examination technique by writing essays; ability to earn and learn at the same time, and so on. Equally, postal tuition produces disadvantages: isolation of students; need for perseverance and determination; no comparative standard of judgment; uneven standard of courses. Over the last ten years, criticism has mounted and official opinion has condemned the use of correspondence tuition.[51]

Reliance upon postal courses results in non-institutionalized higher education; a system under which individuals remain out of contact with fellow-students, without free discussion of topics, educated along the narrowest of examination lines, educated in their own spare time. Yet what alternatives are there? For younger students, part-time day release classes might prove an answer, but in 1939, National Certificates in Commerce were introduced without much success. The scheme failed because Qualifying Associations refused to grant exemptions from their examinations. Only the two associations of secretaries and the *Institute of Bankers* recognized the certificates. Also employers were reluctant to allow time off during the day. Though reconstituted in 1951, the National Certificates still proved unsatisfactory. A new Certificate in Business Studies was announced in March 1961, with courses beginning in autumn 1961. Ten associations will give subject-for-subject exemption from their Intermediate examinations.[52] Another problem arises in commercial education because a great many people only begin to study late in life, when correspondence courses or evening classes supply the available alternatives. In their late twenties or thirties, they see, or hope they see, the possibility of future promotion by obtaining 'professional qualifications', especially in commerce. Thus Qualifying Associations benefit through these late-developers seeking qualifications. Similarly, associations gain from the universities' lack of enthusiasm for commercial subjects. Insurance has never been accepted by universities. Secretarial practice has faded from their work. Accountancy struggled long before acceptance. Management studies are just beginning to find a place. Reliance of Qualifying Associations on postal tuition and evening classes has created a second order in higher education.

National Certificate schemes firmly link the associations to technical colleges. In 1921, the Board of Education discussed with the *Institution of Mechanical Engineers* the foundation of certificates and diplomas for apprentices and students in engineering works. Subsequently the Ordinary and Higher National Certificates and Diplomas were introduced. Normally the Ordinary National is a three-year-course (part-time day and evening) and the Higher National a further two years. Endorsements can be obtained for subjects in the Higher National, following one to three years extra study. Higher National Certificate, especially with endorsements, became an important form of entry into engineering institutions, as it gave exemption from examination requirements. Certificates are awarded and supervised jointly by the Ministry of Education and the appropriate association, in conjunction with the local technical colleges.

Two points are worth notice. Firstly, the high wastage and failure rates in National Certificate courses. In one survey, of all students entering National Certificate courses without exemption from the first, or subsequent years, only 23 per cent eventually obtained an O.N.C., and 10 per cent an H.N.C. Of students without exemptions, only half of those successful at O.N.C. or H.N.C. managed to complete the course in standard time (three and two years respectively).[53] While it would be difficult to apportion part of the blame on to the associations concerned, they are responsible for the changing value of National Certificates, so creating a second problem. Standards of the science and engineering associations' examinations have risen a great deal since the last war. As a result, holders of Higher National Certificates find it increasingly impracticable to gain exemption from Graduate examinations. Before the war, National Certificate gave complete or substantial exemption, now further study is often required to take parts of the Graduate examinations of the engineering institutions. Only an Honours Degree, Diploma in Technology or an equivalent can secure complete or partial exemption. Higher National no longer provides an alternative route to professional qualification, comparable to a university degree as an exempting qualification. National Certificate constitutes a poor second, and more ardous road, toward the achievement of corporate membership.[54] Table 5.3 lists the years in which various National Certificates were introduced.

TABLE 5.3. SHOWING THE YEARS IN WHICH NATIONAL CERTIFICATES AND DIPLOMAS WERE INTRODUCED

Year Certificate Introduced	*Subject*
1921	Mechanical Engineering,* Chemistry
1923	Electrical Engineering*†
1926	Naval Architecture
1929	Building (Reconstituted 1948)
1934	Textiles
1939	Commerce (Reconstituted 1951, replaced 1961)
1941	Production Engineering
1943	Civil Engineering
1945	Metallurgy, Applied Physics
1947	Applied Chemistry
1951	Chemical Engineering
1952	Mining and Mine Surveying
1954	National Diploma in Design
1961	Business Studies (Replaced Certificates in Commerce)
1962	Foundry Technology

* O.N.C. replaced in 1963 by Ordinary Certificate in Engineering
† H.N.C. replaced in 1963 by Electrical and Electronic Engineering

Another important aspect of associations' educational work is their role in co-ordinating, and advising, external educational institutions and committees. Members of associations can be found on an extensive range of education committees, either in an individual capacity, or as official representatives of their organizations. Typical committees are: regional advisory committees; governing bodies of technical colleges and other institutions, and Courts of universities; departmental advisory committees and boards; committees of the City and Guilds Institute; Government joint committees; committees for National Certificate awards; National Council for Technological Awards. Associations may have five, ten, even fifty or more representatives. Some organizations ensure that these connections remain active, two-way lines of communication and influence. Others regard the positions as a form of prestige and very little else. Differences occur between associations. First, associations concerned with science, applied science, technology and engineering generally show greater representation than other types. Second, representation is confined within areas directly related to the association's work. Third, the largest, most dignified and respected usually have the largest representation, though a few are apparently more interested in outside technical committees. Fourth, associations connected with commerce show comparatively little interest in wide representation. Table 5.4 gives some idea of the extent of representation on various committees.

Dr. Venables has demonstrated the importance attached by some colleges to Advisory Committees. In 1955, taking 195 colleges, 131 had no Advisory Committees, because they were too small and/or insufficiently specialized, 64 colleges had 263 Advisory Committees, 23 had between 5 and 13 each.[55]

Besides these continuous bonds, associations serve on specially appointed government committees, inter-association committees, international committees, either by invitation, or by accident when committee members happen to be association members. These factors suggest the possible influence of certain Qualifying Associations, as well-connected interest groups in higher education.

Benefit to the Individual

Qualifying Associations basically offer two advantages to the individual: a means of obtaining a qualification; a means of making wider contact with more professionals and keeping up to date in the field.

In some ways, associations' qualifications present special opportunities. They deal with areas of study and work not covered by existing qualifications, for example, advertising, certain kinds of engineering, applied science, management. University degrees and diplomas may span approximately the identical subject-areas, yet often the necessity of a sound practical background can make the association's qualification more useful, for example, accountancy, architecture, estate-manage-

TABLE 5.4. SHOWING THE NUMBER OF EXTERNAL EDUCATION COMMITTEES ON WHICH CERTAIN QUALIFYING ASSOCIATIONS WERE REPRESENTED IN 1961–62

Note: Selection determined by information available (*Sources:* Annual Reports and Yearbooks)

Title of Association	Universities and Colleges of Universities		Technical Colleges		Other Colleges		Regional and District Advisory Comms.	National Council for Tech. Awards Board of Studies	Joint Comms. for National Cert. Awards	City & Guilds Comms.	National Advisory Comms.	Other Educational Comms.	Total Number of Outside Education Comms.
	Courts	Advisory Comms.	Governing Bodies	Advisory Comms.	Governing Bodies	Advisory Comms.							
Royal Institute of Chemistry	4		20	45			3	1				1		74
Institute of Physics & the Physical Society	3		10	22		6	9	1	3	4			58
Institution of Civil Engineers	1		5	1			6	1	1	1		1	17
Institution of Structural Engineers	1	1	3	10	3	4	12	1	4	4		1	44
Institution of Chemical Engineers	2	2	3	7		1	8	1	3	4			31
Institution of Mining Engineers	1				2		1	1	1	1		2	9
British Institution of Radio Engineers			1	17			3	1	3	4		3	31
Royal Institute of British Architects	2		1	6	2	2	1						14
Pharmaceutical Society	4		2										6
Textile Institute	1		1	5		2	6	1	1	12			28
Institute of Builders			5	23	5	6	3	1	2	7	1	2	55
Institution of Mining and Metallurgy	1	1	1	1	3				2	2		1	12

ment, engineering. To attain stages of corporate membership demands the ability to pass an examination, to show evidence of experience and achieved responsibility in the case of engineering and science. Therefore the association's corporate membership serves as a better guide than, say, a university degree, especially if examinations are seen as a uniform National standard. Unintentionally perhaps, associations furnish supplementary or extra qualifications, by allowing exemption from the qualifying examinations. Finally, associations provide a way for individuals to specialize, and qualify, after a more general training. For example, a chemist or physicist might move into specialized fields: metallurgy, radio, textile technology, plastics or management.

Of course, an incorrect assumption has been made so far. All available qualifications of the associations are not equally good and acceptable. There can be real differences in the standards of associations within the same occupational fields, and between associations in dissimilar fields. Wide gaps may separate the standards of, say, the *Royal Institution of Chartered Surveyors* and the *Building Surveyors' Institute*, the *Institute of Chartered Accountants* and the *Association of International Accountants*. Sometimes the differences are real, occasionally they can be artificial. Spurious disparities arise when the more senior association claims a higher standard, though in fact, very little separates examination levels and entrance requirements. Older associations feel their status threatened. Yet, as already suggested, nearly all associations follow a similar evolutionary pattern. This can be a very long and slow process. The associations tend to proceed through the three stages: firstly, no examination, or limited use of examinations; secondly, an examination for young entrants, plus special allowances for older, experienced personnel; thirdly, entrance by examination only or suitable exemption. Acquisition of professional status is partially determined by the soundness of membership, in turn founded upon high standards of entrance requirements.

Educational opportunity has always been confined to a narrow section of our society. The prospect of more extensive full-time higher education only emerged after the last war. Nevertheless for the last fifty or a hundred years, the formation of Qualifying Associations has given many people a first, or second, chance to obtain qualifications and improve their economic status. Associations cater: for people unwilling to take university examinations, because they are inapplicable to particular occupations; for individuals who need to earn and learn; for those who require more specialized training and qualifications; for those who decide, late in life, to become qualified in their own field, or to qualify in another field enabling occupational mobility. In conjunction with part-time education and postal tuition, associations have vastly expanded educational opportunity into sections of society, otherwise untouched by adequate provisions of facilities and specialist qualification.

Chapter Six

QUALIFYING ASSOCIATIONS AND PROFESSIONAL CONDUCT

INTRODUCTION

QUALIFYING Associations would seem to show a remarkable lack of concern with the problem of professional conduct.
Perhaps this view contradicts the impression given by many
commentators on professionalism, who readily assume that professional associations are established to control conduct, or that
a code of conduct forms an essential part of professionalism. Yet
if every possible Qualifying Association in England and Wales
is taken, less than one-fifth (out of approximately 160) have a
written code of conduct, and many codes are quite unsophisti-
cated.[1] Codes are not necessarily confined to the largest, more
senior and most important associations. Thus the situation con-
trasts strikingly with the United States, where practically every
professional group takes pride in an elaborately written code,
detailed interpretative books, articles, pamphlets, committees
and conferences.[2] Does this absence of codes indicate a high
level of professional morality in Britain? Does it demonstrate a
greater tolerance of, or a lower sensitivity toward unethical conduct? Are professional associations in Britain unable to control
unethical conduct? Questions like these are impossible to answer accurately. A much easier task is to determine the amount
of interest displayed by associations, the methods they use to
control conduct and their apparent effectiveness.

WHAT IS PROFESSIONAL CONDUCT?

Definition

Professional Conduct refers to the mode of behaviour controlling
the inter-professional, intra-professional, professional-client or
professional-public relationship. These relationships are gov-

148

erned by an implicit or explicit code of conduct determined by some authority within the profession, or an authority established external to it, usually with the profession's sanction.

Obviously professional conduct covers a wide range of activities and attitudes: the correct behaviour to be observed toward clients and colleagues; the limits and rule of competition with others; remuneration and quality of service, and so on. Really, every aspect of the professional's work and bearing is bounded, more or less, by his membership of a particular profession. Awareness of, and adherence to, standards of professional conduct help to determine the role and status of individual professionals in society.

Professional conduct presents a complex which ought to be divided into parts: first, the separation into Professional Practice and Professional Ethics; secondly, the breakdown of Professional Ethics into Rules and Etiquette.

(a) *Professional Practice* relates to the adoption of schedules of uniform professional fees and charges, standard forms of contract, regulation of competition for projects.

(b) *Professional Ethics* are concerned with moral directives, which guide the relationship between the professional and others. They are designed to distinguish right from wrong action. Professional ethics are composed of Rules and Etiquette. *Rules* are obligatory customs, which may be implicit or explicit codes enforced by a recognized authority. *Etiquette* is a loose form of permissive conventions observed generally, but not enforced by any central authority, though a breach can lead to censure by colleagues.

A professional ethic may be a formal code, or an informal understanding. Whether implicit or explicit, the ethic is the product of a group, and membership of the group implies acceptance of the group's values or norms. The principles of professional conduct, as devised by the group, are relative rather than absolute. There is no foundation of universal professional dogma. For while rules may be common to several organizations and professions, this does not necessarily indicate a single professional ethic for all. Circumstances and needs vary from occupation to occupation. Temptation and chance, or deliberate violation depend on the type and extent of professional services, strength of belief, vigilance of the group and so on. Because a particular organization constructs an elaborate code, it does not consequently display a more 'moral' attitude, it does not show that a code must be essential, or even that members completely accept and abide by those principles. Therefore, two questions ought to be asked. What may determine the need for an ethical code? What may determine the possibility of a code being introduced?

A much more difficult problem to solve is 'Why do professional ethics exist in the first place?' The history of professional ethics has never been investigated very thoroughly. Most explanations merely demonstrate the high colouration of their originators' own theoretical bias.

THE SOCIOLOGICAL DETERMINANTS OF AN ETHICAL CODE

Writers on the nature of professionalism, and the function of professional organization, often stress control over professional conduct as a key to the problem of defining a profession. They presume the extensive adoption of detailed codes of conduct, and strict policing by associations. Yet the presence or absence of a code of conduct does not make an association 'professional', any more than the sheer existence of organization determines whether or not, a collection of individuals can be legitimately styled a profession. Certain occupations require stricter control than others, for example, law, medicine, accountancy, banking, advertising. Actually, any occupation connected with life and property, entailing some trust or advantageous influence, ought to be regulated. Statutes help to contain possible corruption and misapplication, even so, a code of conduct serves to guide practitioners. Not only does a code protect the public, it also protects the practitioners themselves.

To answer the questions, 'What determines the need for an ethical code?' and 'What determines the possibility of introducing a code?', both structural and functional elements must be considered. 'Need' is governed structurally by the professional situation. 'Possibility' is produced by the structure of the occupation. Chart 6.1 outlines the nature of the structural elements determining 'need'. Chart 6.2 shows the structural elements determining 'possibility'.

Elements Determining the Need for Introducing an Ethical Code

The PROFESSIONAL SITUATION is the operational area, in which the individual professional provides his service. It consists primarily of three components: practice; technique; client. Each component breaks down into two parts. Each part further subdivides to represent extremes in the range of need.

(1) *Practice*

   (*a*) Type of Practice

The professional may be involved in institutional, or non-institutional practice. In a non-institutional practice, he can work alone or in a group. This means he does not operate in a large organization, such as a big company, civil service, local authority, etc. He works alone and gives a personal service, or he is one of a small group of fellow-practitioners, for example, solicitors, barristers, architects, accountants, consultant engineers and scientists. In opposition to the single, or small group practice, the professional may work within an institutional setting. Then he can be enclosed in a bureaucratic structure, conflicting with, and possibly dominating, his professional ideals and status. Thus a professional working alone in a non-institutional practice would need the guidance of an ethical code, much more than the individual in an institutional setting.

   (*b*) Nature of the Practice

A great deal depends on the nature of practice. It may be fiduciary, or non-fiduciary. The trust may involve life or property. Responsibility created for physicians, surgeons, barristers, solicitors or accountants differs from that normally devolving upon the industrial chemist or the artist.

(2) *Technique*

   (*a*) Technique Involved

Technique may be a complex intellectual, or practical undertaking demanding the conscientious application of skill and knowledge. A code of conduct might be necessary to remind the professional of his duty to provide the best possible service.

CHART 6.1 SHOWING STRUCTURAL ELEMENTS DETERMINING NEED
FOR INTRODUCING AN ETHICAL CODE WITHIN AN OCCUPATION

PROFESSIONAL SITUATION DETERMINING NEED FOR THE CODE

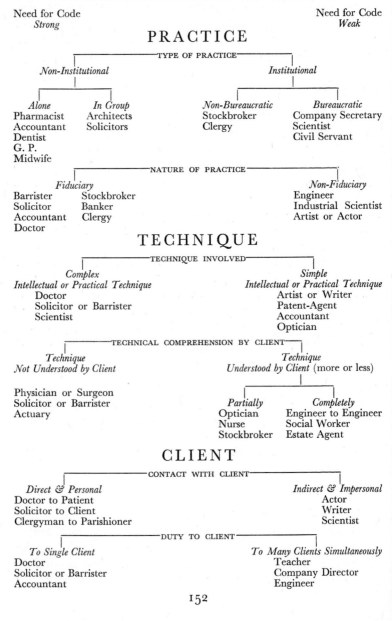

Need for Code
Strong

Need for Code
Weak

PRACTICE

TYPE OF PRACTICE

Non-Institutional

Institutional

Alone	*In Group*	*Non-Bureaucratic*	*Bureaucratic*
Pharmacist	Architects	Stockbroker	Company Secretary
Accountant	Solicitors	Clergy	Scientist
Dentist			Civil Servant
G. P.			
Midwife			

NATURE OF PRACTICE

Fiduciary		*Non-Fiduciary*
Barrister	Stockbroker	Engineer
Solicitor	Banker	Industrial Scientist
Accountant	Clergy	Artist or Actor
Doctor		

TECHNIQUE

TECHNIQUE INVOLVED

Complex
Intellectual or Practical Technique
Doctor
Solicitor or Barrister
Scientist

Simple
Intellectual or Practical Technique
Artist or Writer
Patent-Agent
Accountant
Optician

TECHNICAL COMPREHENSION BY CLIENT

Technique
Not Understood by Client

Physician or Surgeon
Solicitor or Barrister
Actuary

Technique
Understood by Client (more or less)

Partially	*Completely*
Optician	Engineer to Engineer
Nurse	Social Worker
Stockbroker	Estate Agent

CLIENT

CONTACT WITH CLIENT

Direct & Personal
Doctor to Patient
Solicitor to Client
Clergyman to Parishioner

Indirect & Impersonal
Actor
Writer
Scientist

DUTY TO CLIENT

To Single Client
Doctor
Solicitor or Barrister
Accountant

To Many Clients Simultaneously
Teacher
Company Director
Engineer

(*b*) Technical Comprehension by Clients

Coupled with the technique involved is the ability of clients to understand fully, or partially, the professional's technique. What he does, how he does it, why he does it, the theory and practice of the mechanisms composing the technique. A sales engineer selling equipment to another engineer faces a different situation from that of the patient, who visits his doctor with a pain in his back. Where the client cannot be expected to understand the professional's work, a code is required for protection of the client.

(3) *Client*

(*a*) Contact with the Client

The client-contact may be a distinct, direct, personal contact with the professional, for example, a normal doctor-patient relationship, or a solicitor-client relationship. Such contact is open to possible abuse, owing to its intimacy. Confidential information is surrendered and so on. Therefore a code protects professionals and clients. On the other hand, an architect or engineer generally does not deal with a single client, as a variety of other specialists know full details of the project. Here, a different form of abuse appears, the possibility of bribery through gifts, commissions and concessions. A code is essential. When contact with the client is indirect and impersonal, then a code is not required.

(*b*) Duty toward the Client

A professional may owe a duty to a single client, or to many 'clients' simultaneously. The teacher serves the child, the parents, the school authorities and the community, in different ways and for different reasons, all at once. The Director of a public company owes a duty to shareholders, the company and to the public. Naturally, the demands and extent of duty vary from one multiple-set to another, and from one client to another within the set. With a single client, duty must be clearly defined by a code. With multiple clients, there is less chance of hiding responsibility.

Elements Determining the Possibility of Introducing an Ethical Code

The STRUCTURE OF THE OCCUPATION is the factor determining the possibility of introducing a code. Four components make up this structural feature: education and training; occupational diversity; nature of employer; occupational control.

(1) *Education and Training*

If particular work requires training, encroachment by other occupations is reduced. But there may be one, or more, methods of training which lead, or do not lead, to a qualification. Similarly the training might enable the professional to practise in adjacent occupations, thereby finding fresh clients for his main activity. Many avenues of entrance to the occupation, differences in qualifications of practitioners and forms of training, easy access for untrained personnel—all these factors cause separation within the occupation, reducing the possible enforcement area of an ethical code.

(2) *Occupational Diversity*

An occupation is seldom 'pure', in the sense that all practitioners do much the same work. Occasionally specialism does not override the common background. For example, the practising barrister specializes in specific kinds of work. He may practise at the Chancery Bar, being concerned with conveyancing and company law; at the Common Law Bar, concerned with criminal and commercial law; at the Parliamentary Bar, Admiralty Bar, etc. Despite variations in the type of practice, he remains fundamentally a barrister. Engineering is entirely different, for 'the engineer' does not exist. Specialization turns engineers into radically contrasting sorts of worker. Variations in tasks cannot produce a uniform outlook, a common attitude towards an ethical code. Some types of engineer may need a code owing to the professional situation, rather than because they perform as engineers. The existence of one main, dominating kind of work allows a fair code to be introduced.

CHART 6.2. SHOWING STRUCTURAL ELEMENTS DETERMINING
POSSIBILITY OF INTRODUCING AN ETHICAL CODE WITHIN AN
OCCUPATION

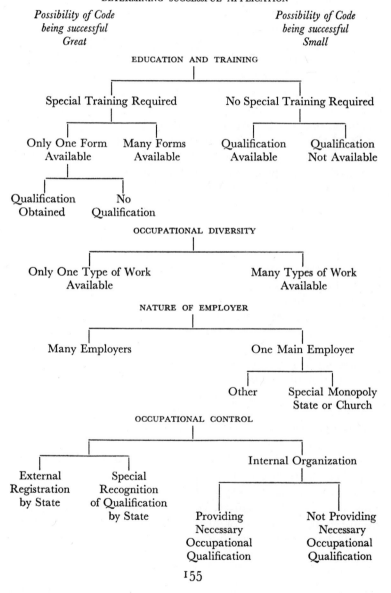

STRUCTURE OF PROFESSION
DETERMINING SUCCESSFUL APPLICATION

Possibility of Code being successful Great

Possibility of Code being successful Small

EDUCATION AND TRAINING

Special Training Required

No Special Training Required

Only One Form Available

Many Forms Available

Qualification Available

Qualification Not Available

Qualification Obtained

No Qualification

OCCUPATIONAL DIVERSITY

Only One Type of Work Available

Many Types of Work Available

NATURE OF EMPLOYER

Many Employers

One Main Employer

Other

Special Monopoly State or Church

OCCUPATIONAL CONTROL

External Registration by State

Special Recognition of Qualification by State

Internal Organization

Providing Necessary Occupational Qualification

Not Providing Necessary Occupational Qualification

(3) *Nature of Employer*

One employer may predominate, as in the case of teaching. That single employer can be the State. Alternatively, the occupation may hold a special institutional position in society, for example, the armed forces, or the Church. But the professional may have a variety of potential employers. The engineer or scientist can be a teacher, or a straightforward field and laboratory worker. He may work for Central or Local Government, in private practice or for industry. A single employer reduces the need for an ethical code, though making it easier to introduce rules. In addition, a single employer superimposes a new classification, which covers many diverse occupations at once, all fitted together into an institutional hierarchy. Where many employers occur simultaneously, there is a greater chance of considering the professional first as an engineer, scientist, accountant, etc. So, a code may be initiated.

(4) *Occupational Control*

An occupation may, or may not, be organized. Of the various types of organization, the Qualifying Association probably offers the greatest opportunity to control conduct, providing professionals rely on the association as a means of qualification. Severe misconduct results in expulsion, so removing the individual's qualification. But unless the profession is registered by Statute, nothing really prevents continued practice, unless colleagues, clients and employers refuse to accept the offender. Ultimately, only a Statutory-registered profession can hope to possess an ethical code, which is strictly enforceable and guarantees legally to restrict a serious offender, thus protecting both clients and the profession. When specific kinds of work are governed by Statute, an individual may be deemed qualified, through membership of designated associations. Loss of membership then deprives the offender of any legal right to carry out such work. In these cases, professional conduct can be supervised with a level of security. Where membership of an organization remains optional, or inessential, in an occupation, there is little hope of maintaining a firm control over professional conduct.

Summary

These two sets of structural elements present a polarization of the need for, and the possibility of establishing a code of professional conduct, within a professional group. For example, a professional who practises alone, in a direct personal client relationship, involving a fiduciary service and a complex intellectual or practical technique, which is not understood by the client. This case offers an extreme situation demanding a strong code. At the opposite end, there is the professional in a bureaucratic institutional setting, involved with many clients simultaneously and practising an intellectual or practical technique, which is simple or fully understood by the client. Possibility is conditioned by the structure of the occupation. Here, certain factors provide a strong possibility of success, if a code is introduced. For example, the greatest success might be expected, when a code is introduced among professionals who undergo a single form of specialized training, leading to a qualification, who are involved in one main type of work, for many employers in a strongly organized and registered profession.

Functional Elements Determining the Need for, and Possibility of Introducing a Code within an Occupation

Besides structural factors, there are functional requisites derived from the structure. These consist of: tradition; unity of attitude; demand for service; supply of professionals; image of the profession.

(1) *Tradition*

Tradition can be based on the profession's own developing background, or upon the background of another profession. Particular elements of etiquette, or specific rules can be absorbed from established practice in other professions. These could become dysfunctional for the profession adopting them, as they may not have been translated into a new context. They may erect limitations, which are not necessarily required. Similarly, tradition can be a dysfunctional element in the occupation, if it hinders change. Adjustments are essential to meet new circumstances, thus a code must be flexible.

(2) *Unity of Attitude*

Unity is expressed by organization, though organization does not signify unity of attitude. A scientist may teach, work in industrial research, work in a government laboratory on secret research, practise as a consultant and so on. The accountant may be in practice, or he may work within a large industrial concern, or in an institution, as a teacher, etc. These examples suggest differing levels of responsibility and need, contributing various professional attitudes of mind.

(3) *Demand for Service*

Unless a profession is registered, or protected in another way, a heavy demand for particular services encourages encroachment by those in allied fields, if they can perform the same functions. Also it may increase temptation to violate any code, as commissions and similar perquisites are more readily offered. A low demand for professional services intensifies competition and tempts professionals to under-cut, to seek methods of obtaining business, to create unnecessary work and so on. Therefore, demand for professional services must strain any effort to build and maintain a code of conduct.

(4) *Supply of Professionals*

Supply is largely related to the available forms of training and education. Training and education constitute important factors in the formation of professional conscience. If the aspirant professional goes through a period of service with an established practitioner, there is an opportunity to inculcate the essential meaning of professional conduct. Alternatively, pure institutionalized training seems less likely to induce a knowledge of professional ethics, unless deliberate instruction takes place. Even then, lectures are a poor substitute for observing the code in action.

(5) *Image of the Profession*

The image of a profession contains three elements: the image held within the profession of itself; the image held by other professionals; the image held by the lay-public. Image content is a complex of perceptions, attitudes and beliefs about: the educational attainments and background of professionals; their conditions of work; income; style of life; affiliations and loyalties to intra-professional and extra-professional groups. Content is determined by: contact; traditional accounts of the profession; understanding of the professional's techniques; assessment of the profession's power position, value to the community, etc. To some extent the self-image, or group-image, of the profession creates a role-expectation, predetermining and reinforcing the content of, and adherence to, the code of conduct. Thus a client, who informs the professional of intimate personal details, expects the doctor, solicitor, etc., to maintain complete secrecy. Again, the professional does not denigrate colleagues, in case of indirect damage to his own reputation or that of the profession. Similarly, to receive commissions and bribes from clients and other professionals is degrading, as it destroys independence and impartiality.

QUALIFYING ASSOCIATIONS' CONCERN WITH PROFESSIONAL CONDUCT

Qualifying Associations have always shown a reluctance to establish a rigid written code of ethics. In the nineteenth century, most associations possessed constitutional means for dealing with unprofessional conduct, yet a long delay usually occurred before an association attempted to present a formal code.[3] Why was this?

Several factors might explain unwillingness to formulate codes. Firstly, most associations have shown greater interest in educational standards. For many, they aimed at establishing a competent membership, by setting examinations, arranging education and training. Firm and trustworthy organization is required before either the public or the membership becomes prepared to accept the 'moral' intentions of an association. Secondly, associations often display a feeling of distrust for structured codes. They dislike written codes, preferring instead a general clause in the constitution, which allows wider scope for disciplinary action. One of the best arguments has been put forward by D. V. House, a Past-President of the *Institute of Chartered Accountants in England and Wales*.[4]

In this country we do not favour written codes. As a nation, we prefer a man to be judged by his peers rather than be condemned or exonerated by the written word and we can still pride ourselves upon knowing instinctively what is 'done' or 'not done'; what is 'cricket' or 'not cricket'.

He suggested three objections to a written code.[5]

(a) It is impossible to lay down a written code which operates fairly and remains without loopholes.

(b) A written code includes much that must be obvious to anyone who has served a rigorous professional training.

(c) Without a written code, disciplinary decisions are unlikely to be upset by the Courts. The complaint can be tried on its merits. If tried fairly, the Courts will not interfere in domestic affairs.

Thirdly, there may be a sense of satisfaction, based on the belief that careful selection of members initially suffices to preserve probity. A written code might cast doubts on the very claim of the occupation to describe itself as a profession. Therefore, ethical conduct becomes a question of trust.[6] Fourthly, where a formal code has developed, it has evolved from generally accepted practice, built up over years. Fifthly, neither the medical profession, nor the legal profession relied on elaborately structured codes. If law and medicine had produced manifest codes, aspiring professions would probably have copied their example.

In medicine, the Hippocratic Oath has guided practitioners since the fifth century B.C.[7] The Royal Colleges have always investigated and disciplined their members in cases of unprofessional conduct, though without a clear framework of rules. Probably today they leave matters of unethical conduct mainly to the General Medical Council. While not a qualifying body, the *British Medical Association* took an early interest in professional ethics. On formation of the Association in 1832, one object was the 'maintenance of the Honour and Respectability of the Profession generally', but not until the 1840s was the matter seriously tackled. In 1853, the Association appointed a committee to frame a code of ethical rules. Subsequently various additional codes appeared, and now a Central Ethical Committee considers all cases of unprofessional conduct.[8] Since the Medical Act, 1858, the medical profession has been supervised by the General Medical Council. By Statute, only the Council can register qualified medical practitioners, or erase the names of any found guilty of unprofessional conduct. Nevertheless, the Council only issued the first formal 'Notice' relating to professional conduct in 1905.[9]

In the legal profession, a mass of customs grew up without written formulation. For example, solicitors must normally intervene between Counsel and client; Counsel cannot sue a client for fees; a client cannot sue Counsel for negligence or non-attendance at Court; confidential communications between Counsel and client are privileged, etc.[10] Despite the fact that many customs were not formally written and collected together, Benchers would still act on them. Before 1873, disciplinary jurisdiction over solicitors was exercised by different Courts, then by the Supreme Court. The Solicitors Act, 1888, appointed a Disciplinary Tribunal of Council members of the *Law Society*. Disciplinary powers were given to a Statutory Committee of past and present Council members in 1919. Finally, the Act of 1933 empowered the *Law Society* to make rules governing professional conduct.[11] Again, discipline had been enforced without a written code.

Even in the absence of structured codes of conduct, Qualifying Associations investigated unprofessional conduct, prepared schedules to guide fees and charges, laid down standard forms of contract. Two or three examples will illustrate their interest.

The (*Royal*) *Institute of British Architects* established its first Professional Practice Committee in 1845, eleven years after foundation. The committee was 'to enquire as to the custom of architects in respect to professional charges and other matters connected with the practice of the profession, with such recommendations as they may think fit to insure a uniformity in such proceedings. To establish an honourable remuneration for the professional man and at the same time to protect the employer'. After delving into the history of professional fees, the committee decided on a basic charge of 5 per cent. In 1862, a document was published in the Journal—'Professional Practice and Charges of Architects being those now usually and properly made'. From time to time, the Scale of Charges has been revised.[12] How effective was the measure? Membership of the R.I.B.A. in 1862 represented less than one-tenth of the practising architects.[13] Clearly the scale was a model used by more honest architects. Nothing prevented architects from demanding larger fees. And if the Institute ejected a member, he could continue to practise.

In 1870, the Professional Practice Committee considered 'Conditions of Building Contracts'. In consultation with the *London Builders' Society*, the committee produced a standard 'Heads of Conditions of Builders' Contract'. Two years later, the first general regulations for architectural competitions were drawn up and adopted. These rules resulted from discussion and disagreement beginning in 1838, when the first committee had been appointed.[14] Up to 1869, the Professional Practice Committee investigated all cases of unprofessional conduct. From 1869 to 1886, Council dealt with the matter. Then in 1886, the Professional Practice Committee resumed its investigating role, leaving Council to act as the disciplinary body. Occasionally members received guidance about professional conduct from the Journal, still, no written code appeared until 1900.

When first incorporated in 1877, the (*Royal*) *Institute of Chemistry* provided for the election of Censors, to investigate misconduct and infringement of regulations. The designation 'Censors' was probably derived from the old procedure of the Royal Colleges, for they each appointed a group of Council members to investigate members' misconduct.

On 8 December 1881, the Institute held a conference on 'Professional Ethics'. Like the architects, the chemists seemed mainly concerned with problems of practice, for example, methods of taking chemical samples, methods of analysis and so on. A specific committee had been appointed in November 1881, to prepare a scale of minimum charges for analysis and other services. Eventually Council decided not to proceed further. In February 1883, Council appointed a committee on Professional Practice, to consider 'the advisability of establishing a definite code'. Apart from a recommendation to discourage members from advertising, nothing substantial followed.[15] Early in 1893, Council discussed a report from the Censors, which drew attention to the prevalence of unprofessional conduct, and proposed establishing a more definite code of conduct. Now there were nearly 830 Fellows and Associates. The Council called an Extraordinary General Meeting in April, to discuss the Censors' resolution declaring certain activities to be discreditable to the profession, viz., advertising in papers and journals or by post, undercutting the usual fees for analyses, providing 'puffing' testimonials for products, using fictitious designatory letters. The meeting felt that the best check on unprofessional conduct must be mass condemnation by the profession. The resolution was passed, without any further action being taken.[16]

Doubtless the most concerted effort of any allied associations is shown in the 'land' profession, containing surveyors, land agents, auctioneers, estate agents and valuers. Inter-association co-operation dates from 1932. Up until then, associations enforced ethical codes, which remained more or less unwritten and uncodified. The *Auctioneers and Estate Agents Institute* was probably the only body possessing written rules, incorporated in the constitution. These had been adopted in 1920. The Institute was about to issue a revised version of the code in 1932, when the *Chartered Surveyors' Institution* (now the *Royal Institution of Chartered Surveyors*) invited three associations to help secure uniformity of action. The associations held a conference. Later they formed a Code of Conduct Liaison Committee, composed of four representatives from each association (the Institute, the Institution, the *Land Agents' Society* and the *Incorporated Society of Auctioneers and Landed Property Agents*). They reached agreement on a basic Code of Conduct, leaving each organization to adopt the rules separately. Subsequently the *Valuers Institution* and *Rating and Valuation Association* also adopted the Code.[17] In 1935, after several conferences, the four associations prepared a revised schedule of charges. Each association then circulated a Scale of Charges common to all bodies, followed by scales applicable to that particular association.

Summarizing the emerging attitude in the nineteenth century, it appears to have been one of trust. Associations relied on the personal integrity of members. Of all associations, the *Institute of Chartered Accountants* alone prescribed written rules from the very beginning. Understandably, the Institute's examinations and 'Fundamental Rules' aimed to promote public confidence in an occupation, otherwise assumed to consist of disreputable, untrustworthy, incompetent characters. New associations continued a traditional confidence in the fine, upstanding nature and noble qualities inherent in the English gentleman. Every professional, or aspiring professional, should automatically possess a sense of honour, fair play and an instinctive understanding of right and wrong. To acquire professional status, the first move was to ensure competence by examinations. Nevertheless, a fair undercurrent of latent action can be traced. Associations usually inserted a flexible clause in the Articles of Association, enabling Council to examine erring members and expel the 'black-sheep'. Where direct economic competition exposed members to temptation, associations tried to construct scales of common fees and standard contracts.

THE NATURE OF THE CODE

B. Y. Landis's classic analysis of code-types cannot be easily applied to English associations. Written codes are a comparative rarity, whereas in the United States they seem a commonplace necessity. Codes seldom show extensive formulation. No attempt is made to devise comprehensive statements. They float like icebergs on the professional sea, more being concealed below, than revealed above the surface. Associations much prefer to leave the matter open, empowering Council or some designated authority to investigate and caution, suspend or expel guilty members, on the basis of past experience and uncodified practice. Further complications in the English scene arise from the process of registration by Statute, when an external authority is appointed to discipline the profession.

Landis found four types of documents.[18]
(*a*) A collection of specific rules.
(*b*) A mixture of specific rules, plus general principles which set no standard.
(*c*) Only general principles.
(*d*) General principles constantly applied by the rulings of practice committees.

This distinction drawn between specific rules and general principles is not as useful as might be expected. Level of enforcement seems more important. At what point is the regulating authority prepared to act? It does not matter whether a code is implicit or explicit; an idealistic objective or a working reference; a positive statement allowing action or a negative statement limiting behaviour. The essential consideration remains the point and degree of enforcement.

A valuable separation has been made by R. M. MacIver.[19] He divides the contents of codes into three elements:

- (a) EXTRINSIC INTEREST: the part devoted to economic and social status 'the reputation, authority, success and emoluments attaching to the profession as a body',
- (b) TECHNICAL INTEREST: directed to the maintenance and improvement of technical standards,
- (c) CULTURAL INTEREST: the intrinsic 'truth and beauty', pride in workmanship, as opposed to the plain technical modes of investigation or expression.

Although these three elements may be present in an entire code of conduct, identification constitutes a real problem, owing to the tacit assumption underlying the attitudes of most associations. For example, they do not state that a member must give the best service, uphold the honour and dignity of the profession, maintain loyalty to colleagues, etc. Presumably these principles must be taken for granted; a professional naturally behaves honourably.

Another method of analysing content and implications of codes entails the abstraction of principles, and classification in two dimensions. One dimension concerns the relationship involved, i.e. professional-client, professional-professional, professional-public relationship. The second dimension separates the elements in terms of characteristic quality, i.e. loyalty, service, responsibility, independence, remuneration, advertising. Moving through the different relationships involved, gives a different implication to the quality. Table 6.1 presents a classification of typical statements made about professional conduct. Table 6.2 analyses a number of codes, a choice determined by availability.

This break-down of statements taken from associations' codes, reveals the direction of interest. Associations show greatest concern over competition: firstly, in terms of finding work; secondly, with the method of payment. Very little emphasis appears to centre on service to clients, or on any duty to expose professional incompetence. Over four-fifths of the codes prohibit soliciting or attempts to supplant colleagues, four-fifths restrict advertising to specified limits. Two-thirds of codes contain statements

TABLE 6.I. SHOWING AN ANALYSIS OF STATEMENTS ABSTRACTED FROM ETHICAL CODES

Professional Relationship	Professional Standards			Regulation of Competition		
	Loyalty	Service	Responsibility	Independence	Remuneration	Advertising
Professional and Client	1. Must maintain secrecy 2. Must remain loyal to client, inspire confidence and trust	3. Must not create unnecessary work 4. Must seek help of experienced colleague when necessary 5. Must provide best impartial service	6. Must not avoid responsibility by forming a company	7. Must not become involved in client's business or profits, or make payments on client's behalf except by issuing certificates	8. Must only receive salary/professional fee 9. Must not directly or indirectly profit from protected article used on client's work unless authorized 10. Must maintain prof. charges or standard agreements	11. Must not solicit or seek to supplant a professional colleague
Professional and Professional	12. Must not criticize colleagues or otherprofessional 13. Must maintain good relations with colleagues 14. Must only take part in properly regulated competitions	15. Must expose incompetence 16. Must assist colleagues when called upon 17. Must not aid, use or associate with unqualified practitioners	18. Must consult client's previous advisers, or only undertake work if previous adviser no longer engaged 19. Principal must be responsible for juniors	20. Must not secretly engage in another occupation which brings work or may compromise position 21. Must not encroach on legitimate work of other profs.	22. Must not give or receive commission or discount 23. Must only share remuneration with partners/employees 24. Ought to give free service or help in colleague's personal problems	25. Must not advertise except in the prescribed ways
Professional and Public	26. Must uphold dignity of profession and/or honour and dignity of the Association	27. Must provide service when called upon	28. Must not undertake work in conflict with professional duty 29. Must remember duty to Community	30. Must maintain independence and impartiality	31. Must be willing to adjust fee for necessitous clients	32. Must not allow name and/or designation to be used indiscriminately

166

Notes: (1) Selection is determined by information available. (2) Only direct statements or implications have been analysed. There may be other implicit aspects, which are assumed. (3) ★ indicates that code is primarily for members acting as consultants, although parts may apply to all members.

Elements—Taken over from Table 6.1

Title of Association	1	2	3	4	5	6	7	8	9	10	11	12	13	14	15	16	17	18	19	20	21	22	23	24	25	26	27	28	29	30	31	32
Institute of Chartered Accountants																				+		+	+			+						+
Royal Institute of British Architects						+		+		+								+		+		+		+								+
Town Planning Institute								+		+	+			+						+				+								
Royal Instn. of Chartered Surveyors / Chartered Land Agents Society / Chart. Auct. & Estate Agents Inst. / Incorp. Society of Auct. & Landed Property Agents / Valuers Institution						+				+									+			+	+		+	+						
Institute of Quantity Surveyors									+	+	+											+			+							
Incorporated Association of Architects & Surveyors		+							+	+	+									+		+		+	+			+				
Institution of Civil Engineers ★		+				+	+	+	+	+	+	+	+	+						+				+	+	+						
Institution of Electrical Engineers ★		+				+	+	+	+	+	+	+	+							+		+		+	+	+						
Institution of Structural Engineers ★						+	+	+	+	+	+							+		+		+		+	+	+						
Association of Consulting Engineers ★		+					+	+	+	+	+			+						+		+				+		+				
Society of Engineers ★		+			+	+	+	+	+	+	+							+		+	+	+			+							
Institute of Actuaries				+					+											+												
Chartered Institute of Patent Agents	+					+	+													+	+			+	+		+	+				
Chartered Society of Physiotherapy										+	+									+		+		+	+							
Society of Chiropodists											+	+	+								+	+		+							+	
British Optical Association		+			+	+				+	+	+												+	+	+					+	+
Institute of Physics and the Physical Society ★							+		+										+				+									
Textile Institute ★																		+		+		+				+		+				
Institution of Mining and Metallurgy					+	+		+		+								+		+		+		+	+	+						
Institute of Public Relations	+							+	+	+	+											+		+	+							
Institute of Linguists	+	+			+				+	+	+													+								

condemning practice in other occupations, which may provide opportunities to obtain clients surreptitiously. Half the codes stipulate that practitioners must not give, or receive, any discount or commission. The only remuneration must be a salary or professional fee. They must maintain professional charges, or standard agreements.

Unexpectedly, many reputable and highly respectable associations do not possess a code. Few engineering institutions have a code. Instead, they tend to rely on that devised by the *Association of Consulting Engineers*. The Chartered Accountants have a code, the Certified Accountants do not. Chemists have a disciplinary mechanism, but no code. Physicists have a code. Neither the *Chartered Insurance Institute*, nor the *Chartered Institute of Secretaries* has a code.

A number of associations lay down scales of charges to be observed by members, for example, the *Law Society, Royal Institute of British Architects, Town Planning Institute, Institution of Structural Engineers, Royal Institution of Chartered Surveyors, Institute of Quantity Surveyors, Chartered Land Agents Society, Institute of Chartered Shipbrokers*.

Taking all Qualifying Associations, they fall into five distinct groups. There is:

(*a*) A formal code, plus special standing committees for investigating and disciplinary procedure.
EXAMPLES: *Royal Institute of British Architects, Institute of Chartered Accountants, Royal Institution of Chartered Surveyors*.

(*b*) A formal code, but no regular standing committees for disciplinary procedure. Either committees are set up as required, or Council deals with each problem as it arises.
EXAMPLES: *Institution of Civil Engineers, Rating and Valuation Association*.

(*c*) No formal code, but regular disciplinary procedure.
EXAMPLES: *Association of Certified and Corporate Accountants, Institute of Practitioners in Advertising, Institute of Housing*.

(*d*) No formal code, no regular disciplinary procedure, but power to act under the Charter Bye-laws, or Articles of Association, if necessary.
EXAMPLES: *Institute of Municipal Treasurers and Accountants, Advertising Association, Royal Aeronautical Society, Corporation of Insurance Brokers*, most engineering institutions.

(*e*) No formal code, no regular disciplinary procedure, apparently no power to act except for a breach of Articles or Bye-laws, conviction for criminal offence, larceny, or non-payment of subscriptions.

EXAMPLES: *Institute of Transport, Institute of Bankers, Museums Association.*

A few associations have selective codes, applicable solely or mainly to a section of the membership. This arrangement acts as a reasonable compromise, for the code applies to those who need it, for example, to private consultants, or workers in vulnerable positions. Codes of engineering institutions seem chiefly constructed for members acting as consultant engineers. The *British Institute of Management* does not have a code of conduct. However, in 1948, the Institute established a Register of Management and Industrial Consultants, controlled by a Consultants' Registration Committee—a committee of Council.[20] A code of conduct governs only the Management Consultants. The Registration Committee examines any case of misconduct.[21]

Occasionally, associations develop codes which apply so specifically to the work situation, and very little else, that they might be considered as 'work codes' rather than statements of a generalized professional ethic. For example, the *Pharmaceutical Society* issues a 'Statement Upon Matters of Professional Conduct', which is 'for the guidance of pharmacists and corporate bodies carrying on business under the Pharmacy Acts'.[22] Under the Solicitors' Act, 1933, the *Law Society* received powers to make rules regulating conduct. Three sets of rules have emerged so far: the Solicitors' Practice Rules, 1936, dealing with touting, advertising, profit sharing, etc.; the Solicitors' Accounts Rules, 1945–56, concerning the handling of clients' money; the Solicitors' Trust Accounts Rules, 1945, governing the handling of trusts. Thus in both the case of the *Pharmaceutical Society* and the *Law Society*, these narrowly focused rules represent a clarification of particularly vital issues, they are not intended as comprehensive statements on all matters.[23] The *Institute of Practitioners in Advertising* does not have a code of conduct, though Council has the power 'to determine upon and decide any questions with regard to professional conduct', and Bye-laws have been introduced to prevent soliciting and undercutting.[24] But the Institute helps to administer the 'British Code of Standards for the Advertising of Medicines and Treatment',[25] and supports the 'British Code of Advertising Practice'.[26] The *Market Research Society*, which started examinations in 1962, issued 'Standards in Market Research' as a guide to practice in 1954.[27]

THE PROBLEM OF IMPLEMENTING A CODE

As suggested in Chapter One, the position of professionals today needs redefining. The greatest single change in professions has been the steady decline in the proportion of independent, individually practising professionals. This slow transformation has resulted from the rise of new professions, plus the shifting emphasis in older professions. It is no longer realistic to visualize the professional worker mainly as a sole practitioner. The movement provokes many questions. How applicable is a code of conduct? What problems are introduced by a changing professional situation? How far does the new situation strain the structure of an existing code?

Another problem looks more central. How does the professional grow aware of professional ethics? Very few associations demand pupilage, perhaps the simplest means of ensuring some acquaintance with the basic elements of ethical conduct. Otherwise the only normal contact for the professional comes via a copy of the Charter Bye-laws, or Articles of Association, briefly stating the rules, or the single expansive clause providing for disciplinary procedure. Copies of the Code and Schedule of Charges would be sent to new members. The Journal may include 'Practice Notes', or the occasional notice of disciplinary action by Council. Associations make very little continuous effort to describe, interpret and discuss the problems of professional conduct. There are exceptions. The *Institute of Chartered Accountants* takes considerable trouble to keep members informed of disciplinary action, implications of the Code and so on. The *Royal Institute of British Architects* examines students' knowledge of their Code, standard agreements and charges.

In Britain, the situation becomes complicated by the nature of authority over practitioners. Three possibilities exist:

    (*a*) The profession is registered by Statute and controlled by a representative Council. For a practitioner found guilty of misconduct, the consequences are serious. Suspension or erasure from the Register prohibits further practice by law. Table 6.3 lists the registered professions.[28]

(*b*) The profession is unregistered, but dominated by one or two associations. Membership of the association may be recognized as a qualification by certain Statutes, and/or by various employers, institutions, etc. Expulsion will result in disqualification from specific appointments and types of practice, otherwise nothing prevents continued practice.

(*c*) The profession is unregistered and not dominated by particular associations, or membership of the association is not essential in the occupation. Expulsion does not stop practice.

Thus, three levels of authority imply three degrees of control, with two extremes of effectiveness. Disciplinary action can mean the virtual end of a professional career, or a momentary unpleasantness providing temporary disusance.

Finally, there is the problem of vigilance. How can an association ensure that all cases of misconduct are brought to its attention? Firstly, clients must know when the professional's behaviour constitutes a breach of ethical conduct. This awareness cannot be expected at all times. Secondly, the client must take action by reporting the incident. Perhaps more important than clients' understanding is the attitude of colleagues who are in a better position to judge the seriousness of unethical actions. Alternatively the association's officers, Council and committee members are left to keep watch by themselves. Any realistic assessment of efficiency is impossible, as professional misconduct forms a feature of the association's life, confidentially and discretely handled. Associations do not issue much concrete information.

INVESTIGATION OF UNPROFESSIONAL CONDUCT

For the Statutory-registered professions, investigation of misconduct and disciplinary action are determined by the individual General Councils, regulated by Statute. In the case of the Bar, Barristers undergo investigation by the Bar Council, while discipline remains in the hands of the Benchers of the

TABLE 6.3. SHOWING PROFESSIONS REGISTERED BY STATUTE ARRANGED IN CHRONOLOGICAL ORDER OF REGISTRATION

Profession	First Statute Introducing Registration	Title of Statutory Committee Controlling Professional Conduct	Year Introduced	Authorizing Statute	Present Statute Governing Committee
Solicitors	Probably the 1729 Act 2 Geo. II, c. 23	Statutory Comm. of Law Society Investigating powers in— Disciplinary powers in—	1888 1919	Solicitors Act, 1888 51 & 52 Vict. II, c. 65, Solicitors Act, 1919 9 & 10 Geo. V, c. 56	Solicitors Act, 1957 5 & 6 Eliz. II, c. 27, s. 46–8 & Solicitors (Amendment) Act, 1959
Pharmacists	Pharmacy Act, 1852 15 & 16 Vict., c. 56	Statutory Committee of the Pharmaceutical Society	1934	Pharmacy & Poisons Act, 1933 23 & 24 Geo. V, c. 25	Pharmacy Act, 1954
Medical Practitioners	Medical Act, 1858 21 & 22 Vict., c. 90	General Medical Council	1858	Medical Act, 1858	Medical Act, 1956 4 & 5 Eliz. II, c. 76
Dentists	Dentists Act, 1878 41 & 42 Vict., c. 33	General Dental Council (previously the Dental Board of General Medical Council)	1956	Dentists Act, 1956 4 & 5 Eliz. II, c. 29	Dentists Act, 1956
Veterinary Surgeons	Veterinary Surgeons Act, 1881 44 & 45 Vict., c. 62	Disciplinary Committee of Council of Royal College of Veterinary Surgeons	1881	Veterinary Surgeons Act, 1881 (Restricted Powers)	Veterinary Surgeons Act, 1948 11 & 12 Geo. VI, c. 52, s. 13–19 (Powers extended by 1900 Act)
Patent Agents	Patents, Designs & Trade Marks Act, 1888	Council of Chart Institute of Patent Agents	1907	Patents & Designs Act, 1907	Patents Act, 1949 12, 13 & 14 Geo. VI, c. 52 s. 88
Midwives	Midwives Act, 1902 2 Edward VII, c. 17	Central Midwives Board	1902	Midwives Act, 1902	Midwives Act, 1918 8 & 9 Geo. V, c. 43 & Midwives Act, 1902
Nurses	Nurses Registration Act, 1919 9 & 10 Geo. V, c. 94	General Nursing Council	1919	Nurses Registration Act, 1919	Nurses Act, 1957 5 & 6 Eliz. II, c. 15
Architects	Architects Registration Act, 1931 21 & 22 Geo. V, c. 94	Architects Registration Council	1931	Architects Registration Act, 1931	Architects Registration Act, 1931 (The 1938 Act did not affect powers)
Opticians	Opticians Act, 1958 6 & 7 Eliz. II, c. 32	General Optical Council	1958	Opticians Act, 1958	Opticians Act, 1958
Medical Auxiliaries	Professions Supplementary to Medicine Act, 1960 8 & 9 Eliz. II, c. 66	Council for Professions Supplementary to Medicine. Separate Boards for each of seven concerned	1960	Professions Supplementary to Medicine Act, 1960	Professions Supplementary to Medicine Act, 1960

Notes:

(1) *Barristers*—Power was assumed by the Inns of Court in fourteenth and fifteenth centuries to control entry to the Bar, and disciplinary power of members. These powers have never been seriously challenged and they have never been verified by Statute, but the Bar is a closed profession.

(2) *Solicitors*—By the 1729 Act all Solicitors had to be admitted to the Roll of the Court in which they wished to practise—all Court Rolls were united by the Supreme Court of Judicature Act, 1873—Control over Solicitors was gradually passed to the Law Society Control over Examinations (Solicitors Act, 1877); Power to investigate misconduct (Solicitors Act, 1888); Disciplinary powers (Solicitors Act, 1919); Power to make rules governing conduct (Solicitors Act, 1933).

(3) *Teachers*—Registration of Teachers was initiated by the Board of Education Act, 1899. The scheme proved unsuccessful—the previous power was repealed in 1906 and a new Registration Council proposed—today, teaching cannot be considered a closed registered profession.

(4) *Certain other occupations are closed*—since the Merchant Shipping Act, 1850, 1854 all Merchant Navy Officers have been certificated by the Board of Trade. After the Coal Mines Regulations Acts, 1872, 1877, 1887, all Mine Managers have had to be certificated by the Board of Trade.

offender's Inn. The *Law Society* investigates complaints against solicitors. Disciplinary action is carried out by a Statutory Committee of up to eighteen past and present Council members, appointed by the Master of the Rolls. Veterinary surgeons are disciplined by a Statutory Committee of the *Royal College of Veterinary Surgeons'* Council. Similarly, pharmacists are dealt with by a Statutory Committee of the *Pharmaceutical Society*. In addition to the powers of General Councils, individual Qualifying Associations connected with the profession normally possess their own disciplinary procedures.

Methods for dealing with misconduct vary slightly from one association to another. Chart 6.3 shows the general procedure for investigating and disciplinary action. This outline presents the most elaborate pattern. Not all associations follow the 'ideal type'. Variations occur at three stages:

(a) The Secretary may have considerable, or comparatively little responsibility for advising members about problems of professional conduct, on a day-to-day basis. Also great, or little power to decide whether a prima facie case exists for further action.

(b) The Investigation and Disciplinary Committees may be separated from the Council, although composed of Council members. Alternatively, an *ad hoc* investigating committee can be established as required; or Council, in part or whole, will act both as the investigating and disciplinary agency.

(c) Very few associations contain appeal machinery. Usually Council's decision is regarded as final. In registered professions, practitioners generally have opportunity for appeal.

The Advisory Council on Tribunals, initiated by the Tribunals and Inquiries Act, 1958, does not exercise any discretion in the case of professional disciplinary tribunals. Normally, Courts cannot interfere in the proceedings.[29] For registered professions, the General Councils are carefully constituted to represent the various aspects of the profession, professional organization, examining bodies, relevant Government departments and other interested parties. In each registered profession, the authorizing Statute specifies the composition of Council and disciplinary committees, and may outline proceedings and powers.

CHART 6.3. SHOWING GENERAL PROCEDURE FOR INVESTIGATING UNPROFESSIONAL CONDUCT

	AGENCY INVOLVED	NATURE OF ACTION	PROCEDURE
OFFENCE	ASSOCIATION OR OFFENDED PARTY	*Offence committed:* The offence may be— (1) Against a client or external body (2) Breach of association Bye-laws (3) Court conviction, i.e. misdemeanour/felony (4) Discreditable act to profession or member	Charge submitted in writing
	➡ SECRETARIAT		SECRETARIAT — EITHER (1) Decides whether case needs investigation (2) If prima facie case established, then charge passed to investigating committee OR Passes case directly to a permanent Investigation Committee
INVESTIGATION — EITHER these committees and procedures are separate OR (as in many cases) both procedures are carried out simultaneously by the whole or part of the Council	SECRETARIAT	*Investigation of Offence* If complaint is substantiated it is formally framed (perhaps by a solicitor) before presentation to offender and to Disciplinary Committee — (Defender is informed, usually by registered letter)	
	➡ INVESTIGATION COMMITTEE (composed of Council members)		INVESTIGATING COMMITTEE (1) Requests full written and/or oral evidence from offender and offended (2) *Either* committee decides to make formal complaint to Disciplinary Committee Or once satisfied that no offence has been committed, dismisses the case
DISCIPLINE	➡ DISCIPLINARY COMMITTEE (composed of Council members)	*Decision as to Disciplinary Action* Range of possible action: expulsion, suspension, reprimand or admonishment (Few bodies can impose fines)	DISCIPLINARY COMMITTEE (1) Reviews evidence and hears the offender, who is sometimes allowed legal representation (2) If satisfied that a formal complaint is proved, decision is made about action
	SECRETARIAT	*Enforcement of Decision*	SECRETARIAT (1) Council is officially informed (2) Offender informed of decision in writing (usually by registered post) (3) Decision published in journal etc.
	OFFENDER ➡ SECRETARIAT	*Appeal against Decision* (Few un-registered professions have the advantage of an appeals procedure in their associations)	SECRETARIAT (1) Offender lodges appeal with secretary within a specified time (21–28 days) (2) Appeal passed to Committee
APPEAL AND RE-EXAMINATION	➡ APPEAL COMMITTEE (Council members not previously involved)		APPEALS COMMITTEE (1) Re-affirms or reverses previous decision (2) Committee informs Council (3) Secretary informs offender (4) Decision published in journal

Disciplinary procedure for Qualifying Associations may be laid down completely by the Charter Bye-laws, or Articles of Association. Often, a single clause empowers Council to act as necessary, without indicating the method. Then Council relies on Standing Orders or Bye-laws. Regardless of the detail expressed in these instructions, offenders are given a fair hearing. Evidence is submitted in writing. The offender appears personally before the requisite committees. The accuser may also have to appear. Council takes care to safeguard the association's procedure for dealing with unprofessional conduct, because ultimately it is answerable to the corporate membership.

Broad external criticism of the whole system becomes dangerous, owing to the apparent variations in standards. At one end of the scale, stands the impeccable procedure of the *Institute of Chartered Accountants, Royal Institute of British Architects* and similar bodies. At the opposite end, there exists the more casual, *ad hoc* method of the smaller associations. A serious defect shows throughout, in the lack of wide publicity given to findings. Frequently, associations merely publish a brief passing reference to the occurrence in the journal, almost hidden away in a corner. Some associations make a real effort to use the incident to full advantage, reminding members of their obligations and guiding them in future practice. For example, the Chartered Accountants receive complete information about findings and decisions, first in the journal, later in the Annual Report. Understandably, no association is anxious to expose a grave matter to a wide audience. Continuous revelations of unethical practice might cause a loss of confidence outside the association, even a fall in morale within the organization. Yet, better treatment of cases could only help to improve members' awareness, strengthen their consciences and build public confidence.

THE ROLE OF PROFESSIONAL ETHICS

No comprehensive and accurate picture can be given of the extent of professional misconduct, or the treatment of malpractice. Associations sparingly provide adequate figures and analyses. Superficial inquiries reveal a remarkably low incidence. For example, there are about 2,000 practising barristers in England and Wales. The Bar Council's Professional Conduct

Committee only deals with roughly thirty-five to forty complaints annually. Of these, perhaps four or five are serious, the Committee rejecting the rest on the grounds that no prima facie case existed.[30] The *Law Society* considers approximately forty cases each year, although there are nearly 20,000 solicitors on the Society's Roll.

One of the rare opportunities for analysis of the situation is afforded by the *Institute of Chartered Accountants*. The Institute issues sufficient information to enable some kind of appraisal. Tables 6.4 and 6.5 give the basic facts about cases of unethical conduct considered during the period 1949 to 1962.[31]

TABLE 6.4. SHOWING THE NUMBER OF CASES DEALT WITH BY THE DISCIPLINARY COMMITTEE OF THE INSTITUTE OF CHARTERED ACCOUNTANTS IN ENGLAND AND WALES, INDICATING THE ACTION TAKEN, FOR THE YEARS 1949–62

| Year | Disciplinary Action ‡ | | | | | At 1 January | |
	Expulsion	Suspension	Reprimand	Admonishment	Total in Year	Total Members in Practice	Total Corporate Members †
1949	2	—	5	1	8	5,660	14,133
1950	3	—	1	5	9	5,830	14,632
1951	4	1	2	3	10	6,014	15,260
1952	7	1	8	—	16	6,236	16,079
1953	10	3	3	—	16	6,419	16,856
1954	9	1	2	—	12	6,595	17,561
1955	8	1	5	1	15	6,753	18,151
1956	10	—	5	2	17	6,904	18,772
1957	8	—	5	2	15	7,050	19,414
1958	7	—	8	2	17	7,179	20,124
1959*	9	1	7	1	18	9,827	31,381
1960	7	—	9	4	20	9,991	32,579
1961	10	1	8	2	21	10,201	33,867
1962	11	2	9	2	24	10,476	35,228
Total	105	11	77	25	218		

* During 1959, the *Society of Incorporated Accountants'* membership was integrated with the Institute's membership.

† Includes members not in practice and those not in the United Kingdom (for 1961 and 1962), not in England and Wales (for the years 1949 to 1960 inclusive).

‡ The figures below do not include action taken for failure to pay subscriptions within a certain time.

Table 6.4 shows the number of cases which led to disciplinary action. Of the 218 occurrences, 53 per cent resulted in Expulsion or Suspension, 35 per cent of members were Reprimanded and the rest Admonished. The total number of cases represents a very small fraction of all members in practice (about 0.2 per cent each year).

Table 6.5 gives an idea of disciplinary action in relation to type of offence committed. Of all 218 cases, 51 per cent constituted serious breaches of professional conduct, i.e. Court convictions or Statutory violations, mainly in connection with work (Categories 1–11). Disciplinary action caused 76 per cent of these members to be expelled or suspended, 19 per cent reprimanded, the rest admonished. Separating the other categories roughly into two parts: offences largely committed against clients (12, 14, 17, 18, 19); offences against other professionals (13, 15, 16). In the former situation, 25 were expelled or suspended out of 56, 28 were reprimanded. In the latter, only 2 were expelled out of 40, 24 reprimanded, 15 admonished.

Here then is some indication of the Institute's sense of responsibility. Any breach endangering public trust means expulsion. Conviction for a civil or criminal offence obviously casts doubt on the integrity or competence of the individual, and besmirches the profession's good name. For an accountant acting as an auditor to public companies, expulsion or suspension prevents him, by law, from certificating public company accounts. Another implication is that the Institute only notices, or deals with, serious misconduct. Only 11 per cent were admonished. Perhaps this low figure gives a wrong impression. Through the 1948 Supplemental Charter, the Institute completely revised the disciplinary procedure. A three-stage committee system was adopted: Investigation Committee; Disciplinary Committee; Appeals Committee. Powers to reprimand and admonish were added to those of exclusion and suspension. As a result of the new system, the Investigating Committee decides whether a prima facie case exists, it also advises members on points of ethical conduct.[32] Consequently, there must be many cases, which do not reach the Disciplinary Committee.

A survey of approximately forty of the more important Qualifying Associations revealed very little. Most associations declared that a breach of professional conduct was rare. Some

TABLE 6.5. SHOWING AN ANALYSIS OF OFFENCES COMMITTED BY MEMBERS OF THE INSTITUTE OF CHARTERED ACCOUNTANTS IN ENGLAND AND WALES AND DISCIPLINARY ACTION TAKEN BY COUNCIL DURING THE YEARS 1949 TO 1962

Offence	*Disciplinary Action Taken by Council* (number of cases)			
	Expulsion	*Suspension*	*Reprimand*	*Admonishment*
(1) Failure to file returns with Registrar of Companies	1	1	1	—
(2) Failure to send returns as liquidator	10	2	9	3
(3) Failure as Trustee	4	—	2	—
(4) Conspiracy	3	—	—	1
(5) Fraud	9	—	—	—
(6) Larceny or embezzlement	4	—	—	—
(7) Misappropriation	6	—	—	—
(8) Falsification of company accounts to avoid taxation	11	—	—	—
(9) Other convictions connected with accountancy work	6	1	2	1
(10) Other convictions (non-accountancy matters)	4	1	4	1
(11) Bankruptcy and/or failure to meet judgment debts	22	—	3	—
(12) Mis-use of designation 'Chartered Accountant'	1	—	—	2
(13) Circularization, soliciting or advertising	1	—	10	5
(14) Improper basis of charges to client	—	—	2	—
(15) Acceptance of nomination as auditor, without contacting previous auditor	—	—	12	9
(16) Failure in duty to articled clerk	1	—	2	1
(17) Failure to hand over papers etc. to client or successor	9	3	5	—
(18) Signing certificates without proper audit	1	1	11	1
(19) Failure to carry out work	9	1	10	—
(20) Other offences	3	1	4	1
Totals	105	11	77	25

refused the information outright. A large association such as the *Royal Institution of Chartered Surveyors*, has an average of only three cases a year. The *Institute of Practitioners in Advertising* deals with about twenty-five to thirty cases a year, about ten serious, of which five are important.

Unstructured disciplinary procedure and absence of formal codes, evident in most associations, apparently indicates the relative unimportance of misconduct. It is doubtful whether these factors really show unconcern, or lack of vigilance on the part of associations. On the other hand, lack of codes and procedure does not demonstrate an extremely high level of professional morality in Britain.

Unethical conduct is based on a relative rather than an absolute standard. For the individual, violation depends on many factors: temptation offered by the work situation (including the type and extent of possible gain, ease of violation, etc.); chance of discovery; range of possible punishments; probable effect of punishment on the professional's future. In the profession as a whole, attitude toward professional misconduct depends on: the scope of actions considered unethical; attitude of practitioners; extent of punishments; efficiency of policing. To combat unprofessional conduct, most associations rely on a general clause in Articles or Bye-laws, giving Council wide disciplinary powers. Perhaps a single, short, all-inclusive directive functions better than a detailed formal code, because of the greater freedom of action. Yet members may have no clear idea what constitutes an infringement. Again, expulsion comprises the worst penalty. However, outside registered professions, few associations possess the power to deprive a member of his professional livelihood, simply by excluding him from membership. Expulsion can only be effective, where membership furnishes a necessary qualification for performing work under certain Statutes, or where employers regard corporate membership as a qualification for employment. Otherwise deprivation from membership does practically nothing to eliminate the worst practitioners.

For the modern Qualifying Associations, investigation of professional ethics by social theorists has evolved an idealistic picture of the situation, rather than an actual representation. Probably the best examination of professional ethics is by Emile

Durkheim, who argued from the standpoint of a drive toward social solidarity. He suggests that every social activity requires its appropriate form of moral discipline. If a group is to persist, every individual must behave as part of the whole group. Association provides the natural resort of men in the same kind of work. Professional organization results from individuals being attracted by their similarities, and seeking each other out to form agreements and limited groups. Once a group has been founded, individuals gain a sense of the whole and rules evolve to manage the association. Distinct professional groups give rise to localized ethics. The stronger and more stable the group, the greater is its authority and the more numerous are the moral rules. A more developed professional ethic brings more stable and improved organization.[33]

Apart from his assumption that a professional ethic must automatically develop, Durkheim basically neglects the external work situation, which creates different demands for ethical codes. Need for a code is chiefly generated outside the organization, by the factors previously discussed. Internal organization only contributes to the possibility of introducing the code.

Historically, the modern associations have concentrated on building educational standards and level of competence, partly influenced by an inadequate, undeveloped National system of education and training. In view of associations' normal self-conscious concern with inter-association status, the failure to concentrate on codes of conduct seems surprising. In fact, sophisticated regulation of professional conduct remains the exception. Social theorists, such as Durkheim, Max Weber and Taeusch, all appear to assume that a profession is a closed regulated system. This might well be true of law, medicine and the Church, and other professions later controlled by Statute. But today it is difficult to regard all possible professions as closed, in terms of entrance, methods of training, qualification and regulation. Probably members look to associations as a means of qualification, and not necessarily as guardians of occupational morals.

Chapter Seven

THE QUALIFYING ASSOCIATION
IN SOCIETY

THE DEVELOPMENT OF ASSOCIATIONS

(1) *Origins and Types of Organization*

ANY analysis of professional organization soon exposes two essential features: the existence of different types of organization; the variety of different basic reasons for foundation.

Chapter Two suggested that four distinct types of professional organization can be found: the Prestige Association; the Study Association; the Qualifying Association; the Occupational Association. Such a classification becomes necessary as the structure and functions of each kind determines objectives, means and success of action.

The Prestige Association may enhance an individual's status, but it rarely improves the collective status of an occupational group. Inability to improve group status results from wide aims and a membership drawn from many occupations, or from an unwillingness to adopt the techniques of organizations striving to gain professional status for members. Study Associations seek to extend knowledge in a special field, by encouraging research and dissemination of information. Invariably, these associations aim to improve the subject itself, rather than the qualifications, working conditions and salaries of practitioners. Of course, indirectly, professionals may also be improved through being better informed, or stimulated by discussion.

Occupational Associations directly concern themselves with professional status, for they try to improve salaries and working conditions, and recognition of the occupation's individuality. But Occupational Associations can be separated into Coordinating and Protective Associations. It is the Protective Association, which might be popularly described as a professional 'trade union', though a number of these organizations would reject the idea. Objection to the term 'trade union' normally rests on three propositions. First, organizations express reluctance to take normal manual-worker, trade union action to obtain their ends, because of obligations to clients and public, also because of possible danger to the 'public image'. Second, the associations claim to undertake technical research, publishing useful, objective information. Third, they suggest that the aim to improve members' status is always related to the need for public protection. While these claims may be warranted in some cases, often they provide a flexible ideal to be modified as appropriate.[1] Occupational Associations face two limitations in their struggle for professional status. First, they are reduced to pressure group methods and militant tactics in order to improve conditions, though there tends to be a widespread belief that their sense of public duty will always finally prevail and prevent strike action. Any resort to these methods damages the professional image and causes status to deteriorate. Second, membership consists of individuals already qualified, or examined by an external authority. They neither examine prospective members, nor make provision for students. This restricts control over a valuable element in building professional status, namely, provision of a qualification.

Of all types of organization, Qualifying Associations stand out in their ability to offer a demonstrable qualification to aspirant professionals. Side by side with the qualifying function, aspects of other organizational forms are found: the individual may acquire prestige through membership the association will foster study functions. However, Qualifying Associations seldom take part in direct negotiations over members' remuneration and working conditions. This point will be examined later. Because they act as qualifying bodies and rely on a traditional pattern of organization, Qualifying Associations can achieve status more readily, or, at least, attain vestiges of status in an uninformed world.

Clearly all Qualifying Associations did not begin as straightforward attempts to gain professional status. Immediate causes, as far as they can be traced, reveal a variety of reasons for establishing an association: to co-ordinate the activities of workers within an occupation; to offer facilities not otherwise available; to provide for new technological development. Subsequently these associations introduced examinations and sought to improve members' status.

Foundation of associations often failed to follow a simple chain of events: technological advance and/or commercial adjustment —demand for personnel—organization of personnel. More important, such a notion ignores the variable time-lag between first appearance of personnel and ultimate organization. Sometimes formation anticipated an expanding demand in an occupational area, the establishment of specialists and consequent need for 'qualified people'. Occasionally further development of the association justified the founders' foresight. At times, slow development of the association suggested the evident inability of the association to satisfy requirements for qualified personnel, or a false anticipation of need for organization.

(2) *Expansion of Numbers*

The number of Qualifying Associations steadily increased from the 1870s, and more especially from the 1880s. Approximately a dozen new associations appeared in each decade between 1880 and 1910. The main emphasis was on the organization of engineers (Electrical 1871, Municipal 1873, Marine 1889, Mining 1889, Gas 1890, Sanitary 1895, Water 1896, Heating and Ventilating 1897, Automobile 1906, plus at least three others). Undoubtedly, the success of the Institutions of Civil and Mechanical Engineers influenced the foundation of new engineering associations. The *Institution of Civil Engineers* had 5,000 members in 1886, and 9,266 members in 1914, plus a solid dignity and status in the professional world. The *Institution of Mechanical Engineers* had also achieved some position, with about 5,000 members in 1905. Determined efforts by accountants to reform the profession and reduce malpractice, produced the *Institute of Chartered Accountants in England and Wales*. Five other accountancy associations were formed in England and Wales, before 1910. A third area prone to organization covered surveyors, estate agents, valuers and auctioneers. These three occupational areas (engineering, accountancy and the broad field involving surveyors, estate agents, valuers and auctioneers) have continued to erupt in the twentieth century.

From 1910 to 1950, formation rate of new associations increased to roughly two dozen in each decade. Once again, engineering, accountancy and the 'land profession' generated new organizations: eighteen engineering; eight accountancy; seven surveying, auctioneering and valuation associations. Management and administration became another general occupational area subject to organization. Eight associations were formed. Auxiliary medical services produced organizations, particularly during the 1920s and 1930s. By mid-century, taking all associations, important and insignificant, examining and relying on external examinations, these five areas account for just over half of the associations in England and Wales (Engineering 25 per cent, 'land profession' 5 per cent, management and administration 10 per cent, medical auxiliaries 5 per cent, accountancy 8 per cent). No other occupational areas show so much saturation, except perhaps for insurance, which has four associations. Thus the spread of organization is not as wide as might be expected.

How can expansion be explained? Prolificity stems from many factors. First, there is increasing specialization within an occupation. Specialization might be regarded as legitimate grounds for extending organization. Yet often the alleged differences seem quite subtle, even trivial, mere excuses rather than genuine reasons. In the case of accountancy, a division has grown up between practising and non-practising accountants; the needs of the accountant in practice, being different from those of the internal auditor within industry or some institution. Really a three-way division separates 'pure' accountants, cost accountants in industry and accountants working for local authorities. How far are dissimilarities sufficiently distinct to justify the existence of a dozen accountancy bodies?[2] Additional factors must help to interpret causes of multiplication. To take another example, management has also yielded extensive organization apparently based on pseudo-specialization, for example, office, works, personnel, credit, institutional, sales, printing management. Could more be accomplished by one organization, with a series of optional subjects in examinations?[3] Today, engineering has seventeen examining and about nine non-examining associations. Is this large number the result of developing specialization, or unnecessary superimposition of diversity for the sake of creating fresh organization? The question of duplication and consolidation will be looked at more closely later.

Second, joined to the problem of specialization is the lack of facilities for training and education. As a specialized form of work evolves into a distinct occupation, then, sooner or later, those employed will seek a means of preparing incomers. Training entrants helps to ensure better standards, and to raise the level of the occupation's exclusiveness. Combined with obvious benefits obtained from co-ordinating ideas and experience, a Qualifying Association supplies the easiest way of organizing training and education. By establishing examinations, tuition can be encouraged.

Third, new associations can be formed as a reaction to the work, scope or administration of existing associations. Surprisingly, this seldom happens, either internal differences resolve themselves, or dissenting members leave the association. The one notable modern example has already been cited; the breakaway of architects from the R.I.B.A., to found the *Society of Architects* in 1884.

Fourth, a more likely cause of formation springs from the reaction to entrance requirements of existing organizations. Where examination standards are considered too high, and limited allowances are made for experience, then older, experienced personnel have formed new associations. Examples can be detected in accountancy, insurance and engineering. Expressed disagreements with established organization may hide an unwillingness to enter via an arduous examination route.

Fifth, lack or absence of a widely acceptable foundation of basic knowledge and technique tends to induce duplication. As a corollary, where the theory and technique are relatively simple, false specialization can be created, leading to organization. Management illustrates the problem of doubt over theory and practice. From the foundation of the *Institute of Industrial Administration* in 1919, no one apparently had a clear idea of management needs; the Institute found difficulty in deciding upon the essential constituent parts of a suitable curriculum.[4] Continuous formation of management associations before 1939 must be related to the uncertainty.

Sixth, duplication and overlapping organization result from

a situation allowing individuals to enter an occupation, then gain experience and promotion without needing to obtain a qualification based on examined competence. These circumstances occurred in accountancy, engineering and the building industry (including architecture, surveying and actual construction). Then, individuals in senior or executive positions attempt to consolidate and improve status by forming an association.

Seventh, linked with the previous case, there is the desire of insignificant occupational groups to gain status, or to seek recognition as a profession.

Eighth, perhaps the greatest contributory factor has been the ease of formation. By the 1890s, the accomplishments of established associations demonstrated the value of organization and the procedure for organizing. Since 1900, part of the enormous expansion must be due to the noticeable status acquired by organized groups, for accountants, pharmacists, engineers, architects. Details of structure and methods of these bodies were plainly visible, ready for copying by any collection of people engaged in any occupation. Often existing associations were prepared to help in 'legitimate' cases. Founding a Qualifying Association is reasonably easy; maintenance and development prove more difficult.

(3) *Progress of Associations*

Of the numerous Qualifying Associations, how many have achieved success, or stand a chance of succeeding? But what constitutes success for an association? How can success be measured? Success, or development, defies any simple interpretation. Is it international recognition of the association, or recognition within our own society? Is it recognition by everyone, including public and professionals, or just acknowledgment by those inside or connected with the occupation? Is it acceptance by all other associations, or by the eminent well-established bodies? Is development measured by size, by regular growth, by number of examinees, by ability to extend services for members, by a Royal Charter?

Progress for associations depends on both internal and external factors. Internally, there are primarily three elements. Firstly, administration by secretariat, Council and committees furnishes a central component. Policy is directed by Council and implemented through the secretariat. Active Council members and Honorary Officers aid development by supervising activities, initiating change, promoting research, fostering good public relations, etc. These efforts can only prosper with the help of a progressive secretariat. If Council and secretariat are not alive to issues inside and outside the occupation, if they remain unwilling to act, if they regard their appointments as sinecures, then the association will suffer.

Secondly, internal finance can be a severe limiting factor on development. For most associations, sources of income are restricted to subscriptions, donations, examination fees and sale of publications. Maintaining the associations demands expenditure on premises, staff, publications (including large quantities of publicity literature), examinations, possibly a library, and investment to safeguard the future. Initially, associations must rely on subscriptions and donations, therefore membership growth becomes imperative. Encouraging members to join can result in extensive concessions to experienced people, thus holding back standards and eventual quality of membership for many years, and so delaying acceptance of the association.

Thirdly, attitude and activity of members help determine association's development. If members view the association solely as a convenient source of prestige, or just as a necessary qualification for work, then the association might easily continue in an amorphous, unprogressive state. If members fail to take any interest in elections, the association may stagger on with a decrepit Council, unable or unprepared to cause change. Also an associations' members are individual ambassadors for the organization, for they can contribute to the association's honour and value, by expressing their attitudes and taking part in various activities outside the association.

External to the association, many features add to, or restrict the association's progress. One set of factors ensues from the occupational area covered by the association.

Firstly, the number of workers in the occupation, or bordering occupations covered by the association, must dictate the potential size of membership, so controlling the scope for expansion. A smaller number gives opportunity for comprehensive coverage, inclusive membership and probably confined resources.

Secondly, the success of an association is unsure, where experience continues as a powerful determinant of occupational promotion, mobility and security, while theoretical knowledge and qualifications are less important. If qualifications do not matter in the occupation, the association endures hardship, because it hopes to raise status by means of a qualification based on examinations.

Thirdly, where members of an occupation look upon themselves as competitors, each depending on his own skill, special techniques or ability, an association has less chance of success.

Fourthly, appreciation of the association's value, plus acceptance of the qualification within the occupation, undoubtedly enhances the association. Executives and senior workers, who are members of the association, can patronize the qualification and association by giving preference to members, also by advising juniors to train for the qualification, allowing trainees time and facilities for study.

Finally, external to the association exists another significant contributor to the association's progress: knowledge of the association outside the occupation by the public, the Government, various official bodies and kindred professional organizations. Such knowledge permits recognition of the qualification, recruitment, acceptance of advice and opinion when proffered or solicited.

THE NATURE OF QUALIFYING ASSOCIATIONS

Early professional organization (the *Inns of Court, Royal College of Physicians, Royal College of Surgeons*) introduced a rigid structure of government and membership. Emphasis was on the qualifying ability of the associations, members were offered few facilities beyond occasional lectures and extensive libraries. Except for barristers, practice did not require membership of the organization.

Today, the state and operation of these old corporations remain deceptively unchanged. From the outside, members still appear to be mainly diploma-holders, without access to comprehensive services. Voting rights are restricted. Despite these facts, fundamental changes have taken place. The Inns now delegate substantial power to the Council of Legal Education. The Inns of Court Executive Committee and the General Council of the Bar compose two very influential bodies. The *Royal College of Surgeons* provides extensive research and post-graduate teaching facilities.[5] The *Royal College of Physicians* promotes research, organizes conferences, endows lectures on various topics. Special research committees prepare reports on aspects of medicine.

New organizations came into existence during the early nineteenth century, for solicitors (the *Law Society*, 1825), pharmacists (the *Pharmaceutical Society*, 1841), veterinary surgeons (the *Royal College of Veterinary Surgeons*, 1844). Each of these associations assumed unusual features (structure of government, membership structure, facilities), originally determined by the older organizations and special occupational demands, then later by responsibilities devolving from Statutory functions. Of other registered professions, the *Chartered Institute of Patent Agents* alone maintains similar dominance over the occupation. Most registered professions have Qualifying Associations for their practitioners, with Statutory control in the hands of a central representative Board or Council.

Foundation of the *Institution of Civil Engineers* (1818), the *(Royal) Institute of British Architects* (1834), the *Institution of Mechanical Engineers* (1847) and the *Institute of Actuaries* (1848) established a fresh organizational pattern, evolving into a regular, standardized structure. The new form of organization combined the idea of a diploma-awarding body, with the concept of a 'learned society'. It was probably the constitutional framework of these four organizations which provided the example and model for all subsequent Qualifying Associations. The basic structure eventually devised consisted of:

(*a*) Government by Council elected from, and by, corporate members, with Council functions entrusted to committees.

(*b*) Administration by a paid secretariat.

(*c*) Multi-grade membership, including provision for students, with corporate members selected by examinations and additional requirements.

(*d*) Facilities for members, such as regular lectures and discussions, regular publication of technical papers and news of the association.

189

Chapter Three considered the general structure of associations in some detail. However, analysis of formal organization does not completely portray the true nature of associations, for it neglects the status-hierarchy existing throughout the entire range of Qualifying Associations.

Quite feasibly, Qualifying Associations could be assigned to various categories, as hotels are classified in a tourist guide: from a five-star high-quality association of international repute and solid national status, down to a one-star (or no-star) organization of doubtful merit. Facilities could be similarly ranked. Such grading would be mischievous; the action being applauded by some associations and resented by others. Yet, an élite set of associations can be identified, plus another band of respectable lesser associations, followed by the nondescripts and the insignificant. Most associations would admit the fact, even if they fail to agree about the pattern. Status and effectiveness of an association depend on recognition of value within the occupational area, bounded by acceptance outside. Some associations have achieved inter-professional status. Some have achieved intra-professional status only. Some have achieved neither inter-, nor intra-professional status. In addition, there are associations gradually achieving status, moving from one level to another, and some almost inextricably condemned to obscurity.

What determines individual status for an association? How is status measured? Contributory factors have already been outlined: acceptance of the standardized structure for associations; recognition by individuals in the occupation, by clients and employers, by other associations, by society as a whole. Now the content of recognition must be examined more closely.

Recognition is a complex, for it involves subtle judgments. Assessments rest very much on individual and relative opinion. But common components begin to emerge.

First, membership size and length of establishment seem important: partly through an assumption that age brings experience, maturity and dignity; partly because a steady accumulation of funds enables extension of facilities, together with a more open display of grandeur. Rate of growth is taken as a better indicator than absolute size, as rapid expansion implies successful organization. Age does not necessarily bring higher status owing to: (a) internal problems: inactive Council or secretariat; extensive apathy among members; conflict within the association, (*b*) external worries: competition from rival associations (although competition often improves one or more parties); failure to obtain recognition for the association's qualification; too intensive specialization, which restricts the contact area between the association, members, and a wider section of society.

Second, recognition is conditioned by quality of membership (i.e. the kind of people who join) and the subject-matter or area of concern. Associations can be handicapped by their area of concern, even by the title chosen. Either the subject-matter appears too specialized, or the subject is generally unacceptable. Some subjects are felt to be an unsuitable basis for a 'professional' occupation. In fact, if certain associations try hard to build up a sound examination, a useful technical journal and high-quality meetings, they can still remain under-valued and obscure. Established associations, and perhaps society at large, continue unwilling to discard preconceived attitudes and beliefs about the subject. It is not enough to call the organization the 'Institute of . . .', the 'Institution of . . .', the 'Association of . . .'. Quality of membership is primarily based on ease of entry. Too many concessions to individuals unprepared to take examinations, reduce quality. Young associations often attempt to counter-balance low entrance standard by injecting 'quality', persuading prominent people to accept honorary membership, or honorary office.

Third, building an association's reputation demands continuous effort. Generally, associations seek recognition in various ways:

(*a*) by representation to employers, to gain acceptance for the qualification,

(*b*) by securing senior workers in the occupation as members of the association, as Council members and Honorary Officers (often by direct canvassing),

(*c*) by inducing educational institutions to organize courses for the association's examinations,

(*d*) by publications, conferences and joint meetings with similar associations,

(*e*) by acquiring a good name for sound judgment and useful impartial advice in representations to official committees and inquiries.

Fourth, recognition of associations arises from the adoption of conventional association status symbols. Five marks of prestige are commonly employed:

(*a*) A suitable London address. Associations tend to gravitate towards London squares and particular streets. Obviously large, spacious, Georgian houses provide ample room for administration. At the same time, they add a quiet dignity and a sense of age impressive to the visitor.

(*b*) Incorporation under the Companies Act. It hardly forms a true status symbol, for incorporation is a necessary safeguard. Nevertheless, the word 'Limited' must be added to the association's title, unless a licence has been obtained to omit it, from the Board of Trade. The concession tends to be regarded as a sign of progress.

(*c*) Armorial Bearings. A Grant of Arms has very nearly grown into an essential symbol for Qualifying Associations. In modern times, the award means virtually nothing beyond the power to display a coat of Arms.

(*d*) A Royal Charter. Of all symbols, a Royal Charter is probably the most coveted; though a Charter extends, rather than reduces a corporate body's obligations to an external authority. Associations believe a Royal Charter signifies recognition of an ability to serve and represent the occupation. If nothing else, a Charter inspires an association with a new sense of duty and purpose. Often an association will undertake preparation over a period of years, before feeling sufficiently developed and irreproachable to petition for this valuable indicator of prestige. Other associations, especially Chartered bodies, maintain a careful watch on petitions, supporting worthy claims and strongly opposing petitions from associations thought to threaten their status and work.

(*e*) Royal Patronage. The last symbol is Royal Patronage. Some associations have obtained the consent of members of the Royal family to act as patrons. The addition of the word 'Royal' to the association's title also acts as another prestige mark. Apart from the Royal Colleges, the concession has only been granted four times to associations, after petition.

Is it totally wrong to suggest that such status symbols exist for associations? In fact, several pieces of evidence point to the utilization and appreciation of symbols. Applications for a licence to omit 'Limited' from the title, petition for a Grant of Arms, or a Royal Charter, or Royal patronage are all deliberate actions taken by associations, all unnecessary for the real functioning of the organization. Obtaining a Charter or Grant of Arms can mean considerable expense. Lastly, Presidential Addresses, Annual Reports and Editorials in journals imply a vision of a clear path toward professional status, marked at various stages by appropriate signs.

Is it worthwhile seeking association status symbols? Pursuit of professional status through prestige symbols dissipates part of the association's energy and resources, while exhorting Council and members to improve standards. Symbols may add honour to an association, though they reflect an active concern with an inter-association rating, not a direct aim at improvement by means of examinations and better services. Perhaps a member looks upon his qualification more appreciatively, as the association attains these stages and makes visible progress. Certainly, a Charter helps an association, for people seem to take a Chartered body more seriously. And other associations, particularly Chartered associations, show greater willingness to co-operate.

Since the last war, extra methods of prestige-building have emerged, ranging through communication services: special publications and reports, joint meetings, national and international conferences. Coupled with communication, more associations are undertaking research, preparing evidence for committees, etc. Standard of presentation and content of journals have improved noticeably in the face of competition from commercial publications, and the example of progressive associations. Journals are much less stodgy and unappealing.

Two elements help to explain the quest for symbols. Firstly, organizations feel a need to obtain identification with leading associations, in a belief that the action demonstrates professional status. Secondly, associations aim to sustain members' interest and confidence, by convincing them of development in clearly observable terms.

DILEMMAS OF QUALIFYING ASSOCIATIONS

In a mature industrial society, slowly becoming more conscious of the value of qualifications and the danger of relying completely on experience, the Qualifying Associations assume greater responsibilities. But the associations increasingly face very fundamental problems.

(1) *Size*

Since 1900, the number of associations has multiplied four or five times. Sixty years ago, possibly ten out of forty or fifty associations were important, in that they had gained respectability, acceptance and a reasonable size. None was larger than 9,500, most of the big organizations consisted of 4–5,000 members. Today, twenty-eight associations contain over 10,000, fourteen have a total membership over 20,000.

Expanding size has resulted in a series of troubles: increasing complexity of administration; greater separation of ordinary members from each other and from government; accumulation of capital; changing significance of local organization; diversity of members' specialization; representation of membership on the Council, and Council's size.

The main issue is administration. Complex administration and organization strain the traditional voluntary basis of government. Inevitably, older men are left to undertake Council work, as they alone can obtain enough time from their normal jobs, and committees may demand considerable sacrifice of personal free time. While ultimately administrative control must stay with an elected Council, more authority could be delegated to full-time officials. Some associations have been forced to concede power. Some associations' members are probably ignorant of the actual extent of administration in the hands of the Secretariat. Other associations seem reluctant to modify their old structure. During the late 1950s, much reorganization and streamlining was started or completed, and the greatest modification has been separation of administration into manageable divisions.

(2) *Examinations*

Associations undertake an ever-increasing role as examining

bodies, specially the organizations connected with commerce: accountancy, secretaryship, insurance, banking. Many associations still count candidates in tens or hundreds; some deal with thousands or tens of thousands.[6] In engineering, science, architecture and pharmacy, growing numbers of candidates for corporate membership gain exemption from practically all examinations by means of university and college degrees and diplomas.

An outstanding danger arises from maintaining large-scale examinations, supervising institutions and adjusting syllabuses to meet changing needs. The sheer volume of work encourages a concentration on examinations, encouraging the neglect of other functions. Emphasis on the qualifying role endangers study activities and development of membership facilities. A large, financially secure association can cope with the vast amount of work, by employing more staff; smaller associations struggle. Not enough co-operation exists between associations to reduce the load by sharing common papers. For example, seven associations connected with commerce appear to cover similar ground in parts of their Intermediate examinations, viz. Elements of English Law, Commercial Practice, Economics, Auditing/Accounting, Costing.[7] Several factors might explain the lack of co-operation: different occupational needs; different standards; certain associations' unwillingness to work with other associations, adjudged inferior.

Examination success rates vary from one association to another, from year to year, level to level. Normally the range lies between 30 per cent and 45 per cent, occasionally more or less.[8] High failure rates may be due to: high standards (hard papers and strict marking); poor quality candidates; poor tuition; difficulty of earning and learning, and so on. The problem has never been thoroughly investigated. Inadequate, or indifferent, tuition must help to account for the enormous failure rates. Often, there is insufficient liaison between associations and teaching institutions. Too many associations rely too much on correspondence tuition. Smaller associations, with small numbers of examinees spread throughout the country, cannot easily arrange suitable tuition. Technical colleges understandably decline to organize and maintain courses for doubtful numbers. The simple, convenient answer is correspondence teaching. However, postal courses are like hire-purchase agreements, people do not immediately realize the extent of commitment.

(3) Technical Communication

Demand for technical communication by members and outside bodies is constantly expanding. Quality and quantity of associations' publications vary greatly; commercial competition does not necessarily modify quality. Associations connected with science, engineering and technology have always been heavily involved in technical communication. Now most associations find themselves more and more engaged in preparing and publishing technical information, for example, in accountancy, architecture and management. Provision can go far beyond a single journal and monthly meetings. The *Institute of Physics and the Physical Society* publishes four scientific periodicals, plus a monthly *Bulletin* for private circulation, it assists in the management of *Scientific Abstracts* and sponsors two series of monographs. In the case of the *Royal Institute of Chemistry*, the main burden of publishing falls on the *Chemical Society* and R.I.C. members join a special subscription scheme.

Specialization inside the occupation forces complex internal group structures on to associations, though special group arrangements only operate efficiently in very large organizations.[9] Group structures can be extremely elaborate. Both the *Institution of Electrical Engineers* and the *Institution of Mechanical Engineers* found it necessary to reconstruct their internal group schemes in order to give better service. The mechanical engineers (over 56,000 members) finally approved a thirteen-group structure in 1960.[10] The I.E.E., now 50,000 strong, drastically altered internal structure, replacing four sections by three divisions. The scheme began working in October 1962, each division with an elected Board and four representatives on Council.[11] Internal specialist groups may not be generally possible or desirable. Despite this fact, too few associations contain specialist groups, catering for radically different needs and interests, which emerge among members. Some associations have apparently neglected their study functions. In the future, they may be compelled to provide more than just a qualification to satisfy members. Specialist groups seem an inevitable step to cope with changing needs.

(4) *Recruitment*

How can associations gain new members, or capture the interest of potential young entrants to the occupation? Associations consider direct canvassing for members 'unethical', or 'unprofessional'. Still, associations resort to gentle soliciting: an advertisement announcing examination dates, or examination successes, or the existence of an appointments register; careers talks to schools, colleges, etc.; articles or pamphlets about the occupation, injected with information about the association; encouragement of members to invite colleagues to join.

Potential members can be found at two stages: as school-leavers; as adults. Before the last war, associations were able to tap a reservoir of frustrated 'talent'; clever boys unable to continue at school, or move on to full-time higher education. Now 'Eleven-plus' selection, plus greater opportunities for higher education, tend to filter-off the 'clever' people. Additionally, competition intensifies as more occupational fields seek to attract qualified personnel, or those prepared to undergo extended training and education, also as more associations develop keener interest in education.

Once at University or technical college, students may study subjects related to associations' examinations, as in science, engineering, architecture, pharmacy and so on. After graduation, degree-holders may become association members through examination exemptions. Some associations seem less fortunate. Universities offer little or no instruction in their subjects (insurance, accountancy, secretaryship, aspects of engineering, management, advertising), consequently these associations do not immediately attract graduates. Sometimes associations believe the establishment of a university course means a sign of progress. They do not necessarily understand that a university course may not supply the best training for a specific occupation.[12]

Examining the literature from approximately forty to fifty associations, aimed at encouraging young entrants into the occupation, two major features were revealed. Firstly, the information frequently consists of blatant propaganda for the association and not much more. Too few take the trouble to clearly explain: the nature of the work; length, cost and alternative forms of training; entrance requirements (special personal characteristics); remuneration and prospects. The main concern was to emphasize the association, ITS achievements, ITS requirements. Vagueness probably stems from a desire to prolong the life of pamphlets. Secondly, presentation of material was often poor and unattractive, unillustrated and badly written. Not many associations appeared to have commissioned commercial designers for preparation of layout. Of course, lavishly illustrated brochures are expensive to produce, and obviously some occupations can be made to look more inviting and satisfying than others. While competitive campaigns are unpleasant and unnecessary, associations could make a greater effort to keep the right people informed with the aid of good quality, useful literature.[13]

(5) *Public Relations*

During the last five or ten years, associations have grown more conscious of their 'public image', or at least, the image of the occupations they represent.[14] Awakened interest must be partly due to the post-war emergence of the public relations experts—and their organization. Concern shows itself in the appointment of a public relations/professional status committee, and the appearance of the Information/Press/Public Relations Officer.[15] Naturally, associations interpret public relations in a liberal fashion. It can mean: distribution of information to press, radio and television; liaison with schools and non-technical organizations; presentation of literature, conferences, popular lectures and exhibitions; furtherance of the subject.

Limited finances leave associations unable to explore all legitimate facets of publicity.[16] Even so, many associations have been slow in appreciating that public relations constitutes, not so much a nefarious activity, as a natural adjunct to organizational life. How can an uninformed public use or evaluate any occupation properly? An association benefits by demonstrating alertness and interest in public welfare. Besides establishing public awareness, good publicity helps to build morale. Not enough associations understand the concept of the 'professional image', or the process of image improvement.

(6) *Salaries and Working Conditions of Members*

The majority of Qualifying Associations will not directly negotiate with employers over members' salaries and working conditions. Firstly, they consider the practice unethical, or detrimental to status. Secondly, associations may contain employers (principals) and employees together as members (as in architecture, accountancy, pharmacy). Distressing consequences might follow interference. Thirdly, there may be legal prohibitions, either written into the constitution, or the result of litigation.[17]

In spite of general disapproval, some associations of social workers and medical auxiliaries appoint a Salaries Committee, with representatives on national negotiating bodies.[18] One organization of medical auxiliaries has a special negotiating officer. This unusual situation arises from occupational rather than organizational features. The main employers are public authorities possessing special negotiating machinery, for example, Whitley Councils. Historically, some associations began as Protective Occupational Associations, not as Qualifying Associations, so they retain their previous negotiating role.

Though associations refrain from negotiation, they adopt protective tactics. First, remuneration surveys are conducted among members.[19] Second, advice is given to individual members on terms of contract and suitability of salaries. Third, contact is made with employers to discuss and advise on agreements and contracts of service. Fourth, the journal carries announcements of appointments vacant, and/or the association maintains an appointments register. Fifth, they support formation of suitable negotiating bodies.[20] Sixth, they may warn members against taking up a particular appointment.

Extension of employment by Central and Local Government and public corporations, comparison of incomes by various surveys, Government economic policy in the 1960s, plus similar incidental factors have contributed to widespread unrest and dissatisfaction. 'Status', largely measured by income, therefore emerges as the real problem for professionals. In the future, associations are bound to face mounting pressure from members to participate actively in the betterment of economic status.

(7) *Further Specialization*

Specialization composes a constant threat to organization. Occupational development can produce internal specialisms, disrupting unified training and outlook. Associations may need to adjust their examinations, area of concern and perhaps aim, or tolerate formation of new organization. Fortunately, the process of internal specialization normally occurs fairly slowly, thus permitting adjustment. But adjustment offers problems. Surveying is a good example of excessive internal specialization, for the subject broadly covers the work of: the land surveyor; agricultural surveyor or land agent; property valuer and manager; housing manager; quantity surveyor; building surveyor; mining surveyor. Specialization, or quasi-specialization, continuously generated associations of surveyors and resulted in adaptation of the *Royal Institution of Chartered Surveyors*.[21] Another example comes from electrical engineering and the development of radio and electronics. The *Institution of Electrical Engineers* has undergone internal modifications, in order to contain radio and the broad field of electronics.

Over a period of time, occupational emphasis changes: fewer members may be employers or principals, a larger proportion employees; the chief form of employment may alter. Different types of work can reflect different needs and interests. Too few associations take full account of the type of employment in Council representation, or arrangement of meetings.

(8) *Competition, Status and Over-organization*

To the outside observer, associations give the impression of a preoccupation with 'status'. Today, associations seem to stress inter-association prestige, possibly pursuing objectives not directly beneficial to members. The source of anxiety is not just duplication and overlapping; clearly, the older well-established associations resent the spread of extra organization.

Resentment springs from numerous true and false beliefs about new organizations. Objection is expressed in various ways.[22] What forms the basis of indignation? First, they feel that too many associations utilize the trappings of professional organization (examinations, a journal, designatory letters, etc.), without ensuring, or attempting to build, reasonable standards of entrance. Second, they believe that certain occupations, or activities, do not deserve recognition as professions. Third, fresh organization introduces a threat to collective status, as extension of 'professionalism' dilutes its meaning. Fourth, status can only be measured by size, possession of a Royal Charter and length of establishment.

Indeed, there are numerous inferior organizations, remaining insignificant because of failure to fulfil early promise, or inability to raise standards. By assuming the standard organizational pattern, and gathering association status symbols, they portray an outward air of respectability and value. And danger mounts as people pretend to be experts, using designatory letters to mislead and invest themselves with an aura of specialism. On the other hand, who is deceived by bogus qualifications? Surely employers ought to know the difference between the qualifications in their own fields. How far is the public in peril? Ordinary members of the public seldom encounter, or need to consult a great variety of professionals, except through specially organized channels. Specific types of work, controlled by Statute, must only be carried out by personnel possessing designated qualifications. However, the general public does regularly use estate agents, builders, radio engineers, travel agents and other workers, who are subject to almost no control.[23]

At times, the large, dignified associations seem unjust and mistaken in their attitudes toward newer organizations. They forget their own past struggles and unimportance. Often their own standards and status have only leapt forward during the last twenty years, owing to extended educational opportunity, plus greater recognition of, and demand for, qualifications from employers and employees. They fail to appreciate the fact, that some associations are bound to remain small and unappealing to the outside world, as the subject-areas are remote and unattractive. Restricted size and limited scope do not prevent new associations from performing a valuable function inside the occupation, by setting and maintaining qualification standards, and organizing technical communication.

There are associations formed with immediate, inbuilt advantages: wide acceptance by influential members in the occupation, by educational institutions, by other organizations, etc.; a sound financial base, or a guarantee of help; an assured future.[24] They are projected into the professional world. They contrast with the majority of new associations, which begin almost as pioneers or missionaries in a hostile environment, where their efforts may be decried and sabotaged by older organizations.

(9) *Extension, Amalgamation and Co-operation*

Where and when will association formation stop? Has a saturation point been reached? Will there be a slow reduction in numbers?

As previously shown, particular occupational areas yield an excessive number of associations. Engineering, the 'land profession', management and administration, medical auxiliary services, accountancy and insurance contain approximately two-thirds of all associations. This concentration suggests that further extension might well occur in these already oversaturated areas. Formation is much less frequent in other occupations, then usually it reflects a genuine need to organize education and standards, where none existed before.

Will there be any consolidation? Since 1900, several prominent associations have absorbed rivals or lesser bodies, amalgamated to strengthen organization, endeavoured to reach understandings. Table 7.1 shows the more important changes.

Recently, at least four amalgamations were considered and dropped. In May 1959, the *Institution of Metallurgists* called an Extraordinary General Meeting to discuss a proposed amalgamation of the Institution with the *Institute of Metals* and the *Iron and Steel Institute*. Discussion between the three bodies led to closer co-operation and inter-change of services, but no amalgamation.[25] A possible amalgamation was considered between the *Institution of the Rubber Industry* and the *Plastics Institute*, owing to overlapping interests. They decided to shelve the idea and prepare a joint examination scheme to cover common papers in chemistry. In 1961, an amalgamation was proposed between the *Institution of Civil Engineers* and *Institution of Municipal*

TABLE 7.1. SHOWING THE MAIN EXAMPLES OF CONSOLIDATION
AMONG QUALIFYING ASSOCIATIONS IN THE TWENTIETH CENTURY

(Foundation dates are given in parentheses)

Amalgamation Year	Associations Involved
1925	*Royal Institute of British Architects* (1834) incorporated the *Society of Architects* (1884)
1927	*Royal Aeronautical Society* (1866) incorporated the *Institution of Aeronautical Engineers* (1919)
1934	*Chartered Insurance Institute* (1897) absorbed the *Faculty of Insurance* (1912)
1937	*Chartered Institute of Secretaries* (1891) absorbed the *Incorporated Secretaries Association* (1907)
1945	*Institution of Mechanical Engineers* (1847) incorporated the *Institution of Automobile Engineers* (1906)
1951	*British Institute of Management* (1948) incorporated the *Institute of Industrial Administration* (1919)
1957	*Institute of Chartered Accountants in England and Wales* (1880) incorporated the *Society of Incorporated Accountants* (1885)
1960	*Institute of Physics* (1918) amalgamated with the *Physical Society* (1874)

Note: The *Royal Institution of Chartered Surveyors* has incorporated six other
associations (1905, 1922, two in 1937, 1938, 1953).
The *Association of Certified and Corporate Accountants* resulted from a
series of amalgamations. For details, see Appendix II.

Engineers. Further action was approved by I.C.E. members, and
rejected by a postal vote of the municipal engineers.[26] Possible
integration of the Chartered Accountants and Certified Accountants was discussed between 1958 and 1960. Eventually,
they dropped the matter.

These examples indicate that consolidation does take place,
and associations do discuss amalgamation. Definite opportunities
remain in the cases of accountancy, surveying, management,
engineering, the two associations of secretaries, and the two
advertising associations. However, extensive future amalgamations cannot be expected.[27] First, enmity often prevails between
associations, or more accurately, they sustain a curious mixture
of avoidance and surreptitious contact, which defines their relationship in somewhat vague terms. Second, once associations

have struggled independently to achieve standards and status, they become less willing to surrender their independence. Third, associations fear, real or imaginary, loss of identity and dilution of standards. Fourth, present and future expansion of education and demand for qualifications, encourages associations to stay individualists. Fifth, the gap separating 'the best' from 'the indifferent' has widened since the last war.

While association formation will continue, even inside areas already over-organized, and the prospect of far-reaching amalgamation looks gloomy, associations are co-operating more and more. Signs of greater co-operation show in joint examinations, joint conferences, joint meetings, joint publications and use of joint facilities. On the whole, the movement is more visible among the engineering, technological and scientific associations.

THE ROLE OF QUALIFYING ASSOCIATIONS

(1) *As a means of ensuring professional standards*

A corporate member of the mature, well-run association has satisfied specific requirements. He, or she, must have (*a*) reached a minimum age, (*b*) passed the association's examinations or obtained exemption from them, (*c*) served an approved period of training and experience, (*d*) (often) attained a position of responsibility in the occupation, (*e*) shown evidence of good character. Admittedly, this outline disguises the multifarious interpretations and standards employed by associations. Disregarding variations, the Qualifying Associations present a qualification, which supplies a basic standard for those in the occupation and for people employing their services.

By acquiring corporate membership, assuming the qualification is recognized, the professional obtains a national, uniform standard. This fact can make it easier when seeking employment, as employers know roughly what to expect in terms of qualification. Sometimes, as in architecture, accountancy, to some extent science and branches of engineering, and insurance, the professional qualification might be preferred to a university degree. Corporate membership denotes examination success *plus* minimal approved experience, also those hiring employees may be corporate members of that association themselves. Where associations maintain employment registers, members benefit from special contacts. Meetings and publications assist the professional to retain and better his knowledge and practice, at the same time continuing his sense of belonging to the profession. Standards of service benefit from association's prescriptions about the principles of professional practice and ethics.

For clients, employers and the public, associations furnish a measure of anticipated basic competence. And they might presume that the professional is conversant with current methods of practice and new developments, through being kept up to date by his association's publications. Where available, a code of conduct, or a schedule of charges ought to predetermine fair, impartial treatment and redress for incompetence, or excessive charges.

Yet how far are the above 'advantages' realistic or idealistic? What is this 'standard'? Is the public satisfactorily protected against incompetence and abuse? Does the professional bother to keep up to date? Does the association really provide opportunities to keep up to date? Such questions are not easily answered, as much depends on the individual, the association and the services demanded. To some extent, they centre around the vexed problem 'How can one tell "good" associations from "bad"?'

Whereas examination levels and entrance requirements of leading associations are reliable, particularly since the last war, some 'qualifications' arouse suspicion. Ultimately, no universal standard prevails for all organizations. One association's qualification seems better than that of another, as one university's degrees may be superior to those of another, because of more searching selection, better tuition, stiffer marking in examinations, and the fact that the university has built up a reputation.

An examination syllabus conveys a limited amount of meaning to the non-specialist. Examination questions provide a relatively poor guide, unless the level of marking is known. Frequently, associations' students can take the whole examination, or section by section, or even paper by paper. Opportunity for preparation can be hopelessly restricted. Inevitably, failure rates give only approximate estimates of examination standards, ignoring the state of examinees. Another important factor is the impossibility of making reasonable comparisons between, say, chemists, surveyors, architects, accountants, electrical engineers, and librarians. The final gauge must be the estimated standard and valuation within the occupation, judged by practitioners and co-workers. Either the public and clients trust an association to devise and keep a high standard, or they must reject the possibility of qualification altogether.

Chapter Six indicated that few associations possess a code of conduct, though practically all constitut:ons contain provisions for disciplining unprofessional conduct. Need for a code, and ability to introduce rules successfully, must be considered when any attempt is made to evaluate the significance of presence or absence of codes. Better to have codes when, and where, they can be effective, than to reduce the principle to a form of 'window dressing', for impressing the uninformed. Assuming a code does exist, how much are practitioners aware of the code, the reasons for each clause, the interpretation of the code in a changing work situation? What are the chances of unethical conduct being detected, if clients are ignorant of distinctions involved, if they fail to report the matter? Nothing usually prevents further practice of members ejected from associations.

(2) *Role as an organized voice of the professions*

Qualifying Associations hold a crucial position among professional organizations for, at their best, they consist of concentrated bodies of expert technical opinion. Therefore, potentially, they constitute a strong, organized voice of narrowly specialized sections of society, serving as sources of powerful pressure groups. During the last ten years, intensified exposure of pressure group activities has led to many articles and general studies.[28] These accounts tend to present a false impression of Qualifying Associations' activities, as no real distinction is drawn between various types of professional grouping. Separation of types suggests the special character of Qualifying Associations as interest, rather than pressure groups.[29]

What methods are chosen by associations to express their views? Quite accidentally, M.P.s may be corporate members of an association due to their previous professional training, but associations do not sponsor candidates. The *Pharmaceutical Society* remains unique in possessing a 'Parliamentary Fund' to promote or assist candidates. Since 1942, Sir Hugh Linstead, a Joint-Secretary of the Society, has been Member of Parliament for the Putney Division of Wandsworth.[30] Generally speaking, associations use different means of influence. Association members are commonly invited to sit on advisory or investigating committees, Royal Commissions, etc., either in a private capacity or as representatives of the organization.[31] Certain associations appoint a 'Law and Parliamentary Committee' to watch the progress of legislation affecting their members' work.[32] The chief form of representation is submission of written and/or oral evidence to committees; advice, assistance and critiques to Local and Central Government, educational authorities, employers and so on.

Reservations must be included. First, some associations receive greater attention than others, either because of their special status and valued opinion, or through an established reputation for sound non-partisan advice. Second, while associations offer evidence and issue memoranda, much advice is requested from associations. Automatically, particular organizations will be asked to submit recommendations and present their views. Third, some associations appear very active, others inactive. Fourth, associations keep to their own subjects. Fifth, the effect is two-way; associations try to influence outside groups, equally, outside bodies seek to influence associations. Sixth, associations normally take great care in preparing evidence, they aim to give expert advice and to remain as impartial as possible.

How active are associations? Actual extent is indeterminate. Usually associations publish their recommendations in the journal, summarizing the year's work in the Annual Report. Unfortunately precise details are seldom offered. And in view of associations' efforts to impress members by demonstrations of activity and progress, absence of information must suggest comparatively limited action. Of course, associations may be inhibited by real and imaginary barriers. More likely, the administration is not geared to continuous pressure group activities, owing to the sheer weight of everyday association work—examinations, inquiries, publication of the journal, etc.

On the whole, association involvement looks less than might be supposed. They act as interest groups, promoting measures and submitting evidence occasionally, as special issues come up. They do not persistently pester authorities, though legislation, directives and orders are carefully watched. A review of Annual Reports and journals of about fifty associations suggested that intensity depends on several factors:

(*a*) The association's overall level of activity, measured by publications, extent of lectures and meetings, etc. More widely active associations show keener interest.

(*b*) The area of concern. Associations connected with accountancy and commerce, architecture and the 'land profession' submit the greatest number of pieces of evidence.

(*c*) The available opportunities. Some associations possess greater scope, as items of legislation and administration frequently occur in their fields.[33] Some topics of inquiry committees develop wider interest than others (e.g. the Jenkins Committee on Company Law Reform, or the Robbins Committee on Higher Education).

(3) *Role as a means of extending educational, industrial and other facilities*

Associations can provide an extensive range of services: meetings, publications, instruction, library, technical advice, appointments register, social activities and so on. However, not all all members in all associations have an equal quantity and quality of services available to them. Provision of services and their quality depend on many elements.

First, size of membership determines finance for activities and potential numbers of participants for branch activities, conferences, etc. Taking the examining Qualifying Associations in Appendix I, about a quarter have total membership under 2,000, a half under 4,000, three-quarters under 8,500, plus six of 20–30,000, six of 30–50,000, two over 50,000. A majority of associations are quite small. A membership scattered throughout the country reduces the concentration of active members. If half, or more, of members are students and other non-corporate grades, the supply of contributors to lectures and the journal is restricted.

Second, limited finance curtails services, preventing employment of sufficient staff, establishment of a modern comprehensive library, even adequate housing. The journal distributed free to members, can quickly suffer from a low budget.

Third, inclination and attitude of 'Headquarters' may hinder development of services. A large, rich organization does not necessarily provide the most for members. Some small associations stretch their resources by enthusiastic help and attractive presentation of publications.

Fourth, inclination and attitude of members are equally important. If members simply regard the association as a source of designatory letters, poor participation weakens the effectiveness of facilities. Rudimentary local organization decreases opportunity for meetings.

Fifth, a less obvious factor is the association's area of concern. Science, engineering and technology generate a need for publications, meetings, reports and research. Commerce, say, develops a need either for day-to-day information, which an association cannot supply, or general summaries of trends and background knowledge. Research is less important. Thus, the amount of material prepared by scientific and engineering associations might falsely imply a larger capacity of, and consideration for, members.

Sixth, competition usually helps an association. Commercial publications can make an association design-conscious, modifying presentation and content. Competition from similar associations tends to enliven, also to stultify, as syllabuses, requirements and facilities may be copied.

Bearing in mind the above remarks, what have associations done to extend facilities? Perhaps half the associations add an apparently dubious qualification, an indifferent journal and extra mystification for everyone. Alternatively, the best make significant contributions. Their extension of educational institutions has been described. Expansion of technical colleges and correspondence tuition owes a lot to associations' examinations, though this expansion has produced evils: emphasis on part-time education; continuation of uneven standards; stagnation of higher education; encouragement of worthless associations and correspondence colleges. Associations aided the dispersion of educational opportunity. By setting qualifications as objectives for self-improvement, they assisted a majority excluded from higher education.

Industry has gained both directly and indirectly. The British Standards Institution was founded in 1901, by three engineering institutions and two other associations. Today, most scientific, engineering and technological associations are heavily represented on B.S.I. committees. The *British Nuclear Energy Society*, constituted in January 1962, began as the *British Nuclear Energy Conference* in 1954, organized by the engineering institutions to study and further the use of nuclear energy. Associations are closely linked to industrial research organizations, by representatives and day-to-day exchanges. Industry has close contact with educational institutions, where executives are association members, and representatives, on governing and advisory committees of technical colleges and similar institutions. Practically all technological and engineering associations are well represented on City and Guilds Examinations committees. It is hard to say how far associations exploit all the chances offered by an intricate pattern of contact with industry and educational institutions. Many times, they give the impression of a failure to realize the full potential of the situation. Benefits seem accidentally achieved, not the result of deliberate action.

Associations have helped to create better qualified staff, co-ordination of ideas and experience, regularization of the approach to work-problems. Gains vary from occupation to occupation. Whether an individual needs to study and qualify, in order to obtain establishment and promotion, depends on employers and pressure from associations, unless Statutory requirements demand qualified personnel. In Central and Local Government, the intensively graded structure makes qualifications important. In teaching, qualifications influence salary. But in commerce, paper qualifications retain relative unimportance, except in accountancy, banking and insurance. Changes may occur, as executives become firmly conscious of management training and qualifications.

Outside education and industry, associations have long served another valuable function, acting as expert watch-dogs in the progress of law, regulations and administration. Large, well-established organizations really possess a sense of public duty, their vigilance has produced many improvements without the knowledge of the public.

The Qualifying Association in Society

What have Qualifying Associations accomplished or contributed in the wider context of society?

First, they modified the concept of professional organization. Early professional associations had a narrow function. Their main purpose was to qualify practitioners. Once examined, or admitted, members were not bound to their organizations by subscriptions and facilities, they had practically no control over their own government. The new Qualifying Associations of the nineteenth century destroyed the sterility of older organizations, by introducing elected Councils, membership participation in regular meetings and published accounts of proceedings. By combining the merits of the old qualifying bodies and the learned societies, an entirely new form of organization was conceived.

Second, they transformed the professional ideal. During the eighteenth and nineteenth centuries, the professional ideal was solidly formed by the rapidly changing social and economic structure. The professional (doctor, lawyer, clergyman and to lesser extent engineer, architect, apothecary) possessed recognizable qualities: training was chiefly via pupilage (later institutionalized for doctors and clergy); he practised alone as a principal; he acknowledged a keen sense of professional conduct, due to a close professional-client relationship, and a desire to contrast with unscrupulous practitioners; he held a respectable position in society, reinforced by a tendency toward occupational self-recruitment and a need to practise in the open. Over the last hundred years, Qualifying Associations have altered this ideal: opportunities for training have increased, accompanied by a reduction in the importance of full-time institutionalized education; no longer is the professional necessarily a sole-practitioner or principal, working in a close professional single-client relationship, in complete public view; self-recruitment is almost unimportant in the selection of personnel. Has the concept of a 'profession' suffered any loss through liberalization? Has the content of professionalism been destroyed? These are perennial problems encountered by analysts of the professional scene. Quite wrongly, critics try to match recently developed occupations against early 'professions'. Comparison is misleading. Work-situation, training and education are entirely different. This fact does not make engineers, managers or scientists less professional, because they are not lone practitioners in private practice, in direct contact with the public. Either doctors, clergy, dentists, barristers, solicitors and accountants in practice, etc., alone are specified as professionals, owing to the special professional-client relationship, or, more realistically, the term 'professional' ought to be applied freely to anyone able to demonstrate a high standard of examined competence, experience, achieved responsibility and good character. And the best associations demand these very qualities, when admitting candidates to corporate membership.

Third, they created, sponsored or encouraged educational facilities in a society, which neglected its educational system and allowed educational opportunity to be dominated by social class membership. In addition to conducting examinations, providing tuition and inspecting teaching institutions, associations have performed a valuable service by circulating ideas and attitudes. Yet development of associations and their examinations stimulated the growth of part-time education and correspondence tuition. This movement helped to delay the evolution of a sound national system of further and higher education. Gaps were filled, thus giving a false impression of educational provision. The multitude of examinations prevented efficient use of resources and augmented the state of confusion. Because of limited teaching facilities, associations have frequently appeared to adopt and adapt subjects and syllabuses to fit existing provisions. At times, associations seem to have been hard pressed to discover suitable theoretical principles, so they could establish the prerequisite examination and claim professional status. Examinations present an impressive and persuasive inducement for potential recruits and a gullible public, though only the experienced observer can assess their true value.

Fourth, associations introduced qualifications for personnel in occupations which previously lacked any measure of ability except experience. And by devising and organizing theoretical background, associations facilitated standardization of practice, systematization of training, rationalization of selection, formation of a basis for development within the subject itself. If examinations and qualifications result in better quality, greater efficiency, higher standards and ensure regular, supervised training, then any occupation must benefit. However, to improve status, members of an occupation have to separate themselves from other workers, in and around the same field. Separation concentrates on differences rather than similarities, perhaps extending specialization unnecessarily. Formation of associations stresses variance. Over-specialization constitutes a menace in any industrial society, owing to the problems generated in training, demarcation, promotion, remuneration, etc. Though associations ensure a higher acceptable level of entrance to many occupations, by doing so, they help to affirm faith in 'the expert'. 'Experts' are presumed to be essential. Anyone claiming 'expert knowledge' and displaying designatory letters may find a favourable reception. Every society requires specialists, but associations add confusion by multiplying variations and blurring distinctions between essential and inessential.

Lastly, associations contribute to the co-ordination and flow of technical communication, though standards of content and presentation vary extremely. The best associations offer good opportunities for discussion and technical communication. The rest provide indifferent facilities, restricted by available resources, subject-matter and quality of membership. In many fields, commercial publications give better coverage, superior presentation and a larger proportion of useful information. Membership services are deceitfully inviting to the unwary, for they may consist of just a narrow range of valueless meetings and a pathetic magazine.

Chapter Eight

CONCLUSION

THE development of any industrial society is bound to extend occupational specialization, multiplying the demand for, and supply of, skilled personnel. Over-specialization and unnecessary occupational sub-division may also result from the growth. Whether or not society continuously needs the break-down of skills, does not always seem to be considered. Sooner or later, organization occurs to establish a new occupation, a fresh variation of skills. Appearance of a number of people in the same kind of work generates a feeling for organization: to obtain outside recognition of their status; to increase efficiency and exclusiveness; to ensure selective recruitment; to improve internal occupational standards. This process of generation has taken place regularly over the last hundred years, among high-grade, skilled and supervisory workers in industry, commerce and administration, where a superior level of knowledge and practice have permitted separation from workers in the same general occupational area.

The high occupational status of professions is a comparatively recent phenomenon in English society, dating from the eighteenth century. Great consolidation of status was achieved in the nineteenth century, aided by legislation and deliberate organization. During the nineteenth century, new forms of professional association evolved, creating a pattern of organization clearly visible by the beginning of the twentieth century. Of the four principal types of professional organization which emerged, the Qualifying Association is by far the most interesting, owing to the widespread use in raising occupational status.

Qualifying Associations founded between 1800 and 1850 devised a model system of government and facilities, differing from that established in the old qualifying bodies. They attempted to provide more than a qualification for members, by arranging regular lectures and discussions and publishing an account of their proceedings. Ever since then, all new associations have adopted the same basic constitutional framework. And today there are approximately one hundred and sixty Qualifying Associations, or pseudo-qualifying bodies in England and Wales.

Bearing in mind the ease of formation and protection offered after the Companies Act, 1862, the availability of a well-tried constitutional pattern and the achievements of maturing associations, it was not surprising to find occupations tempted to copy by setting up new organizations, thereby hoping to gain professional status. But looking at all associations, the spread throughout occupations is not as wide as expected. Five occupational areas account for just over half the associations. Unlikely, unnecessary and speculative organizations evidently exist to exploit acceptance of more respectable bodies, who have worked for many years to build up public confidence. Are people easily fooled by spurious organizations? True, most disreputable or badly organized associations usually fail to stand the tests of time and close scrutiny. Perhaps the members alone benefit from an internally conceived sense of self-importance. But a gullible public might be convinced by impressive designatory letters. Possible abuse of 'the means of professionalization', causes new progressive and hard-working associations to suffer from unwarranted criticism and opposition. If an association genuinely performs a valuable service within an occupation, by raising standards of competence and efficiency, then it deserves recognition.

Direct comparison of associations is neither easy, nor desirable, owing to dissimilar and changing occupational needs. Nevertheless a distinct hierarchy of organizations can be recognized, supported by a conglomeration of real and unreal factors defining prestige. Expenditure of time, money and effort on actual progress constitutes good policy. Improved facilities for members, better training and educational programmes, a sound examination system, recognition of the qualification are all worthwhile, legitimate aims. However, the attempts of long-established associations to separate themselves from the rest, have resulted in the propagation of a belief in false development, denoted by a succession of status symbols. The pursuit of digressive objectives allows useful bodies to disguise their true value.

Ideally, greater control ought to be exercised over associations, preventing abuse of the system, duplication, sterility and unnecessary formation. Introduction of any kind of supervision seems improbable, so that nothing will stop extension of organization. When an association applies for incorporation under the Companies Act, the Board of Trade investigates the case, just to make certain that Statutory requirements have been met. No further demands are made, beyond the deposit of an annual financial statement with the Registrar of Companies. When application is presented for incorporation, a caveat can be lodged by another organization. Such a move will not terminate the application, though it may secure an alteration of title, or even aims. More effective action materializes when associations petition for a Royal Charter. A number of petitions have been rejected through opposition from leading organizations; sometimes counter-action seems to arise from spite, or a jealous concern with privilege. The aloofness of old-established associations does not discourage or disrupt new organizations. Legislation can produce some control, either by registration of the profession and definition of acceptable qualifications, or by designating specific associations as qualifying bodies for performing work governed by Statute. But the past history of Registration suggests a reluctance to impose such a measure, which restricts entrance to the profession and prohibits 'unqualified' practice. All registration Acts have only been obtained after protracted negotiation and compromise; often, practitioners have felt disappointed with the final legislation.

As already pointed out, intensive or extensive amalgamation and absorption may not happen in the future, though ample scope exists in engineering, accountancy, management and parts of commerce. A general register of professional bodies might offer a solution, as in the case of trade unions, friendly societies and charities. Of course, many objections must be answered. First, certain senior bodies would oppose such action, unwilling to surrender their autonomy, or to mix with lesser organizations. Second, there is the problem of devising standards and supervisory mechanism, for organizations meeting different requirements and at different stages of development. Third, setting up registration would mean compromise and perhaps undeserved elevation of some organizations and occupations. Fourth, a real difficulty would be the task of informing the public, and convincing professions of the necessity for general registration. Regardless of objections, some future government may be forced to take steps controlling organization, as the volume of 'experts' expands.

Structurally, associations remain practically unchanged after a century of operation. Despite increased size, extended educational role, and the pressures of technical communication, they continue fundamentally unaltered. Councils are either too large owing to complex representation, or too small to be truly representative. Is voluntary government still a useful constitutional device? Voluntary government does not pose the crucial issue, for much work, and many preliminary decisions, must be left to Council committees and the Secretariat. More dangerous in large Councils is the growth of power among inner factions of senior people within associations. Also greater reliance placed on the Secretariat extends its influence. Another structural problem stems from the multiplication of membership grades: most associations have three, some seven, eight or more. While distinction must be drawn between Students (unqualified) and Corporate Members (qualified), further division of corporate grades causes confusion. The outside world is not always aware of tenuous differences separating Members and Associate Members, Fellows and Associates. Inside occupations, differentials serve an essential function, if indeed they demonstrate superior qualification. Within associations, many members do not bother to apply for upgrading, although eligible, as the change means extra subscription and no extra privileges. Complications occur as additional classifications mark off students, successful examinees (otherwise unqualified), qualified and senior qualified, distinguished qualified and notable unqualified, retired members, foreign members. Most associations require just two grades dividing qualified from unqualified, some need three, a few function better with four. Science, engineering and technology call for three or four grades, due to the ease and value of separating levels of competence and experience.

Members primarily join Qualifying Associations to obtain a qualification and, probably indirectly, for access to a regular flow of technical information. Associations distribute information through meetings and publications. Perhaps a majority of members would prefer the bulk of information via publications, owing to their location, hours of work, other interests, alternative information sources and inclination. Yet how many associations arrange a comprehensive variety of meetings? How many associations pay sufficient attention to internal occupational specialization, developing distinct groups for particular needs? More inter-association meetings and co-operation would benefit members and associations, spreading costs and responsibility, increasing the size of potential audiences, encouraging more ambitious enterprises.

Associations possess substantial opportunities for the co-ordination and dissemination of information. Unfortunately, too many fail to explore actual requirements and possibilities. The journal often rates as a poor, unattractive, uninformative magazine, with amateurish and uninspired presentation. Naturally, the best journals set a very high standard. Unless associations take more trouble to stimulate membership participation in meetings and publications, many organizations may decline even deeper into pure diploma-awarding bodies, the majority of members being solely interested in the designatory letters and unconcerned with corporate life.

The role of associations in education has been stressed. During the nineteenth century, they evolved in an inadequate national system of secondary and higher education, producing individual provision of tuition, uncertainty about curricula and tolerance of low standards. Multiplication of associations and their examinations in the twentieth century has promoted: expansion of local technical and commercial colleges; the expansion of part-time and evening study; the inefficient overlapping of subjects and growth of devious requirements; the assisted delay of adequate provision for higher education; the supply of qualifications for occupations, where none previously existed. Accomplishments seem both advantageous and detrimental to the educational system. Today, the situation is not altogether satisfactory. There is excessive duplication. Too many individual courses are offered. Associations do not always competently supervise facilities and students. Insufficient inter-association co-operation accounts for part of the problem, also the failure of associations to employ fully their power as co-ordinating links. But this plight is not universal, for the best associations carefully watch the education, training and examination of their students. The smaller, younger associations are seldom as vigilant.

Having assumed a responsibility for qualifying individuals, associations rarely venture a thorough control of practice, thus maintaining high standards and integrity. As the exhibition of a code of conduct and disciplinary mechanism constitute a means of instilling public confidence, as well as a professional conscience, the omission looks puzzling at first. Some associations explain that a code and elaborate disciplinary procedure are unnecessary, because of the low incidence of unprofessional conduct. But as already indicated, detection methods are limited. Many associations only become conscious of misconduct, when a member faces Civil or Criminal proceedings, or if he loses his job. Analysis of the situation exposes more reasonable grounds for neglecting to furnish a code and complete disciplinary procedure: not every occupation needs a code; some occupations permit easier introduction of a code. Associations show reluctance to produce a comprehensive code, due to the hazard of foreseeing all contingencies. On the whole, associations do not exploit 'professional conduct' as a form of window dressing, and that stands to their credit.

To the outside world, associations may act as a form of professional 'trade union', selfishly thrusting members' demands forward, or as an intense political voice in society. No evidence supports either view. In fact, associations are too big, too dignified and unprepared to behave as irresponsible pressure groups; or they are too small and insignificant to succeed. There are a few exceptions to the general rejection of direct political action, or 'trade union principles', but most associations discard these ideas as being 'unprofessional'.

For all their disabilities and errors, their misconceptions and prejudices, the Qualifying Associations contribute a great deal to the standardization of practice, the determination of technical standards. Taking these qualities, spread throughout many branches of industry and commerce, Central and Local Government and many technological fields, the benefits are undeniable and immeasurable. Forgetting the dubious organizations, the uneven standards, the over-concentration on status symbols, the over-lapping and unnecessary associations, the best were founded as sincere attempts to gain self-improvement, reaching a recognized status by means of a long and determined effort. Our society profits by their presence.

APPENDIX I

A List of Qualifying Associations in England and Wales

SHOWING YEAR FOUNDED AND INCORPORATED, YEAR
EXAMINATIONS INTRODUCED, MEMBERSHIP GRADES,
MEMBERSHIP SIZE, TITLE(S) OF REGULAR JOURNAL(S)

NOTES:

(1) This list contains approximately 80–90% of all the Qualifying and Pseudo-Qualifying Associations in England and Wales. All the major associations are included and many of the minor ones; no important organization is excluded. Most associations give rise to designatory letters.

(2) It is impossible to indicate the relative status of organizations within professional fields, i.e. within a specific profession, or amongst all professions. Some associations are much more senior and have greater prestige than others. No significance, in terms of status, must be attached to the inclusion, or exclusion, of any association in this list. The common element is the fact that all qualify, or attempt to qualify, by setting examinations or accepting external evidence of examinations and/or experience.

(3) Although the year, in which examinations were introduced, is important, even more important is the year when examinations were made compulsory for entrance. This is not always easy to determine. In all cases, the year given is for the introduction of examinations. Another difficulty is the determination of examination standards.

(4) Membership Size. In some cases, only total membership size was available. In fact, it is valuable to distinguish between: corporate and non-corporate membership; different membership grades; home and overseas membership. As far as possible, the date for the figure is shown.

ABBREVIATIONS USED:

(?) Indicates information unknown or uncertain.

IN CONNECTION WITH TITLES: (COL. 1) Assoc. = Association, Inst. = Institute, Instn. = Institution, Soc. = Society, Chart. = Chartered, Incorp. = Incorporated.

IN CONNECTION WITH FOUNDATION DATES: (COL. 2) R.C. = year of first Royal Charter, Incorp. = year of incorporation under various Companies Acts.

IN CONNECTION WITH MEMBERSHIP GRADES: (COL. 4) Hon. F. = Honorary Fellow, Ret. F. = Retired Fellow, F. = Fellow, A.F. = Associate Fellow, Hon. M. = Honorary Member, Ret. M. = Retired Member, M. = Member, A.M. = Associate Member, A. = Associate, L. or Lic. = Licentiate, G. or Grad. = Graduate, C. or Comp. = Companion, Prob. = Probationer, Affil. = Affiliate, Cert. = Certificated, S. or Stud. = Student, Sub. = Subscriber.

IN CONNECTION WITH MEMBERSHIP SIZE: (COL. 5) Corp. = Corporate Members, Non. = Non-corporate Members.

IN CONNECTION WITH PUBLICATIONS: (COL. 6) J. or Journ. = Journal, T. or Trans. = Transactions, Bull. = Bulletin, Proc. = Proceedings; (Frequency: example (12X) = issued 12 times a year); (1921–) means published from 1921.

(A) ASSOCIATIONS HOLDING THEIR OWN EXAMINATIONS

ACCOUNTANCY
(NOTES: (1) Only members of the Inst. of Chart. Accts. and Assoc. of Cert. & Corp. Accts. are qualified under the Companies Act, 1948, as Auditors to Public Companies.
(2) Two other accountancy bodies not included 'Inst. of Internal Auditors', 'Faculty of Auditors'.)

FIELD AND TITLE OF ASSOCIATION	YEAR FOUNDED AND INCORPORATED	YEAR EXAM INTRODUCED	MEMBERSHIP GRADES	MEMBERSHIP SIZE	REGULAR JOURNAL
Inst. of Chart. Accountants	1880 R.C. 1880	1880	F.C.A., A.C.A., Stud.	36,581 Corp. c. 15,000 Art. Clerks 1/1/63	*Accountancy* (12×) (1938–) (As 'Incorp.Accts.Journ.' (1889–))
Assoc. of Cert. & Corporate Accountants	1904 1939 as A.C.C.A.	1906	F.A.C.C.A., A.A.C.C.A., Stud.	11,199 Corp. 12,520 Studs. 31/10/63	*Accountants Journ.* (12×) (1946–) (As 'Cert. Accts. J.' (1905–1946))
Inst. of Municipal Treas. & Accountants	1885 R.C. 1959	1905	F.I.M.T.A., A.I.M.T.A., Stud.	3,723 Corp. 2,196 Studs. Aug. 1963	*Local Govt. Finance* (12×) (1935–) (As 'Financial Circular' (1896–1935))
Institute of Cost and Works Accountants	Incorp. 1919	1920 Fellowship Exam 1952	F.C.W.A., A.C.W.A., Stud.	8,274 Corp. 17,312 Studs. 31/7/63	*The Cost Accountant* (12×) (1921–)
Assoc. of International Accts.	1928 Incorp. 1932	1932	F.A.I.A., A.A.I.A., Licentiates, Students	1,303 Corp. 3,928 Non. 1963	*International Accts. Journ.* (4×) (1930–)
British Association of Accountants and Auditors	Incorp. 1923	1923	F.B.A.A., A.B.A.A., Stud.	1,030 Corp. 260 Studs. Oct. 1963	*The Registered Acct.* (4×) (1925–)

Incorp. Assoc. of Cost and Industrial Accts. 'The Cost Accts. Assoc.'	Incorp. 1937	1951	M.C.I.A., A.M.C.I.A., Lic.C.I.A., Student	c. 500 c. 1,000 Studs. 1963	Costing (14×) (1962–) (6×) (1937–62)
Institute of Company Accts.	1928 Incorp. 1929	1929	F.I.A.C., A.I.A.C., Student	5,156 Corp. 935 Studs. 1/1/63	Company Accountant (12×) (1931–) (incorporating 'Taxation Review for Comp. Accts.' in 1938)
Society of Commercial Accountants	1942 Incorp. 1943	1943?	F.Comm.A., A.Comm.A., Studs.	3,500 Corp. +1,400 Studs. 1963	The Commercial Accountant (4×) (1949–)
ACTUARIES Institute of Actuaries	1848 R.C. 1884	1849	F.I.A, A.I.A, Student	1,463 Corp. 1,164 Studs. 31/3/63	Journ. (3×) (1851–)
ADVERTISING Advertising Association	1926 Incorp. 1931	1931	M.A.A. (Indiv. qualif membership only introd. in 1958)	523 M.A.A.s +Studs. +869 firms Aug. 1963	Journ. (4×) (1936–) Newsletter (12×) (1952–)
Inst. of Practitioners in Advertising	1917 Incorp. 1927	1927	F.I.P.A., M.I.P.A., A.M.I.P.A., Hon.F., Hon.M., Ret.F., Ret.M., Ret.A.M., Stud.	1,800 + Studs. 1/10/63	I.P.A. News (12×) (1953–)
AERONAUTICS Royal Aeronautical Society	1866 R.C. 1949	1922	Founder M, F.R.Ae.S., A.F.R.Ae.S., Assoc., Grad., Comp., Stud.	5,977 Corp. 5,290 Non. 30/6/63	Journ. (12×) (1918–) (As 'Aeronautical J.' (1897–1918)) Aeronautical Quarterly (1949–)

223

FIELD AND TITLE OF ASSOCIATION	YEAR FOUNDED AND INCORPORATED	YEAR EXAM INTRODUCED	MEMBERSHIP GRADES	MEMBERSHIP SIZE	REGULAR JOURNAL
ALMONERS Institute of Almoners	1903 Incorp. 1945	1912 By Hospital Almoners' Council	Hon.M., 'A' 'B' 'C' Mems., A.M.I.A. for those on Register	1,232 'A', 544 'B' Aug. 1963	*The Almoner* (12×) (1948–)
ARCHITECTURE Royal Institute of British Architects	1834 R.C. 1837	1863	F.R.I.B.A., A.R.I.B.A., L.R.I.B.A., Studs.	20,417 Corp. 752 Ret.M. 193 Hon.M. 3 Subs. 5,544 Studs. 31/12/62	*Journ.* (12×) (1893–) (new series) *Trans.* (1886–93) *Proc.* (1835–93)
Architectural Association	1847 Incorp. 1920	1860's?	Members, Prob. Mem. (A.A. Dip. recognized by A.R.C.U.K.)	3,681 31/12/63	*Arch. Assoc. J.* (12×) (1905–) (As 'A.A. Notes' 1886–1905)
Incorp. Assoc. of Architects and Surveyors	Incorp. 1925	c. 1935	*Architects:* F.I.A.A., A.I.A.A., Prob., Stud., *Surveyors:* F.I.A.S., A.I.A.S., Stud.	c. 3,500 1963	*Architect & Surveyor* (24×) (1956–) (As 'Parthenon' (1926–56))
Faculty of Architects and Surveyors (Architectural qualification not recognized by A.R.C.U.K.)	Incorp. 1926	1930s	*Architects:* F.F.A.S., A.F.A.S., L.F.A.S. *Surveyors:* F.F.S., A.F.S., L.F.S., Students	1,941 Corp. 35 Studs. 1/6/63	*Portico* (4×) (1926–)

AUCTIONEERS Chartered Auctioneers' and Estate Agents Institute	1886 R.C. 1947	1892	F.A.I., A.A.I., Lic., Hon.F., Hon.M., Student	8,014 Corp. 2,459 Non. July 1963	*Journ.* (12×) (1921–) (As 'Notes on Pract.' (1909–1920) and 'Annual Record' (1911–1920))
Incorp. Society of Auctioneers and Landed Property Agents	Incorp. 1924	1926	F.A.L.P.A., A.A.L.P.A., Licentiate, Student	4,381 31/12/63	*Incorp. Auctioneers Journ.* (12×) (1927–)
BANKERS Institute of Bankers	1879	1880	F.I.B., A.I.B., Ordinary Members	19,459 F.s and A.s 40,961 Ord. Ms. Oct. 1963	*Journ.* (6×) (1879–)
BARRISTERS Inns of Court (Lincoln's Inn, Gray's Inn, Middle Temple, Inner Temple)	14th cent. Unincorporated	1853 voluntary exam.; 1872 compulsory exam.	No designatory letters	c. 2,000 in practice	None
BOOK-KEEPERS Inst. of Book-keepers	Incorp. 1916	1916	F.B.I., A.B.I., Studs.	1,850 1/10/63	*Book-keepers Journ.* (4×) (1920–)
BOOT & SHOE TECHNOLOGY British Boot & Shoe Instn.	1927 Incorp. 1927	1953	F.B.S.I., A.B.S.I., Ordinary Members, Grad. Studs.	2,931 Corp. 593 Non. 31/12/63	*Journ.* (9×)
BREWING Institute of Brewing	1886 Incorp. 1907	1916 but postponed until 1920)	M., A.M., Dip.M., Hon. M., Stud.	c. 2,400 (1963)	*Journ.* (12×) (1887–)

225

FIELD AND TITLE OF ASSOCIATION	YEAR FOUNDED AND INCORPORATED	YEAR EXAM INTRODUCED	MEMBERSHIP GRADES	MEMBERSHIP SIZE	REGULAR JOURNAL
BUILDING Institute of Builders	1834 Incorp. 1884	1923	F.I.O.B., A.I.O.B., L.I.O.B., Hon. F.I.O.B., M.I.O.B., Prob., Stud.	2,455 Corp. 3,126 Non. June 1963	*Building : Technology and Management* (4×) (1963–) (Previously as 'The J.')
BUILDING SOCIETIES Building Societies Inst.	1934	1936	F.B.S., A.B.S., Hon. M., Ordin. M., Studs.	3,935 1/1/63	*BSI Quarterly* (4×) (1947–)
CERAMICS Institute of Ceramics	Incorp. 1955	1958 L.I.Ceram.	F.I.Ceram., A.I.Ceram., L.I.Ceram., Student	c. 500 (1963)	*Trans.* (12×) (1900–) (of Brit. Ceramic Soc.)
CHEMISTRY Royal Institute of Chemistry	1877 R.C. 1885	1878	F.R.I.C., A.R.I.C., G.R.I.C., L.R.I.C., Stud.	16,069 Corp. 991 Grad. 888 Lic. 2,280 Studs. 2/7/63	*Journ.* (12×) (1877–) 'Lecture Series' replaced 'Lectures, Monographs & Reports (6×) (1926–60)
COMMERCE Institute of Commerce	1906 Incorp. 1908	1909?	F.C.I., A.C.I., Studs.	1,677 (1963)	*Journal* (4×)
DECORATORS Incorp. Inst. of British Decorators & Interior Designers	1894 Incorp. 1899	1922	F.I.B.D., A.I.B.D., L.I.B.D., Hon. M., Ret. M., Stud.	c. 1,000 (1963)	*The Record* (4×) (1932–)
ENGINEERS Institution of Agricultural Engineers	1930 Incorp. 1960	1958	M.I.Agr.E., A.M.I.Agr.E., Hon. M., Comp., Grad., Stud.	c. 1,900 Oct. 1963	*Journ.* (4×) (1944–)

226

Institution of Chemical Engineers	1922 R.C. 1957	1925	M.I.Chem.E., A.M.I.Chem.E., Hon. M., Grad., Stud.	3,703 Corp. 2,592 Non. 31/12/62	*The Chemical Engineer* (12×) *Trans.* (6×) (1923–) *The Diary* (12×)
Institution of Civil Engineers	1818 R.C. 1828	1897	M.I.C.E., A.M.I.C.E., Hon. M., Assoc., Grad., Stud.	18,703 Corp. 11,690 Non. Oct. 1963	*Proc.* (12×) (1957–), (1952–56) *Journ.* (6×) (1935–51) *Proc.* (1837–1935) *Trans.* (1836, 1838, 1842) *Geotechnique* (4×)(1948–) (pub. by I.C.E. since 1950)
Institution of Electrical Engineers	1871 R.C. 1921	1913	Hon.M.I.E.E., M.I.E.E., A.M.I.E.E., Comp., Assoc., Grad., Stud.	26,404 Corp. 24,893 Non. 30/9/63	*Electronics & Power* (12×) (1964–) (As 'J. of I.E.E.' (1889–1962), as 'J of Soc. of Telegraph Engs.' (1877–99)) *Electronics Record* (6×) (1964–) *Power Record* (4×) (1964–) *Science & General Record* (4×) (1964–) (As 'Quarterlies' (1963)) *Proc.* (12×) (1963–) (Previously in parts from 1949, 'Proc.' commenced 1898) *I.E.E. Studs.' Quart. J.* (1930–)

FIELD AND TITLE OF ASSOCIATION	YEAR FOUNDED AND INCORPORATED	YEAR EXAM INTRODUCED	MEMBERSHIP GRADES	MEMBERSHIP SIZE	REGULAR JOURNAL
Institution of Engineering Inspection	1919 Incorp. 1922	1960	M.I.E.I., A.M.I.E.I., Comp., Grad., Assoc., Stud.	2,564 Corp. 493 Non. 31/12/63	*The Quality Engineer* (6×) (1960–) (As 'Inspection Engineer' incorporating 'Quality Control' (1956–59) as 'Engineering Inspection' (1935–55), as 'Inspection' (1930–34))
Institution of Fire Engineers	1918 Incorp. 1924	1924	M.I.Fire.E., A.M.I.Fire.E., Grad.I.Fire.E., Hon.M.I.Fire.E, Lic., Stud., Subscribers	4.753 (1963)	*Journ.* (4×) (1941–) (New Series)
Institution of Gas Engineers	1863 R.C. 1929	1926 A.M. exam. 1952	Hon. Life M., Hon. M.Inst.Gas.E., M.Inst.Gas.E., A.M.Inst.Gas.E., Grad., Assoc., Stud.	2,937 Corp. 913 Non. 31/12/62	*Journal* (12×) (1961–) (Replaced '*Trans.* (12×) (1898–1960) and Bull. (?–1960))
Institution of Heating and Ventilating Engineers	1897 Incorp. 1926	1920	M.I.H.V.E., A.M.I.H.V.E., Assoc.I.H.V.E., Grad., Stud.	2,071 Corp. 3,782 Non. 31/12/62	*Journ.* (12×) (1933–) (As monthly supplement to 'Domestic Engineering' (1897–1933))
Institute of Marine Engineers	1889 R.C. 1933	1935	M.I.Mar.E., A.M.I.Mar.E., Comp., Assoc., Grad., Stud., Prob. Stud.	c. 15,500 (1963)	*Trans.* (12×) (1889–) *Stud. Trans.* (12×) (1955–)

Association	Founded	Date	Qualifications	Membership	Publications
Institution of Mechanical Engineers	1847 R.C. 1930	1913	M.I.Mech.E., A.M.I.Mech.E., Comp., Grad., Stud.	32,871 Corp. 25,178 Non. 31/12/62	*Proc.* (1847–) (irregular) *The Chart. Mech. Eng.* (12×) (1954–) *J. of Mech. Eng. Science* (4×) (1959–)
Institution of Mining Engineers	1889 R.C. 1915	1947	Hon.M.I.Min.E., M.I.Min.E., A.M.I.Min.E., Assoc., Stud.	c. 4,400 (1963)	*Trans.* (12×) (1889–) *The Mining Eng.* (12×)
Institution of Municipal Engineers	1873 R.C. 1948	1886	Hon.M.I.Mun.E., M.I.Mun.E., A.M.I.Mun.E., Assoc., Stud.	6,043 Corp. 1,895 Non. 31/12/62	*The Chart. Mun. Eng.* (12×) (1962–) *Journ.* (12×) (1913–61) *Proc.* (1873–)
Institution of Production Engineers	1921 Incorp. 1931	1932 A.M. exam. 1951	M.I.Prod.E., A.M.I.Prod.E., Assoc.I.Prod.E., Grad., Stud.	7,884 Corp. 5,624 Non. 31/7/63	*The Production Engineer* (12×) New Series (1953–) Old Series (1925–53)
Institution of Public Health Engineers	1895 Incorp. 1916	c. 1900	F.I.P.H.E., M.I.P.H.E., A.M.I.P.H.E., A.I.P.H.E., Stud.I.P.H.E.	c. 1,600 Nov. 1963	*Journ.* (4×) (1895–)
British Institution of Radio Engineers*	1925 R.C. 1961	1929	Hon. M., Comp., M.Brit.I.R.E., A.M.Brit.I.R.E., Assoc.Brit.I.R.E., Grad., Stud.	3,066 Corp. 5,982 Non. 1/9/63	*The Radio & Electronic Engineer* (12×) (1963–) (As 'J.' (1926–1962))

229

* At the time of going to press, the name was in the process of being changed to the 'Institution of Electronic and Radio Engineers'.

FIELD AND TITLE OF ASSOCIATION	YEAR FOUNDED AND INCORPORATED	YEAR EXAM INTRODUCED	MEMBERSHIP GRADES	MEMBERSHIP SIZE	REGULAR JOURNAL
Institution of Railway Signal Engineers	Incorp. 1912	1946	Hon.M.I.R.S.E., M.I.R.S.E., A.M.I.R.S.E., Assoc., Grad., Stud., Technician M.	c. 1,550 (1963)	*Journ.* (Annually) (1913–)
Institution of Structural Engineers	1908 R.C. 1934	1920	Hon. M., Hon. A., M.I.Struct.E., A.M.I.Struct.E., Assoc., Grad., Stud., Retired M.	6,085 Corp. 3,896 Non. 1/8/63	*The Struct. Eng.* (12×) (1924–) *Trans. & Notes* (1908–1920) *Journ.* (1922–23)
Society of Engineers	1854 Incorp. 1910	1912	Hon. F., F.S.E., M.S.E., A.M.S.E., A.S.E., Grad.S.E., Stud.	1,584 Corp. 2,071 Non. Oct. 1963	*Journ. & Trans.* (4×) (1911?–)
HOTEL MANAGEMENT AND CATERING Hotel & Catering Institute	Incorp. 1949	1953	F.H.C.I., A.H.C.I., Grad., Stud.	4,241 Corp. 2,126 Non. 30/6/63	*Journ.* (12×) (1950–)
HOUSING Institute of Housing	Incorp. 1931	1938	F.I.Hsg., A.I.Hsg., Hon. M., Stud., Retired M.	1,037 Corp. 741 Studs. Oct. 1963	*Housing* (4×) (1938–)
INSURANCE Chart. Insurance Institute	1897 R.C. 1912	1899	F.C.I.I., A.C.I.I., Hon. M., Hon. F., Hon. A., Corr. M., Stud.	17,797 Corp. 31,557 Non. 30/6/63	*J.* (Annually) (1899–) *Contact* (2×) (1955–)

	Founded	Exam.	Membership grades	Numbers	Publications
Corporation of Insurance Brokers	1906 Incorp. 1910	1919 (now Corp. uses the C.I.I.'s exam.)	F.C.I.B, A.C.I.B., Temp. Assoc., Stud.	c. 2,000 +870 Firms Dec. 1963	*Journ.* (12×) (1906–39) Resumed (4×) (1952–)
Chartered Institute of Loss Adjusters	1941 R.C. 1961	1948	F.C.I.L.A., A.C.I.L.A., Hon. M., Overseas Corr., Lic., Stud.	401 Aug. 1963	*Newsletter* (2×)
LAND AGENTS Chart. Land Agents' Society	1902 R.C. 1929	1921	F.L.A.S., Q.A.L.A.S. (Qualified A.), A.L.A.S., Stud.	1,462 +255 Studs. Aug. 1963	*Journ.* (12×) (1902–)
LANDSCAPE ARCHITECTS Institute of Landscape Architects	Incorp. 1929	1946	F.I.L.A, A.I.L.A., Prob. Subs, Hon. F., Hon. A., Hon. Corr. M., Lic., Stud.	216 Prof. Ms. 26 Hon. Ms. 308 Others Aug. 1963	*Journ.* (4×) (1941–) (*Previously used* 'Landscape & Garden') *Quarterly Notes* (1929–?)
LEGAL EXECUTIVES Institute of Legal Executives	1962	1964	F.Inst.L.Ex., A.Inst.L.Ex., Studs.	c. 6,000 Fs. & As. c. 1,000 Studs. (1963)	*The Legal Executive* (12×)
LIBRARIANS Library Association	1877 R.C. 1898	1896	Personal Ms. (F.L.A., A.L.A.), Hon. F., Instl.M, Corr. Instl.M.	11,900 Personal 790 Affil. Ms. 1,524 Corr. Personal 371 Corr. Affil. 31/12/62	*The Lib. Assoc. Record* (12×) (1899–) *Library Science Abstracts* (4×) (1950–) *Brit. Humanities Index* (4×) *Brit. Technology Index* (11×) *Brit. Education Index* (irregular)

231

FIELD AND TITLE OF ASSOCIATION	YEAR FOUNDED AND INCORPORATED	YEAR EXAM INTRODUCED	MEMBERSHIP GRADES	MEMBERSHIP SIZE	REGULAR JOURNAL
LINGUISTS Institute of Linguists	1910 Incorp. 1958	1910 (suspended 1914–23)	Qualified Ms. (F.I.L., A.I.L.), Elected Ms., Ordin. M., Affil. M., Studs.	2,249 31/7/63	*The Incorp. Linguist* (4×) (As 'Linguists' Rev.', 1951–60) as 'Inst. of Linguists' Rev.' (1924–51))
MANAGEMENT AND ADMINISTRATION British Institute of Management	Incorp. 1947	1927* as Exam. of Inst. of Indust. Admin.	F.B.I.M., M.B.I.M., A.M.B.I.M., Grad., Assoc., Stud., Collect., Subscriber	6,834 Corp. 8,981 Non. 30/9/63	*The Manager* (12×) (1948–) (Prev. as 'Industry' (1932–48))
Institute of Hospital Administrators	1902 Incorp. 1910	1915	F.H.A., A.H.A., Ordinary M., Stud.	2,436 Corp. 67 Ord.M. 1,224 Studs. 30/9/62	*The Hospital* (12×) (1929–) (As 'The Hosp. Gazette' (1904–29). Incorp. 'J. of Incorp. Assoc. of Clerks & Stewards of Mental Hosp.'))
Institutional Management Association	1938 Incorp. 1960	1947	M.I.M.A., A.M.I.M.A., Hon. M., Affil., Studs.	2,806 +1,012 Studs. 30/4/63	*I.M.A. Journ.* (12×) (1950–)
Institute of Office Management	1915 Incorp. 1960 (as Inst.)	1946 Dip. in Office Management	F.I.O.M., M.I.O.M., Assoc., Patron	3,190 (1963)	*Office Management* (12×) (1946–)

* The British Institute of Management will cease to conduct examinations in management subjects from October 1966.

Institute of Personnel Management	1913 Incorp. 1924	1956	F.I.M.P., M.I.P.M., A.M.I.P.M., Grad., Stud., Reg. External S., Affiliates	2,959 Corp. 2,771 Non. 30/6/63	*Personnel Management* (4×) (1963–) (As 'J.' (1946–62), as 'Labour Management' (1931–46) as 'Welfare Work' (1920–31)) *Mems. Bull.* (4×) (1952–)
Institute of Public Relations	1948 Incorp. 1963	1949	F.I.P.R., M.I.P.R., Assoc., Affil., Overseas Assoc., Corp. Ms.	1,843 1/10/63	*Public Relations* (4×) (1952–) (As 'J.' of Inst.' (1948–52)) *Members Newsletter* (12×) (1948–)
Institution of Works Managers	1931 Incorp. 1936	1951	Hon.F.I.W.M., F.I.W.M., M.I.W.M., A.M.I.W.M., Comp. Grad, Affil, Stud.	3,302 Corp. 1,862 Non. 30/6/63	*Works Management* (12×) (1950–) (Prev. as 'Journ. of Inst.')
Institute of Credit Management	Incorp. 1939	1949	F.I.C.M, M.I.C.M., Studs.	c. 750 (1962)	*Journ.* (12×) (1947–)
Institute of Marketing and Sales Management	1911 Incorp.	1928	F.Inst.M.S.M., M.Inst.M.S.M., A.Inst.M.S.M., Grad., Stud.	10,101 1/9/63	*Marketing* (12×) (1931–)
MARKET RESEARCH Market Research Society	1947 Incorp. 1953	1962	Full M, Assoc.	1,225 31/3/63	*Commentary* (3×)
MEDICINE Royal College of Obstetricians and Gynaecologists	1929 R.C. 1946	1931	F.R.C.O.G., M.R.C.O.G., D.Obst., R.C.O.G.	646 Fs. 1,684 Ms. 1/1/63	*Journal of Obstetrics & Gynaecology of the Brit. Commonwealth* (6×) (1954–)

FIELD AND TITLE OF ASSOCIATION	YEAR FOUNDED AND INCORPORATED	YEAR EXAM INTRODUCED	MEMBERSHIP GRADES	MEMBERSHIP SIZE	REGULAR JOURNAL
Royal College of Physicians of London	R.C. 1518	16th cent. Joint Exam. R.C.P./R.C.S. 1886	F.R.C.P., M.R.C.P., L.R.C.P.	1,023 Fs. 4,246 Ms. + Lics. and diploma holders 1/11/63	None
Royal College of Surgeons of England	R.C. 1800 (Previously as Company of Surgeons founded 1745)	1745 M.C.S. 1800 M.R.C.S. 1843 F.R.C.S. 1859 L.D.S.R.C.S. 1886 M.R.C.S./L.R.C.P. 1947 F.D.S.R.C.S. 1948 F.F.A.R.C.S.	F.R.C.S., M.R.C.S., L.D.S.R.C.S., F.D.S.R.C.S., F.F.A.R.C.S.	c. 5,500 Fs. 650 F.D.S. 5,827 L.D.S. 1,600 F.F.A. + Members (1963)	*Annals* (12×) (1941–)

MEDICAL AUXILIARIES

NOTE: The following are designated under the 'Professions Supplementary to Medicine Act, 1960'. 'The British Dietetic Association' is shown in Part B.

FIELD AND TITLE OF ASSOCIATION	YEAR FOUNDED AND INCORPORATED	YEAR EXAM INTRODUCED	MEMBERSHIP GRADES	MEMBERSHIP SIZE	REGULAR JOURNAL
Society of Chiropodists	Incorp. 1945	1945	F.Ch.S., M.Ch.S., A.Ch.S.	3,761 31/12/63	*The Chiropodist* (12×) (1945–)
Association of Occupational Therapists	1936 Incorp. 1935	1955	M.A.C.T., T.M.A.C.T., Assoc. M., Overseas M.	2,676 Aug. 1963	*Occupational Therapy* (12×) (1938–)
Chart. Society of Physiotherapy	1894 R.C. 1920	1895	M.C.S.P., Students	25,560 registered since 1920 17,201 on verified Register c. 2,600 Studs. Oct. 1963	*Physiotherapy* (12×) (1948–) (Prev. as 'J. of Soc. of Masseurs & Med. Gymnasts' (1915–44) as 'J. of Chart. Soc. of Physioth' (1944–48)

Association					Publications
Institute of Medical Laboratory Technology	1912 Incorp. 1942	1921	Hon. F., Life F., F.I.M.L.T., A.I.M.L.T., Ordin. M., Stud.	c. 7,500 Corp. c. 2,500 Studs. (1963)	Journ. (4×) (1951–) (Prev. as 'The Laboratory J.' (1913–51)) The Gazette (12×) (As 'The Bull.' (1934–))
Society of Radiographers	1920 Incorp.	1920	Hon. F., Hon. M., F.S.R., M.S.R.	c. 250 Fs. c. 5,000 Ms. (1963)	Radiography (12×) (1935–)
Society of Remedial Gymnasts	1945 Incorp.	1945 (When training introduced) 1958 (External exam.)	M.S.R.G.	c. 330 (1963)	The Remedial Gymnast (4×) (1949–)
METALLURGY Institution of Metallurgists	1945 Incorp. 1946	1947	F.I.M., A.I.M., L.I.M., Enrolled Grads., Enrolled Studs.	3,878 Corp. 2,340 Non. 31/7/63	The Metallurgist (12×) (1960–) (Prev. as "The Bull. of the Inst.' (1952?–59))
Institution of Mining and Metallurgy	1892 R.C. 1915	1950	M.I.M.M., A.M.I.M.M., Hon.M.I.M.M., Affil., Stud.	3,150 30/6/63	Trans. (Annually) (1892–) Bull. (12×) (1904–) Abstracts (24×) (1950–)
MOTOR INDUSTRY Inst. of the Motor Industry	1920 Incorp. 1927	1925	F.I.M.I., M.I.M.I., A.M.I.M.I., Assoc., Grad., Stud.	6,600 (1963)	Journ. (4×) (1947–)
MUSEUMS Museums Association	1889 Incorp. 1920	1938	F.M.A., A.M.A., Hon. F., Prof. M., Non.Prof. M., Instl. M., Stud.	1,458 Aug. 1963	Museums J. (4×) (1901–) Bull. (12×) (1961–)

235

FIELD AND TITLE OF ASSOCIATION	YEAR FOUNDED AND INCORPORATED	YEAR EXAM INTRODUCED	MEMBERSHIP GRADES	MEMBERSHIP SIZE	REGULAR JOURNAL
OPTICIANS British Optical Association	Incorp. 1895	1896	F.B.O.A., F.B.O.A. Hons., Assoc., Reg. M.	4,929 Fs. 357 As. 459 Reg. Ms. 31/12/63	*Ophthalmic Optician* (24×) (1960–) (As 'Dioptric News' (1931–60)) *Brit. J. of Physiological Optics* (4×) (c. 1927–)
PACKAGING Institute of Packaging	1948	1957	F.Inst.Pkg., M.Inst.Pkg., Affiliates, Hon. F.	c. 3,000 (1963)	*Journ.* (24×) (1951–)
PATENT AGENTS Chart. Inst. of Patent Agents	1882 R.C. 1891	1889	F.I.P.A., A.I.P.A. Brit. Overseas M., Foreign M., Hon. M., Stud.	955 +277 Stud. 30/4/63	*Trans.* (12×) (1882–)
PHARMACISTS Pharmaceutical Society of G.B.	1841 R.C. 1843	1842	F.P.S., M.P.S., Hon. F., Hon. M., Corr. M., Stud.	28,847 Reg. Pharm. Chemists 535 Studs. 31/12/63	*Pharmaceutical Journ.* (weekly) (1841–) *J. of Pharmacy and Pharmacology* (12×)
PHOTOGRAPHERS Institute of British Photographers	1901 Incorp. 1921	1942	F.I.B.P, A.I.B.P, Lic., Affil. M., Stud.	2,083 Corp. 1,308 Non. 31/12/63	*I.B.P. Record* (12×) (1938–) (Prev. as 'Prof. Photo Alliance Record' (1923–38))

PHYSICS Inst. of Physics and the Physical Soc.	1918 Amalgamated 1960	1920	Hon. F.Inst.P., F.Inst.P., A.Inst.P., Grad.Inst.P., F. of Phys. Soc., Stud., Subs., Group Subs.	8,300 Corp. (inc. 7,020 Prof. M.) 1,400 Studs. and Subs. Dec. 1963	*Proc. of the Phys. Soc.* (12×) (1878–) *Bull.* (12×) *J. of Scientific Instruments* (12×) (1922–) *Brit. J. of Applied Phys.* (12×) (1950–) *Reports on Progress in Phys.* (Annually) (1934–)
PLASTICS Plastics Institute	Incorp. 1931	1937 via G.&Gs. 1950 own exam	F.P.I, A.P.I, Grad., Ordin. M., Junr. M., Hon. Life M., Stud.	4,389 31/7/63	*Trans. and Journ.* (24×) (1959–), (4×) (1939–59), (2×) (1932–39)
PRINTING Inst. of Printing	Incorp. 1961	1962	F.I.O.P., Hon.F.I.O.P., A.M.I.O.P., Grad.I.O.P., Affil., Stud.	869 Aug. 1963	*Printing Technology* (2×) (1957–) (Prev. by Assoc. of Printing Technologists) *Bulletin* (4×) (1963–)
PUBLIC CLEANSING Inst. of Public Cleansing	1898 Incorp. 1928	1910	F.Inst.P.C, M.Inst.P.C., A.M.Inst.P.C., Hon. F., Assoc., Stud.	c. 600 (1963)	*Public Cleansing* (12×) (1910–)
PURCHASING OFFICERS Purchasing Officers Association	1931 Incorp. 1935	1946	M.P.O.A., A.M.P.O.A., Grad., Reg. Stud.	5,219 1,406 Studs. 31/12/63	*The Purchasing Bull.* (52×) (1951–) *The Purchasing Journ.* (12×) (1944–)

237

FIELD AND TITLE OF ASSOCIATION	YEAR FOUNDED AND INCORPORATED	YEAR EXAM INTRODUCED	MEMBERSHIP GRADES	MEMBERSHIP SIZE	REGULAR JOURNAL
Inst. of Public Supplies	1949	1950	F.Inst.P.S., M.Inst.P.S.(Dip.), Assoc., Stud.	2,700 (1963)	*Supplies* (12×) (1949–)
QUARRYING Institute of Quarrying	1917 Incorp. 1958	1948	F.I.Q., M.I.Q., A.M.I.Q., Hon. M., Assoc., Grad., Stud.	1,702 31/7/63	*The Quarry Managers' J.* (12×) (1919–) *Cement, Lime & Gravel* (1926–)
RUBBER TECHNOLOGY Institution of the Rubber Industry	Incorp. 1921	1927	F.I.R.I., A.I.R.A., L.I.R.I., Stud., Manuf. M., Merchant M.	3,603 (1962)	*Proc.* (1954–) *Trans.* (12×) (1925–) *Progress of Rubber Tech.* (1×) (1938–)
SECRETARIES Chart. Institute of Secretaries	1891 R.C. 1902	1897	F.C.I.S., A.C.I.S., Lic., Stud.	28,695 Corp. 343 Uc. 20,716 Studs. Oct. 1963	*The Chartered Secretary* (11×) (1961–) (As 'The Secretary' (1892–1960))
Corporation of Secretaries	Incorp. 1923	1924	F.C.C.S., A.C.C.S., Lic., Stud.	10,010 Corp. 215 Lics. 13,464 Studs. 16/10/63	*Secretaries Chronicle* (12×) (1924–)
SEWAGE PURIFICATION Institute of Sewage Purification	1901 Incorp. 1932	1915	F.Inst.S.P., M.Inst.S.P., A.M.Inst.S.P., Hon. M., Assoc., Affil, Stud.	1,194 31/12/62	*Journ. and Proc.* (6×) (1902–)

A List of Qualifying Associations in England and Wales

	Founded / Incorporated	Examination	Designatory letters	Membership	Journal
SHIPBROKERS Institute of Chart. Shipbrokers	1911 R.C. 1920	1923	F.I.C.S., A.I.C.S., Hon. M., Studs.	3,311 31/5/63	*The Shipbroker* (2×) (1931–)
SHIPPING AND FORWARDING AGENTS Inst. of Shipping and Forwarding Agents	1944 Incorp.	1948	F.S.F., A.S.F., Stud.	c. 1,900 c. 650 Studs. (1963)	*Shipping and Forwarding* (4×) (1944–)
SOLICITORS Law Society	1825 R.C. 1831	Introd. by Courts 1835–37 Taken over by the Society 1877	Members, Assoc. M. (no designatory letters)	18,287 30/4/63	*Law Society Gazette* (12×) (1903–) (As 'Law Society's Registry' (1888–1903))
STATISTICIANS Inst. of Statisticians	Incorp. 1948	1949	F.I.S., A.I.S., Reg. Stat. Asst., Stud.	436 Corp. 214 Reg. Stat. Assts. 998 Studs. 31/12/62	*The Statistician* (12×) (1962–) (As 'Incorp. Statistician' (1949–61))
SURVEYORS Institute of Quantity Surveyors	1938 Incorp. 1941	1941	F.I.Q.S., A.I.Q.S., Hon. F.I.Q.S., Prob., Stud.	1,950 Corp. 2,350 Non. Aug. 1963	*The Quantity Surveyor* (24×) (1941–)
Royal Institution of Chart. Surveyors	1868 R.C. 1881	1881	F.R.I.C.S., A.R.I.C.S., Hon. M., Stud.	16,745 Corp. 9,507 Non. Aug. 1963	*The Chart. Surveyor* (12×) (1955–) (Prev. as 'J. of R.I.C.S.' (1946–55), 'J. of Chart. Surv. Inst.' (1921–46) *Professional Notes* (1886–1921) plus *Trans.* (1868–1955))

FIELD AND TITLE OF ASSOCIATION	YEAR FOUNDED AND INCORPORATED	YEAR EXAM INTRODUCED	MEMBERSHIP GRADES	MEMBERSHIP SIZE	REGULAR JOURNAL
TAXATION Institute of Taxation	1930 Incorp. 1934	1932	F.T.I.I., A.T.I.I., Subs.	3,550 +600 Subs. Aug. 1963	*Digest of Tax Cases* (2 ×) *Circular on Spec. Taxation Subjects* (12 ×)
TEXTILES Textile Institute	1910 R.C. 1925	1926	F.T.I., A.T.I., Lic.T.I., Comp., Ordin. M., Stud.	7,486 31/12/62	*Journ.* (1910–) (12 ×) since 1918. *Trans.* (pub. separately since 1949) *Review of Textile Progress* (1949–)
TOWN PLANNING Town Planning Institute	1914 R.C. 1959	1920	M.T.P.I., L.M.T.P.I. (Legal M.), A.M.T.P.I., L.A.M.T.P.I. (Legal A.M.), Hon. M. Hon. Corr. M., Hon. Assoc., Stud.	3,123 Corp. 1,404 Non. 31/12/63	*Journ.* (10 ×) (1914–)
TRANSPORT Institute of Transport	1919 R.C. 1926	1926	M.Inst.T., A.M.Inst.T., Assoc.Inst.T., Grad., Stud.	3,766 Corp. 7,116 Non. 12/3/62	*Journ.* (6 ×) (1920–)
TRAVEL AGENTS Inst. of Travel Agents	1956	1957	Hon.M.T.A.I., M.T.A.I., A.T.A.I., Grad. T.A.I., Stud., A.T.A.I.	1,500 Aug. 1963	*Journ.* (12 ×) (1960–)

240

VALUATION Rating and Valuation Association	1882 Incorp. 1927	1912	F.R.V.A., A.R.V.A., Lic., Stud.	2,995 Corp. 1,611 Subs. 30/11/63	*Rating & Valuation* (12×) (1953–) *J. of Incorp. Assoc. of Rating & Valuation Officers* (12×) (1950–53), (irregular) (1912–1950)
Valuers Institution	Incorp. 1929	1940	F.V.I., A.V.I., Lic., Stud.	4,740 1/12/63	*The Valuer* (6×) (1953–) (Prev. the journ. of the 'Valuers' Assoc.') (The 'Valuers' Instns. journ. was 'Valtion' (1928– 36), then as 'J.' (1936– 53). The 'Nat. Assoc. of Estate Agents' also had a 'Journ.' (1924–28)
VETERINARY SURGEONS Royal College of Veterinary Surgeons	R.C. 1844	1844	F.R.C.V.S., M.R.C.V.S.	7,112 on register 16/12/63	None
WEIGHTS AND MEASURES Inst. of Weights and Measures Administration	1892 Incorp. 1893	1950 Weights and Measures Testamur 1957 Petroleum Testamur	F.I.W.M.A., M.I.W.M.A., A.I.W.M.A.	c. 1,000 (1963)	*The Monthly Review* (12×) (1892–)
WELDING Institute of Welding	Incorp. 1923	1947	Hon. F.Inst.W., Hon. M.Inst.W., F.Inst.W., M.Inst.W., A.M.Inst.W., C.Inst.W. Assoc., Grad., Stud.	2,815 Corp. 2,316 Non. 31/3/63	*British Welding Journ.* (12×) (1954–) (Replaced 'Trans. of Inst. of Welding' (1938–54) and 'Welding Research')

241

FIELD AND TITLE OF ASSOCIATION	YEAR FOUNDED AND INCORPORATED	YEAR EXAM INTRODUCED	MEMBERSHIP GRADES	MEMBERSHIP SIZE	REGULAR JOURNAL
WELFARE OFFICERS Inst. of Welfare Officers	1945 Reg. in 1945 under the Friendly Societies Act 1896	1956	F.W.I., M.W.I., A.M.W.I., Grad.W.I., Stud.	not available	*Welfare Officer* (4×) (1951–) *Bull.* (12×) (1946–)
WORK STUDY Institute of Work Study	1944 Incorp. 1956	1943	F.Inst.W.S., M.Inst.W.S., A.M.Inst.W.S, Grad., Affil., Stud.	2,758 Corp. 2,349 Non. Aug. 1963	*Work Study & Management* (12×)

(B) ASSOCIATIONS WITHOUT EXAMINATION—BUT USING EVIDENCE OF EXTERNAL EXAMINATIONS

FIELD AND TITLE OF ASSOCIATION	YEAR FOUNDED AND INCORPORATED	YEAR EXAM INTRODUCED	MEMBERSHIP GRADES	MEMBERSHIP SIZE	REGULAR JOURNAL
ARBITRATION Institute of Arbitrators	1915 Incorp. 1925	Uses Corp. Membership of Prof. Assocs. Also own exam.	F.I.Arb., A.I.Arb.,	c. 1,100 Dec. 1963	*Arbitration* (4×) (1955–) (As 'J. of Inst.' (1915–55))
BIOLOGY Institute of Biology*	Incorp. 1950	Uses Hons. Deg. or equivalent	F.I.Biol., M.I.Biol., Assoc., Stud., Subs.	3,233 31/12/63	*Journ.* (4×) (1953–)

* Examinations will be introduced in 1965.

DAIRY TECHNOLOGY

DIETITIANS

ENGINEERS

Association	Founded / Incorp.	Examination	Grades	Membership	Journal
Society of Dairy Technology	1943	Unspecified	Ordin. M., Hon. M., Assoc. M., Stud.	2,500 Aug. 1963	*Journ.* (4×) (1947–)
British Dietetic Association	1936 Incorp. 1947	Uses Dip. in Dietetics at recog. Instn.	Full M., Stud. Assoc. M., Affil. M., Hon. M.	846 Full Ms. 60 Studs. 54 Others 1/3/63	*Nutrition* (4×) (1947–)
Instn. of Engineers-in-Charge	1895 Incorp. 1923	Unspecified	M.I.E.C., A.M.I.E.C., J.M.I.E.C., A.I.E.C., C.I.E.C., Hon. M.I.E.C.	c. 700 (1963)	*Trans.* (12×) (1895–)
Institute of Engineering Designers	1945	Uses O.N.C. and H.N.C.	F.I.E.D., M.I.E.D., A.M.I.E.D., Grad., Comp., Stud.	2,061 Corp. 1,648 Non. 31/6/63	*The Engineering Designer* (12×) (1947–)
Institution of Locomotive Engineers	1911 Incorp. 1915	Uses degree or Grad. Exam. of I.E.E., I.C.E., I.Mech.E.	Hon. M.I.Loco.E., M.I.Loco.E., A.M.I.Loco.E., Assoc., Grad., Student	2,270 Dec. 1963	*Journ.* (6×) (1911–)
Institution of Plant Engineers	Incorp. 1946	Uses Full Tech. Cert. C.&Gs.	F.I.Plant.E., M.I.Plant.E., A.M.I.Plant.E., Hon. M., Grad., Assoc., Stud.	4,353 31/12/62	*Journ.* (6×) (1947)
Institute of Road Transport Engineers	Incorp. 1945	Uses C.&Gs., O.N.C., etc.	M.I.R.T.E., A.M.I.R.T.E., A.I.R.T.E., Hon. M., Affil., Grad., Stud.	2,574 30/6/63	*Journ. & Proc.* (4×) (1946–)

243

FIELD AND TITLE OF ASSOCIATION	YEAR FOUNDED AND INCORPORATED	YEAR EXAM INTRODUCED	MEMBERSHIP GRADES	MEMBERSHIP SIZE	REGULAR JOURNAL
Institution of Water Engineers	1896 Incorp. 1911	Uses Corp. Membership of I.E.E., I.C.E., I.Mech.E. and I.C.E. in hydraulics or equiv.	M.I.W.E., A.M.I.W.E., Prof. Assoc., P.A.I.W.E., A.I.W.E., Stud.	2,212 Aug. 1963	*Journ.* (7×) (1947–) *Trans.* (?–1946) *Water & Water Eng.* (1899–1947)
FOUNDRY MEN Institute of British Foundrymen	1904 R.C. 1921	Uses degree or H.N.C.	Hon. M., F.I.B.F., M.I.B.F., A.M.I.B.F., Assoc., Stud.	6,713 Aug. 1963	*The British Foundryman* (12×) (1957–) (Incorp. 'Proc.' (1946-57)) *Foundry Trade Journ.* (6×) (1902–)
FUEL Institute of Fuel	1927 R.C. 1946	Uses Univ. degree A.R.I.C., H.N.D., H.N.C.	Hon. M.Inst.F., F.Inst.F., M.Inst.F., A.M.Inst.F., Assoc., Collective M., Rep. Nomin. M., Stud.	5,892 31/12/62	*Journ.* (12×) (1927–) *Fuel Abstracts & Current Titles* (12×) (1960–)
Institute of Petroleum	1913 Incorp. 1914	Degree, etc., plus experience	Hon. M.Inst.Pet., M.Inst.Pet., A.M.Inst.Pet., Hon. F.Inst.Pet., F.Inst.Pet., Stud.Inst.Pet.	c. 5,000 (1963)	*Journ.* (12×) (1938–) *Inst. of Pet. Review* (12×) (1947–) (*Journ.*—prev. as 'J. of Inst. of Pet. Tech.' (1914–37))
GLASS TECHNOLOGY Society of Glass Technology	1916	Uses degree, for F.S.G.T. under certain rules	F.S.G.T., Ordin.M., Assoc. M., Hon. F., Collective M.	1,430 31/12/63	*Journ.* (1917–1959) *Glass Technology* (6×) (1960–) *Phys. & Chem. of Glasses* (6×) (1960–)

MANAGEMENT Inst. of Printing Management	1950 Incorp. 1961	Uses B.I.M. exams., H.N.C. in Bus. Studies, Full Tech. Cert. C.&Gs. with Advanced Admin.	F.I.Ptg.M., M.I.Ptg.M., A.M.I.Ptg.M., Grad., Hon. F., Stud.	c. 650 (1963)	*Managing Printer* (12×) (via Printers' Managers & Overseas Assoc.)
MEDICINE College of General Practitioners	1952 Incorp. 1961	Medical degree or equiv.	M., Assoc. (no designatory letters)	6,785 Oct. 1963	*The Practitioner* (12×) (1952–) *Journ.* (4×)
METALLURGY Institute of Metals	1908 Incorp. 1910	Unspecified	Fellow Hon. M., Ordin. M., Junr. M., Stud.	6,250 Aug. 1963	*Journ.* (12×) (1909–) *Bull.* (1951–) *Monographs & Reports Series* (1936–)
NAVAL ARCHITECTS Royal Instn. of Naval Architects	1860 R.C. 1910	Uses degree, R.N. Cert. for Eng. Officers H.N.C. plus	M.R.I.N.A., A.M.R.I.N.A., Hon. M., Assoc., Stud.	3,571 Corp. 1,204 Non. Aug. 1963	*Trans.* (4×) (1860–)
REFRIGERATION Institute of Refrigeration	1899	Uses Full Tech. Cert. C.&Gs. (73) since 1944	M.Inst.R., A.M.Inst.R., Comp., Assoc., Grad., Stud.	1,070 July 1963	*Proc.* (Annually) (1900–)
SURGICAL TECHNICIANS Inst. of Brit. Surgical Technicians	1936	Uses Full Tech. Cert C.&Gs.	F.I.B.S.T., L.I.B.S.T., Assoc. M., Stud. Assoc.	1,100 Aug. 1963	*Journ.* (2×) (1960–) *Trans.* (4×) (1957–)

APPENDIX II

Chronological List of Existing Qualifying and Non-Qualifying Associations in England and Wales

PART A—QUALIFYING ASSOCIATIONS AND PSEUDO-QUALIFYING ASSOCIATIONS

NOTE: No significance, in terms of professional status, must be attached to the inclusion, or exclusion, of any association in this list. The standards and prestige of these associations vary widely. All the following are examining bodies and/or they give rise to designatory letters. Designatory letters are not associated with membership of the Inns of Court, or the Law Society. Non-examining organizations are marked (*). Many associations are included in order to indicate the growth of organization, and direction of expansion.

If some estimate of importance has to be made, it would probably be true to say that: 10–15% are very important (undisputed status); 25–30% important in the occupation (disputed inter-professional status); 10% useful within their occupations (not generally recognized); 50% vary from struggling unrecognized organizations down to useless associations.

Inns of Court (14th–15th centuries)
(probably appeared during the 14th century)—earliest recorded dates given are:

1391 Gray's Inn

1404 Middle Temple

1422 Lincoln's Inn

1440 Inner Temple

1518 Royal College of Physicians of London

1617 Society of Apothecaries

1629 Worshipful Company of Spectacle Makers

1800 Royal College of Surgeons of England
   (As 'Guild of Surgeons' 14th century, as 'Company of Barber-Surgeons' 1540, as 'Company of Surgeons 1745, as 'R.C.S. of London 1800, as 'R.C.S. of England' 1843.)

1818 Institution of Civil Engineers

1825 Law Society
   (Connected with earlier 'Society of Gentlemen Practisers in Courts of Law and Equity', founded in 1739, and its successor 'The Metropolitan Law Association' (1819). Founded as 'The Society of Attorneys, Solicitors, Proctors and others not being Barristers practising in the Courts of Law and Equity of the United Kingdom'. Renamed 'The Law Society' in the Supplemental Charter of 1903.)

1834 Royal Institute of British Architects
   (As 'Institute of British Architects', incorporating the 'Architectural Society' (1831) in 1842, and the 'Society of Architects' (1884) in 1925. Title 'Royal' granted in 1887.)

1834 Institute of Builders
   (As 'The Builders' Society', incorporated in 1884 as the 'Institute of Builders'.)

1841 Pharmaceutical Society of Great Britain
1844 Royal College of Veterinary Surgeons
1847 Institution of Mechanical Engineers
   (Incorporating the 'Institution of Automobile Engineers' (1906) in 1945.)

1847 Architectural Association
   (From the 'Association of Architectural Draughtsmen' formed in 1842.)

1848 Institute of Actuaries

1854 Society of Engineers
   (Incorporating the 'Civil and Mechanical Engineers' Society' (1859) in 1910.)

1860 Royal Institution of Naval Architects*
   (Title 'Royal' granted 1959.)

1863 Institution of Gas Engineers
   (The 'British Association of Gas Managers' (1863) was renamed 'The Gas Institute' in 1881 and amalgamated with the 'Incorporated Institution of Gas Engineers' (1890) in 1902 to form the present Institution.)

1866 Royal Aeronautical Society
   (Incorporating the 'Institution of Aeronautical Engineers' (1919) in 1927, and the 'Helicopter Association of G.B.' (1945) in 1960.)

1868 Royal Institution of Chartered Surveyors
(As 'Institute of Surveyors', renamed the 'The Surveyors' Institution', renamed the 'Royal Institution of Chartered Surveyors' in 1930. Incorporating the 'Irish Land Agents' Association' in 1905, the 'Quantity Surveyors' Association' (1904) in 1922, the 'Scottish Estate Factors' Society' in 1937, the 'Faculty of Surveyors of Scotland' in 1937, the 'Irish Quantity Surveyors' Association' in 1938, the 'Institute of Mining Surveyors' in 1953.)

1871 Institution of Electrical Engineers
(As the 'Society of Telegraph Engineers', renamed the 'Society of Telegraph Engineers and Electricians' in 1880, renamed as the 'I.E.E.' in 1888.)

1873 Institution of Municipal Engineers
(As the 'Association of Municipal & Sanitary Engineers and Surveyors', as 'Incorporated Association of Municipal & County Engineers' in 1910, then as 'Institution of Municipal & County Engineers'.)

1877 Royal Institute of Chemistry
(As the 'Institute of Chemistry'—title 'Royal' granted in 1944.)

1877 Library Association

1879 Institute of Bankers

1880 Institute of Chartered Accountants of England and Wales
(Formed on grant of Royal Charter to: 'Institute of Accountants, London' (1870), 'Society of Accountants, Liverpool' (1870), 'Society of Accountants, Manchester' (1871), Society of Accountants in England' (1872), Society of Accountants, Sheffield' (1877), and incorporating the 'Society of Incorporated Accountants and Auditors' (1885) in 1957.)

1882 Rating and Valuation Association
(The 'Association of Rate Collectors and Assistant Overseers' was formed in 1882. In 1927, the Association was joined by other organizations of rating officers, to form the 'Incorporated Association of Rating and Valuation Officers'. Renamed in 1953.)

1882 Institute of Clerks-of-Works of Great Britain

1882 Chartered Institute of Patent Agents

1885 Institute of Municipal Treasurers and Accountants
(As the 'Corporate Treasurers' and Accountants' Institute', incorporated with present title in 1901.)

1886 Chartered Auctioneers' and Estate Agents' Institute
(As the 'Institute of Auctioneers and Surveyors of the U.K.' in 1889, amalgamated with the 'Estate Agents' Institute' in 1912 (previously the 'Estate Agents' Institute' had been founded as the 'Institute of Estate and House Agents', renamed in 1904.)

1886 Institute of Brewing
(As the 'Laboratory Club', renamed the 'Institute of Brewing' in 1890, amalgamated with a Yorkshire Institute (1893) in 1900. In

1903, the 'North of England Institute of Technical Brewing' (1891) and 'Midland Counties Institute of Brewing' (1894) also amalgamated, the present Institute being constituted in 1904.)

1889   Institute of Marine Engineers

1889   Institution of Mining Engineers

(Formed as Federation of: 'North of England Institute of Mining and Mechanical Engineers' (1852), 'Mining Institute of Scotland' (1878), 'Manchester Geological and Mining Society' (1838), 'Midland Institute of Mining Engineers' (1857), 'Midland Counties Institution of Engineers' (1871), 'North Staffordshire Institute of Mining Engineers' (1872), 'South Staffordshire & Warwickshire Institute of Mining Engineers' (1857). Joined by 'Southern Counties Institute of Mining Engineers' (1958) in 1958.)

1891   Chartered Institute of Secretaries

(As the 'Institute of Secretaries', absorbed 'Incorporated Secretaries Association' (1907) in 1937.)

1892   Institution of Mining and Metallurgy

1892   Institute of Weights and Measures Administration

(As the 'Incorporated Society of Inspectors of Weights and Measures'.)

1894   Chartered Society of Physiotherapy

(As the 'Society of Trained Masseuses', as 'Incorporated Society of Trained Masseuses' in 1900, amalgamated with the 'Institute of Massage & Remedial Gymnasts' in 1919 to form the 'Chartered Society of Massage and Medical Gymnasts', renamed the 'Chartered Society of Physiotherapy' in 1942.)

1895   British Optical Association

(Amalgamated with 'National Association of Opticians', in 1956, amalgamated with the 'Institute of Optical Science' (1910) in 1963.)

1895   Institution of Public Health Engineers

(As 'Institute of Sanitary Engineers', renamed in 1955.)

1895   Institution of Engineers-in-Charge

(As 'Association of Parochial Engineers', renamed in 1923.)

1896   Institution of Water Engineers

(As 'British Association of Waterworks Engineers', renamed in 1911.)

1897   Institution of Heating and Ventilating Engineers

1897   Chartered Insurance Institute

(Formed from the 'Federation of Insurance Institutes of Great Britain & Ireland' founded by ten local Insurance Institutes—modified and renamed in 1908. Absorbed the 'Faculty of Insurance' (1912) in 1934.)

1898   Institute of Public Cleansing

(As the 'Association of Cleansing Superintendents', renamed 1928.)

1899   Incorporated Institute of British Decorators and Interior Designers

(As the 'Institute of British Decorators', renamed about 1946.)

1899   Institute of Refrigeration
      (As 'The Cold Storage and Ice Association', name changed in 1922, 1927—present name 1944.)

1901   Institute of British Photographers
      (As the 'Professional Photographers' Association', renamed in 1938.)

1901   Institute of Sewage Purification
      (As the 'Association of Managers of Sewage Disposal Works', renamed in 1932.)

1902   Chartered Land Agents' Society
      (As the 'Landed Estate Agents' Society'—title quickly modified to 'Land Agents Society'.)

1902   Institute of Hospital Administrators
      (As the 'Hospital Officers' Association', incorporated in 1910 as the 'Incorporated Association of Hospital Officers', fused in 1942 with the 'Association of Clerks and Stewards of Mental Hospitals' (1904) to form the 'Incorporated Association of Hospital Administrators', renamed in 1945.)

1903   Institute of Almoners
      (As the 'Hospital Almoners' Association', joined by the 'Hospital Almoner's Council' (1907) and incorporated as the 'Institute of Hospital Almoners', renamed in 1945.)

1904   Institute of British Foundrymen
      (As the 'British Foundrymen's Association', renamed in 1923.)

1906   Institute of Commerce

1906   Corporation of Insurance Brokers

1908   Institution of Structural Engineers
      (As 'The Concrete Institute', renamed in 1922.)

1909   Institute of Certified Grocers

1910   Textile Institute

1910   Institute of Linguists

1911   Institute of Marketing and Sales Management
      (As 'Sales Managers Association' then as 'Incorporated Sales Managers' Association', renamed in 1960.)

1911   Institution of Locomotive Engineers*
      (As the 'Junior Institution of Locomotive Engineers', soon after renamed.)

1911   Institute of Chartered Shipbrokers

1912   Institute of Railway Signal Engineers

1912   Institute of Medical Laboratory Technology
      (As the 'Pathological and Bacteriological Laboratory Assistants' Association', renamed on incorporation in 1942.)

1913   Institute of Personnel Management
      (As the 'Welfare Workers' Association', renamed 'Welfare Workers' Institute' in 1919, renamed 'Institute of Industrial Welfare Workers' in 1924, renamed 'Institute of Labour Management' in 1931, present name in 1946.)

1914   Town Planning Institute

1914   Association of Supervising Electrical Engineers*

1915   Institute of Office Management
       (As 'Office Machine Users' Association', merged with 'Office Management Association' (1932) in 1935, renamed in 1960.)

1915   Institute of Arbitrators

1916   Institute of Book-keepers

1917   Institute of Quarrying
       (As 'The Quarry Managers' Association', renamed in 1919.)

1917   Institute of Practitioners in Advertising
       (As the 'Association of British Advertising Agents', renamed in 1927 'Institute of Incorporated Practitioners in Advertising', present name in 1954.)

1918   Institution of Fire Engineers

1918   Institute of Physics and the Physical Society
       (As the 'Institute of Physics', amalgamated with the 'Physical Society' (1874) in 1960.)

1919   Institute of Transport

1919   Institute of Cost and Works Accountants

1919   Institute of Engineering Inspection
       (Previously as 'Technical Inspection Association', renamed 1922 on incorporation.)

1920   Society of Radiographers

1920   Institute of the Motor Industry

1921   Institution of the Rubber Industry
       (As the 'Rubber Club of Great Britain', renamed in 1923.)

1921   Institution of Production Engineers

1922   Corporation of Certified Secretaries

1922   Institution of Chemical Engineers

1923   British Association of Accountants and Auditors
       (As 'British Association of Accountants', incorporating in 1935 'The Professional Accountants Alliance' (1927), amalgamated with the 'Association of Practising and Commercial Accountants' in 1961.)

1923   Institute of Welding
       (As the 'Institute of Welding Engineers', renamed in 1935.)

1924   Incorporated Society of Auctioneers and Landed Property Agents

1925   Incorporated Association of Architects and Surveyors

1925   Institution of Electronic and Radio Engineers
       (As the 'Institute of Wireless Technology', renamed 'British Institution of Radio Engineers' in 1941, present title in 1964.)

1926   Advertising Association

1926   Faculty of Architects and Surveyors
       (Incorporating the 'Faculty of Surveyors', and in 1956 the 'Architectural and Building Surveyors' Society'.)

1927   British Boot and Shoe Institution
       (As 'The National Institution of the Boot & Shoe Industry', renamed in 1951.)

1927 Institute of Fuel*
    (Formed from a merger of the 'Institution of Fuel Economy Engineers' and 'Institution of Fuel Technologists' (1925).)

1928 Valuers Institution
    (Amalgamted in 1949 with the 'National Association of Estate Agents, Auctioneers, House Agents, Rating Surveyors and Valuers' (1924), fused with the 'Valuers' Association' (1937) in 1953, and with the 'Northern Ireland Auctioneers' Association' in 1959.)

1928 Faculty of Auditors

1928 Institute of Company Accountants

1929 Royal College of Obstetricians and Gynaecologists
    (As the 'British College of Obstetricians and Gynaecologists', title 'Royal' granted in 1938.)

1929 Institute of Landscape Architects

1930 Institute of Taxation

1930 Institute of Electronics

1930 Institute of Highway Engineers

1931 Plastics Institute
    (As the 'Institute of the Plastics Industry', renamed in 1947.)

1931 Purchasing Officers' Association
    (As 'British Industrial Purchasing Officers' Association', renamed 1935.)

1931 Institution of Works Managers
    (As the 'Works Managers' Association', incorporating the 'Institution of Factory Managers'.)

1931 Institute of Housing

1932 Association of International Accountants

1933 Institute of Registered Architects*

1934 Building Societies Institute

1934 Faculty of Radiologists

1934 Institute of British Surgical Technicians

1936 British Dietetic Association*

1936 Association of Occupational Therapists

1937 Institute of Export

1937 Incorporated Association of Cost and Works Accountants
    ('The Cost Accountants' Association'.)

1938 Institute of Works and Highways Superintendents

1938 Institution of Agricultural Engineers
    (As 'Institution of British Agricultural Engineers', renamed 1959.)

1938 Institutional Management Association

1939 Faculty of Radiographers
    (From the 'British Association of Radiologists' (1934), and the 'Society of Radiotherapists' (1935).)

1939 Institute of Automobile Assessors*

1939 Association of Certified and Corporate Accountants
    (Formed from the 'London Association of Accountants' (1904) which included the 'Central Association of Accountants' (1905))

and the 'Corporation of Accountants' (1891), amalgamated with
the 'Institution of Certified Public Accountants' (1903) in 1941.)

1939   Institute of Credit Management
(As 'Institute of Creditmen', renamed 1947.)

1941   Chartered Institute of Loss Adjusters
(As 'Association of Fire Loss Adjusters', renamed 1962.)

1942   Society of Commercial Accountants
(As the 'Northern-Southern Union of Commercial Accountants'.)

1943   Society of Dairy Technology*

1944   Institute of Shipping and Forwarding Agents
(Formed from local associations: London (1897), Liverpool (1901),
Manchester (1926), Southampton (1938), Glasgow (1941),
Bristol (1942), the 'British Association of Shipping and Forwarding
Agents' (1928) and the 'U.K.-Canada Westbound Forwarding
Agents'.)

1944   Institute of Traffic Administration*

1944   Institute of Work Study
(As the 'Motion Study Society of G.B.', now incorporating the
'Society of Industrial Engineers' (a previous fusion of the 'Institute
of Economic Engineering' (1941) and the 'Production Control
Research Group'), as 'Work Study Society', renamed in 1961.)

1945   Incorporated Institute of Road Transport Engineers*
1945   Institution of Metallurgists
1945   Institute of Welfare Officers
1945   Society of Remedial Gymnasts
1945   Institute of Engineering Designers*
1945   Faculty of Ophthalmologists
1945   Society of Chiropodists
(In 1945, the present Society was incorporated as an amalgamation of: the 'Incorporated Society of Chiropodists' (1912), the
'Northern Chiropodists' Association' (1925), the 'Chelsea Chiropodists' Association' (1926), the 'British Association of Chiropodists' (1931), and the 'Chiropody Practitioners' (1942).)

1946   Institution of Plant Engineers*
(As the 'Incorporated Plant Engineers', renamed in 1959.)

1946   Institute of Meat
1946   Faculty of Builders*
1947   Market Research Society
(As 'Business Research Association of G.B.'.)

1948   British Institute of Management
(Incorporating the 'Institute of Industrial Administration' (1919)
in 1951.)

1948   Clothing Institute
1948   Institute of Public Relations
1948   Institute of Packaging
1948   Society of Cardiological Technicians of G.B.*

1949   Institute of Statisticians
       (As 'Association of Incorporated Statisticians', renamed 1961.)
1949   Institute of Public Supplies
1949   Hotel & Catering Institute

1950   Institute of Biology*
1950   Institute of Printing Management*
1952   Building Surveyors Institute*
1952   Institute of Building Estimators*
1953   Institute of Municipal Building Management*
1955   Institute of Ceramics
1956   Institute of Travel Agents
1958   Institution of Nuclear Engineers*

1961   Institute of Printing
       (Merged with 'Association of Printing Technologists' (1956) in
       1962.)
1962   Institute of Management Consultants*
1962   Institute of Legal Executives
       (Reconstituted from 'Solicitors' Managing Clerks' Association')

PART B—NON-QUALIFYING ASSOCIATIONS
IN EXISTENCE TODAY

NOTE: This list is not comprehensive. Choice of associations is determined by available information. Study Associations marked thus (*).

1660   Royal Society

1717   Society of Antiquaries*
       (Reconstituted from the Society founded in 1707.)

1754   Royal Society of Arts*
       (As 'Society for the Encouragement of Arts Manufacturers and
       Commerce', as R.S.A. 1908, includes 'Faculty of Royal Designers
       for Industry' (1936).)

1768   Royal Academy

1773   Medical Society of London*

1788   Linnean Society of London*

1804   Royal Society of Painters in Water Colours
1804   Royal Horticultural Society*
       (As 'Horticultural Society'.)

1807   Geological Society*

1819   Hunterian Society*

1820   Royal Astronomical Society*
      (As 'Astronomical Society'.)
1823   Royal Asiatic Society*
      (As 'Asiatic Society'.)
1823   Royal Society of British Artists
1823   Royal Society of Literature*
1826   Zoological Society*

1830   Royal Geographical Society
      (As the 'Geographical Society', incorporating in 1831 the 'African
      Association' (1788) and 'Palestine Association' (1805) in 1834.)
1831   Royal Institute of Painters in Water Colours
1831   Harveian Society of London*
1832   British Medical Association
      (As the 'Provincial Medical & Surgical Association', renamed in
      1856.)
1833   Royal Entomological Society*
      (As the 'Entomological Society'.)
1834   Royal Statistical Society*
1836   Botanical Society of the British Isles*
1836   Royal Numismatic Society*
1839   Royal Botanic Society of London*
1839   Royal Microscopical Society*
1839   Justices' Clerks Society

1841   Chemical Society*
1841   Royal Medico-Psychological Association*
1842   Philological Society*
1843   Royal Anthropological Institute*
      (As the 'Ethnological Society', renamed 'R.A.I.' in 1871 on
      amalgamation with 'Anthropological Society' (1863).)
1843   Royal Archaeological Institute of Great Britain & Ireland*
1843   British Archaeological Association*
1846   Hakluyt Society*
1847   Palaeontographical Society*

1850   Royal Meteorological Society*
      (As the 'British Meteorological Society'.)
1853   Society of Medical Officers of Health
1854   Royal Photographic Society*
1855   Geologists' Association*
1858   British Ornithologists' Union*

1865   Mathematical Society, London*

1868   Royal Historical Society*
1869   Iron and Steel Institute*
1869   Harleian Society*

1870   National Union of Teachers
       (As 'National Union of Elementary Teachers', renamed 'N.U.T.' in 1889.)
1871   Mathematical Association*
1874   Society of Analytical Chemists*
       (As 'Society of Public Analysts and other Analytical Chemists'.)
1874   Association of Headmistresses
1876   Mineralogical Society*
1876   Royal Society of Health*
1876   Physiological Society*
1877   Agricultural Engineers' Association

1880   British Dental Association
1880   Royal Society of Painters, Etchers and Engravers
1881   Royal College of Midwives
1881   National Veterinary Medical Association
       (As 'National Veterinary Association', reconstituted in 1912 and 1919.)
1881   Society of Chemical Industry*
1882   Society for Psychical Research*
1883   Royal Institute of Oil Painters
1883   Association of Public Health Inspectors
1884   County Surveyors' Society
1884   Society of Dyers and Colourists
1884   Ray Society*
1884   Association of Assistant Mistresses in Secondary Schools
1887   Royal British Nurses' Association
1888   National Association of Colliery Managers
1889   Institute of Journalists
       (From 'National Association of Journalists' (1883).)

1890   Royal Economic Society*
1890   Association of Headmasters
1890   Royal Society of Miniature Painters, Sculptors and Gravers
1891   Association of Assistant Masters in Secondary Schools
1891   Royal Society of Portrait Painters
1892   Bibliographical Society*
1893   Geographical Association*
1895   Association of Headmistresses
1896   British Mycological Society*
1898   Association of Hospital and Welfare Administration
       (As 'National Association of Administrators of Local Government Establishments'.)

1901 British Academy
1902 British Psychological Society*
1903 Faraday Society*
1903 Classical Association*
1903 Institute of Directors
1903 Society of County Treasurers
    (As 'County Accountants' Association'.)
1904 Association of Applied Biologists
1906 English Association*
1906 Historical Association*
1907 Eugenics Society*
1907 British Association of Chemists
1907 Royal Society of Medicine*
    (Formed as a result of a Supplemental Royal Charter obtained by
    the 'Royal Medical and Chirurgical Society of London' (1805)
    amalgamating with fourteen other medical societies.)
1908 Institute of Metals*
1909 Illuminating Engineering Society*

1911 Biochemical Society*
1912 British Engineers' Association
1913 British Ecological Society*
1913 Incorporated Association of Consulting Engineers
1913 Institute of Petroleum*
    (As the 'Institution of Petroleum Technologists', renamed in 1938.)
1916 Royal College of Nursing
1916 Society of Glass Technology
1917 British Insurance Association
1918 Oil and Colour Chemists' Association
1919 Association of Officers of Executive Councils and Pricing Committees
    (As 'Association of Insurance Committee Officers'.)
1919 Association of Hospital Matrons

1920 Society of Graphic Artists
1920 Newcomen Society*
1920 Magistrates Association
1920 Society of Consulting Marine Engineers and Ship Surveyors
1921 British Society of Master Glass Painters
1921 National Pharmaceutical Union
1922 Association of Public Lighting Engineers
1925 Association of Dispensing Opticians
1928 Society of Town Clerks

1930 Society of Industrial Artists
1932 Advertising Managers' Association
1933 British Interplanetary Society*
1938 Engineers' Guild

1947   Society of Cosmetic Chemists

1951   British Sociological Association*
1952   College of General Practitioners
1959   British Academy of Forensic Science*

1962   British Nuclear Energy Society*

NOTES

CHAPTER ONE

[1] M. L. Cogan, 'Towards a Definition of a Profession', *Harvard Educational Review*, 1953, XXIII, 33–50 (p. 47).

[2] M. L. Cogan, 'The Problem of Defining a Profession', *The Annals* (*The Annals of the American Academy of Political and Social Science*), 1955, CCXCVII, 105–11 (pp. 106–9).

[3] For example, see:
H. W. Jessup, 'The Ethics of the Legal Profession', *The Annals*, 1922, CI, 16–29.
H. S. Drinker, *Legal Ethics*, New York, 1953.

[4] For example, see:
J. L. Carey, *Professional Ethics of Certified Public Accountants*, New York, 1956, Chapter 2.
K. L. Milne, *The Accountant in Public Practice*, London, 1959, Chapter 1.
Sir Harold Howitt, 'The Profession of Accountancy', *The Accountant*, 1950, CXXII, 537–40.
Sir Harold Howitt, 'Training for the Professions: Accountancy', *Journal of the Royal Society of Arts*, 1951, XCIX, 741–8 (p. 743).

[5] A. M. Carr-Saunders and P. A. Wilson, *The Professions*, Oxford, 1933 (particularly pp. 284–7).
Examples of heavy influence:
R. Lewis and A. Maude, *Professional People*, London, 1952.
Milne, op. cit.
B. Kaye, *The Development of the Architectural Profession in Britain*, London, 1960.

[6] Special Supplement on Professional Associations (by S. and B. Webb), *The New Statesman* (21, 28 April) 1917, IX, 211, 212 (pp. 4–5).

[7] R. H. Tawney, *The Acquisitive Society*, London, 1922, pp. 106–11.
Examples of heavy influence:
R. H. Kohn, 'The Significance of the Professional Ideal: Professional Ethics', *The Annals*, 1922, CI, 1–4 (p. 1).
A. Crew, *The Profession of a Secretary*, Cambridge, 1942, pp. 1–5.

[8] H. Spencer, *The Principles of Sociology*, London, 1896, Vol. III, Part VII, pp. 179–80, 181–4.

[9] Emile Durkheim, *On the Division of Labour in Society* (English Translation), London, 1949.

Emile Durkheim, *Professional Ethics and Civic Morals* (English Translation), London, 1957, pp. 14–15, 23–24.

(For a criticism of Durkheim's view, see:

Leopold von Wiese, *Systematic Sociology* (Translated and Edited by H. Becker), New York, 1932, pp. 407–12).

[10] Sources of definitions used in Table 1.1:

in works already cited above: Drinker, Milne, Crew, Howitt, Tawney, Webbs, Cogan, Kaye, Carr-Saunders and Wilson, Lewis and Maude;

in other works:

T. Parsons, The Professions and Social Structure, *Essays in Sociological Theory*, Glencoe, Ill., Rev. Ed. 1954.

T. H. Marshall, 'The Recent History of Professionalism in Relation to Social Structure and Social Policy, *The Canadian Journal of Economics and Political Science*, 1939, V (3) (reprinted in *Citizenship and Social Class*, Cambridge, 1950, pp. 128–55).

Lord Simon (*The Accountant*, 5 May 1951), quoted by G. F. Saunders, 'The Accountant in General Practice', paper to *6th International Congress on Accountancy*, 1952.

A. G. Christie, 'A Proposed Code of Ethics for All Engineers', *The Annals*, 1922, CI, 97.

A. Flexner, 'Is Social Work a Profession?', *School and Society*, (26 January) 1915, I, 904.

A. N. Whitehead, *Adventures of Ideas* (Penguin Edition), London, 1948, pp. 73–4.

W. E. Wickenden, quoted in full by Lewis and Maude (op. cit. pp. 55–6).

H. R. Bowen, 'Business Management: A Profession?', *The Annals*, 1955, CCXCVII, 105–11.

E. Greenwood, 'Attributes of a Profession', *Social Work*, 1957, II, 45–55.

E. A. Ross, *Principles of Sociology*, New York, (3rd Ed.) 1938, Chapter XLVII (particularly pp. 570–3).

R. D. Leigh, *The Public Library in the U.S.*, New York, 1950, pp. 86–88. Some definitions seem a little fatuous, for example:

A profession is '. . . a limited and clearly marked group of men who are trained by education and experience to perform certain functions better than their fellow men'. (C. E. Taeusch, *Professional and Business Ethics*, New York, 1926, p. 5.)

Some definitions are overwhelming. For example:

E. W. Roddenberry, 'Achieving Professionalism', *Journal of Criminal Law, Criminology and Police Science*, 1953, XLIV (1), 109–15.

[11] For example, see *Report of the Royal Commission on Doctors' and Dentists' Remuneration*, Part I, Cmnd. 939, February 1960. Table 14 (p. 48) indicates the proportion of principals in private practice: Accountants 33%, Actuaries 4%, Architects 25%, Solicitors (England and Wales) 62%, Surveyors 27%, Engineers 2%—for Scientists the figure is probably less than 2%.

[12] No Q.C. (Queen's Counsel) should accept a fee of less than £3 5s 6d for any work, no junior should accept less than £2 4s 6d. W. W. Boulton, *A Guide to Conduct and Etiquette at the Bar of England and Wales*, London, 1957, pp. 39–46.

[13] An early example is the classification offered by the Webbs: (*a*) learned professions (law, medicine, teaching), (*b*) technicians of industry (engineers, architects, surveyors, scientists), (*c*) technicians of the office (accountant, actuary, secretary), (*d*) manipulators of men (managers, superintendents, foremen), (*e*) professional artists, *The New Statesman*, Supplement, op. cit., p. 4.

Carr-Saunders and Wilson offer a classification. See also R. Lewis and A. Maude, *The English Middle Classes* (Penguin Edition), London, 1953, pp. 114–15.

[14] There are many books, pamphlets and articles, which argue the case. For example:

L. D. Brandeis, *Business: A Profession*, Boston, 1914.
Six articles in *The Annals*, 1922, CI (May) (Part IX, 'Ethics in Business').
H. R. Bowen, *Social Responsibilities of the Business Man*, New York, 1953.
L. F. Urwick, *Is Management a Profession?* London, (2nd Ed.) 1958.

[15] In the case of writing, painting, acting, music, etc., the position is not the same. The work involves high-level individual creativity in a very competitive field. Success depends on differences in individual performance, rather than upon conformity to group standards. Practitioners will hardly make much effort toward collective action. This does not exclude them from professional status. Individual achievement may create status for the occupation as a whole. Opportunity to earn money may be spasmodic and so force trade unions to appear.

[16] Apothecaries were descendants of the twelfth-century 'pepperers', a type of merchant. In the fourteenth century, they were absorbed into the *Grocers' Company* of London, previously formed in 1345 by the pepperers, canvas dealers and traders in foreign spices. Apothecaries still retained their name within the Company. After incorporation in 1428, the *Grocers' Company* obtained exclusive powers in 1447 (from Henry VI), to inspect all spices and drugs and prevent adulteration of the products. From then on, the Grocers maintained their hold over apothecaries. Because of increasing competition from other grocers selling inferior drugs, and as physicians became less willing to compound their own medicines, apothecaries decided to form their own company. Meanwhile, the Grocers secured a Royal Charter in 1606, to prevent the apothecaries from gaining independent corporate existence. But the apothecaries continued to struggle and finally they obtained a Charter in 1617, establishing the *Society of Apothecaries*. Every apothecary in the City of London and within seven miles, had to serve seven years as an apprentice, then submit to an examination. No apothecary was to be a grocer, no grocer could act as an apothecary, no surgeon could sell drugs.
See:

Cecil Wall, *A History of the Worshipful Society of Apothecaries of London*, Vol. I (1617–1815), London, 1963.
C. R. B. Barrett, *The History of the Society of Apothecaries of London*, London, 1905.
Walter Rivington, *The Medical Profession of the United Kingdom*, London, 1888, pp. 21–5.

London surgeons formed an unincorporated guild in 1435, and in 1495, an understanding was reached between barbers and surgeons. Barbers surrendered their power over surgeons. It is said that barbers originally became associated with surgery through a decree of 1092 forbidding monks to wear beards. Barbers assisted the monks in their medical work, later taking over surgical operations when ecclesiastics were prevented from undertaking operations. The *Barbers' Company*, established about 1308, was made a livery company in 1387, and received a Royal Charter in 1462. The Barbers reorganized their company in 1530, and a Statute of 1540 united barbers and surgeons in the *Company of Barber-Surgeons*. All barbers in the City of London, and within one mile, had to stop practising surgery, except for the drawing of teeth.

By the eighteenth century, barbers outnumbered surgeons (about 20 to 1), although most of the Company's income was provided by surgeons. Also, the status of barbers and surgeons had diverged. Surgeons made several unsuccessful attempts to break-away from the barbers. Separation was finally achieved, largely through William Cheseldon (1688–1752), a celebrated London surgeon who had served the Company in many capacities. In December 1744, the surgeons suddenly announced their intention of separating from the barbers. Parliament was petitioned and Dr Cotes (Cheseldon's son-in-law) was Chairman of the Parliamentary investigating committee. The petition was granted and the subsequent Act incorporated the *Company of Surgeons* in May 1745. Quite accidentally, through the sale and purchase of property, the Company violated its corporate status in 1796. A Bill was rushed through Parliament to reincorporate the Company. The Bill failed and instead the Company petitioned for a Royal Charter. This was granted in February 1800, incorporating the Company as the *Royal College of Surgeons of London*.

See: Rivington, op. cit., p. 37.

Cecil Wall, *The History of the Surgeons' Company 1745–1800*, London, 1937.

Sir Zachary Cope, *The Royal College of Surgeons of England*, London, 1957.

B. Holt-Smith, 'The Medical Profession in the Eighteenth Century', *Economic History Review*, 1951, IV, 141–69 (pp. 149–59).

[17] See: Dom David Knowles, 'Religious Life and Organization', Ch. XII in A. L. Poole (Editor), *Medieval England*, Vol. II (Revised Edition), Oxford, 1958.

[18] For decline in discipline, decay and increasing contempt, see:

Dom David Knowles, *The Religious Orders in England*, Cambridge, 1955, Vol. II, pp. 204–18, Vol. III, pp. 62–86.

A. Hamilton Thompson, *The English Clergy and their Organization in the Later Middle Ages*, Oxford, 1947.

Eileen Power, *Medieval People*, London, 1924, Chapter III.

J. Huizinga, *The Waning of the Middle Ages*, London, 1924, Chapter XIII.

[19] The Council of Lateran (1139) prohibited monks from acting as physicians. In 1163, the Council of Tours prevented monks from leaving monastries for more than two months at a time, it also condemned teaching and practice of medicine. An Ordinance of Pope Innocent III in 1215, for-

bade any surgical operation shedding blood. Decrees by Pope Boniface VIII (1300) and Clement V absolutely prohibited the practice of surgery. (The trouble was that monks neglected their spiritual duties, and medical practice was often very lucrative.)

See:

Rivington, op. cit., p. 8.

Dom David Knowles, *The Monastic Order in England 943–1216*, Cambridge, 1940, pp. 516–18.

In 1217, the clergy were first restrained from practising Common Law, by an Edict of Richard Poor, Bishop of Salisbury. But ecclesiastics continued to serve as judges until about 1278.

See:

William Dugdale, *Origines Juridicales, or Historical Memorials of the English Laws, Courts of Justice* . . . London, 1671, pp. 141–3.

[20] See:

Sir Frederick Pollock and F. W. Maitland, *The History of English Law Before the Time of Edward I*, Cambridge, (2nd Ed.) 1896.

H. J. Cohen, *History of the English Bar and Attornatus to 1450*, London, 1929.

T. F. T. Plucknett, *A Concise History of the Common Law*, London, (5th Ed.) 1956, Chapter 5.

[21] See:

Dugdale, op. cit., pp. 141–4, 159–60.

Cohen, op. cit., pp. 444–56, and Appendix XV, pp. 589–95.

Earliest recorded dates claimed for foundation of the Inns of Court: Gray's Inn 1391, Middle Temple 1404, Lincoln's Inn 1422, Inner Temple 1440. Cohen suggests that the system was rudimentary in 1300 and fully established by 1400. In the time of Sir John Fortescue (about 1470), there were four Inns of Court and ten Inns of Chancery. John Stow (1598) listed two serjeants' Inns (plus the defunct Scrop's Inn). By Dugdale's time (1671), there were eight Inns of Chancery, all unimportant except for Thavies Inn and Clifford's Inn. The Order of Serjeants was dissolved in 1877, and the remaining serjeants' Inn was sold.

(Dugdale gives the best account of the Inns.)

[22] In a number of English boroughs, barber-surgeons were unable to confine their guilds to their own occupation. The Kingston-upon-Hull guild contained wigmakers; that in Kinsdale, apothecaries; in Shrewsbury, wig-makers, apothecaries, wax and tallow chandlers. Some joined very unrelated trades. In Lancaster, they united with plumbers, glaziers, saddlers, white-smiths and cutlers; in Ripon, with drapers, dyers and apothecaries. In Ipswich, Dorchester and Devizes, they lost their identity completely in miscellaneous craft guilds.

See: Stella Kramer, *The English Craft Guilds: Studies in their Progress and Decline*, New York, 1927, pp. 18, 135–45.

[23] An Act in 1511 (3 Henry VIII, c. 11) stated that all physicians and surgeons (except Oxford and Cambridge graduates) practising in London, had to be examined, approved and admitted to practise by the Bishop of London, or Dean of St Paul's, aided by four Doctors of Physic and expert

surgeons. Outside London, physicians and surgeons were to be examined by the Bishop, or his Vicar-General, of the diocese in which practice was intended. The Statute of 1540, combining barbers and surgeons, prohibited barbers from practising surgery, except for tooth extraction. The Company had thirteen examiners. Four examiners, plus the Master and three Wardens, examined each surgeon. After acceptance, the candidate was licensed by the Bishop.

[24] Some London physicians petitioned Edward IV in 1421. They suggested that only university graduates should be allowed to practise medicine, everyone else to be prevented by a large fine, or long imprisonment. Apparently, instructions were given to implement this, but action was stayed, because the physicians and surgeons obtained permission from the Lord Mayor and Aldermen to establish a conjoint Faculty in the City of London. Within a few years the scheme had broken down. From then on, physicians and surgeons remained divided. (See Rivington, op. cit., pp. 9–10.)

Five hundred years later, physicians and surgeons still maintained the division. A Standing Joint Committee of the three Royal Colleges resolved on 16 December 1941, that it was desirable to bring all three Colleges together in Lincoln's Inn Fields. Each Council confirmed this resolution. In January 1945, correspondence developed in *The Times* supporting an alliance to form an 'Academy of Medicine'. The *Royal College of Surgeons* pledged £100,000 in November. The *Royal College of Obstetricians and Gynaecologists* expressed their willingness to move to Lincoln's Inn Fields. The *Royal College of Physicians* rejected the idea. (See various issues of *The Times* during January 1945, also for 16 November 1945.) The plan had failed. In 1960, the R.C.O.G. opened a new building at Regent's Park. The R.C.P. intends moving in the 1960s to another part of Regent's Park.

[25] The most important confirming Statute was 14 & 15 Henry VIII, c. 5 (1522–3). (There is no modern history of the College. Charles Goodall published a history in 1684. The College library has two manuscript histories written in the nineteenth century.)

See:

William Munk, *The History of the College* (MS. c. 1850–60), pp. 1–4.

Rivington, op. cit., pp. 11–12.

[26] There are many histories of the *Royal Society*: Thomas Spratt (1667), John Wallis (*Defence of the Royal Society*) (1678), Thomas Birch (in four volumes) (1756–57), Thomas Thomson (1812), G. H. Weld (in two volumes) (1848).

Recent histories are:

Sir John Lyons, *The Royal Society 1660–1940*, London, 1944.

Dorothy Stimson, *Scientists and Amateurs*, London, 1949.

Sir Harold Hartley (Editor), *The Royal Society: Its Origins and Founders*, London, 1960.

[27] Joan Evans, *A History of the Society of Antiquaries*, Oxford, 1956, pp. 7–13.

[28] D. Hudson and K. W. Luckhurst, *The Royal Society of Arts 1754–1954*, London, 1954, pp. 5–11, 28.

(Previous histories:

G. K. Menzies, *The Story of the Royal Society of Arts*, London, 1933.

Sir H. Trueman Wood, *History of the Royal Society of Arts*, London, 1913.)
The title 'Royal' was granted in 1908.

[29] Sir Walter Lamb, *The Royal Academy: A Short History of Its Foundation and Development*, London, 1951.

Nikolaus Pevsner, *Academies of Art: Past and Present*, Cambridge, 1940, pp. 124–6.

[30] Robert Robson, *The Attorney in Eighteenth Century England*, Cambridge, 1959, pp. 2–6, 7–17, 20–34.

Michael Birks, *Gentlemen of the Law*, London, 1960, pp. 101–11, 136–7, 143–53.

[31] Sir D'Arcy Power (Editor), *British Medical Societies*, London, 1939.

Maurice Davidson, *The Royal Society of Medicine: The Realization of an Ideal 1805–1955*. London, 1955, pp. 13–27.

Hospital medical societies appeared at Guy's (1771), at Middlesex (1774), at Bart's. (1795). J. C. Lettsom (1744–1815), a physician at St. Thomas', was mainly responsible for foundation of the *Medical Society of London* in 1773.

[32] A. T. Gage, *A History of the Linnean Society of London*, London, 1938, pp. 1–3.

The Society was named after Carl von Linne (Linnaeus), the Swedish doctor and naturalist, who died in 1778. J. E. Smith, who eventually purchased Linnaeus' famous natural history collections, was a leading founder and first President.

[33] The *Society of Engineers* (1771) (resuscitated as *Society of Civil Engineers* in 1793, also called the *Smeatonian Club*).
See:

E. C. Wright, 'The Early Smeatonians', *Transactions of the Newcomen Society*, 1937, XVII, 57; 1938, XVIII, 101–10.

'The Society of Civil Engineers', *Transactions of the Newcomen Society*, 1938, XVII, 51–71.

The *Architects' Club* (1791).
See:

B. Kaye, *The Development of the Architectural Profession in Britain*, London, 1960, pp. 58–60.

The *Society for the Improvement of Naval Architecture* (1791).
See:

K. C. Barnaby, *The Institution of Naval Architects 1860–1960*, London, 1960, pp. 255–7.

The *Surveyors' Club* (1792).
See:

The Surveyors' Club 1792 (Pamphlet), London, 1939.

There were also the *Auctioneers' Society* formed in 1799, and the *Chemical Society* existing about 1781.

[34] Bernice Holt-Smith (née Hamilton), op. cit., pp. 159–69.

Rivington, op. cit., pp. 21–31.

The turning point for apothecaries was the Rose Judgment of 1703. John Searle, a butcher, sent for medicine to an apothecary named Rose. Rose gave free advice, but later charged £50 for drugs. Feeling no better, Searle consulted a physician, who cured him in six weeks and charged two pounds —so he said. The *Royal College of Physicians* decided to prosecute William Rose for illegal practice of medicine. The action was successful at the Queen's Bench, but the *Society of Apothecaries* appealed to the House of Lords and the decision was reversed. From this time, apothecaries practised medicine more and more openly.

³⁵ Robson, op. cit., Appendix V, pp. 168–70.

E. Hughes, 'The Professions in the Eighteenth Century', *Durham University Journal*, 1952, XIII, 46–55.

J. H. Plumb, *England in the Eighteenth Century*, London, 1950, Chapter 5.

C. K. F. Brown, *A History of the English Clergy 1800–1900*, London, 1953, Chapters 1 and 3.

³⁶ From the foundation of the *Royal Society* in 1660, there had always been twice as many non-scientific as scientific Fellows. In 1860, scientific Fellows outnumbered non-scientists for the first time (330 against 300). By now, the Council consisted entirely of scientists, and elections to Fellowship were restricted to fifteen per year.

Lyons, op. cit., pp. 242–75.

Stimson, op. cit., pp. 191–8.

³⁷ The struggle for reform within the *Royal College of Physicians* began in the second half of the eighteenth century. Licentiates complained that they could not become Fellows. Limited concessions were made in 1771.

(Holt-Smith, op. cit., pp. 142–9.)

For a short account of the nineteenth century reforms, see:

Sir Arthur MacNalty, 'The Royal College of Physicians 110 Years Ago', *The Medical Press and Circular*, 7 September, 1949.

³⁸ The *Royal College of Surgeons'* opposition to the rising provincial medical schools, produced protests from many parts of the country. This widened into criticism of the College's administration led by Thomas Wakley, editor of *The Lancet*, also a member of the College, aided by another surgeon named William Lawrence. Wakley continued attacking for many years. Finally, a Supplemental Charter was obtained in 1843.

Cope, op. cit., pp. 3–6, 17–21, 42–56, 83–90.

³⁹ Barrett, op. cit., pp. 197–9.

Charles Newman, *The Evolution of Medical Education in the Nineteenth Century*, Oxford, 1957, Chapter 2.

⁴⁰ *Council of Legal Education: Calendar 1956–57*, 'The Council's First Hundred Years', pp. 2–3.

J. R. V. Marchant, *Barrister-at-Law*, London, 1905, p. 10.

Various parts in, *A Century of Law Reform: Twelve Lectures on the Changes in the Law of England during the Nineteenth Century*, London, 1901.

⁴¹ For the foundation in each case:

H. B. Woodward, *The History of the Geological Society of London*, London, 1907, pp. 6–9.

J. L. F. Breyer and H. H. Turner (Editors), *History of the Royal Astronomical Society 1820–1920*, London, 1923, pp. 7–11.

P. Chalmers Mitchell, *Centenary History of the Zoological Society of London*, London, 1929, Chapter 1.

H. R. Mill, *The Record of the Royal Geographical Society 1830–1930*, London, 1930, Chapter 2.

S. A. Neave, *The History of the Entomological Society of London 1833–1933*, London, 1933, pp. 1–6.

T. S. Moore and J. C. Philip, *The Chemical Society 1841–1941: A Historical View*, London, 1947, pp. 13–18.

[42] Dr Evans' account of the *Society of Antiquaries* shows something of the changing composition of 'learned societies'. From 1793 to 1815, members were drawn from the Church, law, medicine, Parliament, City of London and country gentry. Between 1815 and 1846, still many clergy joined (about a quarter of all candidates for membership). In the late 1840s, elected members included retail and wholesale traders, also more who gained freelance living from antiquarian work. In the second half of the nineteenth century, the Society was liberalized: 1806—93 Peers, 141 Clergy (membership c. 840); 1852—33 Peers, 75 Clergy (524 members); 1870—15 Peers (674 members). The Society had grown less Metropolitan; by 1870, 353 out of 674 members lived in the provinces.

Evans, op. cit. pp., 201–2, 263–64.

[43] For example: Robert Brown (Vice-President of the *Linnean Society*) and Sir Roderick Murchison (on Council of *Geological Society*) helped to devise the constitution of the *Geographical Society*. G. B. Greenough, a founder of the *Geological Society*, became Vice-President of the *Geographical Society* on its formation. Sir Humphry Davy helped to form the *Geological Society* and the *Zoological Society*. Arthur Aikin helped to found the *Geological Society* and the *Chemical Society*. William Allen was active in the foundation of the *Geological Society* and the *Pharmaceutical Society*. The theme could be continued.

[44] The *Yearbook of the Scientific and Learned Societies of Great Britain and Ireland* demonstrates the spread of organization throughout the country. The *Yearbook* for 1884 groups societies under fourteen sections, dividing them into Metropolitan and country. Year of formation and size are given. The majority were founded after 1850. The following numbers of country (England and Wales) societies are listed: General Science 88; Mathematics and Physical Science 18; Biology, including Microscopy and Anthropology, 64; Mechanical Science and Architecture 12; Archaeology 28; Law Societies 43, Medical Societies 42. London societies increase these figures.

[45] An analysis of plurality is given in:
Rev. A. Hume, *The Learned Societies and Printing Clubs of the United Kingdom*, London, 1847 (expanded in 1853).

Hume analyses the *Royal Society*. Of 780 Fellows, 38 belonged to three other societies, 19 to four others, 5 to five, 2 to six. There were 105 Fellows of the *Society of Antiquaries*, 126 Fellows of the *Geological Society*, 80 Fellows of the *Royal Astronomical Society*, 104 Fellows of the *Linnean Society*.

⁴⁶ E. Muirhead Little, *History of the British Medical Association*, London, 1932, pp. 20–30.

Paul Vaughan, *Doctors' Commons: A Short History of the B.M.A.*, London, 1959, pp. 7–17.

⁴⁷ A. Tropp, *The School Teachers*, London, 1957, pp. 44–7, 50–6, 99–100, 108–11.

⁴⁸ Birks, op. cit., pp. 176–80.

Introduction of examinations proved to be an effective control over entrance to the profession. Before 1836, an average of five to six hundred were admitted annually, from 1837–52, the annual average dropped to 391.

Report of the Royal Commission on the Arrangements in the Inns of Court and Inns of Chancery for Promoting the Study of Law and Jurisprudence, 1854, pp. 127–32.

CHAPTER TWO

¹ The original prospectus of the *Provincial Medical and Surgical Association* gave five objects relating to the collection of data, advancement of medico-legal science and the 'maintenance of the Honour and Respectability of the Profession'.

E. M. Little, *History of the British Medical Association 1832–1932*, London, 1932, pp. 21–22.

² The first object in the prospectus of the *Institute of Chemistry* was 'to ensure that consulting and analytical chemists are duly qualified for the proper discharge of the duties they undertake by a thorough study of Chemistry and Allied Sciences in their application to the Arts, Public Health, Agriculture and Technical Industry'.

R. B. Pilcher, *The Institute of Chemistry of Great Britain and Ireland: History of the Institute 1877–1914*, London, 1914, p. 51.

³ A direct search of Royal Charters and Memoranda of Association reveals problems. Often the sole guide is a generalized object, constructed in the nineteenth century. In most cases, especially with associations incorporated under the Companies Acts, a very long list of aims will be found.

⁴ For example, in organizations already described: Jacob Bell and the *Pharmaceutical Society*, Sir Charles Hastings and the *British Medical Association*, Henry Linacre and the *Royal College of Physicians*, William Shipley and the *Royal Society of Arts*, Bryan Holmes and the *Law Society*.

⁵ Some have been known to refuse. Some have been unsure, once elected, Edward Burne-Jones (1833–98) elected A.R.A. 1885, resigned 1893.

W. R. Sickert (1860–1942) elected A.R.A. 1924, R.A. 1934, resigned 1935.

Augustus John (1878–1961) elected A.R.A. 1921, R.A. 1928, resigned 1938, re-elected 1940.

Stanley Spencer (1896–1960) elected A.R.A. 1932, resigned 1935, re-elected as R.A. 1950.

[6] In the *Royal Society*, twenty-five candidates are drawn from a list of over one hundred by a sub-committee of the Council, then Fellows vote. Average age at election is 47. Of 616 Fellows in 1960, 326 were Professors, 107 from Cambridge, 50 from Oxford, 126 London, the rest from provincial universities.

[7] There are schools for Painting and Drawing, Sculpture, Architecture. The average number of students in each is 80, 10 and 10 respectively. But Prof. Pevsner has said 'The Royal Academy remained a small and conservative institution, and were it not for the social glamour of its exhibitions and annual dinners, its role would be negligible.'

N. Pevsner, *Academies of Art: Past and Present*, Cambridge, 1940, p. 186.

[8] Sir Frederick Kenyon, *The British Academy: The First Fifty Years*, Oxford, 1952, pp. 27–31.

[9] In 1959, the *Royal Society* administered 35 special funds and 39 research funds, financed 22 research appointments, 20 overseas bursaries. Gross income from sale of publications was £57,573.

See an article by Sir William Penney—'How Work is Financed', *The Times*, 19 July 1960. (Special Supplement on the *Royal Society* Tercentenary. Published as a book in 1961.)

[10] The *Zoological Society* in an introductory leaflet (May 1959) states, 'Fellows may not use the letters F.Z.S. for business purposes.'

The *Royal Geographical Society* in an introductory leaflet (1960) says, 'The title "F.R.G.S." is not an honorific title. Its purpose is not to convey a distinction but to indicate a Fellowship, in the sense of membership of a scientific society incorporated by Royal Charter.'

[11] Following the Insurance Act of 1911, and increasing discontent with the B.M.A.'s Constitution, the Annual Representatives meeting in 1912 instructed Council to report 'on the desirability of the Association becoming a registered trade union'.

A report in 1913 did not recommend the idea. It suggested three major obstacles: (*a*) the difficulty of organizing scattered workers, (*b*) the inability to provide welfare benefits on a trade union scale, (*c*) the inability to proclaim a strike, or the desire to employ other repugnant weapons.

E. M. Little, *History of the B.M.A. 1832–1932*, London, 1932, pp. 89–91. See also 'Preamble' in Paul Vaughan, *Doctors' Commons*, London, 1959.

[12] On 1 June 1961, new Burnham Committee proposals were announced for increased salaries covering school teachers in England and Wales. On June 3, the N.U.T. Executive decided to recommend strike action to members, if negotiations broke down with the Ministry of Education. They suggested a one-day strike of N.U.T. members in Primary and Secondary schools, plus complete withdrawal of services in selected areas, providing three-quarters of members there voted in favour. On June 17, delegates at a special conference agreed to strike action. On October 18, the N.U.T. Executive accepted the Ministry of Education pay offer and called off official union resistance. But some teachers carried out a one-day unofficial strike.

See *The*) *Times* 2, 5, 15, 19 June, 19, 24, 31 October 1961.)

But the N.U.T. has organized strike action in the past, and threatened action, on several occasions since the 1890s.

(See A. Tropp, *The School Teachers*, London, 1957.)

[13] P.E.P. used the following definition: 'a voluntary non-profit making body formed by independent firms of manufactures to protect and advance certain interests to all.'

Industrial Trade Associations: Activities and Organization, London (Political and Economic Planning), 1957, 'Introduction', p. xiii.

[14] Distribution of Trade Associations in various industries (1957): Engineering, Shipbuilding and Electricity (180); Textiles (170); Metal Manufactures, Metal Goods, Food, Drink and Tobacco (120–140 each); Chemicals and Allied Trades, Non-metalliferous Mining Products, Paper and Printing, Manufactures of Wood and Cork, Clothing and other manufactures (60–100 each); Mining and Quarrying, Vehicles, Precision Instruments and Jewellery, Leather and Leather Goods (less than 50 each).

Ibid., p. 2.

[15] Ibid., Chapter Four.

[16] For example: the British Plastics Federation contains six main groups, each group divided into sections. Besides a main Technical Committee, each group and section has a Technical Committee, each committee able to combine with another for technical investigation. The Federation collates data on aspects of the plastics industry, prepares abstracts from 170 journals, issues a *Monthly Bulletin* and a *Buyers' Guide*, holds technical conferences.

See 'The Work of the British Plastics Federation: Key Role in Industry Affairs' in *Rubber Journal and International Plastics*, 1958, CXXV, 464–5. (See also p. 420 for an account of the F.B.R.A.N.)

[17] *A Guide for Articled Clerks: The Training of a Solicitor*, The Law Society, London, (2nd Ed.) 1962.

[18] Since 1941, the *Royal College of Surgeons of England* has published the *Annals of the Royal College of Surgeons of England*. This is now a monthly publication containing technical papers, notes about Council proceedings and various notices.

CHAPTER THREE

[1] J. Cohen, C. E. M. Hansel, E. F. May, 'Natural History of Learned and Scientific Societies', *Nature*, 1954, CLXXIII, 328–33.

'Scientific and Learned Societies' is a collective expression, left undefined by the authors. Roughly, it appears to coincide with the term 'Study Association', except that many of the societies cited, are not of national importance in terms of prestige and membership.

[2] Jacob Bell and Theophilus Redwood, *Historical Sketch of the Progress of Pharmacy in Great Britain*, London, 1880, p. 142.

[3] Miss J. H. Wicksteed, *The Growth of a Profession: History of the Chartered*

Society of Physiotherapy 1894–1945, London, 1948, Chapters 1–3. (Membership: 1900—141, 1914—959, 1945—*c.* 15,000, 1960—*c.* 16,000.)

⁴ J. P. C. Coast, *The Land Agents' Society 1901–1939*, London, 1939, p. 9 (see also pp. 29–30).

Mr Coast's book indicates the solid work to build status. Between 1901 and 1939, the Society took action in about 100 Parliamentary Acts and Bills, it sent 7 deputations to Government departments, it gave evidence before some 30 committees, it prepared 36 reports and memoranda, and held 14 conferences.

⁵ T. L. Poynton, *The Institute of Municipal Treasurers and Accountants: A Short History 1885–1960*, London, 1960, pp. 5–15.

⁶ J. H. T. Tudsbery, 'Record of the Origin and Progress of the Institution', *Proceedings of the Institution of Civil Engineers*, 1918, CCV, 216–25.

'Civil' was used at this time, to distinguish 'civilian' from 'military' engineering. Tredgold was asked to write a description of the civil engineers' work. This was incorporated in the petition for a Royal Charter, and appears in the first Charter of 1828. (See *Charter, Supplemental Charters, By-Laws and Regulations*, I.C.E., London, 1960, p. 5.)

⁷ J. A. Gotch (Editor), *The Growth and Work of the R.I.B.A. 1834–1934*, London, 1934, pp. 2–4.

Barrington Kaye, *The Development of the Architectural Profession in Great Britain*, London, 1960, pp. 58–64.

⁸ Kaye, op. cit., pp. 74–79.

An address by J. Gwilt outlined the Institute's objects. It was founded '. . . for facilitating the acquirement of architectural knowledge, for the promotion of the different branches of science connected therewith, and for establishing an uniformity and respectability of practice in the profession'.

⁹ The best account of the R.I.B.A.'s structure and work is found in Gotch. There are also two articles in the *Journal* ('The Work of the R.I.B.A.', *R.I.B.A. Journal*, 1948, LV, 483–89, 526–33).

¹⁰ Bell and Redwood, op. cit., pp. 34–39.

¹¹ Bell and Redwood, op. cit., pp. 45–69.

Walter Rivington, *The Medical Profession of the United Kingdom*, London, 1888, pp. 29–31.

¹² Bell and Redwood, op. cit., pp. 77–8, 86–97.

Charles Newman, *The Evolution of Medical Education in the Nineteenth Century*, London, 1957, pp. 149–58.

¹³ Bell and Redwood, op. cit., pp. 98–112.

¹⁴ For many years, candidates could be elected to membership without taking the examinations, providing they had practised for a certain period.

The Society's 'School of Pharmacy' became the 'School of Pharmacy' of London University in 1948.

The Supplemental Charter of 1953 introduced a new class of Fellows (F.P.S.) 'to mark higher educational attainments'.

[15] The entire issue of *The Veterinary Record* for 22 December 1945 commemorated the centenary celebrations of the Royal College. (*The Veterinary Record*, 1945, LVII, 599–678.)
For background history of the profession, see pp. 600–7, 610–12.

[16] Ibid., pp. 629–31.

[17] Ibid., pp. 615–20.

[18] Ibid., pp. 620–3, 627–9.

[19] R. C. Simmons, *The Institute of Actuaries 1848–1948*, London, 1948, pp. 3–36.

[20] T. S. Moore and J. C. Philip, *The Chemical Society 1841–1941: A Historical View*, London, 1947, Chapter 4.
R. B. Pilcher, *The Institute of Chemistry of Great Britain and Ireland: History of the Institute 1877–1914*, London, 1914, p. 23.

[21] Pilcher, op. cit., pp. 23–46.

[22] Kaye, op. cit., pp. 136–8. Gotch. op. cit., pp. 33–4.

[23] Kaye, op. cit., pp. 149–51. Gotch, op. cit., pp. 36–7.

[24] R. H. Parsons, *A History of the Institution of Mechanical Engineers 1847–1947*, London, 1947, pp. 10–15.
Apparently, there is no record of this treatment of Stephenson in the archives of the *Institution of Civil Engineers*. At least two other factors must have helped formation. Firstly, the I.C.E. was a London society; foundation of the *Institution of Mechanical Engineers* took place in the Midlands, where there was no equivalent organization. The mechanical engineers remained a northern society for many years, although some meetings were held in London. Secondly, by the 1840s, mechanical engineering had developed into a separate field. Whereas civil engineers were concerned with construction of bridges, roads, docks, canals, etc., mechanical engineers dealt with steam engines, pumps, the use of steam power and machinery—very different work.
The introductory circular proposed foundation of an Institution 'to enable Mechanics and Engineers engaged in the different Manufactories, Railways and other Establishments in the Kingdom to meet and correspond, and by mutual exchange of ideas respecting improvements in the various branches of Mechanical Science, to increase their knowledge and give an impulse to inventions likely to be useful to the world.' (Parsons, op. cit., p. 11.)

[25] Ibid., pp. 16–19.

[26] Beresford Worthington, *Professional Accountants: An Historical Sketch*, London, 1895, pp. 31, 33, 42, 120–5.

[27] Ibid., pp. 55–7, 68–79.

[28] A. A. Garrett, *History of the Society of Incorporated Accountants 1885–1957*, Oxford, 1961.

[29] F. C. Osbourne and R. T. Bell, *Fifty Years: The Story of the A.C.C.A. 1904–1954*, London, 1954.

[30] Institute of Physics and the Physical Society, *General Information Booklet No. 1*, September, 1960 (and personal communications).

[31] W. E. Ballard, (Presidential Address) *Bulletin of the Institution of Metallurgists*, 1958, VI, 8–17 (particularly pp. 9–11).

[32] *The Metallurgist*, 1960, I, 91 and 1961, I, 260–1, 266–9.

[33] J. W. Bambrick and E. B. Groves, 'The I.S.M.A. Story: A History of the Incorporated Sales Managers' Association', *Marketing*, 1961, XXX (5), 281–97 (Golden Jubilee International Conference Issue).

[34] T. G. Rose, *A History of the Institute of Industrial Administration 1919–1951*, London, 1954, Chapter 1.

[35] Ibid., pp. 123–8, 137, 157.

[36] Richard Brown, *History of Accountancy and Accountants*, Edinburgh, 1905. Additional Scottish associations were formed later. In 1951, all the Scottish organizations were merged into the *Institute of Chartered Accountants in Scotland*.

[37] Institute of Chartered Accountants in England and Wales, *Members' Handbook*, Section A2 (membership size: 500 in 1880, 702 in 1900–2, c. 32,600 in 1960).

[38] H. A. L. Cockerell, *Sixty Years of the Chartered Insurance Institute 1897–1957*, London, 1957, pp. 13–17, 20–28.

[39] Mary M. Niven, 'The Beginnings of the Institute', *Journal of the Institute of Personnel Management*, 1957, XXXIX, 28–34.

[40] W. T. K. Braunholtz, *The Institution of Gas Engineers: The First Hundred Years, 1863–1963*, London, 1963.

[41] Institute of Housing, *Yearbook*, 1958–9, p. 4.

[42] K. C. Barnaby, *The Institution of Naval Architects 1860–1960*, London, 1960, pp. 8–12.

[43] B. C. Curling, *History of the Institute of Marine Engineers*, London, 1961.

[44] 'The Institute of Hospital Administrators: The First Fifty Years 1902–1952', *The Hospital*, 1952, XLVIII, 293–321.
A monthly journal (*The Hospital Gazette*) was started in 1904. From 1908, attention turned toward education, the first examinations being held in 1915.

[45] Three articles in *The Almoner*, 1953, VI (Golden Jubilee Number 1903–1953).
I. C. Marx, 'Early Days', pp. 346–59, M. W. Edminson, 'The Middle Period, or Episode Two 1919–39', pp. 360–72, M. J. Roxburgh, 'Episode Three 1939–53', pp. 373–81.

[46] *Notes on the History and Activities of the Institution of Production Engineers*, July 1961, p. 2.

[47] Institution of Chemical Engineers, *History* (Mimeographed).

[48] G. D. Clifford, *A Twentieth Century Professional Institution: The Story of the Brit. I.R.E.*, London, 1960, pp. 1–2.

⁴⁹ E. Appleyard, *The History of the Institution of Electrical Engineers*, London, 1939, pp. 19–22.

⁵⁰ S. B. Hamilton, 'The History of the Institution of Structural Engineers', pp. 16–20 in the Jubilee Issue of *The Structural Engineer*, 1958.

⁵¹ *Royal Institution of Chartered Surveyors: List of Members 1960–61*, 'History of the Profession', pp. 20–27.

⁵² *Yearbook of the Town Planning Institute*, 1958–59, pp. 6–7.

⁵³ *Yearbook of the Textile Institute 1948–49*, pp. 7–8.
For the work to date, see *Yearbook 1962–63*, pp. 31, 44–54.

⁵⁴ Sir George Cayley (1773–1857), an English squire, is considered to be the inventor of the modern aeroplane. Having determined the basic principles of flight and airframe construction between 1799 and 1810, Cayley made gliders (models and full-size) 1804–53, and achieved manned glider flight. Cayley tried to form an Aeronautical Society in 1816, 1837 and 1840.

Apart from the glider flights of Otto Lilienthal (1846–96), and the experiments of S. P. Langley, the first real step forward was the powered flight of Orville Wright on 17 December 1903.

⁵⁵ J. L. Pritchard, *Eighty Years of British Aviation: The Work of the Royal Aeronautical Society*, London, 1946.
F. H. Smith, 'Oldest Aeronautical Society: The Story of the R.Ae.S.', *Flight*, 1960, LXXVII, 69–71, 154–6, 284–5.

CHAPTER FOUR

¹ The *Institute of Welfare Officers* appear to be the only association registered as a Friendly Society (in 1946).

² An Act in 1522–3 (14 & 15 Henry VIII, c. 5) confirmed the Royal Charter of September 1518. It provided for an increase in the number of Elects (the governing body), also for power to examine anyone wishing 'to exercise or practise in physic' throughout England, except for Oxford or Cambridge graduates. These two provisions were repealed in 1860 (23 & 24 Vict., c. 66). An Act was obtained in 1814 (54 Geo. III, c. 118), to enable the College to hold corporate meetings in Westminster, as the College had moved from the City of London.
The Charter and Byelaws of the Royal College of Physicians of London and the Acts of Parliament especially relating thereto, 1959, pp. v, xiii, xv.

³ Sir Zachary Cope, *The Royal College of Surgeons of England: A History*, London, 1959, p. 19.

⁴ R. B. Pilcher, *The Institute of Chemistry of G.B. and Ireland: A History of the Institute 1877–1914*, London, 1914, p. 78.

⁵ For example, the cost to the *Linnean Society* in 1802 was about £460, the *Geological Society* about £385 in 1825, the *Zoological Society* £326 in 1827, the *Royal Astronomical Society* £268 in 1831 (without legal fees), the *Chemical Society* £330 in 1848. Comparable modern figures are not available.

[6] Recent rejections include the *Institute of Taxation* in 1955, the *Institution of Production Engineers* in 1959. The *British Optical Association* had petitions rejected in 1906 and 1919.

Examples of Charters granted on second petition.

	Association Founded	Petition Rejected	Petition Accepted
Institution of Mechanical Engineers	1847	1878	1929
Institution of Electrical Engineers	1871	1880	1921
Institution of Structural Engineers	1908	1926	1934
Institute of Municipal Treasurers and Accountants	1885	1936	1959

[7] The Board of Trade may request a change of name, or modification of the aims. Incorporation can be delayed by objections of existing associations, or Government departments. Certain conditions may be imposed.

[8] Should the association be wound up, membership liability is limited by guarantee to a nominal sum, generally one to two pounds.

[9] Under the present Companies Act, 1948 (11 & 12 Geo. VI, c. 38), Section 19 (1).

[10] The following associations were considered in the analysis of government:

(Chartered Bodies) *Institute of Chartered Accountants in England and Wales, Institute of Municipal Treasurers and Accountants, Institute of Actuaries, Royal Aeronautical Society, Royal Institute of British Architects, Chartered Auctioneers and Estate Agents Institute, Royal Institute of Chemistry, Institution of Chemical Engineers, Institution of Civil Engineers, Institution of Electrical Engineers, Institution of Gas Engineers, Institution of Mechanical Engineers, Institution of Mining Engineers, Institution of Municipal Engineers, British Institution of Radio Engineers, Institution of Structural Engineers, Chartered Insurance Institute, Chartered Land Agents Society, Library Association, Chartered Institute of Patent Agents, Chartered Society of Physiotherapy, Pharmaceutical Society of Great Britain, Chartered Institute of Secretaries, Royal Institution of Chartered Surveyors, Textile Institute, Town Planning Institute, Institute of Transport;* (Associations incorporated under the Companies Acts) *Association of Certified and Corporate Accountants, Institute of Practitioners in Advertising, Incorporated Society of Auctioneers and Landed Property Agents, Institute of Bankers, Institute of Builders, Society of Chiropodists, Institution of Fire Engineers, Institution of Heating and Ventilating Engineers, Institution of Production Engineers, Institute of Housing, Corporation of Insurance Brokers, British Institute of Management, Institute of Hospital Administrators, Institute of Personnel Management, Institution of Works Managers, Institute of Almoners, Institution of Metallurgists, Museums Association, British Optical Association, Institute of British Photographers, Institute of Physics and the Physical Society, Plastics Institute, Purchasing Officers Association, Society of Radiographers, Rating and Valuation Association, Corporation of Secretaries, Institute of Quantity Surveyors, Valuers Institution, Institute of Welding.*

[11] *The Institution of Municipal Engineers: Charter and Bye-laws* (Revised to October 1955), Bye-law 16 (Elections), p. 14.

[12] Of the sixteen 'Nationally Elected Members' (out of forty Council members), four must be teachers, four in private practice, four employed in any service established under or pursuant of the National Health Service.
Bye-laws of the Chartered Society of Physiotherapy (Revised 1962), Bye-law 37 (1), p. 10.

[13] The *Library Association* Council includes five members appointed annually by the Association of Assistant Librarians (an internal section of the Association), six elected by those employed in National, University, College and Medical Libraries, six elected by librarians in Special Libraries (libraries other than Public, National, University, College or Medical).
The Library Association: Charter and Byelaws (Revised January 1962), Bye-law 15(a) (Council, Committees and Officers: Constitution of Council).

[14] The *Royal Institute of Chemistry* tries to arrange that Council reflects various aspects of chemistry: industry, nationalized industry, industrial research associations, government service, hospitals, independent consultants, universities, technical colleges, schools, etc.
The *Institute of Municipal Treasurers and Accountants* ensures coverage by co-opting additional members on to Council, as required, to maintain representation of all types of local authorities in England, Wales and Scotland.

[15] The *Royal Institute of British Architects* shows a reversal in policy. Old Byelaws (last amended in 1956) provided for nine Fellows, nine Associates and three Licentiates, plus nine other corporate members as ordinary members of Council (Byelaw 28 (1) (e)). New Byelaws (1961) allow for thirty-five nationally elected members, who may be Fellows, Associates or Licentiates (Byelaw 28 (a) (6)).
The Charter, Supplemental Charter and Byelaws of the Royal Institute of British Architects.

[16] *Royal Charter and Byelaws of the Town Planning Institute* (1959), Bye-laws: Part IV (Council), Byelaw 25 (1).

[17] In the *Institution of Metallurgists* Council, of the twenty-six elected members, eleven are elected by Fellows and Associates together, nine by Fellows alone, six by Associates only.

[18] In the R.I.B.A., there are four main departments (plus the Board of Architectural Education): Professional Services Department; Information and Liaison Services; Central Administration; Library. One or more Council committees are connected with each department. The Honorary Officers supervise different functions. Each of the four Vice-Presidents is responsible for one aspect (Professional Services; Information and Liaison Services; Allied Societies and Membership; Education and Library). The Honorary Secretary is responsible for Central Administration and the Honorary Treasurer for Finance.
Annual Report 1962, p. 4 or the *R.I.B.A. Kalendar.*

[19] In the *British Institute of Management*, the Chief Executive generally supervises six main divisions: Management Services; Education; Publications; Administration; Development; Regional Offices. Some divisions are further sub-divided. (Information based on two charts prepared in January 1961.)

[20] 'The four Vice-Presidents shall respectively be responsible to the Council for the following affairs of the Institute and Society: (a) professional matters, educational and membership policy and affairs; (b) the scientific activities and meetings including those concerning education and those of Branches and Groups but excluding scientific publications; (c) scientific publications and library; (d) exhibitions and displays.'

Memorandum and Articles of Association and Bye-laws: Institute of Physics and the Physical Society (1960), Art. 54, p. 23.

[21] The *Chartered Society of Physiotherapy* has a distinguished medical practitioner as President. All Honorary Officers are appointed by Council, they need not be members of the Society. Honorary Officers are not Council members, Council has a separate Chairman.

Chartered Society of Physiotherapy: Royal Charter and Byelaws (1962), Byelaw 36 governs appointment of Honorary Officers.

The *Textile Institute* tends to have a distinguished figure in the textile industry as President. Until comparatively recently, the *Library Association* had a distinguished person as President, rather than a professional member. Some of the younger engineering institutions (and many other newer associations) tend to elect distinguished people, within the field, to Honorary Membership then to the Presidency. On the whole, the practice of electing 'unqualified', distinguished people is vanishing.

[22] The following associations were analysed for the requirements governing election to the first corporate grade (in terms of: minimum age; examination requirements; examination exemption allowed; length of training; position of responsibility; whether late entry is permitted; number of members required to propose candidate): *Institute of Chartered Accountants in England and Wales, Association of Certified and Corporate Accountants, Institute of Municipal Treasurers and Accountants, Institute of Cost and Works Accountants, Institute of Actuaries, Institute of Practitioners in Advertising, Institute of Bankers, Royal Aeronautical Society, Royal Institute of British Architects, Town Planning Institute, Chartered Auctioneers and Estate Agents Institute, Incorporated Society of Auctioneers and Landed Property Agents, British Boot and Shoe Institution, Institute of Builders, Building Societies Institute, Institute of Ceramics, Royal Institute of Chemistry, Institution of Agricultural Engineers, Institution of Chemical Engineers, Institution of Civil Engineers, Institution of Electrical Engineers, Institution of Fire Engineers, Institution of Gas Engineers, Institution of Heating and Ventilating Engineers, Institute of Marine Engineers, Institution of Mechanical Engineers, Institution of Mining Engineers, Institution of Municipal Engineers, Institution of Production Engineers, Institute of Public Health Engineers, British Institution of Radio Engineers, Institution of Structural Engineers, Hotel and Catering Institute, Institute of Housing, Chartered Insurance Institute, Corporation of Insurance Brokers, Chartered Institute of Loss Adjusters, Chartered Land Agents Society, Library Asso-*

ciation, British Institute of Management, Institute of Hospital Administrators, Institute of Personnel Management, Institution of Works Managers, Institute of Public Relations, Institute of Almoners, Society of Chiropodists, Chartered Society of Physiotherapy, Institute of Medical Laboratory Technology, Institute of the Motor Industry, Society of Radiographers, Institution of Metallurgists, Institute of Mining and Metallurgy, Museums Association, British Optical Association, Institute of British Photographers, Chartered Institute of Patent Agents, Pharmaceutical Society of Great Britain, Institute of Physics and the Physical Society, Institute of Printing, Purchasing Officers Association, Institute of Public Supplies, Plastics Institute, Chartered Institute of Secretaries, Corporation of Secretaries, Institute of Chartered Shipbrokers, Institute of Shipping and Forwarding Agents, Institute of Statisticians, Royal Institution of Chartered Surveyors, Institute of Quantity Surveyors, Incorporated Association of Architects and Surveyors, Faculty of Architects and Surveyors, Institute of Taxation, Textile Institute, Institute of Transport, Rating and Valuation Association, Valuers Institution, Institute of Works Study.

CHAPTER FIVE

[1] Throughout the nineteenth century, Oxford and Cambridge remained important sources of clergy. For example, percentages of all deacons ordained, who were Oxford or Cambridge graduates: 1834–43 81.9%, 1854–63 67.8%, 1872–99 60.0%.

C. K. F. Brown, *A History of the English Clergy 1800–1900*, London, 1953, p. 250 (see also, Appendix B 'Training for Holy Orders').

[2] Charles Newman, *The Evolution of Medical Education in the Nineteenth Century*, London, 1957.

'Methods of Education and Teaching Institutions', p. 25–40.

[3] *Report of Royal Commission on the Arrangements in the Inns of Court and Inns of Chancery for Promoting the Study of Law and Jurisprudence* (1854), pp. 13, 148, 205.

A Century of Law Reform: Twelve Lectures on the Changes in the Law of England During the Nineteenth Century, London, 1901, Introductory lecture by W. Blake Odgers.

Council of Legal Education: Calendar 1956–7.

'The Council's First Hundred Years', pp. 2–3.

[4] Michael Birks, *Gentlemen of the Law*, London, 1960, pp. 176–80.

E. B. V. Christian, *Solicitors: An Outline of their History*, London, 1925.

Report of Royal Commission on the Arrangements in the Inns of Court and Inns of Chancery for Promoting the Study of Law and Jurisprudence (1854).

(See evidence by K. Barnes and W. S. Cookson on behalf of the *Law Society*, pp. 127–32.)

[5] The *Institute of Builders* is not included here. It was founded in 1834 as *The Builders' Society*. Byelaws published in 1875 state that it was 'to provide friendly intercourse, the interchange of useful information, increase uniformity and respectability in the conduct of business'. No Council minutes exist before 1859, so very little can be said about the Society's work. But

the Society was always small (about seventy members). In the 1880s, the *Central Association of Master Builders* was unable to obtain a licence from the Board of Trade, to omit the word 'Limited'. The Association sent a deputation (of four Society members) to the Society, requesting it to become incorporated. So, in 1884, the Society was incorporated as the *Institute of Builders*.

[6] The *Society of Apothecaries* began lectures in 1803 and revised examinations in 1815. Up to 1840, the Society examined about 500 candidates a year, then the introduction of written papers caused a fall in the number. About one-fifth of candidates failed, mostly because they lacked knowledge of Latin. Both lectures and examinations were orientated toward medicine. General medical practitioners used the Society's Licentiateship as a qualification.

C. R. B. Barrett, *The History of the Society of Apothecaries of London*, London, 1905, pp. 197–9.

Barrett presents an interesting analysis of candidates' ages in 1855–6. Out of 87 candidates, 49 were aged 25–30, 13 were 30–35, 11 aged 35–40, 11 aged 40–50, 3 over 50 (ibid., p. 245).

Cecil Wall, *A History of the Worshipful Society of Apothecaries of London*, Volume I (1617–1815), London, 1963.

[7] J. Bell and T. Redwood, *Historical Sketch of the Progress of Pharmacy*, London, 1880, pp. 152–9.

A great many experienced pharmacists were admitted to membership without examination, as can be seen from expanding size: September 1841 —450, December 1841—800, May 1842—1,958. About seventy to ninety attended the Society's classes.

[8] R. C. Simmons, *The Institute of Actuaries 1846–1948*, London, 1948, pp. 216–17, and Chapter VII.

[9] *Report of Royal Commission on the Arrangements in the Inns of Court*, etc. (1854). Evidence given by K. Barnes and W. S. Cookson, pp. 127–32.

[10] Between 1849 and 1859, only nine took the Natural Science Tripos, plus three in 1859. It constituted a first degree in 1860. A brief account of the development of science teaching at Oxford and Cambridge is given in:

D. M. Turner, *History of Science Teaching in England*, London, 1927.

[11] Most of the University Colleges formed during the nineteenth century, in different parts of the country, became constituent colleges of London University. Their students took University of London degrees. For example: the Hartley Institution (later University College) Southampton 1850, opened in 1862; the College of Science for the West of England, Bristol, founded 1876; University College, Nottingham, founded 1881; the Exeter Technical and University Extension College, founded 1895. Some thirteen colleges were involved. Eventually, they obtained individual university status.

W. H. G. Armytage, *Civic Universities*, London, 1953.

[12] D. Hudson and K. W. Luckhurst, *The Royal Society of Arts 1754–1954*, London, 1954, Chapter 15.

[13] In 1910, the Board of Education set up a Consultative Committee on Examinations in Secondary Schools (Report: Command 6004, 1911). The Committee found about a hundred different examinations being conducted on different levels. The report led to a new secondary schools examination scheme in 1917.

(See also *Secondary School Examinations other than G.C.E.* (1960), Report of Committee appointed by the Secondary School Examinations Council in July 1958.)

[14] J. A. Gotch (Editor), *The Growth and Work of the R.I.B.A. 1834–1934*, London, 1934, pp. 20–1, 29–30 and the Chapter by H. M. Fletcher, 'The R.I.B.A. and Architectural Education'.

[15] Original subscriber/founders of the *Institute of Chemistry*: E. Frankland (Professor of Chemistry, Royal School of Mines), E. Vine Tuson (Professor of Chemistry, Royal Veterinary College, London), W. N. Hartley (Demonstrator in Chemistry, King's College, London), R. Galloway (Professor of Chemistry, Royal College of Science, Dublin), J. Attfield (Professor of Practical Chemistry, Pharmaceutical Society), C. R. Alder Wright (Lecturer in Chemistry, St Mary's Hospital), M. Cartwright (Examiner in Chemistry to the Pharmaceutical Society), A. Crum Brown (Professor of Chemistry, Edinburgh University), plus eight non-teachers.

R. B. Pilcher, *Institute of Chemistry: History of the Institute 1877–1914*, London, 1914, p. 50.

[16] Ibid., pp. 73–4.

[17] H. A. L. Cockerell, *Sixty Years of the Chartered Insurance Institute: 1897–1957*, London, 1957, pp. 22–4.

W. A. Copeman, 'Insurance Education in Retrospect and Prospect', *Journal of the Chartered Insurance Institute*, 1958, LV, 45–116 (pp. 52–4).

[18] *The Chartered Institute of Secretaries 1891–1951: A Review of Sixty Years*, London, 1951, p. 4.

[19] T. L. Poynton, *The Institute of Municipal Treasurers and Accountants: A Short History 1885–1960*, London, 1960, pp. 92–4, 106–9.

[20] John Minto, *History of the Public Library Movement in Great Britain and Ireland*, London, 1932, pp. 209–13.

[21] For example:
Miss M. S. R. James, 'A Plan for Providing Technical Instruction for Library Assistants', *The Library*, 1892, IV, 313.

H. D. Roberts, 'Some Remarks on the Education of Library Assistants: A Plea', *The Library*, 1897, IX, 103–12.

[22] Minto, op. cit., pp. 223–5.
Classes began in March 1898, but four years later Council arranged with the London School of Economics and Political Science to co-operate in providing classes. These continued until 1917.

[23] There are four dining terms a year, each lasts twenty-three days. Ordinary bar students must dine at least six times each term, for twelve terms. Those at university need only dine three times a term. The student

must be present from the grace before dinner and throughout the dinner, until the concluding grace.

P. Allsop, *The Legal Profession*, London (5th Ed.), 1960, p. 7.

[24] For example: *Association of Certified and Corporate Accountants, Royal Institution of Chartered Surveyors, Institute of Quantity Surveyors, Chartered Auctioneers and Estate Agents Institute, Chartered Land Agents' Society, Institution of Municipal Engineers.*

[25] *Institute of Chartered Accountants: Royal Charter and Byelaws*, February, 1960, *Byelaws*, Chapter V, 'Articled Clerks', Byelaw 51.

[26] W. F. Parker, 'Training for the Profession'.
(Address to the *Institute of Chartered Accountants*' Summer School, July 1957. Summer School proceedings, pp. 55–91. See pp. 64–5.)

See also *Report of the Committee on Education and Training, Institute of Chartered Accountants in England and Wales*, 1961 (Especially paragraphs 135–78, 'Theoretical Study'.)

[27] For example: *Royal Institute of Chemistry* (probably the first), *Pharmaceutical Society of Great Britain and Ireland, Institute of Physics and the Physical Society, Chartered Society of Physiotherapy, Institute of Bankers, Royal Institute of British Architects.*

[28] For example: the *Royal Institute of British Architects*, the associations for medical auxiliaries, the engineering institutions.

[29] *A Scheme for Regulating the Practical Training of Persons under Engineers to Local Authorities.* Issued jointly by the *Institution of Municipal Engineers, Institution of Civil Engineers.*

See also, *Municipal Engineering as a Career* (1960–61).

[30] *Training to be a Housing Manager, Institute of Housing*, February, 1960.

[21] Sir John Summerson, *The Architectural Association 1847–1947*, London, 1947, pp. 1–5.

[32] See *College of Estate Management: Prospectus 1960–61*, Introductory Note, pp. 8–9.

Also F. C. Hawkes, 'The Institute 1886–1946', *Journal of the Chartered Auctioneers and Estate Agents Institute*, November, 1946.

A Royal Charter was granted in 1922. It became a recognized institution for teaching the Internal B.Sc. Estate Management, London University, in 1939. Full-time, part-time evening and postal courses are offered for the B.Sc. (Est. Man.) and the examinations of six Qualifying Associations.

[33] Minto., op. cit., pp. 225–8. (The school started with ninety-eight students.)

[34] See *Yearbook 1958–59* of the *Chartered Insurance Institute*, pp. 49, 92–3 (also the Presidential Address by F. R. Norton).

Mr Cockerell, in his history, indicates the Institute's earlier dissatisfaction.

'In the educational world also there is a lamentable ignorance of the discipline that insurance study offers for the mind. Technical Colleges offer little instruction in insurance except so far as is provided for those already in insurance by members of the Institute. As for Universities, it is fair to say that the word "insurance" hardly figures in their syllabuses at all.' (Cockerell, op. cit., p. 69.)

³⁵ Minto, op. cit., pp. 230–1.
The Association of Assistant Librarians (a section of the *Library Association*) has conducted the correspondence courses. However, following the *Library Association*'s complete overhaul of their examinations, the A.A.L. will not offer courses for the new system beginning in 1964. The last courses will be available in 1968.
The Library Association: Syllabus of Examinations 1962, pp. 40–2, 57–62.

³⁶ Simons, op. cit., pp. 260–6.
Copeman, op. cit., pp. 49–50.
The Institute of Actuaries Year Book 1962–1963, pp. 84–87.

³⁷ Copeman, op. cit., pp. 54–7, 67–73.
Cockerell, op. cit., pp. 49–51.
Chartered Insurance Institute Yearbook 1961–62, Section on: 'The Institute Tuition Service.'

³⁸ *The Chartered Institute of Secretaries 1891–1951: A Review of Sixty Years*, London, 1951, p. 61.

³⁹ For example, see: *Professional Bodies Requirements in Terms of the General Certificate of Education*, London (H.M.S.O.), 1962.

⁴⁰ Practical examinations are enforced by the *Royal Institute of Chemistry, Institute of Physics and the Physical Society, British Institution of Radio Engineers, Royal Institution of Chartered Surveyors*, and other associations where practical technique can be an inherent part of normal work in that occupation. Some associations require candidates to appear before a committee, for a professional interview, as in the case of the *Institution of Civil Engineers*.

⁴¹ For example, in 1960–61, the R.I.B.A. introduced a new entrance requirement. All students in Schools of Architecture preparing for R.I.B.A. examinations or equivalents, must have two 'A' Level passes in the G.C.E. This caused a decrease in the number of entrants during the 1961–62 Session, but the intake increased in the 1962–63 Session. (See *Annual Report 1961*, p. 7, *Annual Report 1962*, p. 37.)
From January 1965, the *Institution of Municipal Engineers* will require a higher minimum level of general education: two 'A' Level passes plus two at 'O' Level, or one at 'A' Level and four at 'O' Level. (See *Annual Report of the Council 1961–62*, pp. 1–2.)
The *Royal Institution of Chartered Surveyors* introduced more rigorous entrance requirements in October 1962.
In 1962, the *Pharmaceutical Society* revised the entrance requirement for students. They must now have three 'A' Level passes at G.C.E.

⁴² For example, see the Presidential Address by Professor A. J. S. Pippard to the *Institution of Civil Engineers* in 1958 ('The Individual, the Profession and the Institution').
Also the Reports of 'The Committee on Scientific Manpower of the

Advisory Council on Scientific Policy' (for example, the 1959 Report, Cmnd. 902, p. 23, Table 15).

The increase in the number of graduates is also apparent in other types of associations. For example, the *Library Association* had 654 university graduates in 1947 (out of 6,414 Personal Members) and 1,434 out of 9,935 in 1957. The increase must be partly due to an expansion in the number of Personal Members working in special libraries, in industry, commerce, research associations, technical colleges, etc.

D. D. Haslam, 'The Fighting Fifties: An Informal History of the Association Activities during 1950–9', *The Library Association Record*, 1960, LXII, 2–22 (p. 3).

[43] Plural or multiple membership is not easily analysed, owing to incomplete information in associations' lists of members. Opportunity, or the need, to qualify for several associations varies from occupation to occupation. Today, it is less likely that an individual can qualify for several associations at once, on the basis of a single previous qualification. Fifteen or more years ago, one qualification could give exemption from several assocations' examination requirements. Now standards have increased, reducing the possibility of multiple exemptions.

[44] The Engineering Institutions' Part I Committee consists of representatives from: *Institution of Civil Engineers, Institution of Mechanical Engineers, Institution of Electrical Engineers, Institution of Municipal Engineers, Institute of Marine Engineers, Institution of Gas Engineers, Institution of Production Engineers, British Institution of Radio Engineers, New Zealand Institution of Engineers, Institution of Engineers, Ceylon.*

[45] *The Corporation of Insurance Brokers: Jubilee 1956*, pp. 9–10.

[46] Originally, four associations took part: the *Town Planning Institute, Royal Institution of Chartered Surveyors, Royal Institute of British Architects, Institution of Municipal Engineers.* The *Institution of Civil Engineers* joined the scheme in 1951. The 'Town Planning Joint Examination Board' was wound up on 31 January 1961.

[47] S. F. Cotgrove examines the past history and present system of part-time technical education. (See especially pp. 200–6, also Chapter 11.)
S. F. Cotgrove, *Technical Education and Social Change*, London, 1958.

[48] Little historical information is available. Four correspondence colleges give some account of their origins.
Pitman's, *The Pleasure of Your Company 1840–1960.*
Metropolitan College: 1910 to 1960.
International Correspondence Schools, *Tomorrows begin Today*, 1960.
Foulks Lynch, *Sixty Years of Progress in Accountancy Education*, 1955.
See also: Borje Holmberg, *On the Methods of Teaching by Correspondence*, Lund (Sweden), 1960, pp. 3–17.

[49] Correspondence colleges are not very communicative. Dr Holmberg's account is a sound introduction. See also, two articles: 'Correspondence Colleges', *The Economist*, 1952, CLXV, 4–6, 74–5.

[50] The six associations considered: the *Institute of Chartered Accountants,*

Association of Certified and Corporate Accountants, Chartered Institute of Secretaries, Corporation of Secretaries, Institute of Bankers, Chartered Insurance Institute. This figure is based on approximate numbers of examination candidates 1959–62.

[51] *Report of a Special Committee on Education for Commerce,* (Carr-Saunders Committee), London, H.M.S.O., 1949.

Further Education for Commerce (Report of an Advisory Committee), (The McMeeking Committee), London, H.M.S.O., 1959.

15 to 18: Report of the Central Advisory Council for Education (The Crowther Report), London, H.M.S.O., 1959. Volume I, Sect. 20. Also, A. A. Part, 'Education for the Professions' (Address to the Annual Conference of the *Royal Institution of Chartered Surveyors,* 31 August 1960).

'Postal Tuition for the Professions Criticized', *The Times,* 1 September 1960.

[52] The associations giving exemption from their Intermediate examinations, on a subject for subject basis: the Advertising Joint Examination Board (*Institute of Practitioners in Advertising, Advertising Association*), *Association of Certified and Corporate Accountants, Chartered Institute of Secretaries, Corporation of Secretaries, Chartered Insurance Institute, Institute of Bankers, Institute of Cost and Works Accountants, Institute of Export, Institute of Transport.*

[53] *15 to 18* (The Crowther Report), London, H.M.S.O., 1959, Volume I, Chapter 31, Volume II, Part 3.

From the 'Technical Courses Survey', the Report suggested that the following factors were related to failure:

'. . . students' age on leaving school, type of school he attended, the condition under which he takes the course (day classes, day and evening, and evening classes), the nature of his home background as shown by his father's occupation, his general vigour as shown by his participation in organized games, and the difficulty he found in certain subjects in the course.' (Volume I, Section 519.)

[54] From September 1965, the *Institution of Civil Engineers* will no longer accept the Higher National Certificate as exemption from their examination requirements. As the *Institution of Electrical Engineers* and the *Institution of Mechanical Engineers* work in close liaison with the *Civil Engineers* on educational matters, probably they will also cease to recognize the National Certificate route.

[55] P. F. R. Venables (Editor), *Technical Education,* London, 1955, pp. 133–5, see Table 14, p. 123 which gives examples of different committees' constitutions.

CHAPTER SIX

[1] In January 1963, the *Institute of British Photographers* published a Code of Professional Conduct. At least two associations were considering the introduction of codes. During 1963, they were discussing the reports of committees.

[2] Two useful sources on the nature and problems of professional ethics will be found in *The Annals* (*The Annals of the American Academy of Political and Social Science*):

'The Ethics of the Professions and of Business', (May) 1922, CI.

'Ethical Standards and Professional Conduct', (January) 1955, CCXCVII.

These suggest the wide interest in ethical conduct in the U.S.A. Also many books and pamphlets can be found dealing with the ethics of law, medicine, accountancy, engineering.

[3] A few examples are:

	Founded	Introduced Formal Code
Institution of Civil Engineers	1818	1910
Royal Institute of British Architects	1834	1900
Institute of Actuaries	1848	1946
Royal Institution of Chartered Surveyors (with other associations)	1868	1934
Chartered Auctioneers and Estate Agents Institute	1886	1920
British Optical Association	1895	1936
Institution of Structural Engineers	1908	1926
Textile Institute	1910	1958

[4] D. V. House, 'Professional Ethics' (Address to the Summer Course of the *Institute of Chartered Accountants in England and Wales*, September 1956), *The Accountant*, 1956, CXXXV, 367–73, 395–403, 425–32, 463–70.

The quotation is from the Summer Course Pamphlet, p. 63.

[5] Ibid., pp. 64–5.

[6] See, for example, R. C. Simmons, *The Institute of Actuaries 1848–1948*. Mr Simmons, a Past-President of the Institute, comments on the Institute's attitude toward professional ethics:

'The aim throughout has been to guide and to trust—not to command.' (p. 180.)

It was only in 1946, that the Institute established a Professional Conduct Committee on a permanent basis and introduced a Code of Conduct. In June 1961, the President (J. H. Gunlake) announced drastic reforms of the whole approach to professional ethics.

Also, F. C. Hawkes (Secretary of the Institute), 'The Institute 1886–1946', *Journal of the Institute of Chartered Auctioneers and Estate Agents Institute*, November, 1946.

'The man of good intent needs no written rules to guide his conduct, but even he needs some protection, and most of us, plunged into the hurly-burly of the daily struggle for existence, welcome some definition of the rules by which the game should be played.'

[7] The general principles of the Hippocratic Oath are that the medical

practitioner must: share knowledge with other practitioners; not harm people by misapplication of knowledge; not undertake treatment outside his own competence; not divulge information obtained from the patient; not abuse the doctor-patient relationship.

In 1949, the World Medical Association produced 'The Declaration of Geneva', which is an extended version of the Hippocratic Oath, also 'The International Code of Ethics', which outlines ethical obligations.

S. J. Hadfield, *Law and Ethics for Doctors*, London, 1958, Chapter 7, 'Medical Ethics', especially pp. 38–43.

[8] E. Muirhead Little, *History of the British Medical Association 1832–1932*, London, 1932, pp. 287–95.

The *British Medical Association* has codes covering: Medical Consultations in Practice; Other Intra-Professional Obligations; Examining Medical Officers; Industrial Medical Officers; Guidance for Professional Code in Relation to Dentists (*a*) consultations, (*b*) anaesthetics.

[9] W. Pyke-Lees, *Centenary History of the General Medical Council 1858–1958: The History and Present Work of the Council*, London, 1958, pp. 12–13.

Even without a code, the G.M.C. investigated and disciplined medical practitioners. Trouble occurred in the very first case. Standing Orders were then drawn up, allowing for preliminary investigation by Branch Councils in England, Scotland and Ireland. Between 1858 and 1886, the G.M.C. took consequential action in twenty-three cases, and, until the Medical Act, 1882, erasure from the Medical Register was irreversible. In 1898, the Executive Committee reported that no rule had been made against advertising and recommended condemnation by Council. This proposal was rejected. Eventually, a formal 'Notice' was issued in 1905 against advertising and canvassing. Other 'Notices' followed against unqualified assistants selling poisons in 'open shops', and false certification. These three 'Notices' were consolidated in a 'Warning Notice' of 1914. In 1916, a 'Notice' was issued against association with uncertified midwives, and in 1923 against abuse of dangerous drugs.

[10] J. R. V. Marchant, *Barrister-at-Law: An Essay on the Legal Position of Counsel in England*, London, 1905.

This book traces the rights, privileges and obligations of English Counsel. For barristers, professional conduct is now codified, more or less, in a succession of 'Annual Statements' issued by the General Council of the Bar.

Established in 1895, to replace the Bar Committee of 1883, the Bar Council is an elected body representing the whole Bar. Rules concerning etiquette and practice are prescribed, definite complaints against barristers may be investigated, though disciplinary action is vested in Benchers of the various Inns of Court.

These rules have been brought together unofficially.

W. W. Boulton, *A Guide to Conduct and Etiquette at the Bar of England and Wales*, London, (3rd Ed.) 1961.

[11] See, Sir Thomas Lund, 'The Professional Discipline of Solicitors' in R. S. Pollard (Editor), *Administrative Tribunals at Work*, London, 1950.

Sir Thomas Lund, Secretary of the *Law Society*, has produced two short introductions to the problems of professional conduct: *A Lecture on Professional Conduct and Etiquette* (1950); *Some Additional Aspects of Professional Conduct and Etiquette* (1951).

[12] See Charles Woodward, 'Professional Practice' in J. A. Gotch (Editor), *Growth and Work of the R.I.B.A. 1834–1934*, London, 1934.

[13] Barrington Kaye, *The Development of the Architectural Profession in Britain*, London, 1960.

Tables 1 and 2, pp. 173–4 provide figures from the Census 1861, and for the size of R.I.B.A. membership in 1860. The 1861 Census gave 3,843 architects. In 1860, there were 512 corporate members of the R.I.B.A., i.e. about 10–12 per cent of architects. Today, just over three-quarters of Registered Architects are corporate members of the *Royal Institute of British Architects*.

[14] See, H. V. Lanchester, 'Competitions' in Gotch, op. cit., pp. 99–115.

The method of conducting architectural competitions had been a problem for many years, even before foundation of the R.I.B.A.

[15] R. B. Pilcher, *The Institute of Chemistry of Great Britain and Ireland: History of the Institute 1877–1914*, London, 1914, pp. 70–1, 74.

[16] Ibid., pp. 116–24.

[17] See, J. P. C. Coast, *The Land Agents Society 1901–1939*, London, 1939, p. 88, and Hawkes, op. cit.

[18] B. Y. Landis, *Professional Codes: A Sociological Analysis to Determine Applications to the Educational Profession*, New York, 1927, pp. ix, 87–8.

[19] R. M. MacIver, 'The Social Significance of Professional Ethics', *The Annals*, 1955, CCXCVII, 118–24 (p. 122).

(A revised version of the essay in *The Annals*, 1922, CI, 5–11.)

[20] This step did not apparently satisfy management consultants, for in 1956, the 'Management Consultants' Association' was founded as an employers' organization. By 1962, members were undertaking about 85 per cent of all management consultant work. In 1962, the Association sponsored formation of the '*Institute of Management Consultants*'.

[21] V. C. Coley, 'B.I.M. Register of Management and Industrial Consultants', *The Manager*, 1960, XXVII, 360–2.

The Code covers items 1, 8, 20, 22, 25, 26 in Table 6.1.

[22] See 'Statement Upon Matters of Professional Conduct' (Revised June 1960).

Pharmaceutical Society of Great Britain: Calendar 1961–1962, pp. 61–3.

[23] The *Pharmaceutical Society* indicates the position clearly: 'It is not implied by the issue of this Statement that all matters which should be the subject of standards of professional conduct are included but only those upon which it is considered that guidance is needed. The Council, in considering whether action should be taken on any matter, are not limited to matters mentioned in this statement, nor on the other hand does it follow that all

instances of conduct at variance with the Statement would, when receiving such consideration, be treated as of equal importance.'

Ibid., p. 61.

[24] *Institute of Practitioners in Advertising: Articles of Association*, Article 56 (A), p. 27. Also see two other documents:

Bye-laws relating to Standards of Practice (Dated November 1957).

The Interpretation of Bye-law No. 2 (Dated April 1958).

While the Institute aims to maintain and improve the standards of advertising practice, action seems hampered by the low proportion of agency staff belonging to the I.P.A. Agency membership is representative of all advertising agencies, but personal membership equals only one-tenth of total advertising personnel. To encourage an expansion in the number of personal members, special concessions were announced in 1961 for experienced advertising staff.

(See Presidential Address by Sinclair Wood to the I.P.A., 12 April 1961.)

[25] The *Proprietory Association of Great Britain* first issued a 'Code of Standards of Advertising Practice' in 1937. The Association, representing the principal advertisers of medicines, has revised the Code several times. The 'British Code of Standards for the Advertising of Medicines and Treatments' was based on the P.A.G.B. Code.

See 'The Advertising of Proprietory Medicines', *Leaflets on Advertising No. 2* (I.P.A., 1959).

[26] The 'British Code of Advertising Practice' was introduced in January 1962, chiefly through the efforts of the *Advertising Association*. Thirteen associations connected with advertising or media, support the code. It makes six main recommendations applicable to advertising generally, plus special references to certain problems. Also the 'Advertising Standards Authority' was set up to secure uniform interpretation and application of the Code.

The British Code of Advertising Practice (1st Ed.) 1962.

How Advertising Disciplines Itself (Advertising Association), 1962.

[27] See *Standards in Market Research, Market Research Society* (adopted in November 1954, revised December 1960).

The document covers: Part I Code of Practice (relating to integrity and standards of work); Part II Responsibilities to Informants; Part III Standard Conditions for Market Research Surveys; Part IV Standards in Reporting on Survey Results.

[28] Registration is not easily obtained. Most Registration Acts seem to be based on the principle, that the public ought to be free to choose between qualified and unqualified practitioners. Some eighteen Medical Bills were presented before Registration was finally obtained in 1858; many more were presented to secure an amending Act in 1882. The architects put forward thirteen Bills between 1888 and 1913, finally obtaining Registration in 1931. Other occupations have also tried to achieve Registration. For example, up until 1912, accountants presented seventeen unsuccessful Bills, and two more afterwards. The following are only the published Bills: Accountants 1880, 1893, 1896, 1900, 1909, 1911, 1912; Auctioneers, Estate Agents, Valuers 1914, 1935–6, 1936–7, 1962–3; Engineers 1920, 1926; Osteopaths

1930–1, 1932–3, 1933–4, 1936–7; Opticians 1927 (obtained 1958); Stock-brokers 1936; Surveyors 1936, 1962–3; Travel Agents 1963.

²⁹ Courts are only concerned with procedure: whether the person accused of misconduct was given a reasonable chance to offer a defence; if the decision was unbiased and reached in good faith. The Courts will not act as an appeal from a domestic tribunal. The association's procedure is not bound by legal rules of evidence on procedure. It may inform its own mind in any way thought fit, providing the accused is given fair opportunity for defence. It is not liable to give any reasons for a decision.

Dennis Lloyd, 'The Disciplinary Powers of Professional Bodies', *The Modern Law Review*, 1950, XIII, 281–306 (pp. 284–85).

³⁰ The General Council of the Bar only appears to have published overall figures since 1957–8. The 'Annual Statement' 1958 gave the following information: 39 complaints—30 rejected, 3 forwarded to the Inns for further action, 3 informed that breach of conduct had taken place but no further action, no decision had been reached in 3 cases. Details since 1958 give much the same picture, fewer cases.

³¹ Tables 6.4 and 6.5 are based on material taken from the *Annual Report and Accounts* of the *Institute of Chartered Accountants in England and Wales* for the years 1949 to 1962. Appendix—'Disciplinary Action: Members'.

³² *Institute of Chartered Accountants in England and Wales: Royal Charters and Bye-laws*, Supplemental Charter 1948, Clause 22, and Bye-laws 103–13 (pp. 19–22).

³³ Emile Durkheim, *Professional Ethics and Civic Morals*, London, English Translation, 1957, pp. 5–9, 14–15, 23–4.

CHAPTER SEVEN

¹ Organizations such as the N.U.T. and B.M.A. are in close contact with institutions and teachers, engaged in training and education of entrants to their professions. They do not hesitate to make representations on education. Both associations actively engage in campaigns for recruitment to the profession.

² Nine accountancy bodies are listed in Appendix I, three others are 'Institute of Internal Auditors', 'Faculty of Auditors', 'Association of Industrial and Commercial Executive Accountants'. The *Institute of Chartered Accountants in England and Wales* has an unequalled reputation. The *Association of Certified and Corporate Accountants, Institute of Municipal Treasurers and Accountants* and *Institute of Cost and Works Accountants* are also important. The rest are small, without much standing outside their own membership.

³ The 'Intermediate Certificate in Management Studies' and 'Diploma in Management Studies' are administered jointly by the *British Institute of Management* and Ministry of Education. These examinations are inducing some uniformity among associations connected with management, apart from the fact that eight associations recognize the Intermediate Certificate as exemption from their Intermediates.

See, *Education and Training in the Field of Management: A Service for Students,* (*British Institute of Management*) (n.d.).

⁴ T. G. Rose, *History of the Institute of Industrial Administration 1919–1951,* London, 1954, pp. 32–6, 42–51, 55–9, 62–71.

⁵ The *Royal College of Surgeons of England* holds examinations for Membership (M.R.C.S.) and Fellowship (F.R.C.S.); examinations in Dental Surgery, Fellowship (F.D.S. R.C.S.) and Licentiateship (L.D.S. R.C.S.); examinations in Anaesthesia, for Fellowship in the Faculty of Anaesthetists (F.F.A., R.C.S.); also conjoint examinations in nine post-graduate diplomas, with the *Royal College of Physicians of London.* There are seven post-graduate teaching and research departments within the College. Twenty-one sets of lectures and demonstrations are given annually. Aware of the slender links binding members to the College, an attempt has been made to build up corporate feeling. The College started a journal, and under the 1957 Charter, a 5gs. annual subscription was introduced for Fellows.
Annual Report of the Royal College of Surgeons of England.
Royal College of Surgeons of England: Postgraduate Education.

⁶ For example, in 1961–62, the numbers of candidates in various associations: *Institute of Bankers* (1962) 29,316, *Chartered Insurance Institute* (1961) 15,327, *Chartered Institute of Secretaries* (1960–1) 12,008, *Institute of Cost and Works Accountants* (1961) 11,346, *Institute of Chartered Accountants in England and Wales* (1962) 8,214, *Library Association* (1962) 8,152, *Association of Certified and Corporate Accountants* (1961) 4,890, *Law Society* (1962) 4,405, *Royal Institute of British Architects* (1962) 1,324.

⁷ All subjects are for the Intermediate Examinations (1964).
Institute of Chartered Accountants in England and Wales
Book-keeping (Two Papers), Auditing, General Paper (including the elements of English Law).
Association of Certified and Corporate Accountants
Section I: Book-keeping and Accounts (Two Papers), Costing, Section II: Mercantile Law, Auditing, Economic and Business Statistics.
Institute of Muncipal Treasurers and Accountants
Accountancy (Two Papers), Auditing, Commercial Law, Elements of Public Administration, Financial Administration.
Institute of Cost and Works Accountants
Part I: Industrial Administration, Book-keeping, Economics, Statistics; Part II: Cost Accountancy—Labour, Cost Accountancy—Materials, Cost Accountancy—Overhead.
Chartered Institute of Secretaries
Accountancy, Economic Theory, English, General Principles of Law.
Corporation of Secretaries
Accountancy, General Principles of Law, Economics, Secretarial Practice, English, Company Law.
Institute of Bankers
Part I: English, Economics, Book-keeping, General Principles of Law, Commercial Geography.

⁸ To measure candidates' success, several years must be analysed. Two recent extensive reports give some details.

Chartered Insurance Institute

In 1951, 300 candidates qualified to start taking the Associateship Part I examination (i.e. first part of the Final Examination). By 1959, about 12 per cent (35) had completed the examinations for the Associateship, without failing at any stage. Altogether about 26 per cent (80) had completed the Associateship, in addition, another 3.6 per cent (11) had gone on to pass the Fellowship Examination. In all, 56 per cent (168) had some success, passing one or more parts of the Associateship examinations.

Handbook of the Annual Conference of the Chartered Insurance Institute 1960, Appendix B, 'Report of the Educational Policy Committee', paragraph 35, p. 61.

Institute of Chartered Accountants in England and Wales

During 1952, 1,388 candidates entered into articles. By May 1960, 40 per cent (479) of those completing articled service (five years) had passed each examination at first attempt (i.e. both the Intermediate and Final Examinations), another 24 per cent (279) passed each examination at not later than the third attempt, 6 per cent (76) passed otherwise. Altogether, 64.9 per cent (901) had passed the Intermediate and Final, 78.9 per cent (1,096) had passed the Intermediate only, or Intermediate and Final.

Institute of Chartered Accountants in England and Wales, Report of the Committee on Education and Training (The 'Parker Report') (1961), paragraph 61, p. 30.

⁹ For example, the following associations have specialist groups: *Institution of Civil Engineers, Institution of Mechanical Engineers, Institution of Electrical Engineers, Institute of Physics and the Physical Society, British Institution of Radio Engineers, Chartered Insurance Institute, Library Association, Plastics Institute, Institute of British Photographers, Purchasing Officers Association.*

¹⁰ Each group holds symposia, meetings and discussions. In 1961, 41,430 members had specially registered for group membership. In 1962, the number had risen to 51,691. The groups cover the following subjects: Applied Mechanics; Automatic Control; Education and Training; Hydraulic Plant and Machinery; Industrial Administration and Engineering Production; Internal Combustion Engines; Lubrication and Wear; Manipulative and Mechanical Handling Machinery; Nuclear Energy; Process Engineering, Refrigeration, Ventilation and Vacuum Plant; Railway Engineering; Steam Plant; Thermodynamics and Fluid Mechanics.

Institution of Mechanical Engineers: Annual Report of the Council for 1961, pp. 11–14; *for 1962 (Proceedings 1963*, CLXXVII, 433–4).

¹¹ *Institution of Electrical Engineers: Royal Charter and Byelaws* (Revised 1962), Byelaw 44, 'Constitution and Election of Council', Byelaw 93, 'Authority to Create Divisions'.

The 'Electronics Division' and 'Power Division' each contain ten professional groups, the 'Science and General Division' has eight groups.

¹² After prolonged negotiation, the 'Universities' Scheme' for accountants was started in 1945. A number of universities in England and Wales agreed

to provide full-time degree courses, which included accountancy subjects. Graduates are given exemption from the Chartered Accountants' and Certified Accountants' Intermediate Examinations, plus a reduction in the period of articles to three years. The Scheme has proved disappointing. Firstly, the intake has been much less than expected, 140 in 1954, 100 in 1959–60 (against 200 p.a. originally estimated). Secondly, less than half of those graduating have entered the profession. Thirdly, there has been no marked difference in practical performance, between these graduates and other graduates who have to take the Intermediate and Final Examinations. *Institute of Chartered Accountants in England and Wales: Report of the Committee on Education and Training* (1961), pp. 53–5.

[13] Only three associations appear to have a Council committee directly concerned with reviewing recruitment and training: *Institute of Actuaries* (Recruitment Committee), *Chartered Insurance Institute* (Careers Committee), *Institute of Practitioners in Advertising* (Recruitment and Training Committee). Probably other associations use their Education Committee for this purpose.

[14] Even the Church of England has shown concern with the 'professional image'. (See *The man He wants*, a Report published by the Church Information Office, February 1962.) Also in 1962, it was announced that a full-time recruitment officer would be appointed, and an illustrated booklet distributed to schools entitled *You?*

[15] A 'Public Relations Committee', or an equivalent, can be found in the following associations: *Royal Institute of British Architects, Institution of Civil Engineers, Royal Institution of Chartered Surveyors, Chartered Institute of Secretaries, Institute of Builders, Institute of Quantity Surveyors, British Optical Association, Society of Radiographers, Institute of Marine Engineers, Advertising Association.*

Three have a 'Professional Status Committee': *Royal Institute of Chemistry, Textile Institute, Institute of Housing.*

The *British Institute of Management* has an 'External Relations Committee'.

About a dozen Associations have a special Information/Press/Public Relations Officer.

[16] The *Law Society* has been associated with a television film (*The Lawyers*) and a paperback book (H. J. B. Cockshutt, *The Services of a Solicitor*, London, 1961). The R.I.B.A. started publishing a series of pamphlets in 1963 (*Your House, How to Choose an Architect, Working With Your Architect*). The *Incorporated Society of Auctioneers and Landed Property Agents* issued a film in 1962 (*The First Years*), outlining the career of a school-leaver up until the time he awaits results of his Final Examinations. In 1963, a film (*Municipal Engineering as a Career*) was made for the *Institution of Municipal Engineers*, to encourage recruitment.

In April 1962, the Stock Exchange began regular advertising of available services.

In July 1962, Sir Thomas Lund (Secretary of the *Law Society*) spoke to the International Bar Association Conference about the problem of publicizing the solicitor. He said the Society had been advised that a minimum of £100,000 would be required each year to make a worthwhile impact. (*The Times*, 21 July 1962.)

[17] In 1920, A. H. Jenkins brought an action against the *Pharmaceutical Society*, to test the Society's powers under the Royal Charter and Pharmacy Acts.

Judgment restrained the Society from (*a*) regulating members' hours of business, (*b*) regulating wages and conditions of employment, between masters and employees who are members, (*c*) regulating prices, (*d*) insuring members.

Jenkins v. The Pharmaceutical Society (1921), I Ch. 392, *The Calendar of the Pharmaceutical Society 1961–62*, p. 139.

The Pharmaceutical Journal, 1920, CV, 586–405.

Dissatisfaction over remuneration has built up since the introduction of the National Health Service. Pressure has again been put on the Society to undertake negotiations. (See Report of a Special General Meeting held in April 1962, *The Pharmaceutical Journal*, 1962, CLXXXVIII, 380–3.)

[18] The following Qualifying Associations for Medical Auxiliaries have a 'Salaries Committee': *Chartered Society of Physiotherapy, Association of Occupational Therapists, Society of Chiropodists* (not the *Institute of Medical Laboratory Technology*). The *Society of Remedial Gymnasts* also negotiates over salaries. Among the social workers, the *Institute of Almoners* has a 'Salaries Committee'. There are about a dozen organizations for social workers, though they are not qualifying bodies. All have negotiating committees.

[19] One of the earliest comprehensive 'Remuneration Surveys' was carried out by the *Royal Institute of Chemistry*, the reports are now triennial (1956, 1959, 1962). Other associations conduct regular surveys: *Institute of Physics and the Physical Society, Institution of Metallurgists, Institution of Works Managers*. The *Institute of Office Management* makes a regular survey of office workers' salaries. At least three other associations are contemplating remuneration surveys (1963).

[20] The 'National Pharmaceutical Union' was the outcome of the Jenkin's Judgment restraining the *Pharmaceutical Society* (See Note 17). Similarly, the 'Association of Official Architects' was formed in 1960 by R.I.B.A. members, as a negotiating body. The 'Association of Local Government Engineers and Surveyors' appeared in 1947, after the *Institution of Municipal Engineers* had petitioned for a Royal Charter, and excluded any 'trade union' objects.

See 'Professional Bodies turn Eyes to Collective Bargaining', *The Times*, 12 November 1962.

[21] The R.I.C.S. examinations were divided into eight sections. The Intermediate Examination for each section contained eight or nine papers, drawn from twenty-three different subjects. Each Final consisted of eight or nine papers drawn from thirty-two subjects.

(See *Rules and Syllabus for the Professional Examinations, Royal Institution of Chartered Surveyors*, 1961.)

In December 1961, the whole examination scheme was revised, and new examinations began in 1963, with the changeover being completed by 1967. Eight sections are reduced to five, making 150 separate papers, instead of 300 papers. This revision followed a report on educational policy published in 1960 (Chairman: H. W. Wells).

See *Rules and Syllabus for the Professional Examinations* and the *Candidates' Guide to the Professional Examinations* (1962).

[22] On 27 June 1961, an advertisement appeared in *The Times* issued by the *Royal Institution of Chartered Surveyors* entitled 'Letters are Letters are Letters', pointing out the difficulty of distinguishing between various designatory letters. In 1961, two private companies were formed (A.C.A. Ltd., and F.C.A. Ltd.) 'to advance and protect the status and interests of the accounting profession'. These were formed by the *Institute of Chartered Accountants in England and Wales* 'as a precaution against the registration of companies with those names by other persons'. (See *Report and Accounts 1961*, paragraph 156, also *The Times*, 7 November 1961.)

In mid-1962, the Privy Council circulated a letter to all Chartered professional organizations, asking them to restrict the use of designatory letters. (*The Times*, 30, 31 July 1962.)

[23] Estate Agents have tried to obtain registration. The latest attempt was in 1963. The *Royal Institution of Chartered Surveyors, Chartered Land Agents' Society, Chartered Auctioneers and Estate Agents Institute* and *Incorporated Society of Auctioneers and Landed Property Agents* had hoped to introduce the Estate Agents (Registration) Bill in Autumn 1961. However, in November, the Home Office invited discussions about details in the Bill, and introduction was postponed. In November 1962, the four bodies were joined by the *Incorporated Association of Architects and Surveyors*, the *Rating and Valuation Association* and the *Valuers Institution* in supporting a Memorandum circulated to all Members of Parliament. The Memorandum explained the need for registration and outlined a private Bill, to be introduced during the 1962–3 Session. Some Estate Agents resented the proposed legislation, so that between December 1961 and February 1962, committees were formed in various parts of the country. Their meetings led to foundation of the 'National Association of Estate Agents' on 6 March 1963. The Association conducted a vigorous campaign against the Bill, with advertisements in the national press, surveys of the number and qualifications of Estate Agents, and publication of *The Case Against: The Estate Agents' Bill*. Eventually, the Bill failed on Second Reading in the House of Commons, on 22 March 1963, defeated by a closure motion.

(See 'Estate Agents Demand More Safeguards for Public', *The Times*, 2 November 1962, also 7 November 1962.)

On 30 May 1962, leave was given to introduce the Travel Agents (Registration) Bill into the House of Commons. This Bill was sponsored by the Association of British Travel Agents, which contains about 90 per cent of travel agents, and promoted formation of the *Institute of Travel Agents* in 1956. Nothing came of the Bill.

[24] Examples in the twentieth century are: the *Institute of Physics* in 1918, the *Institution of Metallurgists* in 1945, the *British Institute of Management* in 1948, and the *Institute of Printing* in 1960.

[25] *The Metallurgist*, 1960, I, 92, 266–9, and 1962, II, 28–30, 41. In 1962, the *Institution of Mining and Metallurgy* joined the three organizations on the Joint Consultative Committee.

[26] *Institution of Civil Engineers: Report of the Council 1961–62*, paragraphs 82–4.

At a Special General Meeting of the Municipal Engineers on 13 June 1961, a poll was demanded of all members in Britian. As a result of the poll, Council decided not to proceed.

Institution of Municipal Engineers: Annual Report of the Council 1961–62, p.5.

[27] In his Presidential Address to the *Institution of Civil Engineers* in November 1961, Sir George McNaughton proposed formation of a high-level co-ordinating board, to speak for all Chartered Civil, Mechanical and Electrical Engineers '. . . so powerful that other Chartered bodies could not afford to stand outside'. The suggestion had a mixed reception. (See correspondence in *The Times*, 10, 13, 15, 16, 17 18 November 1961.) In 1962 discussions took place to establish a 'Professional Engineering Institutions Confederation'. In October 1962, 'The Engineering Institutions' Joint Council' was inaugurated, with representatives from the following associations: *Royal Aeronautical Society, Institution of Chemical Engineers, Institution of Civil Engineers, Institution of Electrical Engineers, Institution of Gas Engineers, Institute of Marine Engineers, Institution of Mechanical Engineers, Institution of Mining Engineers, Institution of Mining and Metallurgy, Institution of Municipal Engineers, Institution of Production Engineers, British Institution of Radio Engineers, Institution of Structural Engineers.*

[28] J. D. Stewart, *British Pressure Groups*, Oxford, 1958.

S. E. Finer, *Anonymous Empire: A Study of the Lobby in Great Britain*, London, 1958.

A. Potter, *Organized Groups in British National Politics*, London, 1961.

[29] Professor Eckstein clarifies the distinction between interest and pressure groups.

H. Eckstein, *Pressure Group Politics: The Case of the B.M.A.*, London, 1960, 'Introduction'.

[30] The *Pharmaceutical Society*'s 'Parliamentary Fund' has a long history. Originally, in 1815, a fund was started for the representation of pharmacy in the House of Commons. Later, the Society itself was founded, in 1841, as a resistance to intended legislation. Jacob Bell, a founder, was supported by the fund in his election as M.P. for St Albans from 1850. He guided the first Pharmacy Act through Parliament. After the 1900s, special funds were raised from time to time, for the support of various candidates. Since the election of Sir Hugh Linstead in 1942, the fund has been on a regular basis, to secure continuity of representation.

The Pharmaceutical Society of Great Britain: Calendar 1961–2, pp. 99–101.

[31] For example:

Between 1954 and 1962, many Chartered Accountants were invited to serve on advisory, inquiry and reviewing committees at a National level, at Home and Abroad, quite apart from local and regional committees. (7 in 1954, 15 in 1955, 4 in 1956, 9 in 1957, 6 in 1958, 17 in 1959, 22 in 1960, 16 in 1961, 9 in 1962.) (See *Institute of Chartered Accountants in England and Wales: Report and Accounts, 1954–62*.)

In the case of the *Institute of Actuaries*, between 1920 and 1960, members sat on nine Royal Commissions. During the period 1958 to 1962, members were sitting on nine Government standing or inquiry committees.

The Institute of Actuaries Yearbook 1962–1963, pp. 66–68.

³² The following associations have 'Law and Parliamentary Committees': *Institute of Chartered Accountants* and *Association of Certified and Corporate Accountants* (Accountants Joint Parliamentary Committee); *Chartered Institute of Secretaries; Corporation of Secretaries; Institute of Housing; Institute of Quantity Surveyors;* six associations connected with the 'land profession'.

³³ For example: the *Royal Institution of Chartered Surveyors* is one of the most active associations.

During 1960–1, the Institution submitted memoranda on, or considered fourteen Bills, and a number of Private Bills dealing with matters affecting the profession. Evidence was invited, or submitted, to Ministries or Government Departments on at least eight other matters. In 1961–2, the Institution considered the Pipelines Bill, Gas (Underground Storage) (Chilcomb) Bill, Housing Act, 1961, also Draft Regulations and recommendations were invited or contemplated on four other matters.

Royal Institution of Chartered Surveyors: Annual Report, 1960–1, 1961–2.

INDEX

Accountants, 3, 9, 20, 24, 31, 51, 56, 69, 70, 74, 151, 152, 167, 168, 175, 176–8, 183, 184, 185, 186, 197, 203, 206, 212, 260, 261, 273, 288

Accountants, Association of Certified and Corporate, 31, 70, 117, 168, 203, 222, 252, 272, 275, 277, 281, 284, 289, 290, 296

Accountants, Association of International, 146, 222, 252

Accountants, Incorporated Association of Cost and Industrial (also called 'The Cost Accountants' Association'), 223, 252

Accountants in England and Wales, Institute of Chartered, 13, 31, 51, 69, 74, 92, 100, 114, 117, 118, 125, 126, 131, 132, 140, 146, 159, 163, 167, 168, 170, 175, 176–8, 183, 203, 222, 248, 273, 275, 277, 281, 283, 289, 290, 291–2, 294, 295, 296

Accountants, Institute of Company, 223, 252

Accountants, Institute of Cost and Works, 72, 222, 251, 277, 284, 289, 290

Accountants, Society of Commercial, 223, 253

Accountants, Society of Incorporated, 68, 74, 176, 203, 248, 272

Accountants and Auditors, British Association of, 222, 251

Act of Parliament, as method of incorporation, 88–9

Actuaries, 24, 64, 86, 152, 232, 260, 261, 279

Actuaries, Institute of, 24, 56, 63–4, 92, 112, 121, 122, 123, 125, 132, 167, 189, 223, 247, 272, 275, 277, 281, 285 292, 295

Advertising, 49, 144, 150, 197, 203, 223, 287, 288

Advertising Association, 106, 139, 168, 223, 251, 284, 288, 292

Advertising, British Code of, 170

Advertising, Institute of Practitioners in, 139, 168, 169, 179, 223, 251, 275, 279, 284, 287, 288, 292

Advertising Joint Intermediate Examination, 139

Advertising Managers' Association, 257

Advisory Committees in technical colleges, 144, 145

Aeronautical Society, Royal, 84–5, 93, 126, 137, 168, 203, 223, 247, 274, 275, 277, 295

Agricultural Engineers' Association, 256

Agricultural Engineers, Institution of, 80, 226, 252, 277

Allsop, P., 281

Almoners, 78, 79, 224

Almoners, Institute of, 78–9, 223, 250, 275, 278, 293

Amalgamation of Qualifying Associations, 202–4

Ambiguities in professional organization, 42–3

Analysis of characteristics of professions, 4–6, 9

Analysis of content of ethical code, 164–8

Analytical Chemists, Society of, 256

Anthropological Institute, Royal, 255

Antiquaries, Society of, 18, 22, 254, 267, 268

Apothecaries, 16, 20, 211, 261, 263, 266, 279

Apothecaries, Society of, 19, 21, 52, 66, 122, 246, 261, 266, 279

Appleyard, E., 274

Applied Biologists, Association of, 257

Arbitrators, Institute of, 242, 251

Archaeological Institute of Great Britain and Ireland, Royal, 255

Architects, 20, 23, 52, 66, 67, 83, 151, 152, 161, 162, 172, 186, 206, 211, 260, 261, 271, 276, 281, 287, 288, 291, 292, 294

Architects, Association of Official, 41, 293

Architects, Royal Institute of British, 23, 56, 58–9, 66–7, 82, 92, 106, 114, 115, 117, 185, 189, 203, 224, 247, 271, 275, 276, 277, 280, 281, 282, 283, 285, 287, 290, 292, 293

Index

Architects, Society of, 66, 185, 203, 247

Architects and Surveyors, Faculty, 67, 224, 251, 278

Architects and Surveyors, Incorporated Association of, 67, 167, 224, 251, 278

Architectural Association, 133, 223, 247

Articled service (pupilage), 130–2

Artists, Royal Society of British, 255

Arts, Royal Society of, 18, 27, 85, 124, 254, 264–5, 268, 279

Asiatic Society, Royal, 255

Assistant Masters in Secondary Schools, Association of, 256

Assistant Mistresses in Secondary Schools, Association of, 256

Associations, contributions to society, 139–49, 204–13

Associations, co-operation between, 138–9, 202–4

Associations, development of, 146, 181–8

Astronomical Society, Royal, 22, 27, 36, 255, 267, 268

Attorneys, Solicitors, Proctors and others not being Barristers practising in the Courts of Law and Equity of the United Kingdom, Society of, (*See* Law Society)

Auctioneers, 24, 163, 183, 184, 225, 288

Auctioneers and Estate Agents Institute, Chartered, 93, 126, 132, 133, 163, 167, 225, 248, 275, 277, 281, 285, 294

Auctioneers and Landed Property Agents, Incorporated Society of, 163, 167, 225, 251, 275, 277, 294

Auditors, Faculty of, 252, 289

Auditors, Institute of Internal, 289

Automobile Assessors, Institute of, 252

Automobile Engineers, Institution of, 203, 247

Ballard, W. E., 273

Bambrick, J. W., 273

Bankers, Institute of, 117, 118, 126, 141, 169, 225, 248, 275, 277, 281, 284, 290

Bar Committee, 22, 286

Bar Council (General Council of the Bar), 42, 130, 171, 175, 286

Bar Students, 21, 42, 121, 280–1

Barbers' Company, 17, 262

Barber-Surgeons, Company of, 17, 19, 66, 247, 262

Barnaby, K. C., 265, 273

Barristers, 6, 7, 17, 18, 42, 121, 125, 151, 152, 154, 171, 172, 175, 212, 225, 286

Bell, Jacob, 52, 53, 61, 268, 270, 271, 279, 295

Bell, R. T., 272

Benchers of Inns of Court, 17, 21, 42, 161, 171, 286

Bibliographical Society, 256

Biochemical Society, 257

Biology, Institute of, 242, 254

Birks, M., 265, 268, 278

Book-keepers, Institute of, 225, 251

Boot and Shoe Institution, British, 225, 251, 277

Botanic Society of London, Royal, 255

Botanical Society of the British Isles, 255

Boulton, W. W., 286

Bowen, H. E., 5, 260, 261

Brandeis, L. D., 261

Braunholtz, W. T. K., 273

Brewing, Institute of, 74, 115, 126, 225, 248

Breyer, J. L. F., 267

British Academy, 26, 34, 257, 269

British Medical Association, 12, 15, 23, 26, 40, 41, 160, 255, 268, 269, 289

British Optical Association, 167, 236, 249, 275, 278, 285, 292

Brown, C. K. F., 266, 278

Brown, Richard, 273

Builders, Faculty of, 253

Builders, Institute of, 145, 226, 247, 275, 277, 278–9

Building Estimators, Institute of, 254

Building Societies Institute, 226, 252, 277

Building Surveyors' Institute, 146, 254

Bureacracy and professionalism, 8–9, 41, 151

Cardiological Technicians of Great Britain, Society of, 253

Carey, J. L., 259

Carr-Saunders, Sir A. M., 3, 5, 259, 260, 261, 284

Ceramics, Institute of, 226, 254, 277

Charges, scales of, 161, 163, 170

Charter, Royal, 89–91, 192, 193, 275

Chartered Qualifying Associations listed, 92–3

Chemical Engineers, Institution of, 80, 145, 251, 273, 275, 277, 295

Chemical Industry, Society of, 29, 256

Chemical Society, 22, 26, 29, 36, 37, 64, 65, 196, 255, 265, 267, 272, 274

Chemistry, Royal Institute of, 26, 29, 31, 64–5, 71, 89, 92, 112, 125, 126–7, 145, 162–3, 196, 226, 248, 268, 272, 274, 275, 276, 277, 281, 282, 292

Chemists, 3, 24, 31, 41, 64, 65, 80, 146, 151, 162, 168, 206, 268

Chemists, Society of Cosmetic, 258

Index

Chemists, British Association of, 41, 257
Chiropodists, Society of, 167, 234, 253, 275, 278, 293
Christian, E. B. V., 278
Christie, A. G., 260
Church, 6, 7, 16, 20, 21, 120, 156, 180, 267, 278, 292
Civil engineers, 23, 24, 52, 58, 68, 272, 295
Civil Engineers, Institution of, 23, 56, 57–8, 65, 67, 92, 121, 132, 137, 145, 167, 168, 183, 189, 202, 203, 227, 247, 271, 272, 275, 277, 281, 282, 283, 284, 285, 292, 295
Client-professional relationship, 7, 151–3, 157, 159, 161, 165–8
Clifford, C. D., 273
Clergy, 22, 125, 152, 211, 212, 267, 278
Clerks-of-Works of Great Britain, Institute of, 248
Clothing Institute, 253
Coast, J. P. C., 271, 287
Cockerell, H. A. L., 273, 280, 281, 282
Cockshutt, H. J. B., 292
Cogan, M. L., 2, 5, 259, 260
Cohen, H. J., 263
Cohen, Prof. J., 50, 270
Commerce, Institute of, 226, 250
Committees of Council, 102–6, 115–16, 292
Companies Acts as method of incorporation, 91, 94, 216, 275
Conduct, codes of, 30, 148 et seq., 205, 206, 219, 287; analysis of, 164–8; introduction of, 154, 155, 157; nature of, 164–70; problems of implementation, 170–1; sociological determinants, 150–9
Conduct, unprofessional, 171–9
Consulting Engineers, Incorporated Association of, 167, 257
Cookson, W. S., 278, 279
Co-ordinating Associations, 33, 39, 41
Co-ordination of practitioners as reason for association formation, 77–79
Cope, Sir Zachary, 262, 266, 274
Copeman, W. A., 280, 282
Corporate membership of associations, 15, 109–14, 118–19, 146, 179, 204, 217
Correspondence tuition: advantages and disadvantages, 141; criticism of, 140, 283; dependence of associations on, 140–1, 195–6, 212; development of, 140, 283; organization by associations, 134–5, 282
Council of Legal Education, 21, 42, 189
Councils of Qualifying Associations: committees, 102–6/composition,

105–6/distribution, 102–5/type, 104; constitution, 94; election of, 97–101; powers and duties, 94–6, 187, 190–1; problems, 96–102, 116–19, 217/co-ordination, 102/democracy, 97–9/experience, 101–2/representativeness, 99–101, 200/size, 96–7, 103, 194; and professional conduct, 163–4, 168–9, 175, 179
Cotgrove, S. F., 283
Craft guilds, 15–16, 263
Crew, A., 5, 259, 260
Crowther Report, 284

Dairy Technology, Society of, 243
Davidson, M., 265
Decorators and Interior Designers, Incorporated Institute of British, 226, 249
Dentists, 152, 172, 212, 286
Development of professional organization, 16–25
Dilemmas of Qualifying Associations: amalgamation, 202–4; competition, 200–2; examinations, 194–5; further specialization, 200; members' working conditions, 199–200; public relations, 198–9; recruitment, 197–8; technical communication, 196–7
Dining clubs in the eighteenth century, 19, 265
Directors, Institute of, 92, 257
Disciplinary action, 171–80
Disciplinary committees, 104, 168–9
Distribution of professional organization, factors determining, 43–6
Doctors, 20, 22, 40, 125, 152, 153, 159, 172, 211, 212, 286
Drinker, H. S., 5, 259, 260
Dugdale, William, 263
Durkheim, Emile, 4, 180, 259, 260, 289
Dyers and Colourists, Society of, 256

Eckstein, Prof. H., 295
Ecological Society, British, 257
Economic Society, Royal, 256
Edminson, M. W., 273
Education: for church, law and medicine in nineteenth century, 6, 120–1; as determinant of ethical code, 154
Education and Qualifying Associations: correspondence tuition, 134–5, 140–1; in nineteenth century, 120–9; National Certificate scheme, 142–3; provision for students, 132–3; provision of teaching institutions, 133–4; representation on external committees, 143–5; supervision of students, 130–2

Index

Educational opportunity and Qualifying Associations, 144, 146–7, 212–3

Election: of Council 97–101; of Honorary Officers, 101–2, 106–7

Electrical engineers, 183, 206, 295

Electrical Engineers, Institution of, 80, 81–82, 93, 117, 126, 137, 167, 196, 200, 227, 248, 274, 275, 277, 283, 284, 291, 295

Electronic and Radio Engineers, Institution of (*See* Radio Engineers, British Institution of)

Electronics, Institute of, 252

Engineering, 20, 40, 44, 45, 137, 144, 185, 196, 197, 200, 203, 204, 209, 216, 217, 281

Engineering Inspection, Institution of, 228, 251

Engineering Institutions' Part I Committee, 138, 283

Engineering Joint Examining Board, 137

Engineers, 9, 20, 24, 41, 51, 67, 68, 80–82, 86, 100, 151, 152, 153, 154, 156, 168, 183, 184, 186, 211, 212, 216, 226, 243, 260, 261, 288, 292, 295

Engineers Association, British, 257

Engineers' Guild, 41, 257

Engineers, Society of, 167, 230, 247

Engineers, Society of (1771), 265

Engineers-in-Charge, Institution of, 243, 249

Entomological Society of London, Royal, 22, 255, 267

Entry to professions, 30–1

Estate Agents (*See* Auctioneers and Estate Agents' Institute, Chartered)

Estate Agents, National Association of, 294

Estate Management, College of, 133, 281

Ethical code: functional determinants of, 157–9; in nineteenth century, 160–3; nature of, 164–5; objections to, 159–60; problems of implementing, 170–1; role of, 175–80; structural determinants of—need for introducing, 150–3/possibility of introducing, 154–6/'work codes', 169

Ethnological Society, 255

Etiquette, professional, 149

Eugenics Society, 257

Examinations in the nineteenth century, 120–1, 124–5

Examinations and Qualifying Associations: nature of examinations, 135–6; problems, 122–3, 125–9, 194–6, 205–6; twentieth century trends—elimination of preliminary,

136–7/exemption from final, 137–8/interassociation co-operation, 138–9

Exclusive Prestige Associations, 33–5

Executive Officers in Qualifying Associations, 96, 107–8, 116–18, 173, 174

Expansion of Qualifying Associations: numbers, 183–4; reasons for, 184–6; size, 117, 194, 222–45

Export, Institute of, 252, 284

Facilities offered to members of Qualifying Associations, 29, 32, 113–14, 196–7, 208–9, 218

Factors determining: distribution of organization, 43–6; emergence of organization, 48–50; expansion in numbers of associations, 184–6; need for ethical code, 151–3; possibility of introducing ethical code, 154–61; progress for associations, 186–8; recognition of associations, 190–2

Faraday Society, 70, 257

Finer, S. E., 295

Fire Engineers, Institution of, 228, 251, 275, 277

Fletcher, H. M., 280

Flexner, A., 5, 260

Forensic Science, British Academy of, 258

Formation of Non-Qualifying Associations, reasons for, 50–1

Formation of Qualifying Associations, reasons for: co-ordination of activities, 77–9; generation from existing organizations, 65–76; offering special facilities, 84–5; response to new developments, 79–84; search for status, 54–65

Foundrymen, Institute of British, 92, 244, 250

Functions of professional organization: primary, 28–30; secondary, 30–2

Future control of Qualifying Associations, 216–17

Fuel, Institute of, 92, 244, 252

Gage, A. T., 265

Garrett, A. A., 272

Gas Engineers, Institution of, 77, 93, 126, 228, 247, 273, 275, 277, 283, 295

General Council of the Bar (*See* Bar Council)

General Medical Council, 160, 172, 286

General Practitioners, College of, 245, 258

Gentlemen Practisers in the Courts of Law and Equity, Society of, 18, 19, 24, 247

Index

Geographical Association, 256
Geographical Society, Royal, 22, 27, 35, 36, 37, 255, 267, 269
Geologists' Association, 255
Geological Society, 37, 255, 267, 268, 274
Glass Painters, British Society of Master, 257
Glass Technology, Society of, 244, 257
Goodall, Charles, 264
Gotch, J. A., 271, 272, 280, 287
Government of Associations: Non-Qualifying Associations, 34–5, 36, 40; Qualifying Associations (*See* Councils of Qualifying Associations)
Greenwood, E., 5, 260
Grant of Arms, 8, 192, 193
Graphic Artists, Society of, 257
Gray's Inn, 246, 263
Grocers' Company, 66, 261
Groves, E. B., 273
Guilds, 15–16, 261, 262, 263

Hadfield, S. J., 286
Hakluyt Society, 255
Hamilton, S. B., 274
Hansel, C. E. M., 270
Harleian Society, 256
Hartley, Sir Harold, 264
Harveian Society of London, 255
Haslam, D. D., 283
Hawkes, F. C., 281, 285
Headmasters, Association of, 256
Headmistresses, Association of, 256
Health, Royal Society of, 256
Heating and Ventilating Engineers, Institution of, 134, 228, 249, 275, 277
Highway Engineers, Institute of, 252
Hippocratic Oath, 160, 285–6
Historical Association, 257
Historical Society, Royal, 256
Holmberg, Borje, 283
Holt-Smith, Bernice, 262, 265, 266
Honorary Officers in associations, 96, 98, 101–2, 106–7, 116, 187, 191, 276, 277
Horticultural Society, Royal, 254
Hospital Administrators, Institute of, 78, 232, 250, 273, 275, 278
Hospital Matrons, Association of, 257
Hotel and Catering Institute, 230, 254, 277
House, D. V., 159, 285
Housing, Institute of, 77, 132, 168, 230, 252, 273, 275, 277, 292, 296
Howitt, Sir Harold, 5, 259, 260
Hudson, D., 264, 279
Hughes, E., 266
Hume, Rev. A., 267

Hunterian Society, 255
Huizinga, J., 262

Illuminating Engineering Society, 257
Incorporation, methods of: by Act of Parliament, 88–9; by Companies Act, 91–4; by Royal Charter, 89–91
Industrial Administration, Institute of, 72–3, 185, 203, 253, 273
Industrial Artists, Society of, 257
Inner Temple, 246, 263
Inns of Court, 15, 17, 19, 21, 42, 65, 121, 130, 172, 188, 225, 246, 263, 289
Inns of Court Executive Committee, 42, 189
Insurance, College of, 134
Insurance Brokers, Corporation of, 139, 168, 231, 250, 275, 277, 283
Insurance Institute, Chartered, 74–6, 93, 112, 114, 115, 117, 126, 134, 135, 168, 203, 230, 249, 273, 275, 277, 280, 282, 284, 290–1, 292
Institutional Management Association, 232, 252
Iron and Steel Institute, 29, 71, 72, 92, 138, 202, 256

James, Miss M. R., 280
Jessup, H. W., 259
Joint examination schemes, 139, 202, 204
Journalists, Institute of, 92, 256
Journals, 113–14, 196–7, 222–45

Kaye, B., 5, 259, 260, 265, 272, 287
Kenyon, Sir Frederick, 269
Kohn, R. H., 259
Knowles, Dom David, 262, 263
Kramer, Stella, 263

Lamb, Sir Walter, 265
Lanchester, H. V., 84, 287
Land agents, 18, 49, 83, 200, 231
Land Agents' Society, Chartered, 55, 93, 133, 163, 167, 168, 231, 250, 271, 275, 277, 281, 294
'Land' profession, 133, 163, 183, 184
Landscape Architects, Institute of, 231, 252
Landis, B. Y., 164, 287
Law Society, 15, 24, 42, 43, 92, 118, 121, 123, 133, 161, 168, 169, 172, 173, 176, 189, 239, 246, 247, 268, 270, 278, 286, 290, 291, 292
Legal Executives, Institute of, 231, 254
Leigh, R. D., 5, 260
Lewis, R., 5, 259, 260, 261

Index

Linguists, Institute of, 167, 232, 250

Little, E. Muirhead, 268, 269, 286

Librarians, 24, 206, 231, 280

Library Association, 100, 112, 126, 133, 134, 231, 248, 275, 276, 277, 282, 283, 290

Lincoln's Inn, 246, 263

Linnean Society, 19, 22, 254, 265, 268, 274

Literature, Royal Society of, 255

Lloyds, 75

Local organization in Qualifying Associations, 100–1, 115–16

Locomotive Engineers, Institution of, 243, 250

Loss Adjusters, Chartered Institute of, 93, 231, 253, 277

Luckhurst, K. W., 264, 279

Lund, Sir Thomas, 286, 292

Lyons, Sir John, 264, 266

MacIver, R. M., 165, 287

MacNalty, Sir Arthur, 266

Maitland, F. W., 263

Marine Engineers, Institute of, 78, 93, 126, 137, 228, 249, 277, 283, 292, 295

Marketing and Sales Management, Institute of, 72, 233, 250, 273

Management, 40, 43, 45, 73, 142, 144, 146, 184, 185, 197, 202, 203, 216, 232, 245, 287, 289

Management, British Institute of, 72–3, 106, 169, 203, 232, 253, 275, 277, 278, 289, 292, 294

Management, Institute of Credit, 233, 253

Management Consultants, Institute of, 254, 287

Marchant, J. R. V., 266, 286

Market Research Society, 170, 233, 253, 288

Marshalcy, 61–2

Marshall, T. H., 5, 260

Marshals, Guild of, 61

Marx, I. C., 273

Maude, A., 5, 259, 260, 261

May, E. F., 270

McNaughton, Sir George, 295

Meat, Institute of, 253

Mechanical engineers, 24, 143, 295

Mechanical Engineers, Institution of, 24, 31, 56, 67–8, 93, 117, 121, 137, 142, 183, 189, 196, 203, 229, 247, 272, 275, 277, 283, 284, 291, 295

Medical auxiliaries, 31, 172, 199, 234

Medical Laboratory Technology, Institute of, 235, 250, 278, 293

Medical Officers of Health, Society of, 41, 255

Medicine, 6, 7, 19, 20, 40, 44, 45, 60, 120, 124, 150, 172, 189, 233, 234, 245, 261, 266, 267, 268, 271, 279

Medicine, Royal Society of, 257, 265

Membership of Qualifying Associations, 109–14, 217–18; advantages of, 30–1, 112–14, 213; general structure of, 109, 111, 118–19; requirements for 109–12

Menzies, G. K., 265

Metals, Institute of, 29, 71, 72, 202, 245, 257

Metallurgy, 143, 146, 235, 245, 294

Metallurgists, Institution of, 29, 71–2, 100, 112, 202, 235, 273, 275, 276, 278, 293, 294

Meteorological Society, Royal, 255

Microscopical Society, Royal, 255

Middle Temple, 246, 263

Midwives, 152, 172

Mill, H. R., 267

Milne, K. L., 5, 259, 260

Mine Managers, 172

Mineralogical Society, 256

Miniature Painters, Sculptors and Gravers, Royal Society of, 256

Mining and Metallurgy, Institution of, 29, 71, 72, 93, 145, 167, 235, 249, 278, 294, 295

Mining Engineers, Institution of, 74, 93, 115, 126, 145, 229, 249, 275, 277, 295

Minto, J., 280, 281, 282

Mitchell, P. Chalmers, 267

Moore, T. S., 267, 272

Motor Industry, Institute of the, 235, 251, 278

Municipal Building Management, Institute of, 254

Municipal engineers, 183, 203, 281, 294

Municipal Engineers, Institution of, 93, 100, 126, 132, 137, 202, 229, 248, 275, 276, 277, 281, 282, 283, 293, 295

Municipal Treasurers and Accountants, Institute of, 55, 93, 105, 117, 126, 168, 222, 248, 271, 275, 276, 277, 280, 289

Munk, W., 264

Museums Association, 169, 235, 275, 278

Mycological Society, British, 256

National Certificate examination scheme, 137–8, 141–4, 284

National Pharmaceutical Union, 257, 293

National Union of Teachers, 15, 23, 40, 41, 256, 269, 270, 289

Naval architects, 77, 78, 245

Index

Naval Architects, Royal Institution of, 77, 92, 126, 138, 245, 247, 273
Neave, S. A., 267
Newcomen Society, 257
Newman, C., 266, 271, 278
Niven, Mary M., 273
Non-Qualifying Associations: list of, 254–8; reasons for formation, 50–1; types—Co-ordinating 39/Exclusive Prestige 33–5/Non-selective Prestige, 37/Protective, 39–41/Study, 35–7
Norton, F. R., 281
Nuclear Energy Society, British, 210, 258
Nuclear Engineers, Institution of, 254
Numismatic Society, Royal, 255
Nursing, Royal College of, 257

Obstacles to formation of organization, 47–50
Obstetricians and Gynaecologists, Royal College of, 43, 93, 233, 252, 264
Occupational Associations, 22–3, 39–41, 181–2
Occupational control as determinant of ethical code, 156, 170–1
Occupational Therapists, Association of, 77, 234, 252, 293
Odgers, W. Blake, 278
Office Management, Institute of, 232, 251, 293
Oil and Colour Chemists' Association, 257
Oil Painters, Royal Institute of, 256
Ophthalmologists, Faculty of, 253
Opticians (See British Optical Association), 152, 172, 236, 288
Organization, Local, 115–16
Organization, origins of, 16–25, 47–87, 181–3
Organization, types of, 26–46, 181–3
Ornithologists' Union, British, 255
Osbourne, F. C., 272
Osteopaths, 288

Packaging, Institute of, 236, 253
Palaeontographical Society, 35, 255
Painters, Etchers and Engravers, Royal Society, 256
Painters in Water Colours, Royal Institute of, 255
Painters in Water Colours, Royal Society of, 254
Parker, W. F., 281
Parsons, R. H., 272
Parsons, Talcott, 5, 260
Patent Agents, Chartered Institute of, 31, 92, 126, 167, 189, 236, 248, 275

Personnel Management, Institute of, 76, 233, 250, 273, 275, 278
Petroleum, Institute of, 244, 257
Pevsner, Prof. N., 265, 269
Pharmaceutical Society of Great Britain, 12, 15, 23, 31, 52, 56, 59–61, 65, 103, 112, 114, 121, 122, 123, 133, 145, 169, 173, 189, 206, 236, 247, 267, 268, 275, 278, 281, 282, 287, 292, 293, 295
Pharmacists, 16, 31, 61, 86, 125, 152, 172, 186, 236
Philip, J. C., 267, 272
Philogical Society, 255
Photographers, Institute of British, 236, 250, 275, 278, 284, 291
Photographic Society, Royal, 255
Physical Society, 29, 70, 106, 145, 167, 196, 203, 237, 251, 273, 275, 277, 278, 282, 291, 293
Physicians, 16, 17, 120, 151, 159, 264, 265
Physicians of London, Royal College of, 17, 19, 21, 26, 42, 43, 56, 65, 89, 92, 160, 162, 188, 189, 192, 234, 246, 264, 266, 268, 274, 290
Physicists, 41, 70, 146, 168
Physics and the Physical Society, Institute of, 29, 70, 106, 145, 167, 196, 203, 237, 251, 273, 275, 278, 281, 282, 291, 293, 294
Physiotherapy, Chartered Society of, 54, 93, 100, 126, 234, 249, 271, 275, 276, 277, 278, 281, 293
Pilcher, R. B., 268, 272, 274, 280
Pippard, Prof. A. J. S., 282
Plant Engineers, Institution of, 243, 253
Plastics Institute, 139, 202, 237, 252, 275, 278, 291
Plucknett, T. F. T., 263
Plumb, J. H., 266
Pollard, R. S., 286
Pollock, Sir Frederick, 263
Poole, A. L., 262
Portrait Painters, Royal Society of, 256
Postal courses (See Correspondence tuition)
Potter, A., 295
Power, Sir D'Arcy, 265
Power, Eileen, 262
Poynton, T. L., 271, 280
Printing, Institute of, 237, 254, 278, 294
Printing Management, Institute of, 245, 254
Pritchard, J. L., 274
Prestige among Qualifying Associations 190–3
Prestige Associations, 33–5, 43, 44, 18,

303

Index

Problems connected with Council: co-ordination, 102; democracy, 97–9; experience, 101–2; representativeness, 99–101; size, 96–7

Problems of defining a profession: semantic confusion, 1–3; structural limitations, 3–6; dynamic realism, 6–9

Problems of Qualifying Associations: competition, 200–2; examinations, 194–6; extension, 202; further specialization, 200; members' working conditions, 199–200; public relations, 198–9; recruitment, 197–8; size, 194; technical communication, 196–7

Production Engineers, Institution of, 72, 80, 229, 251, 273, 275, 277

Professional conduct defined (*See also* Ethical code), 148–9

Professional conduct and Qualifying Associations: analysis of codes, 165–8; classification of procedures, 168–9; concern with professional conduct, 159–64, 218; investigation of unprofessional conduct, 171–5; problems of implementing code, 170–1

Professional-client relationship, 5, 7, 151–3, 157, 159, 161, 165–8, 177–8

Professional ethics: defined, 149; nature of, 149–50; role of, 175–80

Professional etiquette, 149

Professional image, 3, 6–7, 158–9, 182, 198–9, 211–12

Professional organization: ambiguities and variations in, 42–3; contrasted with trade unions, 14–15; development before nineteenth century, 16–21; development during nineteenth century, 21–5; factors determining distribution, 43–6; functions of, 27–32; obstacles to formation, 47–50; reasons for formation, 50–87; types of, 26–46, 181–2.

Professional practice, 149, 151–3

Professional-professional relationship, 166, 167, 177–8

Professional-public relationship, 7, 150, 163, 166, 167, 177, 178

Professional rules defined, 149

Professional status: improvement of, 10–13, 30, 86, 164–5, 190–3, 294; Qualifying Associations and, 54–65, 146, 186–8, 200–2, 211–12, 215–16; recognition of, 9, 12–13, 26, 30, 199–200, 214, 261

Professional status committee, associations with, 292

Professionalism versus business, 8, 261

Professionalization: abuse of the means, 190, 200–1, 205–6, 215–17; defined, 10; factors involved in, 10–13, 47- 50

Professionals, proportions as principals in private practice, 260

Professions: characteristics of, 3–6; classification of, 261; definition, 10; in eighteenth century, 20–1; principles involved in definition, 9; problems of definition, 1–9

Protective Associations, 33, 39–41, 43, 45, 47, 199

Provision for students, 132–3

Provision of correspondence tuition, 134–5, 140–1

Provision of teaching institutions, 122–3, 133–4

Psychical Research, Society for, 256

Psychological Society, British, 257

Public Cleansing, Institute of, 237, 249

Public Health Engineers, Institution of, 229, 249, 277

Public relations, 198, 292

Public Relations, Institute of, 167, 233, 253, 278

Public relations and Qualifying Associations, 198–9, 292

Public Supplies, Institute of, 238, 254, 278

Pupilage, 23, 120, 122, 130–1

Purchasing Officers' Association, 237, 252, 275, 278, 291

Pyke-Lees, W., 286

Qualifying Associations: advantages of membership, 112–14; consolidation of, 202–4; contributions of, 139–47, 211–13; Council, 94–107; development of, 50–85, 181–8; dilemmas of, 194–204; and education, 120–45; and examinations, 122–3, 125–9, 194–6, 205–6; facilities offered to members, 29, 32, 113–14, 196–7, 208–9, 218; future control over, 216–17; inter-association status, 8, 86, 116, 146, 180, 190–3; local organization, 115–16; membership, 109–14, 217–18; methods of incorporation, 85–94; nature of, 188–90; Parliamentary activity, 206–8, 219; professional conduct, 159–75, 218; reasons for formation, 51–85; role of, 139–47, 204–13; status symbols, 192–3; structure of 88–119, 217

Qualifications, nature of, 146, 204–6

Quantity Surveyors, Institute of, 167, 168, 239, 275, 278, 281, 292, 296

Quarrying, Institute of, 77, 238, 251

Index

Radio engineering, 80, 81, 146, 200, 201

Radio Engineers, British Institution of (renamed the 'Institution of Electronic and Radio Engineers' in 1964), 81, 93, 145, 229, 251, 273, 275, 277, 282, 283, 291, 295

Radiographers, 235, 251, 275, 278, 292

Radiographers, Faculty of, 253

Radiographers, Society of, 235, 251, 275, 278, 292

Radiologists, Faculty of, 253

Railway Signal Engineers, Institution of, 230, 250

Rating and Valuation Association, 163, 168, 241, 248, 275, 278, 294

Ray Society, 256

Recruitment of members to Qualifying Associations, 197–8

Redwood, Theophilus, 270, 271, 279

Refrigeration, Institute of, 245, 250

Register of Management Consultants, 169

Registered Architects, Institute of, 252

Registration of professions: attempts to gain, 288; registered professions, 170–3

Remedial Gymnasts, Society of, 77, 235, 253, 293

Remuneration surveys, 199, 293

Rivington, Walter, 261, 262, 264, 265, 271

Road Transport Engineers, Institute of, 243, 253

Roberts, H. D., 280

Robson, R., 265, 266

Roddenberry, E. W., 260

Role of Honorary Officers, 106–7

Role of Qualifying Associations: as interest groups, 206–8; in education, 139–47, 218–9; in ensuring professional standards, 204–6; in society, 211–13

Role of the Secretary, 108

Rose, T. G., 273, 289

Ross, E. A., 5, 260

Roxburgh, M. J., 273

Royal Academy, 18, 26, 34, 35, 254, 265, 269

Royal Charter, 90–3, 192, 193, 216; Chartered Qualifying Associations, 92–3; procedure for obtaining, 90

Royal Patronage, 192, 193

Royal Society, 18, 21, 26, 33, 34, 35, 254, 264, 266, 267, 269

Royal Veterinary College, London, 62, 63

Rubber Industry, Institution of the, 139, 202, 238, 251

Salaries and working conditions of members, 199, 293

Saunders, G. F., 260

School of Law, 133

School of Librarianship, 134

School of Pharmacy, 61, 123, 133, 271

School of Welding Technology, 134

Scientists, 9, 151, 152, 156, 158, 212, 260, 261, 266

Secretaries, Chartered Institute of, 93, 117, 118, 126, 132, 135, 168, 203, 238, 249, 275, 278, 280, 282, 284, 290, 292, 296

Secretaries, Corporation of, 238, 275, 278, 284, 296

Sewage Purification, Institute of, 77, 238, 250

Shipbrokers, Institute of Chartered, 93, 112, 168, 239, 250, 278

Shipping and Forwarding Agents, Institute of, 74, 239, 253, 278

Smith, F. H., 274

Sociological Association, British, 258

Sociological determinants of ethical code: functional elements, 157–9; structural elements determining— need, 150–3/possibility of introducing, 154–6

Solicitors (*See also* Law Society), 6, 18, 24, 121, 122, 125, 151, 152, 153, 159, 172, 176, 212, 239, 260, 286

Spencer, H., 4, 259

Spratt, T., 264

Statistical Society, Royal, 35, 255

Statisticians, Institute of, 239, 254, 278

Structural Engineers, Institution of, 80, 82, 93, 137, 145, 167, 168, 230, 250, 274, 275, 277, 285, 295

Statute, Professions registered by, 170–2

Stewart, J. D., 295

Student members, 130–133

Study Associations, 22, 25, 33, 35–7, 44, 45, 84, 181, 252–8

Summerson, Sir John, 281

Surgeons, 16, 17, 20, 120, 125, 151, 152, 261, 262, 264

Surgeons, Company of, 19, 21, 66, 89, 92, 121, 122, 247, 262

Surgeons of England, Royal College of, 21, 26, 42, 43, 56, 65–6, 92, 121, 122, 188, 192, 234, 247, 262, 264, 266, 267, 272, 290

Surgical Technicians, Institute of British, 245, 252

Surveyors, 20, 24, 66, 67, 74, 83, 100, 163, 183, 184, 186, 208, 239, 260, 261, 288, 294

Surveyors' Club, 83, 265

305

Surveyors, Royal Institution of Chartered Surveyors, 83, 92, 99, 117, 118, 126, 133, 146, 163, 167, 168, 179, 200, 203, 239, 248, 274, 275, 278, 281, 282, 284, 292, 293, 294, 296

Taeusch, C. E., 180, 260
Tawney, R. H., 3, 4, 5, 259, 260
Taxation, Institute of, 240, 252, 275, 278
Technical communication and Qualifying Associations, 29, 113–14, 196–7
Town Clerks, Society of, 257
Textile Institute, 84, 93, 103–4, 145, 167, 240, 250, 274, 275, 277, 278, 285, 292
Thomson, T., 264
Town Planning Institute, 83–4, 93, 100, 130, 167, 168, 240, 251, 274, 275, 276, 277, 283
Town Planning Joint Examination Board, 139, 283
Tropp, A., 268, 270
Trade Associations, 41, 269
Trade Unions contrasted with professional associations, 14–16
Traffic Administration, Institute of, 253
Training (*See also* 'Education'), 159, 180, 185, 198, 200, 213, 215, 218, 278, 281, 289, 291, 292
Transport, Institute of, 93, 169, 240, 251, 275, 278, 284
Travel Agents, Institute of, 240, 254, 294
Tudsbery, J. H. T., 271

Unprofessional conduct, 171–5, 179–80
Urwick, L. F., 261

Valuers, 163, 183, 252, 288
Valuers' Institution, 163, 167, 241, 252, 275, 278, 294
Vaughan, Paul, 268, 269
Venables, P. F. R., 144, 284
Veterinary Surgeons, Royal College of, 24, 56, 61–3, 92, 121, 122, 125, 173, 189, 241, 247

Wall, Cecil, 261, 262, 279
Water Engineers, Institution of, 244, 249
Weld, G. H., 264
Webb, Sidney and Beatrice, 3, 5, 259, 260, 261
Weber, Max, 180
Weights and Measures Administration, Institute of, 241, 249
Welding, Institute of, 134, 241, 251, 275
Welfare Officers, Institute of, 242, 253, 274
Weise, Leopold von, 260
Whitehead, A. N., 5, 260
Wickenden, W. E., 5, 260
Wickstead, Miss J. H., 270
Wilson, P. A., 3, 5, 259, 260, 261
Woodward, C., 287
Wood, Sir H. Trueman, 265
Work Study, Institute of, 242, 253, 278
Works and Highways Superintendents, Institute of, 252
Works Managers, Institution of, 233, 252, 275, 278, 293
Worshipful Company of Spectacle Workers, 246
Worthington, Beresford, 272
Wright, E. C., 265

Zoological Society of London, 22, 27, 35, 36, 37, 255, 267, 269, 274

The International Library of
Sociology
and Social Reconstruction

Edited by W. J. H. SPROTT
Founded by KARL MANNHEIM

ROUTLEDGE & KEGAN PAUL
BROADWAY HOUSE, CARTER LANE, LONDON, E.C.4

CONTENTS

General Sociology	3
Foreign Classics of Sociology	3
Social Structure	4
Sociology and Politics	4
Foreign Affairs, Their Social, Political and Economic Foundations	5
Sociology of Law	5
Criminology	5
Social Psychology	6
Sociology of the Family	7
The Social Services	7
Sociology of Education	8
Sociology of Culture	9
Sociology of Religion	9
Sociology of Art and Literature	9
Sociology of Knowledge	9
Urban Sociology	10
Rural Sociology	10
Sociology of Migration	11
Sociology of Industry and Distribution	11
Anthropology	12
Documentary	13
Reports of the Institute of Community Studies	14

PRINTED IN GREAT BRITAIN BY HEADLEY BROTHERS LTD
109 KINGSWAY LONDON WC2 AND ASHFORD KENT

GENERAL SOCIOLOGY

Brown, Robert. Explanation in Social Science. *208 pp. 1963. (2nd Impression 1964.) 25s.*

Gibson, Quentin. The Logic of Social Enquiry. *240 pp. 1960. (2nd Impression 1963.) 24s.*

Goldschmidt, Professor Walter. Understanding Human Society. *272 pp. 1959. 21s.*

Homans, George C. Sentiments and Activities: Essays in Social Science. *336 pp. 1962. 32s.*

Jarvie, I. C. The Revolution in Anthropology. *Foreword by Ernest Gellner. 272 pp. 1964. 40s.*

Johnson, Harry M. Sociology: a Systematic Introduction. *Foreword by Robert K. Merton. 710 pp. 1961. (3rd Impression 1963.) 42s.*

Mannheim, Karl. Essays on Sociology and Social Psychology. *Edited by Paul Kecskemeti. With Editorial Note by Adolph Lowe. 344 pp. 1953. 30s.*

Systematic Sociology: An Introduction to the Study of Society. *Edited by J. S. Erös and Professor W. A. C. Stewart. 220 pp. 1957. (2nd Impression 1959.) 24s.*

Martindale, Don. The Nature and Types of Sociological Theory. *292 pp. 1961. 35s.*

Maus, Heinz. A Short History of Sociology. *234 pp. 1962. 28s.*

Myrdal, Gunnar. Value in Social Theory: A Collection of Essays on Methodology. *Edited by Paul Streeten. 332 pp. 1958. (2nd Impression 1962.) 32s.*

Ogburn, William F., and **Nimkoff, Meyer F.** A Handbook of Sociology. *Preface by Karl Mannheim. 612 pp. 46 figures. 38 tables. 4th edition (revised) 1960. 35s.*

Parsons, Talcott and **Smelser, Neil J.** Economy and Society: A Study in the Integration of Economic and Social Theory. *362 pp. 1956. (3rd Impression 1964.) 35s.*

Rex, John. Key Problems of Sociological Theory. *220 pp. 1961. (2nd Impression 1963.) 25s.*

Stark, Werner. The Fundamental Forms of Social Thought. *280 pp. 1962. 32s.*

FOREIGN CLASSICS OF SOCIOLOGY

Durkheim, Emile. Suicide. A Study in Sociology. *Edited and with an Introduction by George Simpson. 404 pp. 1952. (2nd Impression 1963.) 30s.*

Socialism and Saint-Simon. *Edited with an Introduction by Alvin W. Gouldner. Translated by Charlotte Sattler from the edition originally edited with an Introduction by Marcel Mauss. 286 pp. 1959. 28s.*

Professional Ethics and Civic Morals. *Translated by Cornelia Brookfield. 288 pp. 1957. 30s.*

Gerth, H. H., and **Wright Mills, C.** From Max Weber: Essays in Sociology. *502 pp. 1948. (4th Impression 1961.) 32s.*

Tönnies, Ferdinand. Community and Association. *(Gemeinschaft und Gesellschaft.) Translated and Supplemented by Charles P. Loomis. Foreword by Pitirim A. Sorokin. 334 pp. 1955. 28s.*

SOCIAL STRUCTURE

Andrzejewski, Stanislaw. Military Organization and Society. *With a Foreword by Professor A. R. Radcliffe-Brown. 226 pp. 1 folder. 1954. 21s.*

Cole, G. D. H. Studies in Class Structure. *220 pp. 1955. (2nd Impression 1961.) 21s.*

Coontz, Sydney H. Population Theories and the Economic Interpretation. *202 pp. 1957. (2nd Impression 1961.) 25s.*

Coser, Lewis. The Functions of Social Conflict. *204 pp. 1956. 18s.*

Glass, D. V. (Ed.). Social Mobility in Britain. *Contributions by J. Berent, T. Bottomore, R. C. Chambers, J. Floud, D. V. Glass, J. R. Hall, H. T. Himmelweit, R. K. Kelsall, F. M. Martin, C. A. Moser, R. Mukherjee, and W. Ziegel. 420 pp. 1954. (2nd Impressions 1963.) 40s.*

Kelsall, R. K. Higher Civil Servants in Britain: From 1870 to the Present Day. *268 pp. 31 tables. 1955. 25s.*

Ossowski, Stanislaw. Class Structure in the Social Consciousness. *212 pp. 1963. 25s.*

SOCIOLOGY AND POLITICS

Barbu, Zevedei. Democracy and Dictatorship: Their Psychology and Patterns of Life. *300 pp. 1956. 28s.*

Benney, Mark, Gray, A. P., and **Pear, R. H.** How People Vote: a Study of Electoral Behaviour in Greenwich. *Foreword by Professor W. A. Robson. 256 pp. 70 tables. 1956. 25s.*

Bramstedt, Dr. E. K. Dictatorship and Political Police: The Technique of Control by Fear. *286 pp. 1945. 20s.*

Crick, Bernard. The American Science of Politics: Its Origins and Conditions. *284 pp. 1959. 28s.*

Hertz, Frederick. Nationality in History and Politics: A Psychology and Sociology of National Sentiment and Nationalism. *440 pp. 1944. (4th Impression 1957.) 32s.*

Kornhauser, William. The Politics of Mass Society. *272 pp. 20 tables. 1960. 25s.*

Laidler, Harry W. Social-Economic Movements: An Historical and Comparative Survey of Socialism, Communism, Co-operation, Utopianism; and other Systems of Reform and Reconstruction. *864 pp. 16 plates. 1 figure. 1949. (3rd Impression 1960.) 50s.*

Mannheim, Karl. Freedom, Power and Democratic Planning. *Edited by Hans Gerth and Ernest K. Bramstedt. 424 pp. 1951. 35s.*

Mansur, Fatma. Process of Independence. *Foreword by A. H. Hanson. 208 pp. 1962. 25s.*

Myrdal, Gunnar. The Political Element in the Development of Economic Theory. *Translated from the German by Paul Streeten. 282 pp. 1953. (3rd Impression 1961.) 25s.*

Polanyi, Michael, F.R.S. The Logic of Liberty: Reflections and Rejoinders. *228 pp. 1951. 18s.*

Verney, Douglas V. The Analysis of Political Systems. *264 pp. 1959. (2nd Impression 1961.) 28s.*

Wootton, Graham. The Politics of Influence: British Ex-Servicemen, Cabinet Decisions and Cultural Changes, 1917 to 1957. *320 pp. 1963. 30s.*

FOREIGN AFFAIRS: THEIR SOCIAL, POLITICAL AND ECONOMIC FOUNDATIONS

Baer, Gabriel. Population and Society in the Arab East. *Translated by Hanna Szöke. 288 pp. 10 maps. 1964. 40s.*

Bonné, Alfred. The Economic Development of the Middle East: An Outline of Planned Reconstruction after the War. *192 pp. 58 tables. 1945. (3rd Impression 1953.) 16s.*
State and Economics in the Middle East: A Society in Transition. *482 pp. 2nd (revised) edition 1955. (2nd Impression 1960.) 40s.*
Studies in Economic Development: with special reference to Conditions in the Under-developed Areas of Western Asia and India. *322 pp. 84 tables. (2nd edition 1960.) 32s.*

Mayer, J. P. Political Thought in France from the Revolution to the Fifth Republic. *164 pp. 3rd edition (revised) 1961. 16s.*

Schenk, H. G. The Aftermath of the Napoleonic Wars: The Concert of Europe—an Experiment. *250 pp. 17 plates. 1947. 18s.*

Schlesinger, Rudolf. Central European Democracy and its Background: Economic and Political Group Organization. *432 pp. 1953. 40s.*

Thomson, David, Meyer, E., and **Briggs, A.** Patterns of Peacemaking. *408 pp. 1945. 25s.*

Trouton, Ruth. Peasant Renaissance in Yugoslavia, 1900-1950: A Study of the Development of Yugoslav Peasant Society as affected by Education. *370 pp. 1 map. 1952. 28s.*

SOCIOLOGY OF LAW

Gurvitch, Dr. Georges. Sociology of Law. *With a Preface by Professor Roscoe Pound. 280 pp. 1947. (2nd Impression 1953.) 24s.*

Renner, Karl. The Institutions of Private Law and Their Social Functions. *Edited, with an Introduction and Notes by O. Kahn-Freund. Translated by Agnes Schwarzschild. 336 pp. 1949. 28s.*

CRIMINOLOGY

Cloward, Richard A., and **Ohlin, Lloyd E.** Delinquency and Opportunity: A Theory of Delinquent Gangs. *248 pp. 1961. 25s.*

Friedländer, Dr. Kate. The Psycho-Analytical Approach to Juvenile Delinquency: Theory, Case Studies, Treatment. *320 pp. 1947. (5th Impression 1961.) 28s.*

Glueck, Sheldon and **Eleanor.** Family Environment and Delinquency. *With the statistical assistance of Rose W. Kneznek. 340 pp. 1962. 35s.*

Mannheim, Hermann. Group Problems in Crime and Punishment, and other Studies in Criminology and Criminal Law. *336 pp. 1955. 28s.*

Morris, Terence. The Criminal Area: A Study in Social Ecology. *Foreword by Hermann Mannheim. 232 pp. 25 tables. 4 maps. 1957. 25s.*

Morris, Terence and **Pauline,** assisted by **Barbara Barer.** Pentonville: a Sociological Study of an English Prison. *416 pp. 16 plates. 1963. 50s.*

Spencer, John C. Crime and the Services. *Foreword by Hermann Mannheim. 336 pp. 1954. 28s.*

Trasler, Gordon. The Explanation of Criminality. *144 pp. 1962. 20s.*

SOCIAL PSYCHOLOGY

Barbu, Zevedei. Problems of Historical Psychology. *248 pp. 1960. 25s.*

Blackburn, Julian. Psychology and the Social Pattern. *184 pp. 1945. (6th Impression 1961.) 16s.*

Fleming, C. M. Adolescence: Its Social Psychology: With an Introduction to recent findings from the fields of Anthropology, Physiology, Medicine, Psychometrics and Sociometry. *271 pp. 2nd edition (revised) 1963. 25s.*
The Social Psychology of Education: An Introduction and Guide to Its Study. *136 pp. 2nd edition (revised) 1959. 11s.*

Fleming, C. M. (Ed.). Studies in the Social Psychology of Adolescence. *Contributions by J. E. Richardson, J. F. Forrester, J. K. Shukla and P. J. Higginbotham. Foreword by the editor. 292 pp. 29 figures. 13 tables. 5 folder tables. 1951. 23s.*

Halmos, Paul. Solitude and Privacy: a Study of Social Isolation, its Causes and Therapy. *With a Foreword by Professor T. H. Marshall. 216 pp. 1952. 21s.*
Towards a Measure of Man: The Frontiers of Normal Adjustment. *276 pp. 1957. 28s.*

Homans, George C. The Human Group. *Foreword by Bernard DeVoto. Introduction by Robert K. Merton. 526 pp. 1951. (4th Impression 1963.) 35s.*
Social Behaviour: its Elementary Forms. *416 pp. 1961. 30s.*

Klein, Josephine. The Study of Groups. *226 pp. 31 figures. 5 tables. 1956. (3rd Impression 1962.) 21s.*

Linton, Ralph. The Cultural Background of Personality. *132 pp. 1947. (4th Impression 1958.) 16s.*
See also Yang, M.

Mayo, Elton. The Social Problems of an Industrial Civilization. With an appendix on the Political Problem. *180 pp. 1949. (4th Impression 1961.) 18s.*

Ridder, J. C. de. The Personality of the Urban African in South Africa. A Thematic Apperception Test Study. *196 pp. 12 plates. 1961. 25s.*

Rose, Arnold M. (Ed.). Mental Health and Mental Disorder: A Sociological Approach. *Chapters by 46 contributors. 654 pp. 1956. 45s.*
Human Behavior and Social Processes: an Interactionist Approach. *Contributions by Arnold M. Ross, Ralph H. Turner, Anselm Strauss, Everett C. Hughes, E. Franklin Frazier, Howard S. Becker, et al. 696 pp. 1962. 56s.*

Smelser, Neil J. Theory of Collective Behavior. *448 pp. 1962. 45s.*

Spinley, Dr. B. M. The Deprived and the Privileged: Personality Development in English Society. *232 pp. 1953. 20s.*

Wolfenstein, Martha. Disaster: A Psychological Essay. *264 pp. 1957. 23s.*

Young, Professor Kimball. Personality and Problems of Adjustment. *742 pp. 12 figures. 9 tables. 2nd edition (revised) 1952. (2nd Impression 1959.) 40s.*
Handbook of Social Psychology. *658 pp. 16 figures. 10 tables. 2nd edition (revised) 1957. (3rd Impression 1963.) 40s.*

SOCIOLOGY OF THE FAMILY

Banks, J. A. Prosperity and Parenthood: A Study of Family Planning among the Victorian Middle Classes. *262 pp. 1954. 24s.*

Chapman, Dennis. The Home and Social Status. *336 pp. 8 plates. 3 figures. 117 tables. 1955. 35s.*

Klein, Viola. The Feminine Character: History of an Ideology. *With a Foreword by Karl Mannheim. 256 pp. 1946. 16s.*

Myrdal, Alva and Klein, Viola. Women's Two Roles: Home and Work. *238 pp. 27 tables. 1956. (2nd Impression 1962.) 25s.*

Parsons, Talcott and Bales, Robert F. Family: Socialization and Interaction Process. *In collaboration with James Olds, Morris Zelditch and Philip E. Slater. 456 pp. 50 figures and tables. 1956. 35s.*

THE SOCIAL SERVICES

Ashdown, Margaret and Brown, S. Clement. Social Service and Mental Health: An Essay on Psychiatric Social Workers. *280 pp. 1953. 21s.*

Hall, M. Penelope. The Social Services of Modern England. *416 pp. 6th edition (revised) 1963. 28s.*

Heywood, Jean S. Children in Care: the Development of the Service for the Deprived Child. *256 pp. 1959. (2nd Impression 1964.) 25s.*
An Introduction to teaching Casework Skills. *192 pp. 1964. In preparation.*

Jones, Kathleen. Lunacy, Law and Conscience, 1744-1845: the Social History of the Care of the Insane. *268 pp. 1955. 25s.*
Mental Health and Social Policy, 1845-1959. *264 pp. 1960. 28s.*

Jones, Kathleen and Sidebotham, Roy. Mental Hospitals at Work. *220 pp. 1962. 30s.*

Kastell, Jean. Casework in Child Care. *Foreword by M. Brooke Willis. 320 pp. 1962. 35s.*

Rooff, Madeline. Voluntary Societies and Social Policy. *350 pp. 15 tables. 1957. 35s.*

Shenfield, B. E. Social Policies for Old Age: A Review of Social Provision for Old Age in Great Britain. *260 pp. 39 tables. 1957. 25s.*

Timms, Noel. Psychiatric Social Work in Great Britain (1939-1962). *280 pp. 1964. 32s.*
Social Casework: Principles and Practice. *256 pp. In preparation.*

Trasler, Gordon. In Place of Parents: A Study in Foster Care. *272 pp. 1960. 25s.*

Young, A. F., and **Ashton, E. T.** British Social Work in the Nineteenth Century. *288 pp. 1956. (2nd Impression 1963.) 28s.*

SOCIOLOGY OF EDUCATION

Banks, Olive. Parity and Prestige in English Secondary Education: a Study in Educational Sociology. *272 pp. 1955. (2nd Impression. 1963.) 28s.*

Collier, K. G. The Social Purposes of Education: Personal and Social Values in Education. *268 pp. 1959. (2nd Impression 1962.) 21s.*

Edmonds, E. L. The School Inspector. *Foreword by Sir William Alexander. 214 pp. 1962. 28s.*

Evans, K. M. Sociometry and Education. *158 pp. 1962. 18s.*

Fraser, W. R. Education and Society in Modern France. *150 pp. 1963. 20s.*

Hans, Nicholas. New Trends in Education in the Eighteenth Century. *278 pp. 19 tables. 1951. 25s.*
Comparative Education: A Study of Educational Factors and Traditions. *360 pp. 3rd (revised) edition 1958. (2nd Impression 1961.) 23s.*

Mannheim, Karl and **Stewart, W. A. C.** An Introduction to the Sociology of Education. *208 pp. 1962. 21s.*

Musgrove, F. Youth and the Social Order. *176 pp. 1964. In preparation.*

Ortega y Gasset, Jose. Mission of the University. *Translated with an Introduction by Howard Lee Nostrand. 88 pp. 1946. (3rd Impression 1963.) 15s.*

Ottaway, A. K. C. Education and Society: An Introduction to the Sociology of Education. *With an Introduction by W. O. Lester Smith. 212 pp. Second edition (revised). 1962. (2nd Impression 1964.) 18s.*

Peers, Robert. Adult Education: A Comparative Study. *398 pp. 2nd edition 1959. 35s.*

Pritchard, D. G. Education and the Handicapped: 1760 to 1960. *258 pp. 1963. 28s.*

Samuel, R. H., and **Thomas, R. Hinton.** Education and Society in Modern Germany. *212 pp. 1949. 16s.*

Simon, Brian and **Joan** (Eds.). Educational Psychology in the U.S.S.R. *Introduction by Brian and Joan Simon. Translation by Joan Simon. Papers by D. N. Bogoiavlenski and N. A. Menchinskaia, D. B. Elkonin, E. A. Fleshner, Z. I. Kalmykova, G. S. Kostiuk, V. A. Krutetski, A. N. Leontiev, A. R. Luria, E. A. Milerian, R. G. Natadze, B. M. Teplov, L. S. Vygotski, L. V. Zankov. 296 pp. 1963. 40s.*

SOCIOLOGY OF CULTURE

Fromm, Erich. The Fear of Freedom. *286 pp. 1942. (8th Impression 1960.) 21s.* The Sane Society. *400 pp. 1956. (3rd Impression 1963.) 28s.*

Mannheim, Karl. Diagnosis of Our Time: Wartime Essays of a Sociologist. *208 pp. 1943. (7th Impression 1962.) 21s.* Essays on the Sociology of Culture. *Edited by Ernst Mannheim in cooperation with Paul Kecskemeti. Editorial Note by Adolph Lowe. 280 pp. 1956. (2nd Impression 1962.) 28s.*

Weber, Alfred. Farewell to European History: or The Conquest of Nihilism. *Translated from the German by R. F. C. Hull. 224 pp. 1947. 18s.*

SOCIOLOGY OF RELIGION

Argyle, Michael. Religious Behaviour. *224 pp. 8 figures. 41 tables. 1958. 25s.*

Knight, Frank H., and **Merriam, Thornton W.** The Economic Order and Religion. *242 pp. 1947. 18s.*

Watt, W. Montgomery. Islam and the Integration of Society. *320 pp. 1961. (2nd Impression.) 32s.*

SOCIOLOGY OF ART AND LITERATURE

Beljame, Alexandre. Men of Letters and the English Public in the Eighteenth Century: 1660-1744, Dryden, Addison, Pope. *Edited with an Introduction and Notes by Bonamy Dobree. Translated by E. O. Lorimer. 532 pp. 1948. 32s.*

Misch, Georg. A History of Autobiography in Antiquity. *Translated by E. W. Dickes. 2 Volumes. Vol. 1, 364 pp., Vol. 2, 372 pp. 1950. 45s. the set.*

Silbermann, Alphons. The Sociology of Music. *224 pp. 1963. 28s.*

SOCIOLOGY OF KNOWLEDGE

Hodges, H. A. The Philosophy of Wilhelm Dilthey. *410 pp. 1952. 30s.*

Mannheim, Karl. Essays on the Sociology of Knowledge. *Edited by Paul Kecskemeti. Editorial note by Adolph Lowe. 352 pp. 1952. (2nd Impression 1959.) 35s.*

Schlesinger, Rudolf. Marx: His Time and Ours. *464 pp. 1950. (2nd Impression 1951.) 32s.*

Stark, W. The History of Economics in its Relation to Social Development. *104 pp. 1944. (4th Impression 1957.) 12s.*
America: Ideal and Reality. The United States of 1776 in Contemporary Philosophy. *136 pp. 1947. 12s.*
The Sociology of Knowledge: An Essay in Aid of a Deeper Understanding of the History of Ideas. *384 pp. 1958. (2nd Impression 1960.) 36s.*
Montesquieu: Pioneer of the Sociology of Knowledge. *244 pp. 1960. 25s.*

URBAN SOCIOLOGY

Anderson, Nels. The Urban Community: A World Perspective. *532 pp. 1960. 35s.*

Ashworth, William. The Genesis of Modern British Town Planning: A Study in Economic and Social History of the Nineteenth and Twentieth Centuries. *288 pp. 1954. 25s.*

Bracey, Howard. Neighbours: Neighbouring and Neighbourliness on New Estates and Subdivisions in England and the U.S.A. *220 pp. 1964.*

Cullingworth, J. B. Housing Needs and Planning Policy: A Restatement of the Problems of Housing Need and "Overspill" in England and Wales. *232 pp. 44 tables. 8 maps. 1960. 28s.*

Dickinson, Robert E. City Region and Regionalism: A Geographical Contribution to Human Ecology. *360 pp. 75 figures. 1947. (4th Impression 1960.)*
The West European City: A Geographical Interpretation. *600 pp. 129 maps. 29 plates. 2nd edition 1962. (2nd Impression 1963.) 55s.*

Dore, R. P. City Life in Japan: A Study of a Tokyo Ward. *498 pp. 8 plates. 4 figures. 24 tables. 1958. (2nd Impression 1963.) 45s.*

Jennings, Hilda. Societies in the Making: a Study of Development and Redevelopment within a County Borough. *Foreword by D. A. Clark. 286 pp. 1962. 32s.*

Kerr, Madeline. The People of Ship Street. *240 pp. 1958. 23s.*

RURAL SOCIOLOGY

Bracey, H. E. English Rural Life: Village Activities, Organizations and Institutions. *302 pp. 1959. 30s.*

Infield, Henrik F. Co-operative Living in Palestine. *With a Foreword by General Sir Arthur Wauchope, G.C.B. 170 pp. 8 plates. 7 tables. 1946. 12s. 6d.*

Littlejohn, James. Westrigg: the Sociology of a Cheviot Parish. *172 pp. 5 figures. 1963. 25s.*

Saville, John. Rural Depopulation in England and Wales, 1851-1951. *Foreword by Leonard Elmhirst. 286 pp. 6 figures. 39 tables. 1 map. 1957. 28s. (Dartington Hall Studies in Rural Sociology.)*

Williams, W. M. The Country Craftsman: A Study of Some Rural Crafts and the Rural Industries Organization in England. *248 pp. 9 figures. 1958. 25s. (Dartington Hall Studies in Rural Sociology.)*
The Sociology of an English Village: Gosforth. *272 pp. 12 figures. 13 tables. 1956. (3rd Impression 1964.) 25s.*

SOCIOLOGY OF MIGRATION

Eisenstadt, S. N. The Absorption of Immigrants: a Comparative Study based mainly on the Jewish Community in Palestine and the State of Israel. *288 pp. 1954. 28s.*

SOCIOLOGY OF INDUSTRY AND DISTRIBUTION

Anderson, Nels. Work and Leisure. *280 pp. 1961. 28s.*

Blau, Peter M., and **Scott, W. Richard.** Formal Organizations: a Comparative approach. *Introduction and Additional Bibliography by J. H. Smith. 328 pp. 1963. 28s.*

Gouldner, Alvin W. Patterns of Industrial Bureaucracy. *298 pp. 1955. 25s.*
Wildcat Strike: A Study of an Unofficial Strike. *202 pp. 10 figures. 1955. 16s.*

Jefferys, Margot, with the assistance of Winifred Moss. Mobility in the Labour Market: Employment Changes in Battersea and Dagenham. *Preface by Barbara Wootton. 186 pp. 51 tables. 1954. 15s.*

Levy, A. B. Private Corporations and Their Control. *Two Volumes. Vol. 1, 464 pp., Vol. 2, 432 pp. 1950. 80s. the set.*

Levy, Hermann. The Shops of Britain: A Study of Retail Distribution. *268 pp. 1948. (2nd Impression 1949.) 21s.*

Liepmann, Kate. The Journey to Work: Its Significance for Industrial and Community Life. *With a Foreword by A. M. Carr-Saunders. 230 pp. 40 tables. 3 folders. 1944. (2nd Impression 1945.) 18s.*
Apprenticeship: An Enquiry into its Adequacy under Modern Conditions. *Foreword by H. D. Dickinson. 232 pp. 6 tables. 1960. (2nd Impression.) 23s.*

Millerson, Geoffrey. The Qualifying Associations: a Study in Professionalization. *320 pp. 1964. In preparation.*

Smelser, Neil J. Social Change in the Industrial Revolution: An Application of Theory to the Lancashire Cotton Industry, 1770-1840. *468 pp. 12 figures. 14 tables. 1959. (2nd Impression 1960.) 40s.*

Williams, Gertrude. Recruitment to Skilled Trades. *240 pp. 1957. 23s.*

Young, A. F. Industrial Injuries Insurance: an Examination of British Policy. *192 pp. 1964. In preparation.*

ANTHROPOLOGY
(*Demy 8vo.*)

Crook, David and **Isabel.** Revolution in a Chinese Village: Ten Mile Inn. *230 pp. 8 plates. 1 map. 1959. 21s.*

Dube, S. C. Indian Village, *Foreword by Morris Edward Opler. 276 pp. 4 plates. 1955. (4th Impression 1961.) 25s.*
India's Changing Villages: Human Factors in Community Development. *260 pp. 8 plates. 1 map. 1958. (2nd Impression 1960.) 25s.*

Fei, Hsiao-Tung. Peasant Life in China: a Field Study of Country Life in the Yangtze Valley. *Foreword by Bronislaw Malinowski. 320 pp. 14 plates. 1939. (5th Impression 1962.) 30s.*

Gulliver, P. H. The Family Herds. A Study of Two Pastoral Tribes in East Africa, The Jie and Turkana. *304 pp. 4 plates. 19 figures. 1955. 25s.*
Social Control in an African Society: a Study of the Arusha, Agricultural Masai of Northern Tanganyika. *320 pp. 8 plates. 10 figures. 1963. 35s.*

Hogbin, Ian. Transformation Scene. The Changing Culture of a New Guinea Village. *340 pp. 22 plates. 2 maps. 1951. 30s.*

Hsu, Francis L. K. Under the Ancestors' Shadow: Chinese Culture and Personality. *346 pp. 26 figures. 1949. 21s.*
Religion, Science and Human Crises: A Study of China in Transition and its Implications for the West. *168 pp. 7 figures. 4 tables. 1952. 16s.*

Lowie, Professor Robert H. Social Organization. *494 pp. 1950. (3rd Impression 1962.) 35s.*

Maunier, René. The Sociology of Colonies: An Introduction to the Study of Race Contact. *Edited and translated by E. O. Lorimer. 2 Volumes. Vol. 1, 430 pp., Vol. 2, 356 pp. 1949. 70s. the set.*

Mayer, Adrian C. Caste and Kinship in Central India: A Village and its Region. *328 pp. 16 plates. 15 figures. 16 tables. 1960. 35s.*
Peasants in the Pacific: A Study of Fiji Indian Rural Society. *232 pp. 16 plates. 10 figures. 14 tables. 1961. 35s.*

Osborne, Harold. Indians of the Andes: Aymaras and Quechuas. *292 pp. 8 plates. 2 maps. 1952. 25s.*

Smith, Raymond T. The Negro Family in British Guiana: Family Structure and Social Status in the Villages. *With a Foreword by Meyer Fortes. 314 pp. 8 plates. 1 figure. 4 maps. 1956. 28s.*

Yang, Martin C. A Chinese Village: Taitou, Shantung Province. *Foreword by Ralph Linton. Introduction by M. L. Wilson. 308 pp. 1947. 23s.*

DOCUMENTARY
(*Demy 8vo.*)

Belov, Fedor. The History of a Soviet Collective Farm. *250 pp. 1956. 21s.*

Meek, Dorothea L. (Ed.). Soviet Youth: Some Achievements and Problems. *Excerpts from the Soviet Press, translated by the editor. 280 pp. 1957. 28s.*

Schlesinger, Rudolf (Ed.). Changing Attitudes in Soviet Russia.
1. The Family in the U.S.S.R. *Documents and Readings, with an Introduction by the editor. 434 pp. 1949. 30s.*
2. The Nationalities Problem and Soviet Administration. Selected Readings on the Development of Soviet Nationalities Policies. *Introduced by the editor. Translated by W. W. Gottlieb. 324 pp. 1956. 30s.*

Reports
of the Institute
of Community Studies

(Demy 8vo.)

Cartwright, Ann. Human Relations and Hospital Care. *272 pp. 1964. In Preparation.*

Jackson, Brian and **Marsden, Dennis.** Education and the Working Class: Some General Themes raised by a Study of 88 Working-class Children in a Northern Industrial City. *268 pp. 2 folders. 1962. (2nd Impression.) 28s.*

Marris, Peter. Widows and their Families. *Foreword by Dr. John Bowlby. 184 pp. 18 tables. Statistical Summary. 1958. 18s.*
Family and Social Change in an African City. A Study of Rehousing in Lagos. *196 pp. 1 map. 4 plates. 53 tables. 1961. 25s.*

Mills, Enid. Living with Mental Illness: a Study in East London. *Foreword by Morris Carstairs. 196 pp. 1962. 28s.*

Townsend, Peter. The Family Life of Old People: An Inquiry in East London. *Foreword by J. H. Sheldon. 300 pp. 3 figures. 63 tables. 1957. (2nd Impression 1961.) 30s.*

Willmott, Peter. The Evolution of a Community: a study of Dagenham after forty years. *168 pp. 2 maps. 1963. 21s.*

Willmott, Peter and **Young, Michael.** Family and Class in a London Suburb. *202 pp. 47 tables. 1960. (2nd Impression 1961.) 21s.*

The British Journal of Sociology. *Edited by D. G. MacRae. Vol. 1, No. 1, March 1950 and Quarterly. Roy. 8vo., £2 p.a.; 12s. 6d. a number, post free. (Vols. 1-12, £3 each.)*

All prices are net and subject to alteration without notice